Front Cover Photo

Grace Church (also known as Jesus Church) is the largest Protestant church in present day Poland with 38,000 members, built soon before the revival there under Steinmetz, in 1719. The church seats 6000 persons today. During the revival there were 70,000 members in 1730. The photo is in the public domain.

Johann Adam Steinmetz
Österreichische Nationalbibliothek – Austrian National Library – 1741
PICRYL Public Domain Image

This map reflects twenty first century national borders, and also superimposes three nation states from 1750 pertinent to this study: Silesia, Bohemia, and Moravia.

The Origin of The Wesleyan Theological Vision for Christian Globalization and the Pursuit of Pentecost in Early Pietist Revivalism

Including a Translation of

The Pentecost Addresses of Johann Adam Steinmetz (1689–1762)

The Asbury Theological Seminary Series in World Christian Revitalization Movements in Pietist/Wesleyan Studies

---

Foreword by Timothy C. Tennent

J. Steven O'Malley

EMETH PRESS
www.emethpress.com

The Origin of the Wesleyan Theological Vision for Christian Globalization and the Pursuit of Pentecost in Early Pietist Revivalism, Including a Translation of The Pentecost Addresses of Johann Adam Steinmetz (1689–1762)

Copyright © 2020 J. Steven O'Malley
Printed in the United States of America on acid-free paper

All rights reserved. No part of this book may be reproduced or transmitted in any form or by any means, electronic or mechanical, including photocopying, recording, or by any information storage and retrieval system, without the written permission of the publisher, except where permitted by law. For permission to reproduce any part or form of the text, contact the publisher. www.emethpress.com.

Library of Congress Cataloging-in-Publication Data

Names: O'Malley, J. Steven (John Steven), 1942- author. | Steinmetz, Johann Adam, 1689-1762. Versiegelung der Glaubigen mit dem heiligen Geist. English.
Title: The origin of the Wesleyan theological vision for Christian globalization and the pursuit of Pentecost in early Pietist revivalism, including a translation of the Pentecost addresses of Johann Adam Steinmetz (1689-1762) / J. Steven O'Malley.
Description: Lexington, Kentucky : Emeth Press, 2020. | Series: The Asbury Theological Seminary series in world Christian revitalization movements in Pietist/Wesleyan studies | Includes bibliographical references. | Summary: "While Moravian influences upon Wesley have long been acknowledged, we have not understood the extent to which the key components of his theology were shaped by Wesley's encounter with the first recorded revival in Protestant history. This study follows the sequence of events from Wesley's encounter at Herrnhut with Christian David from whom he first learned of the urgency of progression from justification to sanctification, understood as the Pentecost sealing by the Holy Spirit"-- Provided by publisher.
Identifiers: LCCN 2020003408 (print) | LCCN 2020003409 (ebook) | ISBN 9781609471514 (paperback) | ISBN 9781609471521 (kindle edition)
Subjects: LCSH: Pentecostalism--Methodist Church--History--18th century. | Wesley, John, 1703-1791. | Salvation--Christianity--History of doctrines--18th century. | Sanctification--Christianity--History of doctrines--18th century. | Globalization--Religious aspects--Christianity. | Methodist Church--Doctrines. | Pietism--Influence. | David, Christian, 1690-1751--Influence. | Steinmetz, Johann Adam, 1689-1762--Influence.
Classification: LCC BX8349.P46 O63 2020 (print) | LCC BX8349.P46 (ebook) | DDC 230/.7--dc23
LC record available at https://lccn.loc.gov/2020003408
LC ebook record available at https://lccn.loc.gov/2020003409

Contents

Foreword / xiii
Acknowledgment / xv

PART ONE: Introduction for the Present Day / 1
Chapter One: Globalization Has a History / 3
Chapter Two: Globalization Here and Now / 13

**PART TWO: Supplying the Missing Document from the Past
Johann Adam Steinmetz: Concerning the Sealing of Believers with
the Holy Spirit, Five Lessons in Pentecost Edification /19**

Foreword by Heinrich Ludwig Brönner, 1857 / 21
The First Pentecost Edification:
1.1 Introduction: The Urgent Benefit of Sealing with the Holy Spirit / 25
1.2. The Biblical Basis / 26
1.3. The Source of Mission Identity: Sealing, Childhood, Adoption, and a Twofold Work of Saving Grace / 29
    (a) Sealing and the Struggle with Satan / 30
    (b) Sealing by Grace vs by Works / 32
    (c) Sealing Grounded on the Blood and Merit of Christ / 34
    (d) The Sealing and Pentecost / 35
1.4. Accessing Sealing: Counsel for the Timid / 39
1.5 Sealing Accessed by Faith / 42
1.6. Overcoming as the Outcome of the Spirit's Sealing: The Path to a Globalized Christianity / 44

CONTENTS

The Second Pentecost Edification / 51

2.1. The Means of Sealing / 51
2.2. The Holy Spirit as the Chief Witness to the Sealing of the Holy Spirit / 54
2.3. Ancillary Seals Accompanying the Holy Spirit: Word, Sacrament, and the Inner Person / 56
2.4. The Efficacy of These Seals Depends upon the Receptivity of the Subject through Conversion / 60
2.5. A Warning against Counterfeit Seals / 62
2.6. Fulfilling the Promise of Pentecost with the Sealing of the Holy Spirit / 63

Third Pentecost Edification / 69

3.1. Sealing in Praxis / 69
3.2. Examples of Spirit-Sealed Lives in History / 67
3.3. A Panoply of Christ-like Virtues in the Body of Christ among Those Sealed through the Holy Spirit/ 72
3.4. The Quest for Authenticity as Christians / 73
3.5. Biblical Grounds for Childlikeness as the Highest Expression of Sealing by the Holy Spirit / 83

Fourth Pentecost Edification / 91

4.1. Sealing as the Identity of the Christian Community / 91
4.2. Hindrances to Sealing withs the Holy Spirit in Community / 94
4.3. When Awakening Shapes the Community of Faith / 98
4.4. Entering the Blood of Jesus as the Core which Forms Community / 100
4.5. The Sins that Cling / 103

Fifth Pentecost Edification / 111

5.1. Community Lives Between Deception and Hope for the Future /111
5.2. Pentecost Delayed: The Problem and Its Resolution / 113
5.3. Avoiding the Pitfall of Ananias and Saphira / 117
5.4. Sealed for the World to Receive / 123
5.5. The Closing Prayer of Steinmetz / 125

CONTENTS

PART THREE: "A Little Child Shall Lead Them" / 127

Chapter One: European Christendom is Awakened to the World / 129
1.1. Introduction / 129
1.2. The Biblical Context / 133
1.3. The Roots of Awakening: The Struggle for the Survival of the Reformation / 135
1.4. The Revival Associated with the Children at Prayer [Kinderbeten] / 137
1.5. The Theological Foundation for the Children's Revival in the Reformation Encounter with the Cross / 140
1.6. The Crisis of Faith Provoked by the Revival: The Struggle for the Completion of the Reformation, Encompassing Polarized Tensions in Protestantism / 144

Chapter Two: "There Are Not Drunken as you Suppose": The Children's Revival as Renewal of Pentecost Confronts the Intellectual World of Pre-Revival European Protestantism / 155
2.1. The Composition of That World, Which Produced Two Ways Forward / 157
2.2. Petersen and the Appeal to Restorationism / 161
2.3. The Voluntary, Dualistic Mysticism of Jacob Böhme / 162
2.4. The Appeal of Federalism / 166
2.5. Steinmetz and Revival: The Linkage of Pentecost to the Cross / 181

Chapter Three: THE PIETIST SOURCE OF THE TWO-STAGED SOTERIOLOGY IN THE WESLEYS / 199
3.1. Steinmetz, David, and the Wesleys: A Comparison of the Themes of Pentecost and Sanctification in the Continental Revival and in the Wesleys / 199
3.2. The Role of Christian David in the Dissemination of Steinmetz's Theology of Pentecost / 200
3.3. Christian David's Narrative as Recorded in John Wesley's Journal / 203

CONTENTS

3.4. Early Guidance from Steinmetz / 204
3.5. David's First Migrants Reach Herrnhut / 205
3.6. Division over Religion in Herrnhut / 206
3.7. The Onset of Awakening in Herrnhut / 209
3.8. Progress in the Moravian World Mission through David / 210
3.9. The Close of the Revival in Teschen and Tensions between Halle and Herrnhut / 212
3.10. David's Later International Mission Ventures Featuring Steinmetz's Two-Stage Approach to Salvation / 214
3.11. John Wesley Meets Christian David at Herrnhut (August, 1738) / 220
3.12. Wesley, David and Steinmetz Seen in Tandem / 221
3.13. Steinmetz's Means for Implementing This New Pentecost Vision of the Redeemed and Globalized Life of the New Humanity in Christ / 225

Addendum to Chapter Three: From the Cross to Pentecost—
A Theological Grid / 237
  (a) The Sinner and the Cross / 237
      Luther / 237
      Steinmetz / 238
      Christian David / 238
      The Wesleys / 239
  (b) Pentecost and Sanctification in Relation to the Cross / 240
      Luther / 240
      Steinmetz / 240
      Christian David / 243
      John Wesley / 245
      Charles Wesley / 245
  (c) The Coming Kingdom / 247
      Luther / 247
      Steinmetz / 247
      Christian David / 248

CONTENTS

John Wesley / 250 *Charles Wesley* / 251
1.2. Conclusion / 252

Chapter Four: Steinmetz Links the Children's Revival to Christian Globalization as the Historical Outworking of a Two-Staged Soteriology / 253

4.1. The Revival in its Silesian and Wesleyan Phases / 254
4.2. Steinmetz's Early Life as Preparatory to the Revival / 256
4.3. The Origin of the Twofold Approach to Christian Soteriology in Steinmetz / 258
4.4. Steinmetz Confronts the Restoration Theory as an Impediment to the Coming of the Kingdom of God / 261
4.5. The Revival and the *Gathering*: Their Connection and Import / 263
4.6. The Mission of the *Gathering* / 270
4.7. Concluding Reflections / 279

A FINAL ADDENDUM: David's Foundations for a Global Ministry Based on the Two-Staged Soteriology that He Learned from Steinmetz and Conveyed to John Wesley / 281

Bibliography / 285

Index / 291

Foreword

The present study by J. Steven O'Malley represents a breakthrough in our knowledge of the origin in Pietist Revivalism for the two stage soteriology and concern for Christian Globalization that constituted the core missional focus of John Wesley and early Methodism. While Moravian influences upon Wesley have long been acknowledged, we have not understood the extent to which the key components of his theology were shaped by Wesley's encounter with the first recorded revival in Protestant history. This study follows the sequence of events from Wesley's encounter at Herrnhut with Christian David, as recorded in his Journal, from whom he first learned of the urgency of progression from justification to sanctification, understood as the Pentecost sealing by the Holy Spirit of the atoning work of Christ on Calvary for the sins of humanity.

From this encounter, the study traces Christian David's prior confirmation in this two-stage event of full salvation in Christ during his participation in the first revival within Protestant history, which occurred in the central European nation of Silesia. The preacher of that revival, who would become David's acknowledged spiritual mentor, was a Lutheran pastor, Johann Adam Steinmetz (b 1689), who preached a series of Pentecost addresses to his Silesian refugee congregation of 70,000 refugees from the raging religious wars which had torn apart their homeland.

The heart of this volume consists of the translation from German by O'Malley of these addresses, based upon an extant copy of a nineteenth century published version of these addresses. The study explains how these addresses embody the message of Christianity's first revival, drawing on the apostolic theme of Pentecost to narrate the necessity of believers to receive the sealing of the Holy Spirit to complete their salvation in the work of the Lamb of God on Calvary. O'Malley joins the presentation of this revival and its theology to the earlier children's revival, which precipitated the event leading up to this major awakening which, in turn, resulted in the first border-crossing event of revival which would give rise to the Moravian mission movement at Herrnhut as well as later British Methodism. The study features contemporary accounts of affirmative and critical witnesses to the Silesian children's revival, and features a careful comparison of the soteriological positions of Luther, Steinmetz, David, and the Wesleys, which trace the lines of influence from each one upon the other. A final chapter traces Steinmetz's personal account of the aftermath of the revival, as its center shifted from Silesia, to Germany, England, Scotland, and North America, and to the ministry of his mentee, Christian David, extending to Switzerland, Scandinavia and Greenland.

The implication of this breakthrough study is that the origins of Methodism need to be revisited in light of the global dimensions of its precursors in the faith. This new approach to the origins of Wesley studies provides a key resource for seminaries like Asbury, which are recovering Wesley's vision for what he called the "General Spread of the Gospel" to all nations and cultures. It is a book destined to open a new conversation on the origin and purpose of the larger Wesleyan movement at this critical point in its history.

Timothy C. Tennent, PhD.
President
Professor of World Christianity
Asbury Theological Seminary

PART ONE

Introduction for the Present

Chapter 1

GLOBALIZATION HAS A HISTORY

The accelerated globalization of Christianity in the twenty-first century has been facilitated by the internet and social media perhaps more than by overt missional strategies of institutional entities. Literature on this decisive movement within contemporary Christianity has given more focus to empirical studies and attention to demographic and cultural features. In the present study, the focus turns to the intellectual roots of the concern for globalization within Protestant Christianity, in which the important theological dimensions are housed within a matrix of cultural features.

To date, an understanding of the origin within Protestantism of the vision for a globalized Christianity has not received definitive attention. It may, then, come as a surprise that it began not in the counsels of ecclesial governance nor in academic theological discourse. On the contrary, a concern for tracking an emerging globalized Christianity will lead to its far more humble origins. The roots of Protestant Christian initiatives in taking the gospel to the larger world beyond Europe can be traced to the voices of praying children in Eastern Europe at the beginning of the eighteenth century. There were multiple players in this narrative whose interests collided over how best to respond to this startling and somewhat condescending impetus. These include (1) its protagonists, who can be traced to a children's prayer and prophecy revival, (2) the Catholic ecclesial adversaries whose invasion of Protestant territory precipitated that revival, (3) the Orthodox Lutheran opponents of the children who were fearful the enthusiastic, open air worship would only exacerbate Catholic aggression against Protestants, and so became the vociferous opponents of the children and their defenders. The Pietist advocates of that revival alone heralded its potential as a beginning for a globalized Christianity.

Vision for the global dimensions of Christianity, in its evangelical Protestant expression, was born in the early eighteenth century amid the manifestation of this spontaneous children's revival set amid religious warfare entailing massive loss of life and property. The aggressors were the Austrian Hapsburgs, Catholics with Jesuit support, who conducted a scorched earth policy to regain their homelands lost to the Protestant Reformation. The protagonists are the children, praying and prophesying spontaneously, and supporters drawn from the ranks of the Pietists within Lutheranism. On the other side was an entrenched Protestant orthodoxy defending its turf within a crumbling corpus Christianum.

The date is 1707, and the place is the imperial province of Silesia, in the Polish/Czech/German border region of the Holy Roman Empire, situated within the context of the scorched earth policy of the Counter-Reformation agenda of the Austrian Hapsburg imperial forces in devastating the Lutheran parishes of that land. The key figures in this human tragedy were children, many orphaned, who found themselves immersed in spontaneous revival without parental oversight. The voices of orthodox Lutheran clergy in Silesia vociferously regarded the children as misguided enthusiasts, whose illegal, spontaneous and out of door gatherings for prayer and prophecy would potentially enrage their Hapsburg adversaries. Consequently, the clergy used this occasion to rekindle the skirmishes between Pietist and Orthodox parties within German Lutheranism by publishing verbal critiques of the revival. This included the contrived narrative that these children were imitators of praying Swedish troops—who arrived rather in response to the children's prayers for liberation from their oppressors, or they were seen as pawns of the Pietists' attempt to undermine parochial authority.

The contention between defenders and opponents of the children recapitulated a struggle from the preceding generation between two readings of church history: the pro-Constantinian or Christendom rendition and the anti-Constantinian radical Pietist rendition which had been sparring over who gets to narrate what is Christian orthodoxy. What was defined as Orthodoxy by clergy constrained by the ancient concept of the corpus Christianum is quite different from the version espoused by a Lutheran historian now turned radical Pietist, Gottfried Arnold. Stepping aside from both Roman Catholic and Orthodox Protestant renditions of orthodoxy, Arnold based his understanding of this term upon the question what does it mean for there to be saving union with Christ, defined apart from any "partisan" confessional understanding of that term.[1] Arnold's formula, which would displace the confessional positions of Magisterial Protestants as well as Roman Catholics, included these features: (1) justification is by Christ alone, owned by a personal encounter of new birth, and (2) with the gift of faith comes power for holiness unto perfection, via Nachfolge (being discipled to Christ).[2]

While Arnold provided the radical Pietist critique of the official pattern of Christendom in Western civilization, there was another Lutheran turned-radical Pietist, Johann Wilhelm Petersen, whose vision was for the future. He read the events of the children's revival as Spirit-endued markers signifying a prophetic announcement of an imminent apocalyptic end to history, with the return of Christ as Judge. However, with the delay of the Parousia, the outcome of the children's revival would be diverted from an expected historical apocalypse into an actual spiritual awakening which would sweep across Europe and into North America within three decades of its origin.

The setting for this turn of events was the erection of the Grace Church in Teschen, Silesia, through the intervention and resourcing of August Hermann Francke and the then resourceful Halle Pietists. Revival had not heretofore been the focus at the Prussian University of Halle, whose forte was renewal—renewal of the existing parishes of European Christendom through an extensive program of education and community outreach led by those reborn in Christ. Revival, signifying a supernatural, redemptive breakthrough from God into history which would also be a breakout from the old order of Christendom, would come only after there was no longer an intact corpus Christianum to renew. And that will take us to the scene we find amid the cataclysmic struggle between Orthodox Lutheran and Habsburg Catholic states in the era known to Protestants as the Counter Reformation. In brief, here was a moment when the light of the Protestant Reformation seemed to be all but snuffed out, amid the carnage of these competing states and the utter devastation of all structures of the old parish system. However, from another perspective, to the devout children in the forest, and their Pietist advocates, this tragic hour appeared as the appointed occasion for God to restart the redemptive project which had

---

1. Gottfried Arnold, *Unparteiische Kirche und Ketzer Historie*. Zwei Bände (1699–1700) (Frankfurt-Main: Thomas Fritsch, 1700).

2. Peter Erb, *Pietists, Protestants and Mysticism: The Use of Late Medieval Texts in the Work of Gottfriend Arnold* (Metuschen, New Jersey: Scarecrow, 1989, 37.

begun with the child of Bethlehem, and which had now succumbed to such mortal demise.³ The recovery of that project could only happen, nevertheless, by overcoming a powerful and also contrived apocalyptic resolution of the problem of theodicy.

By attending to historical narrative and to theological documents, our intent will be to disclose how an implicit discernment of divine breakthrough amid a tragic human conflict would lead to an extraordinary outcome. Travail would become the seed for a breakout of revival which, for the first time in Protestant history, would show signs of becoming a singular redemptive event for masses of Europeans across numerous national borders. It was an event which would set in motion momentous expressions of Christian revival whose legacies continue to the present time. A closer focus upon these events will disclose evidence supporting the awareness of the children and their advocates serving as the protagonists in a dramatic spiritual struggle involving Orthodox (or, "old school") Protestants and their Roman Catholic adversaries. The outcome was the forging of an alliance between Pietist devotional interests and Revivalist visionaries, who fixed upon a recovery of the apostolic motif of Pentecost to signify the extraordinary difference between a God-appointed revival with global implications, as distinguished from ongoing concerns for church renewal.

Our focus will be to probe the narrative of these events concerning Pietists and Revivalists in their historical milieu, and the texts which address them, with an eye to discern how the interface of depth and breadth is operative.

As Lutherans, these figures had been catechized in the theology of the cross, where the depth dimension of faith is reached when one comes to confess that in bearing his sins unto death, Christ freed that one from the curse of the law, sin and death. In its place, that one now trusts in the reality of the mysterious love exchange whereby He owns my sins while I now gratuitously own His righteousness. Out of the underserving wonder of this blessed exchange ("fröhliche Wechsel"), faith in this Giver now ecstatically overwhelms my unfaithfulness and overflows as love ("quellende Liebe") for that other person who desperately needs such forgiving love, my neighbor. Did our Lord not instruct us that this living for the

---

3. How this plays out becomes evident in the different projects embodied in the strife between mystics like Arnold and federalists like the Cocceians, and also in the contrasting work of Petersen and Steinmetz, respectively.

neighbor is essentially an act of love for Christ himself?[4] When we identify ourselves as the sinners for whom Christ died, that action produces a synergy of love which results in a passion for meeting Christ in the world as fully as He is graciously encountered in the inner depth of the soul. Here is the correlation and synergy between faith and love, where going deeper in personal faith becomes transmuted into a drive to engage Christ in others. Out of this gracious overflow Luther had perceived the members of his Wittenberg congregation could be freed to serve Christ as He now appears within their neighbors, wherever they engaged them in their daily vocations.

However, the Pietists we shall meet who became Revivalists took this dynamic a step further. Luther counseled his congregants to realize their freedom in Christ was restricted to their inner life, which did not allow that they could now lay aside obligations to the temporal estate into which they had been born. Consequently, those of this new generation of Revivalists found their spiritual vocation in taking the message of this Christ across borders of all kinds. Their vision had become an awareness that Christ's Lordship and Kingdom might come to resonate throughout the world of their day, by reaching all those for whom Christ died, that these too might be impacted by the gospel.

There is released a synergy found within those points where the dimension of depth (the personal appeal to the mystical ground of the faith) interfaces with an awareness of breadth—the external realm of the world, and the global impact of that faith is free in the Spirit to be released across time and space. The prevailing vehicle in the early eighteenth century for embracing this "breadth" concern, came in the form of federal theology, and to it was linked a recovery of the apostolic theme of Pentecost, now advancing on a global scale, in early modernity.[5] From another perspective, we are suggesting that with their pneumatology, these Pietists were morphing into Revivalists precisely because of their appropriation of this apostolic theme, long neglected in the era of European Christendom.

---

4. See Martin Luther, *Small Catechism*, Philip Schaff. Ed. "The Creeds of Christendom Volume III" (Grand Rapids: Baker, 1996 Reprint), 74-92; John Dillenberger, Ed., "Freedom of A Christian" in *Martin Luther: Selections from His Writings*. (New York: Anchor Double Day, 1961), 42-85.

5. This impetus has been attributed to the influence of the thirteenth century Calabrian monk, Joachim of Fiore (1131-1202) who advocated a coming Age of the Spirit, as part of his economic rendering of the Trinity which appeared in his exposition of the Revelation of John. See Karl Löwith, *Meaning in History,* (University of Chicago Press, 1964), 145-159.

Since Constantine in the fourth century, the role of the imperial realm had supplanted that apostolic theme of Pentecost. In the Christendom era, Pentecost had become domesticated into a date in the liturgical calendar, observed by all liturgical church bodies, Eastern Orthodox, Roman Catholic, and magisterial Protestant (e.g., Lutherans, Reformed and Anglicans). Now, however, it began to surface in Petersen's descriptions of the inspiration of the children, which he validated as an occurrence of the immediate inspiration of the Holy Spirit. Next, this theme of Pentecost recovered was brought to another level in the revival at Teschen, under its head preacher, Johann Adam Steinmetz (1689-1762), whose catechesis among converts of the great revival at Teschen is found in his *Addresses on Pentecost*, set forth within a megachurch of some 40,000 to 70,000 displaced war refugees. Here the depth and breadth dimensions of the God/human relationship within the Pietist message of the new birth in Christ became transmuted into a twofold schema of redemption, which consisted of an enactment of the Lukan account of the disciples' movement of faith from Calvary to Pentecost. This also signifies a soteriological shift from pardon and freedom in Christ to subsequent empowerment for "building the Kingdom of God" on earth, which Steinmetz presents as being grounded in the "sealing and security" in the Holy Spirit.[6]

Through Steinmetz's connections with the Moravian evangelist, Christian David, this twofold soteriology was first conveyed to John Wesley, the founder of Methodism, through his extensive encounter with David at Herrnhut, following his Aldersgate conversion in May 1738. This is a link which could not be made apart from this author's discovery of the untranslated German addresses on Pentecost which originated with Steinmetz. They occurred in the context of the first Protestant revival, in his megachurch at Teschen, Silesia, a decade before Wesley's visit to Herrnhut.[7]

There is both a polemical and a liturgical side to the nexus of events in the narrative that leads to Christian globalization: Arnold embodies the former by clearing the way for a new paradigmatic meaning of being in community that is Christian: in short, he is offering a pioneering effort to

---

6. Steinmetz, supra. Here we refer to the title of the religious periodical edited by Steinmetz after his ministry at Teschen, will be explored in the chapters that follow.

7. The original phase of the Silesian revival at Teschen, which grew from the children's revival which preceded it (1707), was extended to the revival at Herrnhut under Steinmetz and David in 1727. Wesley visited Herrnhut a decade later, in August 1738, returning to England convinced of the revival's twofold soteriology and soon ready to engage in revival there along those lines (Bristol, 1739).

look beyond Christendom to Christianity on a global scale, and does so in his seminal study, *Die Unparteiische Kirche und Ketzer Historie* (1699). The liturgical side is presented by Gerhard Tersteegen, who goes beyond merely championing an irenic community of faith as an ideal that is genuinely Christian, to personally embodying, in hymns, correspondence, conventicles and revival addresses, the sanctified life as a winsome, living option for persons of every station and circumstance of life in his day.[8] For both, there is an implicit twofold soteriology which forms the Pietist-based platform for a global Christianity in the modern era: it is found in the dynamic between Calvary and Pentecost, or righteousness and empowerment for holiness of life. The one provides the grounding, the other provides the basis for the breadth which reaches to the limits of time and space.

This twofold nexus is the Pietist-based contribution to revivalism leading toward globalization. It is a human venture, but it also proceeds as a kairos work of God and not as a program of renewing human institutions, either clerical or civil. This study acknowledges that the term revival has often been misunderstood as being interchangeable with the word 'renewal'. The inference here is that 'revival' is a human-initiated event (as Charles Finney had argued) designed to produce the qualitative results of morally redeemed humans. What is inferred here is that one is hereby proceeding along the lines of an empiricism ungrounded in any apostolic/biblical mandate, as well as any intellectual grounding capable of being articulated in the history of Christian thought. In comparison with Finney's empirical approach to revival, Steinmetz presented a distinctly Christ-centered approach to globalization analogous to tracking the course of the 'mission of God' (missio Dei) in history.[9]

Case in point: Steinmetz, the early herald of this revival, would effectually argue that, intrinsic to this term is its inherent presentation of a God-initiated globalizing community of faith, not a renewal project for a deconstructed Christendom. He implemented this strategy as a two-stage model for salvation in his "Pentecost Addresses" presented in the context of the great revival centered in an early eighteenth-century "megachurch." And, it is appropriate here to add that Steinmetz's witness to the faith was not

---

8. See W. Reginald Ward, "Mysticism and Revival: The Case of Gerhard Tersteegen," in Jane Garnett and Colin Matthew, ed., *Revival and Religion since 1700; Essays for John Walsh* (London: The Hambledon Press, 1993),41-58.

9. This theme is popularized in the theology of Karl Barth, although it was grounded in Reformation theology, particularly in the Heidelberg Catechism of the German Reformed Church. See a treatment of that tradition in J S O'Malley, *Pilgrimage of Faith: The Legacy of the Otterbeins* (Metuchen NJ: Scarecrow, 1973).

itself the source of the revival, which was rooted in the children's prayers and prophecies beforehand. Rather, it was an appeal to the apostolic witness which conveyed the reality of the Trinitarian work of the crucified Christ, completed in obedience to the Father on behalf of a bondage-burdened humanity, and implemented through the Pentecostal sealing and empowerment of the Holy Spirit.[10]

Regarded as the first event of its kind within Protestant Christianity, the Teschen revival was the ground zero from which emanated the first line of international/interconfessional revival which fanned out over Europe and into the Western hemisphere. Steinmetz's "bush preachers," augmented by revivalist-tinged Moravians like Christian David, found their way from Teschen to Moravia, Bohemia, Saxony, Sweden, the Rhineland, England and Scotland, the Baltic states, Greenland, and New England. Steinmetz personally forged a network linking the far-flung points of this revival as it unfolded through the pages of the chronicle he edited and made available to the public. It was published by an influential Lutheran publisher with Pietist leanings, Samuel Benjamin Walther in Leipzig, enabling it to appear as a widely read German language periodical (*Zeitschrift*) linking the revival in Silesia with the world of that day.[11]

Beginning in 1724, this periodical had its origin under Immanuel Traugott Jerichovius, a co-pastor with Steinmetz in the Teschen revival.

---

10. The original title of Steinmetz's Pentecost Addresses appears as *Die Schriftmäßige Betrachtung von der Versiegelung der Gläubigen mit dem heiligen Geiste aus Ephes. 4,30* in a German reprint published in Frankfurt/Main by Heinrich Ludwig Brönner (1857), the text available to the present author. This edition is a reprint of the original free public lectures by Steinmetz, offered for clergy at Kloster Bergen (between 1732–1762), which in turn was an adaptation of his homilies delivered in the Teschen revival, between 1719 and 1730. This documentation is provided by Steinmetz's nineteenth century editor, Renner (64), who made the following observations: "For thirty years he [Steinmetz] offered popular instruction for clergy at Bergen and built a large hall for this purpose. Steinmetz had been compelled by his superior [the Catholic authority in Teschen] to complete a verbatim text of his homilies [apparently in the interest of monitoring his thought, under the terms mandated by the Altranstädt Convention (1712)]. Renner also observed that, after diligent meditation, Steinetz preached from his Ephesians text using free expression of thought. This spontaneous style of delivery is what is retained in the published version of the Kloster Bergen lectures. His nineteenth century biographer, Renner, observes, "his free lectures seem to have followed the form of speech in which the fullness of his use of the Scripture and his experience are most alive." L. Renner, *Lebensbilder aus der Pietistenzeit: ein Beitrag zur Geschichte und Würdigung des späteren Pietismus*, 64.

11. Rainer Lächele, *Die "Sammlung auserlesener Materien zum Bes Reichs Gottes: zwischen 1730 und 1760* (Halle: Verlag der Franckeschen Stiftungen Halle im Max Niemeyer Verlag Tübingen, 2006, 80–81.

The latter expanded its reach following the death of the founder, as he and other editors whom he groomed continued the project until Steinmetz's death in 1762. The periodical documents the key events during these three critical decades, including several not previously identified, which comprise the rise of revival on the European continent, linked to the rise of Methodism and extending to the First Great Awakening in America. It was viewed from the vantage point of the home base of that revival in eastern Europe. Read today, the *Gathering of Inaccessible Materials for the Building of the Kingdom of God (Sammlung Auserlesene Materialen zum Bau des Reich Gottes)*—hereafter cited as the *Gathering*—reconstructs a framework for the unfolding of events signaling a seismic shift in the development of Christianity from its base in European Christendom toward extending its mission, understood in Protestant evangelical terms, to become global in extent. Inherent to this chronicle are the key voices who articulated, in diverse sociocultural terms, the meaning and scope of that revival.

The core documents from those voices are assembled in this study as well. These represent theological turning points in tracking with this rising tide of Pietist-inspired globalization unfolding in its earliest historical manifestation. From these interpreters, we glean insight into (1) how the motifs rooted in the initial children's revival continue to inform this narrative, and (2) how Steinmetz's presentation of a two-staged soteriology based on an appeal to the meaning of Pentecost in the global fulfillment of the missio Dei has definitive implications for later Wesleyan theology, (3) finally, we may then be able to glean insights into how the current manifestation of global Christianity, with its strong focus on the recovery of the biblicism of apostolic Christianity,[12] might be provided with an intellectual grounding marked by historical depth and apostolic insight.

None of the above can be addressed, however, without the solid documentation of the theology of Pentecost embodied in Steinmetz's long-buried Pentecost addresses originating in the early eighteenth century, which this author has just made available in English translation and presents here in Part 2 of the present volume. In Part 3 interpretive chapters follow.

---

12. This feature of contemporary movements of Christian globalization in the Southern Hemisphere is documented in Philip Jenkins, *The New Face of Christianity: Believing the Bible in the Global South* (Oxford University Press, 2006).

Chapter 2

GLOBALIZATION THEN AND NOW

Though our worlds be centuries apart, the contemporary global expansion of Christianity with its focus upon the Global South can learn from its evangelical Protestant past. Its challenges and opportunities often mirror those of the early eighteenth century, when a lethargic and insular European Christendom, the largest potential transmitter of the apostolic mission of early Christianity, was slowly being awakened from its long slumber. There had long been a Constantinian resignation into a symbiotic arrangement where the state protected the interests of the church while the church provided the spiritual rationale for sustaining that relationship[1]— a process which conveniently enabled its leaders and their adherents to ignore their Lord's Pentecost-empowered mandate to "go into all the world" with the gospel. Now there were initial signs of a breakout occurring. Viewed from the future, we can identify that moment as the waning of the seventeenth century movement of spiritual renewal known as evangelical Pietism and the initial birth of revival in Protestant Christianity, an event which would be accompanied by a new vision for a world to be redeemed for the Christ and His Kingdom.

---

1. The basis for Constantine's coronation rested on the Two Sword theory of Pope Gelasius I (394 AD), which posted a spiritual and a temporal sword as the legacy of Peter to the Roman curia, and so temporal authority may be exercised by civil power operating as a trust for the interests of the church.) See Bloom, Robert L. et al. "7. The Two Swords in Theory and Practice. Pt. III: The Medieval Church," *Ideas and Institutions of Western Man* (Gettysburg College, 1958).

To be sure, such dreams had been entertained before. Columbus and his conquistador successors had seasoned their discovery of the Western Hemisphere and their verification of the Copernican view of a heliocentric, global planet earth, with the declaration that all global residents would now be brought under the sphere of Christ.[2] It was in the wake of those discoveries and their promotion that the recovery of the biblical message of personal salvation in Jesus Christ made its decisive impact upon Europe with the Protestant Reformation.[3] Its rapid rise and decline in the successive era of Protestant Orthodoxy saw that Protestant legacy obscured by the mire of massive European warfare, in which rival religious entities at enmity bequeathed us with the Thirty Years War (1618–1648). The first signs of awareness that this evangelical message based in the Protestant Reformation would find a vehicle to carry to the larger non-European world can be discerned amid the rubble of that era of conflict in eastern Europe.

It is here that we ask how the contemporary breakout of Christianity in the Global South, which has been widely documented,[4] can find resources from the Christian past to inform, guide, and correct the diverse and qualitatively uneven expressions of Global Christianity which are now proliferating. Influences from the Christian past have the potential to become vital resources for the renewal of Christianity in the often declining and increasingly non-influential denominations of the Global North as well. Mainline church bodies in North America have been desperately searching for ways to address their own spiritual lethargy and institutional decline amid the ever-growing challenges of post-Christendom. As Christianity continues to accelerate its global reach, this study is an invitation to pause and ask what are the pathologies within those new movements of Christianity that might be addressed through attention to insights from the past.

For the new globalized Christianity to track with the insights and avoid the pitfalls from the past, the challenges it faces will need to be identified and then addressed head on in the light of those from the past. Further, it is in this reflection that we find what made evangelicalism attractive and

---

2. On this theme see, Peter Marshall, Jr and David Manuel, *The Light and the Glory of God* (Old Tappan, NJ: Fleming Revel, 1977).

3. Beginning with Luther's posting of his 95 Theses in 1517 and continuing through the Peace of Augsburg (1555), when the first Protestant states were sanctioned in Catholic Europe.

4. See Todd Johnson and Kenneth Ross, eds, *Atlas of Global Christianity* {Oxford, 2009).

effective in being an instrument for the globalization of the apostolic message of Christianity in the first place.

As a phenomenon in our day, what has been termed as "world Christianity"[5] has given rise to a "consciousness of the world as a whole" and a "power of global consciousness" acknowledged by its advocates and critics alike.[6] A key catalyst of that emerging awareness has been the Christian missionary movement. The present study offers a historical grounding of what Professor Lalsangkima Pachuau has called the reinforcement of globalization coming from the "Christian practice of foreign mission."[7] It is widely acknowledged that the "worldwide character" of Christianity, rooted in the apostolic mission of the church, came to be owned by peoples of diverse cultures on every continent as a "historical development of the late twentieth century."[8] It is the position of the present study that the salient roots for that historical development can be traced fom the early eighteenth century to the origin of awakeing in Europe and beyond. The present study also elucidates the historical and theological basis for Pachuau's observation that "Christianity's essential nature is to be able to incarnate itself into in any context to transform such contexts for the knowledge and likeness of God in Christ."[9] In particular, our focus here is upon the origin of the two-staged soteriology of later Wesleyan theology in the preaching of that first awakening in Protestant Christianity, which provided the theological basis and rationale for that global mission in its historical context. It was this particular theological construct which denotes what is this "essential nature" of Christianity which, as Langsalmkima observes, is able to "incarnate itself" in any context.[10]

Addressing the important issue of grounding world mission in a theological framework faithful to the norms of apostolic Christianity becomes an imperative when addressing the pathologies often apparent amid the global expansion of Christianity. For example, a debilitating feature of the new Christianity in some quarters of the Global South is when it becomes

---

5. A term first introduced into academic discussion by Henry P. Van Dusen in *World Christianity: Yesterday, Today, Tomorrow* (New York: Abingdon-Cokesbury, 1947), 124.

6. Lalsangkima Pachuau, *World Christianity: A Historical and Theological Introduction* (Nashville: Abingdon, 2018), 1.

7. Ibid., 2

8. Ibid., 2.

9. Ibid., 3.

10. Ibid.

enculturated around particular leaders or cultural values. They become the prey of nominal Christians or also religious seekers lacking Christian catechesis or theological grounding, for whom it is more convenient to let others think or speak for us rather than attend to the means of grace. Then faith is placed in human figures rather than the living Triune God, and, when such leaders fail, so does the faith of many.

If we ask why it is that many in North American mainline Christianity remain aloof from the new life entering Christianity through its Global South expansion, it may have much to do with what William Abraham has called a pervasive sense of alienation in the pews. This is a sense of "discomfort, unease, and restlessness caused by estrangement from the group to which one belongs."[11] He traces the current decline in mainline church membership and impact on the larger society to many becoming alienated from their faith communities to which they belong and in which they are serving as leaders. This is manifest in isolation and purposelessness, causing many to lose heart and unable to get beyond this paralysis.[12] Here we find further evidence of a need to recover the roots of our faith, marked by a surprising work of the Holy Spirit, that is grounded in the saving work of Christ on Calvary for a fallen humanity. That sojourn from Calvary to Pentecost, which empowered apostolic Christianity as well as a moribund European Christendom in the age of awakening, becomes the norm for understanding and parsing the authenticity of Christian globalization in the present day, wherever it occurs.

In brief, "Revival that is global produces communities of people who are crossing borders, denying themselves, taking up their crosses, and following Jesus."[13] This is another way of affirming the cross-centered priority that genuine revival invariably needs to honor. It also puts down any expression of revival that worships the proclaimer of God's Word rather than God Himself. This pathology has been called an "overly contextualized or enculturated movement": they find themselves "promoting cultural values and hopes as a substitute for Gospel norms," as well as becoming bound by the same culture they intend to convert.[14] The mark of avoiding this pathology is made evident by the way in which a missional movement can "jump cultures, languages, ages and geography" by calling persons to

---

11. William Abraham, "A Barrier to Revitalization: Ecclesial Alienation," in *Interpretive Trends,* ed. J. S. O'Malley, 21.
12. Ibid., 22
13. Ibid.
14. Sunquist, 51.

put aside personal dreams in favor of "new and higher purposes not centered on the self."[15]

As we shall discover, the first instance of such border-crossing revival in evangelical Protestant history was that which occurred in eastern Europe at the dawn of the eighteenth century. This movement emerged concurrently with the rise of the Age of Reason, called the Enlightenment, which has also been lamented in Christianity as the nemesis of the Age of Faith which was the Protestant Reformation. This era also saw the origin of revival and the rise of a globalized Christianity,[16] although it was largely unheralded by the new intellectual elite of the Age of Reason. We now know that those who provided leadership to the rise of revival on a global scale were themselves men and women of strong theological vigor. This was true for the leaders of the first awakening in Protestant history, which became border crossing and international in its development. When we turn to the leaders of the first revival in Protestant history, we will be confronted with expansive minds joined to inspired hearts, which brought together head and heart in a powerful fusion, Edwardian in style, that is rarely seen today. That too was a strategic part of the work of God in advancing the *missio Dei*.

The attempt to discern between healthy and unhealthy forms of Christian globalization in the twenty-first century depends on our capacity to discern marks of health and of pathology which are manifested "on the ground" in real lives and cultures, and to be able to analyze not only the streams of Christian globalization as they unfurl but also to discern where they go awry and fall short of their potentiality. This science is not perfected since it is ultimately a divine mystery, but we are given resources in the history of Christianity which offer insights on what has worked in the past and what has not, and on what has been the role of those human agents who rose to the call to spearhead those initiatives which gave rise to what Scott Sunquist has called the "last great Christian century."

What also becomes evident in this study is that each of those human agents, representing different cultures, confessions, ecclesial positions, academic gifts, languages, and geographical locations, shared one common theme: the recovery of the apostolic theme of Pentecost in an age which was far removed from its apostolic origins. It was also a century before the emergence of an ecclesial movement by that name which would

---

15. Ibid., 52.

16. To this time the term "globalization" has largely been limited to the discussion of 21st Christianity, and here it is being introduced to clarify the origins of revival in its proper historical setting.

domesticate and institutionalize that theme through a diversity of denominational and cultural expressions. It was a brief moment when leading voices across the evangelical Protestant world were joining together to pray and to give witness to an imminent eschatological hour when the kingdoms of this world would in fact become the Kingdom of our God and of His Christ. It was an elusive hour, which we recover in this study.

One other feature remains in considering the historical setting for the early rise of revival with a vision for our globe. After a window of half a century, from ca. 1707 through 1760, the hour for a global, revitalized Christianity was spent. In place of the periodicals detailing this revival, which had been read avidly by masses of Europeans and others in North America during this era, there now came an intrusion of the post-Christian Age of Reason. After 1760 the popular religious journals were now devoted to perfecting reason and a moral order, with little reference to Christianity. Now, these were years when movements like Methodism were getting their footing and advancing, but it was without the support and involvement of the Christian public in Europe and America, whose interests had shifted to new cultural trends, first rationalism and then romanticism. Hence, the shift from revitalization to accommodation in the mid-eighteenth century was a pattern that is replicated today when mission occurs that is devoid of a serious and fresh encounter with the God who acts among those who watch and pray for His coming?

In particular, what difference does it make that the former era of expansion was marked by the overall theme of Pentecost being renewed, and in the current era the theme of Pentecost is dominant on the grassroots level in several areas (especially Latin America) but is lacking in acceptance at the intellectual and leadership levels? What is missing in the current narrative that is present in the previous one because of the absence of the dominance of that apostolic theme? Apart from it, what are the theological elements which are the drivers of contemporary movements for a globalized Christianity?

This study presenting the form and content of the first Protestant revival is here set forth with the intent of addressing that void of apostolic urgency which imperils the global witness of the church in our day, and especially those who stand in the Wesleyan tradition.

PART TWO

SUPPLYING THE MISSING DOCUMENT FROM THE PAST

Concerning the Sealing of Believers
with the Holy Spirit
in Five Pentecost Edification Sessions
[*in der Versiegelung der Gläubigen*

mit dem heiligen Geist]

Johann Adam Steinmetz

Frankfurt am Main
Reprinted by Heinrich Ludwig Brönner in 1857
Its Message originates from the era of the Teschen revival
ca.1720–1730, later formatted in addresses delivered by Steinmetz at
Kloster Bergen (between 1732 and 1762) and
first publihed posthumously in Leipzig in 1769
(See complete editions in Foreword by Brönner)
Translated by J. Steven O'Malley

Foreword

by

Heinrich Ludwig Brönner, 1857[1]

The famous Steinmetz, the son of a Silesian preacher, was born on September 21, 1689, at Gross Kniegnitz, and received in baptism the name Johann Adam. From early on he was dedicated to the Lord His Redeemer through faithful parents. With utmost consecration, his father worked on the development of his spirit and heart. The spirit of Spener held sway in his parents' home. Through his attention to prayer, the ten-year-old boy gave himself in his walk of the powerful leading to the Holy Spirit. About this time a private tutor also came alongside the father in training the boy. The great diligence of the boy made the task easy for the both of them. Beside the startling progress there was also the unmistakable leadings, protections, and summons of God, so that all things came together to create an ever so anointed as well as diligent servant of

---

1. This is the first English translation of the "Vorwort" to the 1857 German edition of Steinmetz's Pentecost Addresses, by the publisher, Heinrich Ludwig Brönner. The German text of these addresses is presented without notes or organization of content, except for division into five separate addresses. All sections and titles in the addresses were provided by the translator and author of this work, J. Steven O'Malley. The first German edition was the *Schriftmäßige Betrachtung von der Versiegelung der Gläubigen mit dem heiligen Geiste aus Ephes. 4,30* (herausgegeben von Oberconsistorialrath Silbergschlag, Wernigerode, 1769, 2. Auflage 1770, neu aufgelegt 1825). The present translator located and translated this third or Brönner (1857) edition of the published addresses by Steinmetz. It was not listed in the official list of editions which were published by the printing office of the Lutheran Church in Werniderode (in 1770 and 1825). This third edition from Brönner was published outside the official aegis of the Church for a wider public audience, at the major publishing center of Frankfurt/Main.

the Lord. At the Gymnasium, the classics of Arndt's book *On the True Christianity* and Spener's writings were the most beloved learning tools.

In the year 1710 he began his education at the University of Leipzig. Here he completed his classical education and with extraordinary diligence he launched a study of the great church fathers of the first five centuries of Christianity. He found in Dr. Gottfried Olearius a pious and learned leader in the study of theology. A measure of this man is found in his expression, "Whoever does not seek the grace of God to accept theological study by head and by collar should leave it alone." Steinmetz was a student of theology in this sense. Diligence to accept the godly truth of revelation wholly in itself, and to study and defend it, is what consumed him. Yet in all this he exercised a most childlike piety, lived with devoted love in the church, allowing himself to be led only by the Holy Spirit in all ways and he remained constrained in prayer. So, he became a theologian in the truest sense of the word.

The first time he preached was at Molwitz by Brieg. He so overcame the congregation there that they henceforth desired that Steinmetz would remain as their pastor. A formal call extended this invitation to him. First, however, after all aspects of who he was concurred in this, and after he reached certainty through prayer that such a step would be pleasing to the Lord, he accepted. It was in the year 1715 that he received with great joy the office of preacher at Molwitz and served there until 1717. Then in succession he became pastor in Töppliwode, senior preacher and inspector at Teschen, Superintendent and first preacher at Neustadt an der Aisch, Abbot of the Closter Bergen, consistorial advisor and general superintendent in the principality of Magdeburg (1732–1762). Steinmetz died July 10, 1762.

"I know best within, what kind of overwhelming grace and mercy has befallen me a poor sinner. That should be my funeral text." This was one of his last notable utterances.

What rich blessing the Lord bestowed on this faithful, highly gifted servant cannot be described here in this brief address. How much knowledge and faith his writings have disseminated is only known through all those who bore testimony. What he is and will remain for faithful Christianity touches us in the following witness.

The celebrated Bogatzky penned this verse for him: "Here you know the people stand for righteousness, And you gave to each the full raiment of salvation."

Here the faithful man observed:

This experienced Abbot has expressed and desired, both orally and in print, that the teacher might constantly project the correct order of salvation, whereby the souls learn not only one and another piece of divine truth, but might learn to understand the whole counsel of God and His blessedness, as also the blessed Professor Francke writes, to confess the entire garment of salvation. However it often happens that some good intending teachers probably give much good doctrine and admonitions, and preach with edification for some hearers, but do not project the whole order of salvation, with a true conversion that first presses into a new birth. Instead, they speak as though all are already believers and reborn Christians, since all are in congregations and churches which mostly consist of persons who are unconverted. Often they do not understand what a preacher is saying because it pertains more to those truly converted than for the unconverted person. The preaching of the crucified Christ is to bare human reason and intelligence a theoretical sermon; but before God it is nevertheless godly wisdom and power.

The blessed General Superintendent Hähny wrote poetically about Steinmetz:

> He rests gently in Jesus' arms, Abiding right in spiritual comfort, So, anyway, his element was here.

This man observes:

> We scarcely know any work in current literature which is in a position to make the case for salvation in such an extraordinary manner as we find here. The Lord of the church rule, so that ripe fruit may come forth among us.

THE FIRST PENTECOST EDIFICATION

(1) = [page numbers of the German text]—translator

1.1 Introduction

(a) The Urgent Benefit of the Sealing with the Holy Spirit

The words of our meditation stand: Ephesians 4:30—"And do not grieve the Holy Spirit of God, by whom you were sealed for the day of redemption."

We want to consider under the gracious favor of God and our Lord Jesus Christ the following: *The boundless benefit of the sealing through grace with the Holy Spirit.*

I rejoice that I can speak about such a glorious subject. I bow down however in shame and fear before my Savior Jesus Christ, because I do not find myself in the position to speak with worthiness on this theme. Had we not the longing to handle this truth, given opportunity, I would scarcely had undertaken it. For it pertains to such an insight and manifold experience that scarcely can a well-versed man venture upon it, to address it with his mouth.

As the Lord knows, my intent, under prayer and diligence, (2) is not to set forth my own thought, my wretched experiences, nor other men's thoughts concerning this subject. Instead, so much as it will be possible for me under divine aid, it is to strengthen me to hold to the Word of divine truth, of which I could say nothing apart from being joyful before my Savior Jesus Christ and in some day to come to stand before His judgment stool.

At the beginning of this address we acknowledge that we set forth a circumspect inquiry. [The first four sections concern God's side in the sealing, and the next three sections concern what is the human side].

1.2 The Biblical Basis

What remains to be understood about the sealing with the Holy Spirit: It is to explore what is intended by this term in God's Word and what the apostle intended to impart to the Ephesians as their understanding of it, when he writes to them: "And do not grieve the Holy Spirit of God, by whom you have been sealed for the day of redemption."

It is probably now a known fact what it means for one to encounter a simile (comparison)—where something is spoken or given in sequential pattern, and the matter is not only written but is also sealed, thereby enabling the thing spoken to receive its certainty, power and validity. It is known, because much that is in a testament is situated so that it is not only verbally explained but also confirmed and sealed, and thereby its ratification results. That which is in it for the inheritance is ratified, so that by this process one receives it. By this process, a person's inheritance (3) will not be able to be contested. Now, does not such a testament, or such a contract—presuming one is confirmed (besiegeln) and sealed (versiegeln) by a righteous judge—provide for a greater certainty about the matter at hand, a guarantee that one can also call upon in judgment, as a claim that is secured, lest it be contested by another?

Therefore, God alludes to the Holy Spirit in His Word when He speaks of sealing. If we observe what I have simply introduced, and remind ourselves of this, then we can thereby likewise recognize that this manner of comparison means the following: sealing through the Holy Spirit means nothing other than that the person may thereby endure in a certain, irrefutable, incontestably firm (4) knowledge concerning what has been sealed against all attacks of the devil, the world, unfaith, and evil hearts. There is also the witness of godly judgments, so that one can be peaceful in conscience. All this is given to be understood in the sealing through the Holy Spirit.

Therefore, it is certainly not just a good hope, a good thought, a good concept in the mind. Ah, no! Such a sealing would not last long. Rather, it is needed in daily life to certify the Presence of the Holy Spirit, according to the simple sense of the holy Scripture, as a firm, certain, immovable, incontestable, heart-soothing and quickening sealing. It is one which no devil can render dubious or take from us by theft, and it is one by which we can stand before God's judgment.

If we now want to grasp the entire matter of what it is to become sealed with the Holy Spirit and everything which belongs to that, then we must necessarily refer to the different places of the holy Scripture in which clear, *expansive* words are found which treat this subject.

In the first place note that the more precise explanation stands in Ephesians 1:13:

> In him, you also, after listening to the message of truth, the gospel of your salvation—having also believed you were sealed in Him with the Holy Spirit of promise.

The Ephesians had not only heard the Word. They also believed it. For it is stated, "since they believed."

In this saying we can already see which persons will become participants in such a sealing, namely, none others than those who believe, who come to know through the Holy Spirit, in the ordinance that is heard, concerning the true faith in our Lord and Savior Jesus Christ. These are the ones who receive the Holy Spirit as the treasure and seal of redemption, so that they become God's possession for the praise of His glory.

(5) An important biblical asset in understanding our theme adequately is the text found in 2 Corinthians 1:20 and 22:

> For as many as may be the promises of God, in Him they are yes, wherefore also by Him is our Amen to the glory of God through us ... who also sealed us and gave us the Spirit in our hearts as a pledge.

Here was not an uncertain, but a pure certainty. Therefore, I infer from these words the following: From them we may recognize that the faithful, who allow themselves be brought through faith to the Lord Jesus through the sealing with the Holy Spirit, become certain of the truth of all the promises which God has done in that time through His Son Jesus Christ, which is for all who belong to Him.

To confirm this, Romans 8:14,17 opens us to a deeper level of insight: "For all who are being led by the Spirit of God, these are the sons of God ... and *children*, heirs also, heirs of God and fellow heirs with Christ, if indeed we suffer with Him in order that we may also be glorified with Him."

What we find here is that the Spirit of God seals the faithful so that they become grounded through Him into the truth of all God's promises in Christ. Here we learn that when the Holy Spirit seals the souls of men, He is also doing this to assure that they are no longer the children of wrath, of death and hell, but rather they have become the (6) children of God. In forgiving them of their sins, God gives them the right to *childhood,* and they, enabled by such a right of childhood, now are intended to have eternal participation in the imperishable [unverweltlichen] inheritance of God, and they now become co-heirs with Jesus Christ.[1]

Finally, in this text from I John 5:5-7 the subject at hand is incomparably presented:

> And who is the one who overcomes the world, but he who believes that Jesus is the Son of God? This is the One who came by water and blood, Jesus Christ, not with the water only, but with the water and with the blood.

And it is the Spirit who bears witness, because the Spirit is the truth. (NIV).

This matter is now explained in the eleventh verse, which can be the witness concerning the Holy Spirit and the sealing:[2] And the witness is this, that God has given us eternal life, and this life is in His Son. A person may not receive this through His own power, but only in the grace of Christ.

---

1. Here we find the author connecting the Ephesians text to the experience of the Silesian children's prayer and prophecy revival, which was the basis for the harvest of souls in the Teschen revival where this preaching was based. This is one of the of many reference to children in his addresses, which becomes the main distinguishing feature of his interpretation of Pentecost in the context of revival. All references to children are in italics to make evident how and where the theme is used. For context, read the chapter in this study on the children's revival and the contemporary responses to it.

2. The concept of a text serving as a witness to the reader of the veracity of a biblical assertion is a pedagogy with a distinguished history in biblical interpretation. It was articulate in the post Reformation era with the thought of the French Huguenot scholar, Petrus Ramus, who developed his pedagogical method as a alternative to Aristotelian syllogistic or deductive logic which prevailed in the post Reformation era of Protestant Orthodoxy. His concern was to develop a method of reasoning which would address issues from the standpoint of the witness found in Scripture for a given assertion, instead of basing reason on a priori major premises to a discussion which may have no relationship to revelation found in the biblical text. (This led to charges of biblical proof texting made against Protestant Orthodox theologians because they were searching for texts to support their a priori premises.) This Ramist method was attacked in Protestant and Catholic schools alike, but found its home in centers of Pietist thought, including Halle. Ramus paid dearly for his efforts by becoming a victim of the St Bartholomew's Day Massacre of Huguenots in Paris in 1572. His work also had wide usage among Puritans. See John Eusden, ed., *Introduction, The Marrow of Divinity: The Thought of Willam Ames,* (Baker Books, 1997).

And so the Holy Spirit testifies Himself of what He has wanted to express to us in the holy Scripture, when it is declared that He seals the person.

1.3 The Source of Christian Identity: Sealing, Childhood, and Adoption, and A Two-Staged Process of Saving Grace

(7) Let us take this all together, so we may be able to form a clear comprehension of what is intended through the sealing of the Holy Spirit according to the Word of God. It is such a certain, powerful, grounded assurance of the believer, which also endures in the time of judgment, and against all assaults of Satan as well as those of a person's heart and conscience. Those who know they are worthy of damnation of themselves are not only brought from death unto life, bringing the forgiveness of their sins, but also become participants of adoption as children of God. This new person now lives in the fulness of faith in their Savior Jesus Christ, to the end. What we have here described reflects the biblical meaning in Ephesians 1 that substantiates this life transformation.[3]

However, I want to explain something further, because this cannot be sufficiently comprehended. *Therefore, give attention, you childlike souls*, the sealing consists in your capacity for this, for such a certain and powerful confidence of soul, of a standing in grace, of the forgiveness of your sins, of your blessedness in such certainty whereby you can also stand (8) before the judgment seat of Christ[4]—yes, even if you are condemned by the

---

3. Here again the close connection is being made between the appeal to children as the prototype for genuine revival and the reliance on pneumatic sealing as the bond whereby that filial status is authenticated.

4. Here the author presents pardon and the sealing of the Spirit as a two part yet inseparable ordo salutis, anticipating the two stages of grace, justifying and sanctifying, in later Wesleyan theology. It was this mode of two stage grace which was also introduced directly to John Wesley by Christian David, the Moravian preacher whom Wesley heard while at Herrnhut, following his Aldersgate conversion (autumn, 1738). Note this: David learned of this distinction from the preaching of Steinmetz, under whom he sat and through whom he came to his own sealing in the Holy Spirit. The latter observation was first made by W.R. Ward in his *Protestant Evangelical Awakening* (Cambridge, 1992), 90. "It was Schwedler who converted Christian David, Zinzendorf's turbulent henchman, who was confirmed in the faith by Steinmetz at Teschen, and passed on via the mystic, Melchior Scheffer, at Görlitz, to Herrnhut." Steinmetz's Pentecost addresses date from this era of the revival in Teschen, which David encountered. See also David's *Memoir*, edited by Zinzendorf. Vernon H. Nelson, ed., *Servant of the Lord: A Memoir of Christian David* by Zinzendorf (Bethlehem, PA:

Devil through your own conscience and by the law. If the matter wants to become doubtful for you, know that you can become capable of such confidence of standing before God's judgment.

For a truly faithful Christian not only knows that his Savior died for him with His blood and by His death to attain and grant life for him; but also, his Savior Jesus Christ bequeaths to him all of this in His *testament*, and He has ratified the testament with His death.[5] Yes, a faithful Christian not only knows that, but God also grants that for his assurance through the Holy Spirit, impressed as a living pledge and seal in his heart. God, the great judge of heaven and earth (thereby a believer may certainly become sure of that), has bestowed in His own Person an affective seal for the testament in His blood. Hence, it freely comes that whoever is sealed with the Holy Spirit has an assurance that he Himself stands with it before the judgment seat of God. Every assault, every objection and opposition of the devil and his own evil heart can be defeated. In this section, the author explores how the Holy Spirit brings about the sealing of believers under three heads.

(a) Sealing and the Struggle with Satan

There is a reason for setting forth these matters here. That is, the sealing of the Holy Spirit is placed on the side of a credible and divine action which may be for the devil himself an irrefutable sealing of a soul through the Holy Spirit. Yet, I have done this, *first of all, so that you might very soon notice what a huge distinction is to be made between the sealing of the Holy Spirit and the distressing suffering of our present day "mouth Christians" [e.g., mere professors of the faith]*, who also keep saying, "yes, I also (9) hope to become blessed." Indeed, what a distinction is found between those who give mere cognitive assent to such texts as the sealing of the Holy Spirit and the encounter with life changing grace accompanied by the pledge of the Holy Spirit which occurs when Jesus first awakens persons from their slumber of death and sin. The latter is a spontaneous act occurring for a person who, imprisoned in the misery of sin, looks within, and throws herself before the feet of Jesus, and receives a life changing visitation of grace. God first peers down for a moment from heaven, so to speak, but that certainly is

---

Archives of the Moravian Church, 1962), especially pages 11, 13, 22, 35, 45, 47, 52, 55, 57, 59, 66, 68.

5. Here Steinmetz reflects Luther's instruction on God's promise in the gospel as a testament made in view of a testator who would die to actualize its validity for believers. See Martin Luther, "Pagan Servitude of the Church" in Dillenberger, *Martin Luther*, 279.

not yet the sealing of grace. For such a glance of grace quickly ebbs away. Within an hour that can begin and also end.

Now, if a seal remains in place, as at the time when a judge has imprinted one upon a person in the verdict of a trial, how much more of a living seal is there with the Holy Spirit? And with the Spirit there grows now a grounded, persevering, heaven-focused assurance enduring unto the judgment of God Himself, that, with it, one may *be a child of God. Then, in an instant, a person may stand in a condition in which that one will unfailingly become blessed.*[6] All temptations [Anfechtungen] and doubts concerning that may say whatever they please . . . [They are now impotent]. It is for the sake of this great promise that I have now brought it forth for our consideration. And I have brought attention to it at the beginning so that the sealing of the Holy Spirit *might stand against all the assaults of this world*[7] that it might be a firm and enduring sealing in the judgment of God itself.

With that I might have opportunity here to remind you that a person sealed in the Holy Spirit can still suffer through the devil, the world, and unbelief. Indeed, his own heart probably often fails him. I want to share with you a simple parable about this. We have heard that there probably exists evil people who lay hands on a (10) judicially sealed testament and seek to make a legitimate inheritance by such deceitful means. This, I might say, is what the devil is doing in his distraction of humanity. Faithful souls have such a testament sealed and *confirmed [Bestätig]* in God's judgment.[8] Jesus has not only confirmed humanity with His blood as our intended Redeemer but God has already sealed them in *judgment* and in *righteousness* through His Holy Spirit. Yet the devil seeks the poor heart of

---

6. "Selig" is a term for salvation which includes beatification, suggesting the highest level of holiness before the Lord. Steinmetz speaks here of the distinction between first being awakened from sin and death and a subsequent instant moment of being sealed with the Spirit. It is not surprising that Charles Wesley who through his brother John had learned to speak in a similar manner from Christian David. Charles recorded in his journal on October 3, 1739, that Sarah Townsend testified that while they were singing on Sunday evening, "the Spirit in that *instant* sealing her pardon upon her heart . . . was filled . . . with joy unspeakable." *The Manuscript Journal of the Reverend Charles Wesley*, M.A, ed. S. T. Kimbrough, Jr., and Kenneth G. C. Newport, 2 volumes (Nashville: Kingswood Books, 2008), 1:210. John Wesley highlighted the "instant" moment of being sealed and sanctified through the Spirit, and Charles often spoke of the *instant* moment of "now" in his hymns for the Holy Spirit to seal and sanctify the believer who was already justified and forgiven of sins.

7. Here "world" is used to signify the backside of glorification.

8. This is an inversion of the Anglican/Lutheran Orthodox portrayal of confirmation to reflect the faith development of a lay church member.

humanity to set it in doubt. He also seeks many kinds of scruples with which to agitate them. However, a divine sealing has occurred. The devil comes nevertheless and assails us. And yet our faith triumphs![9]

No devil can take from you the testament, which seals with the Holy Spirit, and is underwritten with Christ's blood. If there is a doubt which stands against the certainty of this sealing, your course is correct and it is proceeding before God. Your seal which triumphs against everything your Enemy directs against you must endure. In the description of the sealing I have delayed in saying something important, a true believer holds, recognizes and knows, namely, that he is a sinner worthy of condemnation. For that reason he does not base his hope of standing before God in grace on the basis of good works, but he is sealed so that his Savior Jesus Christ obtains that with the merit of His blood.

(b) Sealing by Grace versus by Works[10]

(11) A second important reason why I have sought to clarify the sealing in the Holy Spirit is to make evident the proper basis on which the sealing and certainty reside, which is not on our miserable works. O, that protects us before God. That could also strike the tempter with unrivalled force. No, the ground, the rock of hope of our blessedness is the blood hed by

---

9. Here the focus has shifted from freedom for love of neighbor through trust, against the wiles of the law, sin and Satan, in the promise of righteousness through the shed blood at the cross (Luther) to security in the sealing of the Holy Spirit of the believer into the effects of that blood confirmation effected for us by Christ on the cross, to be lived out in a beatified (sanctified) believer who stands against the onslaught of a defeated Satan throughout the world.

10. See Part 3, Chapter 1.3 below, "The Roots of the Awakening: The Struggle for the Survival of the Reformation" to find the historical context for this emphasis on faith vs works, which takes us not only to Luther and the Reformation of the sixteenth century, but also to the Hapsburg Cathoic incursions into Silesia which created the disruption and dislocation of population that resulted in the formation of the "emergency" refugee churches under the treaty that was signed at Altranstädt in 1707. Steinmetz's church, the Grace church at Teschen, was one built with funding from Francke of Halle, who personally intervened at the peace convention on behalf of the Protestant refugees, offering to provide them with sustenance as well as spiritual assistance in the form of a line of "emergency churches" between the warring sides. Their right to worship was sealed by the agreements at Altranstädt between the Hapsburg Emperor Joseph I and the Swedish King Charles XII, who had arrived in Silesia with an army to force the Emperor to come to terms with these Protestants. Altranstädt was appealing to the earlier provisions found in the Peace of Westphalia (1648) which had brought the Thirty Years War (between Protestant and Catholic powers in Europe) to a conclusion.

the Lamb of God who has died for us on the cross, and who has expensively purchased, attained and brought all of us to the way of blessedness.

I have introduced this theme that you might be directed to the distinction between the miserable sealing of a holiness of works and the proper sealing of all true believers through the Holy Spirit. A miserable and pharisaical hypocrite has self-converted not on the basis of the heart and has likewise outwardly built honorably and quietly, out of his own reason and power, thinking he has done this or that good deed, saying "I love worship, I do so much good in the house, or I give alms and so forth. Therefore, God will be gracious unto me." O you miserable Pharisee! Death, floods and hell are what you have earned with all these highly adorned so-called good works.

If you take a look just once in the light of the Spirit, you will observe what horror there is behind (12) your good works if you intend to rely on them within your heart. We know that an authentic Christian will never build or place trust in a single good work. Indeed, if a person had to exhibit the works of angels before God, an upright soul could not build even upon that, for such works can never stand before God. No impurity of any kind can stand before God in heaven. Thus, the Holy Spirit seals us by our standing in grace, not upon our miserable works. If the Holy Spirit first brings a soul to that position, so that it regards all their works as for naught in the presence of God's judgment, and if that soul is relieved of all self righteousness, considering itself as deserving damnation, then its true anchor can become the shed blood of our Savior as the Rock of salvation. Upon that basis we become sealed by the Holy Spirit, who now becomes the ground of the soul, enduring and persisting on our behalf, even in affliction and in death. There anguish and death may rail against us, but that is also where the merit of the blood of my Savior Jesus Christ does not permit me to be cast aside, and can secure me against the demands of the righteousness of God.[11]

Hence, if I stand and remain grounded in His grace, God will not abandon me according to His righteousness. For I have such a righteousness in the blood of my Savior[12] that it endures in the face of the most stringent

---

11. This reads as an Anselmic (satisfaction) version of atonement.

12. His recurring focus on the blood of Jesus as the core of our redemption is consonant with Luther but is emphasized in Steinmetz to reflect the Moravian focus on blood and wounds, a particular phase of Moravian worship tradition under Zinzendorf's leadership. However, unlike Zinzendorf, his friend Steinmetz places greater focus on the pneumatic aspect, with the sealing of Christ's atoning work on our hearts through the Spirit's sealing. Zinzendorf preferred a more subjective emphasis on feeling (das Gefühl) of Jesus' love for

demands of the righteousness of God. That is what we need to observe. The person who builds even a trifle on his own work has no sealing through the Holy Spirit, and the entire ground of his (13) hope does not rest on the merits of Christ.

(c) Sealing Grounded on the Blood and Merit of Christ

There is yet a third cause why we have needed to address the description of the sealing through the Holy Spirit: that the correct sealing and assurance, which comes through the Holy Spirit, may clearly be understood as standing on the blood and the merit of Jesus Christ, so that a person who comes before that cross may know, see and recognize that he is himself a sinner worthy of condemnation.[13] If the occasional wholly sincere souls are not aware of these matters, where would they be? A person who is genuinely gifted with grace and sealed through the Holy Spirit notices and feels within his spirit that he is a condemned sinner, and so must be lost apart from the crucified Jesus who bore his sins.

Because many of these poor sinners do not always understand how to distinguish these matters of salvation, even if they are already sealed, they fall away from their salvation with a thousand unnecessary doubts. However, if they have now come to a correct understanding of these matters, so that the sealing of such souls does occur, only then do they recognize and really feel themselves to be death deserving sinners who, though they recognize themselves as that, yet their entire ground of hope, their entire trust, simply and solely is placed on the bloody merit of Jesus Christ, on the bloody wounds, and so there is no doubt.

Concerning this description of the sealing with the Holy Spirit, that such persons are not so aligned with this truth in their present state of grace that they actually are standing in the state of forgiveness and adoption [Kindschaft] by God. By contrast, they also become sealed unto their future salvation and blessedness, even if they live one hundred years in this world. Here we would focus on a small word in our text: The faithful Ephesians were sealed with the Holy Spirit unto the day of deliverance. What kind of day then is that? That is the last great judgment day, there the

---

me, as in His question to Peter, "do you love me?" as the point of validation for the theology of the cross. Count Nicholas Von Zinzendorf "Concerning Saving Faith" from "Nine Public Lectures (1746)", Peter Erb, Ed. Pietists: Selected Writings (New York: Paulist Press, 1983), 314.

13. See note 12 above.

great faithful assembly in the actual redemption will enter into the company of all of those by whom they are abandoned or rejected. Thus the believers are assured in the forgiveness of the Holy Spirit, so that they have not only now found grace here in this life, but also there, when the Son of God will appear in the great day of judgment, honor and glory will be received, so that they will stand with joy before the great throne of the Lord Jesus and will receive the crown of honor from his loving gracious hand.

Now, beloved souls! Could one possibly wish for anything better? Could God show us a greater good and a greater benefit than this, when He seals us through the Holy Spirit. Ah, if even God demanded something of a soul, I know not what, so should that soul be ready to please Him if only to become a partaker of this goodness of God.

(d) The Sealing and Pentecost

(15) I must now pose a question on this day of the celebration of Pentecost.

To all of you friends who are here before God, what does it mean for you to be well before God? How will you answer that question before God, so that by the time we have become 20, 30, 40 or perhaps 50 years old, we have heard so much about the Holy Spirit and the gracious sealing through the Holy Spirit, but we have probably not once heard that we need to kneel before God and say,

> 'O Lord Jesus! Help me yet, help me yet, seal my soul with the Holy Spirit, so that I may no longer stagger through the world, like a drunken person, who does not know where his foot will land next!'

O, if what I have just said could still and move your soul to come to the conclusion and to sigh,

> 'Lord Jesus, I do not rest until [this is done], and if I should lay at Your feet day and night, [I do so] until even my soul might partake of this great gift of sealing!'

With that, may you now be much more moved, so let me remain standing here for yet a moment, and, with little further discussion, consider what I have said about the greatest good found in the description of sealing. Before one may come to the right sealing, through the Holy Spirit, one goes forth into uncertainty with no joy, and at that point one does not know how he stands with his God in heaven. At times one may have some glimpse of good hope, yes, that is so, as when one builds a house of spider webs, which we find (16) in Job 8:14.[14] There a small insect often comes and stimulates an entire palace of spinning webs enveloping the house. One comes to that point without grace, but all doubt falls for whomever is sealed through the Holy Spirit by the forgiveness of his sins and by his standing in grace and blessedness. It is even as the scales fell from the eyes of the blessed Paul once God bestowed on him through Ananias the assurance of the forgiveness of his sins.

Hence, this is also found with a sealing, and when doubt again enters into one's disposition, then power is there, which is the seal, and one can be certain that all such doubt, all such attacks are of the devil and contradict his own heart. It may be seen in the first epistle of John, among other passages, even if the heart wants to condemn such a soul, that one thinks, 'my heart cannot condemn me, where God has not condemned me.' God is greater than my heart. God is judge over heaven and earth, who also looks upon my heart. Such a thought will not overcome my heart. Instead, it will encounter God's declaration, if I have a seal of God then He has absolved me eternally. That is how I will look upon whoever would condemn me. This apostle writes (I John 8:19-20), "We shall know by this that we are of the truth, and shall assure our heart before Him, in whatever our heart condemns us, for God is greater than our heart, and knows all things."

Those who have not yet arrived at sealing through the Holy Spirit may be able now and then to enter through all kinds of sweet notions of grace and of pardon from sins. But then, such (17) poor souls who once lay hold of courage, then begin to consider death, judgment, and eternity, and ah, how alarming all this is to them. The dictum then occurs to them, "It is given to man once to die and afterward the judgment" (Hebrews 9:27).

However, if their blessedness is certain for them, then they go to meet death with a thousand joys. The judgment seat of God is their grace and their seat of joy (Gnadenstuhl). Eternity is now the time they attain perfected life and should come to their crown. They have pressed from death unto life.

They know they have been eternally absolved of all their sins. They know that Jesus is their brother and so it is true that their blood bridegroom is seated at the right hand of God, even so far as believing I too must sit on Christ's seat, according to Revelation 3:21.

To him who overcomes, I will grant to sit down with Me on My throne,

---

14. The hope of the godless: "[Their] confidence is fragile and [their] trust a 'spider's web.'"

as I also overcame and sat down with My Father on His throne, *so* truly does the [child of God] triumph in the eternity of eternities. For he is sealed in Jesus Christ, he is His member of His body, and there he must also enjoy an eternity of the good. He must now become a partaker of the One who was his Savior in time and eternity.[15]

I want to set forth yet one more thing. So long as a soul does not come into sealing through the Holy Spirit it has no joy, no confidence in God. He prays but knows not whether it has been heard by God. Therefore, he is always somber in prayer and becomes even more somber out of prayer, as he has come to that place, or, if his heart has remained still so he still remains so empty, because he has still received nothing.[16]

How different though it is if a person is sealed, since there he has joy before God, there he knows all supplications have been heard, since he has stepped to the stool of grace where he receives His divine assistance at the right time. The entire heart of God is now open with all the treasures and blessings of salvation, which have been attained through our Savior Jesus. And who can explain everything which flows for the blessed from the sealing through the Holy Spirit.[17]

The sealing through the Holy Spirit is a real source of peace and joy. It is a really full fountain, which by day and night overflows of blessing and life.[18] It is a genuine, whole, wide, and broad sea of unending heavenly

---

15. The implication here is that revival occurring under the promise of Pentecost serves as a foretaste of that heavenly session, when our completed lives in Christ are joined to our common Head, and we become a partaker of Him together with our fellow brothers and sisters in Christ. In brief, Pentecost today anticipates its great manifestation before the court of our Triune Lord. The Wesley brothers also spoke of "sealing" and "sanctification" as an "eanest of our inheritance" and "pledge of heaven, which comes to one subsequently to being justified by faith and after receiving the forgiveness of sins. " Laurence Wood, *Pentecost & Sanctification in the Writings of John Wesley and Charles Wesley with a Proposal for Today*, 29, 57, 82-83.

16. That is, the heart remains still without the seeking of the Holy Spirit and the joy that goes with this seeking: another allusion to the urgency of Pentecost to be now received.

17. At this point, Steinmetz's sola fideism has become transformed into mystical piety, reflecting Ward's observation that Pietism in central Europe, and the revivalism which grows from it, is steeped in this depth dimension in ways less known in the Anglo world.

18. Here is an inversion of Luther's theology of the cross, where the 'quellende Liebe' (overfloving love) serves to connect the believer's faith in Christ to love of neighbor and it occurs at the point of the 'blessed exchange' between alien and proper righteousness; now shifted to the point of the Spirit's sealing of the righteousness of Christ as life and power unto salvation in the outward life as well. See O'Malley, "The Theology of the Cross in Luther and its Reconfiguration in the Pietist and Wesleyan Awakenings," in Douglas Matthews, ed., *Cross and Kingdom*, publication pending (Wipf & Stock, 2019).

excellence [Gütern] and treasures. In addition, whoever comes to the sealing through the Holy Spirit has a firm anchor for his heart if he also begins to struggle in all kinds of exigencies, tribulation, temptation, and persecutions, since his little ship is never allowed to sink. (19) He knows circumstances may go for him as they will, and they may bring what they will. Everything is happening for his best Romans 8:28).

God is now my mine and Jesus Christ, who pardons my sins, and the wonder of eternity, are now mine to lose. There the soul is transfigured into the forevers of one degree of glory after another and views from the distance its reward of grace. [As Romans 8 suggests, all your suffering and tribulations have become lightened and nothing is proscribed against the overwhelming glory, to be revealed to the soul with sudden splendor].

I ask you yet again, whether we do not have the highest incentive, from this perspective, to lie prone day and night on our knees, without ever resting, until we might become partakers of this comfort and grace and blessedness? I am not wrongly concerned that many such poor souls who hear of this then become reprimanded, and yet they fall short of coming to experience this great letter of grace and to learn how a poor, faint-hearted and doubtful human being can become a partaker of this sealing.

Therefore, I now intend to point to the other essential and also most simple thing from God's Word, of how a person can obtain the great good of the sealing through the Holy Spirit, and such a certain and firm assurance of the forgiveness of sins, of the position of grace, and the certainty of blessedness, that he also may triumph in the judgment of God and its outcome.

The fact has already been shown that it may be possible for such a sealing to come (20). We can discover its meaning without any difficulty from our text. For there we expressly hear that the entire host of humanity who believed in Jesus Christ had arrived at this great blessedness and were assured of their standing in grace through the Holy Spirit—not only perchance the teacher, or the strong Christian, no! *All the believing Ephesians were sealed.* Thus, Paul can consider himself comforted by this and say, all you Ephesians, you who believe: grieve not the Holy Spirit, with whom you are sealed.

The sealing through the Holy Spirit is not such a benefit which we must acquire first. On the contrary, it has been acquired for us by our Savior Jesus Christ through suffering and death and He brought and managed *to make this available to all humankind on the face of the earth.*[19] For as the Lord Jesus has died for all persons, therefore through the Holy Spirit he has also acquired this for all based upon the merit of his blood. All the benefits and all the gifts of grace are here acquired under which this sealing through the Holy Spirit depends. There are important reasons why I have presented this as the ground upon which all depends, before I undertake to address the question of how a person can attain this sealing. For this will make the entire matter meaningful and comprehensible for us, and if we properly hold onto this, it cannot only protect us from all errors and aberrations, but can also lead us into (21) a recognition of God's will, those things which God desires from humans if he should seal them and if they would desire to partake of this great benefit of grace.

1.4 Accessing Sealing: Counsel for the Timid

Here I address a question which has come before me, namely, how a poor person who by nature is timid, can nevertheless attain this. He may be one who he still intends for this to be done, which means, he may become sealed with the Holy Spirit; or, he could attain to a truly certain godly, faithful assurance of his standing in grace and his blessedness.

Notice, first, what is desired as preparation for this important work is this: the man who wants to come to this state of grace, so he might be sealed with the Holy Spirit, must first make room in his soul for the Holy Spirit so He can convince him of his evil, sinful, death-deserving condition. He is not asked to be responsible for this and for that coarse sin against God, but also his good works count for nothing. Beyond that, all good works count for naught, and much more likely they are subject to damnation because he had not believed in the Lord Jesus, and thought his own works were sufficient unto his (22) salvation. Although the death of Jesus Christ and the devil are defeated through Jesus Christ, yet out of his own power he had sought to withstand Satan.

---

19. Here is the note of globalization that is rooted in the very heart of human redemption, the work of the cross, which also provides the impetus for the missio Dei as tracked by Steinmetz in his subsequent authorship of the *Sammlung Auserlesene Materien zum Bau des Reich Gottes*, to be examined in this last chapter of this study. This affirmation of salvation for all is also the answer to the question Christian David asked Steinmetz in 1725 in his journey to seek his counsel at Teschen, that led to David's embrace of the message of full salvation in Christ whose death is efficacious for all persons who embrace Him. See discussion in Part Three, chapter 3.6

Notice, a person needs to desire such an outlook, which only the Holy Spirit can impart, so that he recognizes and feels himself to be a condemned sinner, who has not a single drop of good blood to commend him, and in whom there is no single power of soul that is worthy, of the person who has done nothing really good through the days of his life but rather, all his intended good works are an abomination unto God because they have been done apart from any love of God. Also, with regard to his most heralded works, the verdict is ever lost.

That, then, is the preparation which needs to be made in one's heart for such a person to be able to come before God, that he may become sealed and certain of the grace of God, pardoned for sins, and [receive] eternal life. Jesus demonstrates that in John 16:8 and following. "When He comes, the Holy Spirit will convict the world of sin, and righteousness, and judgment." This means that a person who has not wanted to accept the bloody Jesus, who hanged on the cross for us, for the sake of righteousness, has replaced this message to salvation for the sake of works righteousness. One may say, "I go to church, attend the eucharist, give alms to the poor," et al. This he must do first as a human being in recognizing what is right against sin, as recompense to sin, yet it is his to recognize that he also brought forth these good works out of unholy intentions, and (23) therefore this action was done in sin. Further, the fact that He, Jesus, goes to the Father, that He alone acquires righteousness, and finally for the sake of judgment, that the prince of this world is judged, and yet one says, "I cannot admit this, it is not possible. Satan has a great power over my heart, although the devil was not overwhelmed by the Lord Jesus and became defeated."

See, that is the beginning which needs to be laid in the soul if a person should come to sealing, namely, the Holy Spirit must bring him in, so that he feels and finds himself as a cursed sinner worthy of damnation, who has nothing good in himself, and all of whose works are detestable before God. Ask, you souls, why is that then necessary if one is to be sealed by the Holy Spirit?

Ah, dear man, so long as you do not come to that point, and you do not bow yourself before the Lord Jesus and allow the Holy Spirit to have a place within you, do not seek grace and mercy.[20] You think you can help

---

20. This important observation is in accord with Calvin as well, for whom it is only through union with Christ that the Holy Spirit resides within us through faith, and solely on that basis do we receive the benefits of mercy for sins and grace for an empowered life in the Holy Spirit. See John T. McNeill, Ed., John Calvin, *Institutes of the Christian Religion*, The

yourself, you can propitiate our dear Lord yourself despite your sins. You think you can return again to confession and the eucharist, so your sins may be forgiven you. You think you could already do good yourself— you can pray, read God's Word, give alms to the poor, et al. That would already make yourself good. Look, such a condemned person you and all of us together are by nature, if we do not first recognize what kind of disgusting persons we are by the righteousness which is revealed to you in the conscience, then let us first make room for the Holy Spirit so He can actually work in our hearts, and that we might strive less. We should rather be concerned to bring ourselves before the bloody wounds of our Savior.

There comes to my mind a verse from an old gospel hymn which becomes very penetrating. Many have sung this during their lifetime, but its truth has not been clearly perceived. In this hymn we read, "O God and Lord, how great and heavy," etc, then these words: "Therefore, Lord Christ, my refuge is the horror of Your wounds, whenever sin and death have brought me into distress." Previously I did not find myself there. Ah truly, so it is, you souls. One sings and cries out probably 20 or 30 years and does not once come to the bloody wounds of his Savior Jesus Christ, until distress and death brings one there.[21] It is not until one feels sin and death in his heart and conscience, and until one sees that man is a condemned sinner and that one then flees to the wounds of his Lord Jesus. One sees there, in the old simple hymn, how indispensable it is that it must become so for you as well, you poor man.

You must first recognize yourself as a mortal sinner before you can come into the blessing of the bloody wounds of the Lord Jesus: one skirts this and builds on his good works and is thereby forgiven. That is now the ground where the Holy Spirit must begin His ministry with this kind of work. (25) You souls who do not allow yourselves to come to this place of understanding: you will never enter into the sealing. You might flounder in your works, as you will, if you do not at once conform to the way of such penitential sinners, so that you as godless persons would become the rectified, by faith. Hear, apart from the blood of Christ, you receive no pardon for sins.

Library

21. Here again, this is a conviction shared by the Moravian community at Marienborn when they adopted the "blood and wounds" form of devotional piety as the core of their eucharistic observance. W. Reginald Ward, *The Protestant Evangelical Awakening*, "A Time of Sifting" (Oxford, 1992), 155-159.

This is what Paul describes in Romans 5:7, where alone the righteous are sealed by the Holy Spirit—those who do not proceed with works, but with faith in the One who makes the godless ones righteous. Hence, take aim now in the holy Scriptures where a challenge comes forth a thousand times, saying, a man should make repentance. For that is the repentance whereby a person now recognizes his sins, not only in thought, which would make him a good, well-mannered man, until he lets himself become convinced in his soul that it must become necessary for him as well.

And that is the first discussion, and the preparation which the Holy Spirit must undertake if a person would be brought to the sealing. The other, and certainly the chief part, which is here required, concerns what we permit to take place in ourselves so that we now allow faith to lead us to the Lord Jesus. Whenever a person has now learned what sort of death deserving sinner he is, so he must now allow the Holy Spirit to bring him to faith in His Savior Jesus Christ. (26)

1.5 Sealing Accessed by Faith

I have read in advance Ephesians 1:13, where Paul says: "In him you also, who have heard the word of truth, the gospel of your salvation, and have believed in him, were sealed with the promised Holy Spirit."

From this it is apparent that those who believed were first sealed with the Holy Spirit. At that time they turned from their distress to recognize that which was not yet. At that time they felt that they lay in death and lamentation, yet they believed. By this juncture it is necessary for me to explain two points, whereby you may grasp the right understanding of this and make right use of it.

First we ask, what is understood through the faith by which a person actually allows himself to be sealed with the Holy Spirit? In addition, we must know why it is that this faith would be chiefly and indispensably required for one to participate in the sealing?

An initial explanation is provided for knowing what faith is or how faith in the Lord Jesus is to be understood, which is required if a person would become a partaker of the sealing of the Holy Spirit. This is what is primarily meant by faith in the Lord Jesus. If a person now sees that he is a person worthy of damnation, he must become convinced through the Holy Spirit and God's Word that Jesus is and has done what is sufficient to atone for the sins of all humanity, in which and through which (27) every sinner can become righteous and blessed.

Note that I do not remind you of this without due cause: for that does not mean that if you have a notion in your head and if you assent to the fact that the Lord Jesus has died for all humanity, that is sufficient. Our blessed Luther once said about this, "that would be a thought about a cold, dead person." He scarcely came and then he was gone. If someone wants to make use of such a thought, there is nothing to be made of it. Hence, observe if you have the objective knowledge that Jesus has done that which is sufficient for all human sins, and that all humans, including yourself, should have actual forgiveness for your sins in the blood of Christ. All of you must remain in prayer for as long as necessary until your heart is convinced by the Holy Spirit of the truth of the matter, so you may proceed unerringly to believe this. O strive to reach that position!

Another may believe with faith in the Lord that, if one is now convinced through the Holy Spirit of having in this Savior a perfect Redeemer and Reconciler for all one's sins, that one could have forgiveness of sins in His blood, so that such a person then may allow himself to be regulated by the Holy Spirit, and his personal recourse takes him to the Lord Jesus to become His possession and to obey Him as would a disciple.

Lift up your eyes to the elevated serpent as did the wounded Israelites. Lie down before God's throne and before the cross of the Lord Jesus, until (28) this becomes increasingly invigorated in your heart from time to time, so that you could now be and live pleasing to God in this your Savior. That is called simple faith.

Ask further, why is this belief required? First, it is not at all so that a person might gain something from this fact. Everything is already provided for us, but this faith is required because one cannot otherwise make access to the Lord Jesus. It is not asked according to Jesus, but it is also apparent this is such an excellent Jesus, so great a Savior, yet I am such a faithless sinner, so long as I have no faith.

The fact is, one will repeatedly be brought to Jesus by faith, until it becomes an act of the heart. Then the streams of life can flow upon us, for *as long as there is no faith, there is also no life.* Consider then that the promise in Christ goes not no, no, but yes. The Holy Spirit is opposed if one does not come to the Lord Jesus. The Holy Spirit is not held in proper tranquility until He can imprint, so to speak, His image upon the heart. That image is formed when a person believes and allows Him to bring forth this life, which is also when this confidence in Jesus is grasped in faith. He could and would help, His blood should come to my help, and His merit and righteousness should also become mine.

Now I find that a third and quite extraordinary piece is needed, which is required if one would partake of the sealing through the Holy Spirit. It is found in Revelation 2:17, where it is written:

> (29) He who has an ear, let him hear what the Spirit says to the churches. To him who conquers, I will grant to eat of the hidden manna, and will give him a good witness, and with the witness a new name is written, which no one knows, except him who receives it.

Beloved friends, this manna will be able to be received easily to each one among you so that here through eating the forbidden manna there is indicated the enjoyment of the heavenly blessings which are in Jesus. This important witness is actually referring to the sealing through the Holy Spirit, for when the Holy Spirit seals a person, *that one becomes a child of God*. There is the forgiveness of sins and one becomes eternally blessed. However, what may be understood concerning the Holy Spirit through this overcoming?

1.6 Overcoming as the Outcome of the Spirit's Sealing: The Path to a Globalized Christianity

Paul explicitly instructs that no one will otherwise come into the sealing except he who overcomes. This term might appear incomprehensible to many persons. For that reason, I need to offer an explanation. If you are now asking what is meant by this statement concerning the overcoming, which is first required for access to the sealing through the Holy Spirit, note what follows.

As soon as the Holy Spirit begins to convince a person of his corruption, that he is in a condition of condemnation, what does this person feel? What is the prevailing impulse? Here a person rightly considers himself to be errant before God, and that he is. He must forthrightly lie down before God and continue to pray until the distracting thought disappear through the Holy Spirit who convinces him that his circumstances are now under His authority.

Such a soul can and will say to God, "My God! Oh! So much time has been spent as a blind, miserable person, when I thought that I was good. Oh God! Now I see that I am a condemned and forlorn sinner [both male and female tenses are used here!]. Now I am looking at my miserable state. Oh, God! Have mercy upon me. Oh, Jesus! Have mercy upon me."

Behold, soul, you have already won the first victory, for you have become an overcomer of the beginning. There the Holy Spirit is already beginning to triumph. There he has already conquered the evil thoughts which wanted to bind you, that you should now believe. You were such an evil person, until the Holy Spirit began to overcome through you out of God's Word. Now the poor soul, aware of the danger of condemnation, enters a new phase. In order for the grace, life and forgiveness in Jesus to become enough, He begins to show that only in the blood of Jesus is there more than all that is in heaven and earth, (31) so that if a person becomes a partaker of this grace, he could dispense with all the world and all one's own righteousness, and have enough righteousness for time and eternity.

If that is to occur, what begins first? Ah! Has the sinful, unbelieving heart begun to waver in its resistance, much more now than at the outset? How difficult it is for a person then to believe that out of a purely free grace that old self has been eradicated, and out of this gratuitous grace of Christ, he will also become blessed (holy), that out of this purely free grace he now has the pardon of sins. One sees, one has, one knows no longer anything about sin standing for itself, and should yet believe that this one alone, for the sake of Christ, now has the forgiveness of sins.[22]

What evidence is there now of a contradiction in the heart?[23] It comes to the place that one should also believe that in the peerless Jesus, in the crucified Jesus, in the blood-stained Jesus *more benefit is received than there is in the entire world.*[24]

What is now found of repulsiveness? How difficult it is to believe that one must overcome everything in Christ alone, even his dearest pet sins [or addictions]. What to do now? Then the soul must enter again into battle. It must again begin to pray, to cry out, to arrest with Christ's Word, and to surrender itself earnestly again concerning "those remaining things", surrendering them to the Holy Spirit, so long as it takes until it is purified, and now faith can say, "Yes, in the peerless blood of Christ there is enough for my soul. I need to bring nothing further before God's seat of judgment

---

22. These statements are all intended to underscore the purely gratuitous nature of saving grace that comes through Christ's sacrifice on the cross. Here is the heart of the Lutheran theology of the cross, as first delineated in Luther's Freedom of a Christian (1520).

23. The author moves beyond Luther to resolve his unending dialectic between law and gospel in the life of the believing Christian. Compare Luther, "Freedom of a Christian."

24. The 'world' here appears as a realm of reigning sin, in contrast to its subjection to Jesus Christ in His crucified state, which in turn becomes the incentive for engaging that de jure conquered world in Christian globalization to realize de facto the empirical implications of the outcome of the cross for a new humanity.

than the blood of the Son of God, that can be a sufficient repayment for my sins."25 (32)

So long must a person endure, with prayer and struggles, until he believes and can speak in the authentic faith: if I have Jesus, the crucified Savior, then the entire world is rejected, for I have more than all the world can give me and then has grace triumphed in the soul. The Holy Spirit has once again become victorious in a poor sinner.26

25. What Steinmetz called sealing through the Holy Spirit, which is rooted in the blood of the cross, is similar to what John Wesley would soon call Christian perfection. Diverging from the theology of the cross, according to the law/gospel dialectic of Luther, whom he nevertheless calls "beloved," Steinmetz affirms that it was possible to overcome all sin through surrendering all "the remainings things" in the heart that stand in "contradiction" to the Holy Spirit "until it is purified' through persevering prayer in the Holy Spirit. He says this overcoming of all sin represents a condition of "blessedness," which is inseparable from the sealing of the Holy Spirit. It could be said that what Wesley referred to as the life of full sanctification is what Steinmetz called the life of blessedness. Such a life is always manifested in the ongoing appropriation of the sealing of the Holy Spirit. In his lyrical theologizing of John 17:23, Charles Wesley wrote:

> "Jesus, with thy Father come,
> And bring our inward Guide,
> Make our hearts thy humble home,
> And in thine house abide,
> Show us with thy presence filled,
> Filled with glory from thy throne,
> Wholly sanctified, and seal'd,
> And perfected in one."

MS John, MARC: MA 1977/573 (Charles Wesley Notebooks Box 3), 369, cited in Wood, *Pentecost & Sanctification in the Writings of John Wesley and Charles Wesley.* 112-113.

26. It may here be inferred that from this understanding of grace as victorious, overcoming power, Steinmetz has clearly moved from Luther's view of grace as beneficium (God's good will or benefit accrued to sinners), although he presents his message from within the framework of the Lutheran liturgy and catechesis. In his defense, it may be noted that such inferences can indeed be drawn from those statements in Luther which speak of a Christian as being a wholly new man in Christ. However, to a consistent Lutheran, the inference also disrupts the balance in Luther's simul iustus et peccator, which would argue that it is only to the extent that one acknowledges peccator (sinfulness) can one likewise acknowledge iustus (justified and freed from sin), since, for Luther, iustus remains imputed and not imparted, as it becomes in Steinmetz. For Steinmetz, the imputed nature of "Vergebung" (forgiveness) is valid only as a precursor moment to empowerment over the residue of sin remaining in the life of the redeemed believer, and that is the really great and intended victory of Christ, for Steinmetz. Such a view of grace is also the impetus for pursuing the ministry of revival, as a theonomous expression of God's breakthrough into sin-

The devil, sin, and his heart did not want to let him believe. Behold therefore, oh man, whenever you now come to this point and let your heart be diverted by Satan—you enable your own phantasies, thoughts, and other issues to turn you away. You remain, as you were, a slave of the devil, of sin and unfaith.[27]

But if you make it as simple as I have said, and even if you had been the most miserable person, if the Holy Spirit offers grace, begin by getting in touch with your heart. Invest yourself in the work of prayer and supplication, and hold yourself there so long as needed, as with Jacob: "I will not let you go until you bless me." May it go for me as it will, my Savior, but I know now, as I am drawn together with you, my God and Savior. I must know, whether I will be lost or blessed, once must I know, whether I am to have the forgiveness of sins.[28] The person who presses onward is the one who is crowned, and receives the crown as an overcomer, *the gem of blessedness and of the holy ones*[29] not from the merit of works but as a pure gift of grace.

Now, would not that make your soul wise! Ah, how many will God have awakened into (33) such a sense of well-being (Shalom). Ah, how many will be awakened by God into such bliss. How many of you will have the touch of God's Word upon your hearts? Oh, that you even now many may sense there stands that which is not quite right within you, and there must truly be another to come alongside you. You may have begun to have a new look at yourself, to discover that you are in fact a person with misery that is being quietly carried. Ah, dear soul, you no longer need to struggle if

---

ful humanity, as well as vision for a globalized Christianity, which will manifest Christ's victory as Pentecost fulfilled, the renovation of the imago Dei in the new humanity of Jesus Christ. In eschatological terms, that new humanity is not relegated to the other side of the apocalypse (as with Luther and Lutheran Orthodoxy) but within the history of planet earth through the latter day hegemony of the sealing work of the Holy Spirit amid a fallen humanity. To that point, Steinmetz acknowledges in these addresses that there have been no historical precedents for this sealing work of the Holy Spirit within the memory of Protestants in his day.

27. The appeal to Satan as the obstacle seeking to prevent the momentum of the Spirit's ministry from continuing, is a theme also found in Luther's Commentary on Galatians, Dillenberger, 99–100, but the heightened use of it in Steinmetz suggests the influence of the homilies of Macarius, the desert father, which had recently been translated and published by the radical Pietist, Gottfried Arnold. As Benz has shown in his research, this influence was thereafter becoming pervasive in the literature of German Pietism. See *Die Protestantische Thebais. Zur Nachwirkung Makarius des Egypters im Protestantismus 17. Jhdt 18 in Europa und Amerika* (Wiesbaden: Franz Steiner Verlag, 1963).

28. This section is based on the passage found in Genesis 32:24–30.

29. "das Kleinod der Seligkeit und der Heiligen".

you are collapsing within these thoughts. No, that is not the case, and, I am not so evil as to suggest this must continue to be your lot. Ah, for God's sake, you should not hold onto that thought. Instead, may you follow the work of grace, and the prompting of the grace of the Holy Spirit who wants to pursue you now. You need to relinquish yourself in prayer, so long as you are sensitive to this through and through, and until you are rightly persuaded and become aware, that it is truly so. If you had not believed this, you would have become a godless, condemned person. It is now the time for this change to occur within you.[30]

There are also persons here who have already long felt themselves to be mortal sinners. Is this not so? God the Holy Spirit will also be speaking to you a comforting message from God's Word. A little *flame of comfort*[31] will begin to reign in your hearts. There will be impressions in your inward parts, saying "Ah, God will yet be gracious unto me. Jesus is gracious."

Listen, dear souls, all kinds of roadblocks may begin to surface within you to resist these thoughts. For example, your great sins and your long delay of conversion. These thoughts must be opposed, but the good thoughts must continue, with prayer, even with sighing and agony, until you can believe (34) that in the blood of Jesus, there is grace for you; until you can seek shelter in the Lord Jesus and be enveloped in the love of the crucified Jesus. This is your only solace, with all the storms and buffeting of the devil, the threats of hell and temptations to sin which break loose upon you.[32] If you will do that at this moment and will not call it off, oh hear this, your moment will arrive when you will be sealed.[33]

---

30. This important paragraph presents the author's fervent appeal for the conversion and sealing of his hearers in this revival setting. This section makes clear that these addresses were first delivered in the heat of revival, which would date them in the era of his Teschen ministry, which spilled over into adjacent nations as he and his preachers became itinerant revivalists from this home base. However, the ministry at Teschen ended abruptly after a decade, with his expulsion in 1730. See chapter for historical context. See Part Three, Chapter 2.3.

31. This becomes for the author an application of the theme of Pentecost as the sealing of the Holy Spirit now linked to the apostolic Pentecost in Acts 2 which was accompanied by tongues of flame.

32. This is the author's equivalence to the Wesleyan prevenient grace: the summons from the Holy Spirit of the love of Christ on the cross is set before you in your helpless condition amid the buffeting of the Evil One.

33. Comment: the moment of sealing is here presented as the gate to the new birth as well as to the infilling of the Spirit for new life, which Wesleyans call sanctification; recall that Steinmetz is preaching to baptized Lutherans who had not found their way to faith, and so he is careful to avoid calling this drawing of the sinner to the cross the new birth; it is more precisely the awakening to the faith in which you were baptized, but the empirical

However, one thing more! You who are inclined toward this: If you believe God will have persuaded you without doubt, it is still preferable for us to deny the world, since Jesus must become all in all for us, and so we must allow Him to make us more holy.[34] If you have sensed the beckoning of His grace, and yet the sealing of the Holy Spirit has not yet occurred for you, as it should, your soul nevertheless, which truly believes on the Lord Jesus, also has true grace in His blood. We must press further at that point, out of the earthly and passing orb of this life, and our hearts must become more released from its draw.[35]

If you would only consider this matter simply! Many take it not so seriously, saying "I too am also among those who are true Christians, and am fine just the way I am." Ah, that is the devil speaking, whose thoughts we must not heed and that is the point where you need to join battle against such thoughts by entering into prayer, petitioning for the grace which the Savior has acquired for you.

We must make right use of the Word of God which we have heard until it is firmly establihed in our hearts. Yes, my Savior, still wider from the earthly domain, still nearer to Your bloody wounds, and yet still more must I be sealed by You! So we must hasten on longer, (35) until we become absolutely certain about this in our inner persons.

The direction where that line of belief is heading will be in the holy eternity where the sealing remains, firmly fixed in the beautiful gem. On account of this we certainly deserve nothing, so it is probably worth the effort a thousand fold. God will crown the least measure of faithfulness.

Behold, soul, have you formerly tried to walk against God and the trust-

---

results are equivalent and, in his nomenclature, revival happens through the personalized message of the cross rather than through a direct appeal to be born, as in the tradition of Wesleyans and Reformed Pietists. Again, the empirical results for revival that is global in scope are equivalent.

34. This is the author's first direct appeal to holiness as the outcome of sealing through the Holy Spirit.

35 Here is the author's pastoral observation that addresses hesitant hearts which seem to be in accord with the message of the cross but have not yet indicated a volitional choice has been made: these are also 'souls that are being saved' and the pastor is to hold to them for salvation. These are the ones whom John Wesley would call the "almost Christian". If Steinmetz had used the language of new birth here rather than sealing through the Holy Spirit, he would have ecclesially moved into sectarianism, from a Lutheran standpoint. He is pushing the issue, since it is implicit in his message that baptism itself is not salvific, even if administered correctly, if it is not personally appropriated by an intentional moment of inclination – he calls it a "Stundlein"– that moment whereby saving faith is awakened through the impact of the cross and the efficacy of the shed blood of Jesus the Christ upon the soul.

worthy Jesus? Have you, for the sake of His will, denied sin and the world in your heart, have you submerged yourself with faith into His wounds, have you denied Him in your heart for the sake of sin and the world? And have you noticed something remaining in you that is not right and does not please your Lord Jesus? Do not rest at that point, until your heart comes to that place where you can surrender yourself to your Jesus. Then your small faith will crown Him, and will confirm your seal more firmly within your heart. Now, my Savior, grant me and you grace, that we become crowned as overcomers in time and eternity, Amen.

The Second Pentecost Edification

In the first treatment of the important and mystery-laden doctrine of the sealing with the Holy Spirit we presented two aspects, according to Scripture, namely:
1. What is understood by the sealing with the Holy Spirit.
2. What is required from the side of human responsibility, or what first needs to occur for a person to partake of this sealing through the Holy Spirit

Now we consider also:
3. How and with what *means* this sealing through the Holy Spirit happens with a soul (or a person).

I am setting forth here what happens with a person who has come to this victorious faith which overcomes all doubt concerning the grace of Jesus. Namely, that man or woman no longer lies under a love for the world or for the creaturely realm, or under another reigning domain of sin. Instead, this faith comes to birth not by force, power and the reign of the world and a love for transient things, but through faith. (37)

2.1 The Means for Sealing

We now inquire how and by what means a person becomes sealed, wholly sealed, as with a certain imprinted symbol, certifying that one has the forgiveness of sins, and has become a *child of God*, so that, if that person should die in a moment, he or he would become a co-heir with Jesus Christ. That is overall a quite important matter which is basic to understanding other aspects of this discussion. That is, until a person enters into the sealing, becoming convinced of their access to the status of a *child of God*, which is the condition of grace, of the heavenly inheritance, they have this point to heed. This sealing and assurance is the chief means for all persons who are of the character and sort of person who gets through to God in a salvific manner.

First, God makes known His wisdom in many discreet and diverse ways by which He brings persons to faith by means of sealing. For example, many persons whom God brings to faith must wait unusually long for that to occur, or must pour out a great volume of tears, because God considers these measures to be beneficial before one comes to the actual moment of sealing. The reason for this may be attributed to their vacillation or their habitual lack of focus in their pursuit of salvation. Another person can probably receive this in a few hours or days.

We have this example in Saul's conversion, when he arrived at Damascus,[1] he had his seal after three days. He recognized it with great joy, and began to bear witness to his Savior, rather than continuing to persecute him. Now he could risk body and life in the assurance that in Jesus he had found what he was seeking, namely, he had now attained the forgiveness of his sins, and righteousness before God.

What happened to Paul is certainly not something we can now promise will happen to every person. Since God acts in view of the time,[2] anyone can promise but it is God who acts, in consideration of the time, according to His prudent love and great wisdom. God gladly wanted to be gracious to humankind sooner rather than later with the pledge of His sealing. Whenever the person rightly wanted to accommodate himself to that purpose, God gladly wanted to provide sealing for their soul. Hence, it was Jesus who was willing for that to occur. Ah, so gladly did He want pure, sealed souls who could serve Him with joy and the assurance of their hearts. However, God has directed matters according to His great wisdom, and adjudicated when and how the matter of the soul may be the most praiseworthy. Therefore, there is a precise distinction to be found within it.

Second, the seal is imprinted by degrees upon the soul. For some, the matter occurs with a vivid impression within a minute, or within a quarter of an hour, as was the case for me. That sealing thereafter remains intact throughout life into "early" eternity. Then, God does not always prescribe

---

1. A reference to the account of Paul's conversion in Acts 9:1-21.
2. The implication being that God acted in the days of the apostles in ways which sometimes differed from how He would act in the present day.

one particular method, but knows what may be most useful and wholesome for the soul to pursue.

Third, a distinction is to be noticed with regard to the means used by God to seal the souls, to render souls certain of the pardon from their sins and blessedness. (39) For some souls God uses a language from the holy Scripture, for others, God uses one of the sacraments, and for a third, God uses strong and lively sensations [Empfindungen] within the soul, for which some have not yet experienced anything comparable within their lifetimes. These are repeated, as God directs, so that it is best for these souls that the sensations are most in keeping with their particular conditions.

With great joy to the praise of God, I can say that God has deemed me worthy apart from my merit to circulate here with persons who are being sealed by the Holy Spirit. I have repeatedly, and with great amazement, not known what I should say and think, yet God so punctually, wisely, and carefully occupies Himself with each person [within the context of revival]. Whenever one observes a person correctly discovering their soul's condition [by the Spirit's guidance], it becomes astonishing to see how God is occupied with the sealing occurring within them.[3] It is *even as though God had a child completely alone with Himself in His home.* This occurs in each person in whom this movement is occurring, so that in each instance one becomes convinced that these movements of the Spirit of God were not phantasies [Phantasien], as the "clever" men of the world[4] want to call them. When a hundred persons are observed, it becomes evident how punctually and how precisely God discerns and interacts with each according to the condition of the soul.[5]

This brings to full conviction what truly may be called the work of God and of our Savior Jesus Christ. This is what occurs in our midst when one observes how this process of sealing is occurring through the special fore-

---

3. The verb used, umgehen, is also the one used in German for sexual intercourse, understood as a holy act of love among wedded humans.

4. This is a broad category which includes Orthodox Lutheran clergy and seminary faculty, as well as Habsburg Catholic adversaries of all forms of Protestantism. See the discussion of the parties who opposed the children's revival in our chapter on that revival, as well as in the primary study of Eric Swensson, *Kinderbeten,* 46–80.

5. This precise ordering of those assembled for sealing of the Holy Spirit in the revival setting was for Steinmetz directly reminiscent of the way the children had ordered themselves for prayer in the Silesian prayer revival, as found in the records of that revival as reviewed by Swensson. Ibid.

sight of God moving among those who are His own in the gracious and orderly fashioning of their lives as redeemed humans.

Behold, one must above all observe (40) the question to be answered correctly, how and with what do persons seek this great grace of sealing?

Since we have now introduced our subject, beloved, we now intend to proceed to the reply to our question.

2.2 The Holy Spirit as the Chief Witness to the Sealing of the Holy Spirit

In answering the question of how this great mystery of grace interacting with humans is to be understood, let us do so one at the most advanced level by saying, the chief seal whereby souls become sealed may be said to be the Holy Spirit Himself.

However, it is necessary, beloved, that I explain this [circular] answer, namely, when it is said, the Holy Spirit Himself is the chief sign, this means His own Self attends upon God in His fullness.[6] In bringing them to faith He is *certifying (versichern) the grace of His adoption [Kindschaft] and blessed salvation [Seligkeit] of these whom He has now brought into saving faith.*

This does not in any way intend to convey the meaning that any good work, that perchance conveys a sense of pending awakening upon which we would rely, is what we mean by the sealing of the Holy Spirit. No, for thereby it would be in conflict with what was said above in our inspection of the matter.

If it is stated that the Holy Spirit is Himself the chief seal, whereby souls are made certain of their standing in grace and of their blessedness, then here is what is meant: When a person comes to that place whereby the Holy Spirit truly dwells within them, that their heart is His abiding temple, that the Holy Spirit can now gladden the soul as its comforter [Trösters] and enabler [Beistand], its helper, its teacher, its leader, and, with a Word, (41) we are speaking of when the soul has the Holy Spirit as its possession,[7] and that it needs the same in all the circumstances of its life.[8] Further, the indwelling Holy Spirit pulsates upon godless souls, and upon the souls which, as I have said before, are often disturbed. However, to live within a

---

6. An apparent reference to the Father and the Son, in Trinitarian thinking.

7. In the sense of abiding Presence, not possession as private ownership.

8. Here we may substitute person for soul, if our post-modern sensitivities preclude the use of this traditional Christian name, derived from classical thought, for the core of a human being.

person, to penetrate into that person as into a temple is something *the Holy Spirit cannot achieve apart from one who is converted.*[9]

Romans 8:16 points us in this direction: "The Spirit Himself bears witness with our spirit, that we are children of God,"(NAS) in which He has his workplace and dwelling place, in which He can form them according to His good pleasure, who have in the Holy Spirit and their obedience to his impetus which is itself the seal that holds the forgiveness of sins, grace, and blessedness unto eternity.[10]

On this basis the apostle Paul expressly directs us in our text: "And do not grieve the Holy Spirit of God" (Ephesians 4:30). The apostle does not intend to say here, "You Ephesians have good vibes, you have the summons of the Holy Spirit and enjoy the benefit of it." No! On the contrary, he says that you have been sealed with the Holy Spirit. He not only stands at the door of the heart, making some good movements and thereby beckoning persons. No, you have really received Him. Since the seal is imprinted upon a person, so also has the Holy Spirit been given to you within your heart, so that He thereby works, regulates, shadows and holds sway, creates and brings about what is right before God.

(42) Because this great mercy and grace has become your portion, the Holy Spirit who indwells you has not become grieved. He now gives attention to all movements which have this in heart. God is the One who takes delight in giving witness to His Presence amid all things which you encounter in life. Paul addresses this point in Acts 19. There we read in verses one and two among other things that he was embarking upon one of his apostolic trips and came to Ephesus. He had met some people there who were followers, and so were called Christians.

As soon as he had been aware of these people and received opportunity to speak with them, then his first question to them was, "Have you also received the Holy Spirit, and have you now truly become sealed, so that He lives, works, and abides in you, so that He now guides and directs you according to His heart and mind?"[11]

Then they had to reply, "No, we know yet nothing about that." Ah, then

---

9. This is Steinmetz's first use of this core Pietist theme of conversion, which is important in Francke and Halle Pietism, as die Bekehrung, a will-induced change, as distinct from der Wiedergeburt (new birth), a manifestation of redemptive grace based in Christ.

10. The core passage to which he alludes here is Romans 8:13-17: "If you are living according to the flesh, you must die according to the flesh."

11. An allusion to John 16:13a: ""But when He, the Spirit of truth, comes, He will guide you into all truth."

it must be that most among us still continue in such a condition concerning our perceptions of the Holy Spirit's power indwelling our souls. The power of His Presence indwelt and enlivened them. They expressed this in terms of living within His Temple, although they had as yet neither known or experienced anything.

Beloved, after we now know that the Holy Spirit Himself is the chief seal that is communicated to souls for them to become assured of all that which is necessary for their blessedness, we now proceed further, in the Name of God, and observe the following.

2.3 Ancillary Seals Accompanying the Holy Spirit: Word, Sacrament, and the Inner Person

(43) For others, when the Holy Spirit first enters the inner life of a person [soul] as the chief seal, this is accompanied by the fact that He now needs, so to speak, to be accompanied by some ancillary seals. Through these multiple seals, the heart now becomes ever so more certain of all that which is promised in the Word of God for believers.

I now intend to go so far as to say that the Holy Spirit, whether or not He alone is sufficient to dwell within the hearts of believers, still needs other means through which the heart may become assured that it is truly abiding in God, by grace. The foremost among these ancillary seals is the precious Word of God, through which He brings the souls who come to Him into the assurance of the state of grace, by a position of grace attained through the forgiveness of sins. In particular, this occurs through the gospel, with its promises, in addition to the sacraments, instituted by our Lord Himself.[12]

Here I must take care to explain that I can now show how the soul becomes more certain of its standing in grace through the seal of the Word of the gospel. Now notice! Within the Word of God we can find a

---

12. Here the author builds upon the hermeneutic of Luther's law/gospel dialectic, as the twofold expression of the revelation of the Word of God in the Bible. Luther had insisted that the preacher should ever keep both the dimensions of command and promise within focus, to be drawn upon according to the condition of the hearers of the Word. See especially his "Preface to Romans," in Dillenberger, op.cit., 21-23. Now the sacraments are introduced as the ecclesial link to the revivalist's appeal to reliance on the preached Word as the chief means of conveying the truth of the Word of God within a community of faith. Luther would also say that the chief means by which one may be assured of salvation is by remembering your baptism in those moments of soteriological doubt. See here his "Babylonian Captivity of the Church," in Martin Luther, or called "The Pagan Servitude of the Church," in Dillenberger, 294.

great concentration of the most excellent promises of grace. For example, there is nothing damnable for those who are spiritually impoverished. They are blessed who hunger and thirst for righteousness. In addition to these precious promises we also find in God's Word the clearest marks and descriptions of what remains to be appropriated concerning *the fullness of grace for the children of God*, from which we can observe, recognize and form an awareness of that grace found in the forgiveness of sins and in blessedness. *Here is what God does in His heartfelt and inward pity for His children.*

In addition to the godly Word, God has also given to us the blessed sacraments, and especially His holy Last Supper[13] in which the faithful are represented with the seal of the grace of God and the forgiveness of sins. How then, is it with your souls, my beloved children?[14]

Many thousands of persons hear the Word of God, where the foremost promises are read.[15] Many thousands also regularly partake of the blessed sacrament of the Eucharist, yet they have not the slightest feeling of the sealing of the Holy Spirit in relation to this sacrament.[16] This occurs not only among the ungodly but also among many who have bowed in penitential struggle[17] at the feet of the Lord. Is this not so? Many souls prostrate themselves before God, while they read and listen to the most beautiful promises of God, and these make no impression upon their souls![18] They attend the Lord's Supper, under hearty resolution, as

---

13. Steinmetz uses the term "Abendmahl", being the apostolic term for last supper shared by our Lord with His disciples.

14. The author here refers to his readers as "the beloved," spoken in the context of the preceding reference to their being the children of God.

15. It is to be remembered that Steinmetz had ministered to a congregation of forty to seventy thousand members at Teschen, Silesia, where this preaching originated, in the wake of the children's revival of 1707-08.

16. The term for awareness is "Gefühl," translated as "feeling" in Moravian piety, and later in Schleiermacher.

17. This is an important theological term (Busskampf) which comes from Francke, Steinmetz's colleague as a student at the University of Leipzig and later the leader of the chief Pietist center of world renewal at Halle.

18. This language of "making no impression upon their souls" reflects the author's reliance upon the thought of Jonathan Edwards in the context of the North American Great Awakening at Northanpton, Massachusetts, in 1734. Steinmetz read Edwards in the course of his preparation of his massive account of the growth of the revival which began with the children of Silesia and within a generation had impacted the Western hemisphere. Rainer Lächele, *Die Sammlung auserlesener Materien zum Bau des Reiche Gottes zwischen 1730 und 1760* (Tübingen: Verlag der Frankeschen Stiftungen Halle, 2006), 304; and this suggests the dating of these his addresses on Pentecost follow the events of the revival at Teschen under his leadership, which terminated with his expulsion in 1730, much as the awakening under

well as with prayers, tears, and supplications. They are hoping thereby to enable the holy Lord's Supper to become the seal to their assurance that they have the grace of God. Yet, all that occurs is more as though they were dead, without any sensibility toward the movement of God's Spirit through the sacrament.

This instructs the experience of all poor sinners. Often they go forth, before such a poor sinner understands, and the hour comes (45) that is so powerful a promise, to resign themselves within their inward parts,[19] and yet that soul did not know the joy where it should be found.[20] So it also goes with many of the attributes asssociated with our adoption as the children of God (Kindschaft Gottes).[21]

However, the hour comes, when such a person finds himself so "sonnenklar" (in the clarity of sunlight),[22] so bright, so that it actually becomes so for him as it is in holy Scripture. Through such a moment of recognition from the Word of God he becomes rightly assured that he was also now made worthy of that great gift[23] of what God has provided for his in His Word, that one is made worthy of grace, that is, *the status of childhood and the eternal blessedness.*[24] Even so it can be found also in the holy sacrament.[25] There many a soul has often entered in but has found nothing therein.[26] However, all at once they come to a moment of awareness when this is found at the table of the Lord.[27]

Edwards terminated at Northampton with his expulsion from that congregation of Congregationalism within the context of a Puritan community of faith. See Edwards, *The Surprising Work of God in New England*, and his *Treatise on Religious Affections*. Steinmetz received via Isaac Watts a copy of Edwards' narrative of *The Surprising Work of God in New England in 1734* which was translated and edited in a German edition to extend its influence in Europe. See Ward, *Protestant Evangelical Awakening*, 286.

19. "in ihr Inwendiges," ibid., 45.
20. "wo sie sich hinwenden soll." Ibid.
21. Kindschaft Gottes is a a term for adoption. Here again, we notice how deeply the imprint of the children's revival, which initiated the revival Steinmetz led at Teschen, continued to inform his thought.
22. Ibid.
23. That is, her childhood before God.
24. Here "childhood" and "blessedness" are rendered synonymous by Steinmetz.
25. Later appeals to Pentecost ground pneumatology in baptism; for Steinmetz, it is primarily to be located within the eucharist.
26. The author is reflecting the outlook of the sixteenth century Silesian reformer, Steinmetz's national mentor in the faith, whose suspension of the outward commemoration of the eucharist initiated a break with Martin Luther and the origin of the Schwenkfelder church as a separate community of believers in Europe and America.
27. Here Steinmetz may reflect his alignment with Zinzendorf's focus on the feeling of

Now, beloved, what we are addressing is where the Holy Spirit is sealed. There is where the Holy Spirit uses the sacrament and the *Word of God as the seal,* and impresses Himself as seal, so to speak, upon their heart. Ah, this is no human work!

There are, moreover, quite a few references to this in the Bible. There are many who have perused the texts of the Bible and yet within all this perusal have found no power therein. Hence, such persons have occupied themselves with the text but they have permitted no room for the Holy Spirit to imprint His seal upon their hearts. This happens not only among the godless, but also among sincere persons. They read God's Word, containing the most beautiful promises and yet they have perceived nothing whatsoever.

They also make use of the sacraments, (46) yet there is nothing found there either. Why, then? There is where these poor souls should learn to discern His voice, so that everything read is no mere human work that anyone could just appropriate for himself. Then, no one could make use of the power which lies within these texts for themselves, but rather, the Holy Spirit must imprint the seal upon them.

If anyone appropriates the text correctly it becomes for them a blessing and salvation [Seligkeit]. It may also become that for many who previously had grieved their inability to find any perception even among the most beautiful enunciations of the godly Word, or from the reading of the Bible and from the holy[28] Lord's Supper.

At that point, some poor soul might think, "God has repudiated me! My soul hungers for all this and yet nothing can be discerned in its use." Ah, not so, my friend. Avoid such thoughts, lest you find yourself cut off from God and think that God is only present in the shadow of these signs for those who are able to eat and drink sensibly aware of the most beautiful seal to be found there.

Oh, no! Hold on now! If you will only open your eyes to discern your God, and He notices no deception, then He will come, before you even

---

the love for Jesus as the core meaning of the new birth (Wiedergeburt). Steinmetz shows himself in such references as a veritable ecumenical theologian. See W. R. Ward *Christianity under the Ancien Regime, 1648-1789* (Cambridge, 1999), 118. "Something quicker" was needed, Zinzendorf thought, than the "highly structured Hallensian pattern of conversion," which he thought delayed the conversion of many; instead, he preferred a "quicker method," an "imaginative identification with the the Savior."

28. It is to be noted that the author attaches holiness to the Word and the sacrament of eucharist and not to the recipient of those means of grace, in accordance with Luther's simul iustus et peccator.

understand yourself, within a moment (Stunde), when you hear, read, or observe God's Word,29 even where you are only slightly thinking about all this. By a word of proclamation, *by a use of the holy Lord's Supper, your Jesus will come, and will also apply this seal to your soul,* for the blessed means whereby your poor heart might profit both in time and in eternity. Do not abandon your confidence. Hasten only to weep and to pray to your God (47) and to your Savior. Hasten now to make use of the means of grace in simplicity. He will already observe the moment, which will become for you most blessed so that His seal might be able to be imprinted upon your heart.

That is what I have desired to convey to you concerning the sign which is the sacrament, by which the Holy Spirit intends to assist a person to arrive at their assurance of salvation.

2.4 The Efficacy of These Seals Depends upon the Receptivity of the Subject through Conversion

In addition to the seal of the Word and the sacrament, there is yet another excellent means and ancillary seal, which also serves the Holy Spirit in conveying to a person that they have become certain of the matter of their standing in grace and salvation. This means consists of *the Holy Spirit's powerful workings in their inner person [die Seele]*. With forethought, I assert that it would be the effectual operations of the Holy Spirit within one's inner life, whereby I am able to discern that I am not the one who initiates all benevolent operations within my life. Rather, it is through the really powerful operations of the Holy Spirit within the soul, that such a change can occur, through which the entire heart30 of a person is transformed.

Previously, a person was attached to the love of this world. That had been sufficient for him, if only he were able from time to time to increase his worth by such attachments. If that person now affords room for the

---

29. Whereas Luther and Orthodox Lutherans limited the revelation of God to the hearing of the Word, Steinmetz appears to be widening the scope to include the senses of sight and taste in worship as means of enhancing one's awareness of the sealing of the Holy Spirit.

30. The author shifts from the language of soul to heart, when addressing the innermost activities of the Holy Spirit within a person. This would infer an inclination toward an Origenist tripartite classification of the human person, which heart conveying that faculty most conducive to receiving the direct inspiration of the Holy Spirit, beyond the literal or cognitive levels of human perception. To be clear, this is not an explicitly developed anthropology in Steinmetz, who as a Lutheran also seeks to track with Luther's basic distinction between those who are faithful versus the unfaithful, with reference to hearing and obeying the Word of God in thought, word, and deed.

Holy Spirit to bring *true conversion [Bekehrung]*,[31] then the Holy Spirit penetrates, so that this one is now changed. Formerly he had been alive physically and yet was regarded as dead, since he had not the least measure of joy or well-being. Indeed, he only regarded conversion as a matter which concerned his perishable soul, (48) experienced as a longstanding burden for his heart. And so it went in all things that concerned his life.

However, when such a person makes room for the Holy Spirit in the soul, this changes the entire disposition. The most beloved carnal desires are put to death. This is a matter pertaining to all souls, as we find it stated in 2 Corinthians 6:9: "as dying, yet behold, we live, as punished, yet not put to death."

Such beautiful and excellent operations of the Holy Spirit in a human life are predicated upon whether God's Spirit has been received by those who would behold such glorious displays of His Presence. Let us here address such workings of the Spirit.

These kind of operations require the Spirit of God among persons as the seal which *assures them that they are now truly children of God,* because so great a change among them has occurred which is not from nature, nor do they proceed from the devil, but must of necessity proceed only from God. Such a change shows itself quickly. *So long as a person stands in his natural conditions, he has no truly hearty love for God and for the children of God.* He has a thousand times more to do with visible things than with God and God's Word. If a person is truly converted and has undergone a change, as precious as the temporal things of the flesh have been, they will now become a great aversion and irritation. As little as one has previously found satisfaction in God, (49) or in the activities of *the children of God,* in heartfelt devotions, so a hearty lust, joy and delight proceed thereafter in the soul, revolving around God and His own, to sustain themselves with the Word of God in order to strengthen and edify themselves with the *children of God.*

Does not this joy in our religion hearken back to that blessed time which is portrayed for us in I John 3:14 [..], "we know that we have come from death unto life. For what then? *For what then do you have your seal? We love the brethren. Now the children of God are heartily precious to us and we gladly*

---

31. Conversion is the origin of Christian identity for Francke, with whom the author was closely associated as a fellow university student at Leipzig and also through the extended Halle ministry with was responsible for the erection of the Grace church in Teschen, where Steinmetz served as pastor during the first revival in Protestant history, marked by the seal of Pentecost.

have something to do with them. That is a sign that the Holy Spirit is in our hearts, and has made a change, and the impressions of that kind represent a great first installment [of what God is about in His Pentecost mission in the world].[32]

2.5 A Warning against Counterfeit Seals

Before leaving this theme, one word of caution remains to be given. Namely, a Christian cannot by observation make for himself any seal of the Holy Spirit from these powerful impressions at work in his midst. Other persons have discovered this for themselves. After finding themselves in periods of anxiety, doubt, and fear, they may say, "look, this or that change has occurred with regard to these [Anfechtungen[33]]," and so they ask, "do you not notice these changes persisting in your soul? There you have clear evidence that you are a child of God." You can certainly suppose that, when the Holy Spirit observes His time, and sees that such a person is a soul worthy to become sealed, then each circumstance, each impulse that he feels, and each such impression that is produced, which he observes within himself, is *a clear expression within himself that indeed, such a person is a child of God.* On such occasions it may resound in your heart, "how would it be possible that I lay under the weight of the (50) devil. I truly felt it in my heart, I noticed it there and now I can no longer deny that the grace of God is now here, operating, creating and working in my soul." And so he powerfully convinces himself of all of that. However, all that is precisely what you receive from grace. You cannot conjure all that up for yourself.

I intend to say by all of this that the conviction that these observed impressions convey a genuine sign of the Holy Spirit's sealing is itself the work of the Holy Spirit giving witness to our spirits that we are God's

---

32. The enclosure completes the thought that is implicit in the sentence, given its context in the theme of a great working of Pentecost in the form of an awakening bringing to life a devastated people, the Silesians, reaching over borders in all directions. Compare Acts 2:39a, "The promise is for you and your children, and for all who are far off."

33. This is Luther's term to describe such ordeals of the soul as *Anfechtungen* which can only be resolved by faithfully acknowledging the work of Christ on the cross on our behalf. Steinmetz here observes that a sense of relief from such ordeals or temptations of the soul may indeed be inferred to be a sign of the sealing of the Holy Spirit. A psychological inference is here inferred as evidence for a clear act of grace in the soul, which can only be confirmed through prayer to the source of that grace, Christ, the Lamb of God, in His victory on the cross.

children.³⁴ Therefore, you must through prayerful supplication seek that assurance for yourself from Christ Jesus.

Now I should append more such signs and evidences of the standing in grace, although the brevity of time will not permit it. Therefore, I will continue to address this theme by seeking to clarify how it is only possible for this discussion to be profitable for your edification in grace if it is properly grounded in the Word of God.³⁵

We have first of all heard that God and the Holy Spirit ought not be encountered in one kind of way [as in outward forms of worship and Bible reading] and then at another time be encountered internally in our inner lives with certainty for the sealing of our salvation, in such a way that God is allowing for a longer interval to pass for one thing to occur than for the other, or vice versa. What, then, my beloved friends, do we learn from this which will enable us to advance in grace? Here no one particular order of occurrence among these two is to be commended. Whoever intends to prescribe for God how He should navigate the issues of his soul simply hinders God and himself from attaining the certainty of his salvation. Avoid stipulating specific recommendations of what should be done, and in what order, as a basis for a person becoming assured of the sealing.

We do not know what is good for us. We do not know how Jesus knows us. We also do not (51) have such love for God our Father and our Lord Jesus Christ as they have for us. Therefore, my beloved friend,³⁶ you intend soon to arrive at your goal. Simply surrender yourself to your Lord Jesus. Even this day, go unto Him, if you do not yet have your seal.³⁷ Your soul hungers for this, that you might gladly embrace the prize.

2.6 Fulfilling the Promise of Pentecost with the Sealing of the Holy Spirit

Go home today, and lie prostrate before your Savior and say, "Precious Savior, I prostrate myself even as a poor worm. I well know that I do not deserve to become sealed with the forgiveness of sins, rather, I am worthy only to be cast from Your Presence into punishment. But, dear Lord, you are yet summoning me. You have let it be said of me, even the most abominable person may obtain grace."

---

34. Romans 8:16.
35. The author offers biblical grounding for the psychological observations concerning the sealing of the Holy Spirit which have been introduced into the discussion.
36. Steinmetz here simply addresses his hearer as "O soul."
37. The revivalist in Steinmetz is imploring his hearer, after due diligence in rational reflection on the issues of personal salvation.

"Upon this word I come, Lord Jesus, and bear witness to You before Your face, I am not leaving Your Presence, until I know that I have received the forgiveness of sins in Your blood. However, Lord Jesus, may it be with me in accordance with Your will. Let me wait, or grant it to me soon. May it be Granted to me through Your Word or through an inward awareness. Here I am, Lord Jesus, may your will be done unto me, only permit my supplication to be heard so I may be sure of Your blessed salvation. Do unto me according to Your will. "So, O soul, release yourself unto Him, let Your Savior guide and direct you. Direct your prayer into the heart of Jesus, tarry and wait, hold on with sighs, and allow whatever He does to be pleasing unto you. Whether He handles you with sternness or with loving kindness, respond by saying to all, Lord Jesus, it is right and meet, I do not understand it. (52) You know best how to bring it about, only may Your will and good pleasure be done in me." So will your soul be assisted.

For the second time we have heard in these Pentecost addresses, my beloved, that the Holy Spirit is the excellent primary seal whereby you may arrive at a firm assurance.[38] One should attain that surety so that He may dwell within your heart. We should long that our hearts may become His temple and his dwelling place, where He may remain.[39] This concept leads us to consider excellent recollections. Do you now know whether your condition of grace is certain for you? Do you intend to become

---

38. If John Wesley learned from Christian David and his colleagues at Herrnhut about the full assurance of faith as a privilege for all believers through the Spirit, David had first heard this message explained to him from Steinmetz. Wesley heard from David and his coworker, Arvid Gradin, that "the full assurance of faith, meant . . . 'Repose in the blood of Christ; a firm confidence in God, and persuasion of his favour; the highest tranquility, serenity, and peace of mind, with a deliverance from every fleshly desire, and a cessation of all sin, even inward sins'." David, in speaking about his justified faith, said that "neither saw I then that the 'being justified' is widely different from the having the 'full assurance of faith'. I remembered not that our Lord told his apostles before his death, 'ye are clean'; whereas it was not till many days after it that they were fully assured, by the Holy Spirit then received, of their reconciliation to God through his blood." This teaching from Christian David, learned from Steinmetz, had profound significance for the Wesley brothers' understanding of Christian perfection as a subsequent instant moment following justification (forgiveness of sins). Cf. Wood, *Pentecost & Sanctification in the Writings of John Wesley and Charles Wesley*, 40–41.

39. This is a prayer that Pentecost may be fulfilled from the micro level of the sealing in the Holy Spirit of each thirsty soul to the macro level of the greater temple of His dwelling in the completed Body of Christ which will be Christianity in its global dimensions, for which the next Pentecost Address sheds light, as does Steinmetz's subsequent ministry of chronicling the building of the Kingdom of God on earth.

assured of your adoption [Kindschaft] and its blessedness that your heart might indeed become a temple of the Holy Spirit? Ask Him to occupy all the corners of your heart, that He might search for those areas which He has not yet occupied. It is true, beloved friend, that if you intend to be assured and sealed through the Holy Spirit, you need to admit Him to gain access to your entire heart as His dwelling place. If He is to become the Master of your inner person, how can He fulfill this purpose without granting you the godly gift of the sealing? Apart from this, death and the devil remain free to storm through our lives at will. (53)

Do you not know whether the Spirit of God has His dwelling place within you? What parts of your life remain under the claim of the Devil, and what rights does the world hold over you?[40] What then of sin? In what ways can the law condemn you?[41] Do you not know you are the temple

---

40. This theme of bondage analysis and release is an ancient theme traced to the desert fathers, and to Macarius, in particular. This literature was becoming available for the first time in German (and later English) vernacular in the early decades of the eighteenth century, beginning with the first German edition provided by Gottfried Arnold (cf. Benz, *Die Protestantische Thebais. Zur Nachwirkung Makarius des Egypters im Protestantismus 17. Jhdt 18 in Europa und Amerika)** through whose influence this Macarian theme became popular in radical Pietist literature, especially the *Geistliche Fama*, a periodical of networking data for radicals published at their center in Wittgenstein, Berleburg (Germany) and the radical Pietist commentary on the Bible, J.F. Haug, J.J. Haug, and L. C. Schefer, eds, the *Berleburger Bibel* (Berleburg/Wittgenstein, 1726-42), eight volumes. Through this transmission, the theme appears in the first homily preached in North America, within the United Methodist tradition, "The Salvation-bringing Incarnation and Glorious Victory of Jesus Christ Over the Devil and Death" (*Die heilbringende Menschwerdung und herrliche Sieg Jesu Christi über den Teufel und Tod* (Lancaster, Pa, 1763) by the German Reformed pastor Philip Wilhelm Otterbein (1726-1813), co-founder of the United Brethren in Christ and mentor to Methodist Bishop Francis Asbury at Baltimore. It was based on the text from Hebrews 2:14-15: "Since then the children share in flesh and blood, he himself also likewise partook of the same, that through death he might render powerless him who had the power of death, that is, the devil, and might deliver those who through fear of death were subject to slavery all their lives."

41. This question opens a different emphasis in Steinmetz, a Lutheran, than is found in Luther himself, for whom the dialectical struggle between law and gospel remains unabated in the life of a Christian, in that legal accusation provides the incentive for the peace and joy of the gospel's promise of righteousness (expressed in simul iustus ete peccator: simultaneously just and sinner). With Steinmetz, pneumatology has become the focus of the sin/grace struggle, and his notion of the Spirit's indwelling, signified by the Spirit's sealing the believer, shifts the focus to an imperative for the believer to allow the indwelling Spirit to progressively eradicate the vestiges of peccator within their heart. The sealing is initially for conveying certainty regarding pardon of sins through Christ's righteousness; the secondary focus here on temple occupation by the Spirit opens the door to sin eradication as well as a certification of justification through the cross.

of the Holy Spirit? Can such a temple be forfeited? Can then hell and the devil devolve or die away [hineinfallen]?[42]

O my Lord Jesus, give me and all of us the grace for that to happen, even if it should entail the dearest costs to us in order for sin and the devil remaining in the hiddenmost chambers of the heart to be cleared out. Let us with earnestness before God search and prove how it is with our souls.

In the third place, I have said that the orderly seal, which the Holy Spirit uses, when he has come to indwell our hearts, may be the true Word of God, especially the gospel besides the sacraments, as instituted by Jesus, which the Holy Spirit uses in an orderly manner among each person to seal them and to certify their standing in grace. We find the clearest distinguishing marks of this ministry of the Holy Spirit set forth in God's Word.[43]

Beloved, if we have rightly comprehended these matters, what would bring us to a great esteem for the godly Word? Ah, how gladly we would occupy ourselves with its message! How precious would the sacraments become for us?[44] In this way many persons are truly equipped [for their calling to establish God's blessed reign on earth through Christians who have experienced the Pentecost sealing of the Holy Spirit].[45]

There are probably those who do not even intend evil but are not yet diligent enough in God's Word and in the sacraments. Therefore, they cannot be sealed. In particular, many times an undoubted opportunity appears to be slight, where the Word of God is preached, and there are those who think they are beyond needing to make use of the means of grace.

I have also further said that the Holy Spirit not only makes ample use of the Word of God and the sacraments as the seal to certify persons in the faith. He also uses his gracious operations in their hearts, namely, the great

---

42. Steinmetz asks the difficult question which would break from Luther, without stating the conclusion. Instead, he leaves it an open question of what we will allow the Holy Spirit to do once we have admitted Him to be domesticated within the temple of our hearts.

43. A reference to the eucharistic words of institution, as found in the Pauline letters in I Corinthians 11:23–30.

44. An important mark of the church Pietists, who were committed to the official structures of Christendom, was their intent to enliven the personal use of the means of grace, Word and sacraments, along the lines of the new birth. By contrast, radical Pietists advocated separation from those means because of the suppression of the liberty of the children of God in those structures.

45. This statement relates the discussion to the theme of the book as found in its title, which was lived out in Steinmetz's post-Teschen ministry of creating a network for tracking the progress of the Kingdom of God upon earth, which began with the awakening among the children.

transformation which now enables a person to love God and his neighbors heartily. Now, this can give us a powerful incitement as a conclusion to this discussion.

A further area of investigation: have we not often hindered the Holy Spirit in many of His operations of grace? How often have we allowed the Holy Spirit to do this or that work in our inner lives? This topic may not be found as being quite so pleasant. The problem is that persons are often not obedient to the workings of the Holy Spirit and so come to the conclusion that we cannot be sealed. Let us prove before God whether we are still resisting the Holy Spirit through something. Should we also only find one thing as the issue, let us surrender our hearts anew to the Lord Jesus. We do not know through what working of grace He wants to certify us in His Spirit in order that He might have places in which to extend His operations of grace in all circumstances. To that end He comes upon us until He has brought His work to fullness within our souls. May Jesus help us to reach that point through the Holy Spirit. We intend to call upon Him in a most hearty fashion. Amen.

The Third Pentecost Edification

3.1 Sealing in Praxis

It is not to be denied that the Holy Spirit provides a more certain, vigorous and powerful means of rendering service [to God and neighbor] whenever He has wanted to bring persons into sealing or the certainty of forgiveness of their sins, their standing in grace and their coming blessedness. He convinces us of this as well as practical knowledge, and also of the infallible Word of God. Whoever has dealt with persons who wrestle with their standing in grace, of whom many examples could be cited, know how God has brought such persons to a very special position of grace through very powerful, energetic and impressive reminders of the blessedness found in the use of this benefit of grace.

3.2 Examples of Spirit-Sealed Lives in History

In God's Word we find many traces of this. For example, there is the account of David in Psalm 51:10.[1] Here he petitions his God that he wants God to let him experience joy and ecstasy, so that his bones might be quickened which at that time were so dashed to pieces.

We also find a particularly beautiful witness to this matter in Song of

---

1. "Create in me a clean heart O God and renew a right spirit within me" (Psalm 51:10).

Solomon, chapter two. There, (57) it is explained what Jesus, the bridegroom of faithful souls, has used as a means of bringing them from their misery, which had been given special treatment in the first chapter. It had particularly been addressed there, among other places.

Then the Lord Jesus had to address the congregation of his believers concerning whether they did not know to whom they belonged, or how he had actually provided for them. In the second chapter we find that the believers are presented as a rose among thorns in verse two, that is, with respect to their feeling of their sins. Afterward, in the third and sixth verses, they are described as those now sitting under the shadow of the One who loves their souls, the Bridegroom of their souls, who would now taste the fruit of their Lord Jesus, which would be sweet. In verse four, they are led into the wine cellar, and the love of Jesus was made their banner. They refreshed themselves with flowers and delighted themselves with apples, so that they became so overcome by love that they could hardly bear it. Such an experience, and such a feeling, must be brought to bear and impressed upon their inward parts.[2]

When I read here about these sweet affections, whereby the Holy Spirit seals the soul or assures it of the grace of God and the forgiveness of their sins, as well as their future blessedness, I am not here speaking of all sensations and satisfying refreshments which a person may somehow imbibe, even though it soon passes away, and the poor heart is left even less assured than it had been. (58) You will also remember that I have already said that God takes care to grant to persons such a sweet, appealing vision of His grace when they hardly have begun to awaken from their fallen condition of depravity — something so sweet, appealing, satisfying and refreshing within the reading and meditation upon the Word of God, or within the moment of inward prayer.

However, that sensation passes away so fleetingly, as a stream of sunlight in spring, into the soon return of winter storms and cloudbursts. Upon that fleeting experience I must not rest my assurance of a standing in saving grace, for thereby a person can powerfully be deceived, if that is viewed as the assurance and the sealing of the forgiveness of my sins. No, the heart must abide in the realm of certainty, and not that of a transient

---

2. This bridal mysticism, based in the Song of Solomon, had long been a favorite devotional theme in medieval Catholic mysticism. This section takes us to the heart of Steinmetz's mystical piety, characteristic of Pietist authors, which expressed how he grasped the mystical depth of the theology of the cross, from which the breadth of his vision for the building of the Kingdom of God on earth takes its direction.

experience. Therefore, I now speak of the passions and feelings which the Holy Spirit uses as a means. For example, when the Holy Spirit makes use of the godly Word in relation to the soul of a person, that soul lets itself be openly susceptible to this influence and it convinces that person of the reality of their standing in grace, that they could be assured of the grace of God and the forgiveness of their sins. He thereby adds a certain degree of sufficiency to their sense of assurance. For it may likely be a possible experience, especially for a poor worm who has long laid in thousands of doubts, that there often resounds in his heart the thought that, "Ah, I am probably a condemned sinner!" (59) And then there comes a moment when God and His Word become known to him, from which point a certain ground of hope begins to be created, which assists him amid his mortal condition.

And so it goes with the other means and seals, which the Holy Spirit uses among many persons. However, if I say that the Holy Spirit works such a sealing and certainty among persons by bringing forth such powerful sensations I am thereby saying that such powerful foretastes of grace and the love of God have become authentic channels of saving grace. It is to say that I have gained certain assurance by such lively and energizing sensations of peace in the Holy Spirit, such a foretaste of the power of the coming world, which sweeps away all the streams of doubt and hesitation from the soul. By these means I could say, despite death and the devil, that "I now know it. *My God and my Savior have now assured me in a lively manner that I am His child*, that my sins are forgiven, and I am certain of that."

When other persons read that, and see that the Lord has used such means to establish certainty of salvation, it nevertheless is insufficient for me that I have explained myself more clearly about what I understand through such a conviction, whereby the Holy Spirit takes care to seal many souls of their standing in grace. (60)

Nor does that signify that such persons are any better than another. Instead, it indicates that this sealing through these affections[3] [Empfind

---

3. It is appropriate to use this Edwardian term because Steinmetz requested news from Edwards' parish in Northampton, Massachusetts, on the signs of the Great Awakening taking shape there. This is found in his correspondence with Philip Doddridge, the noted British Nonconformist pastor and Steinmetz received, translated, and published a German edition of Edwards' Narrative of the Surprising Work of God in Northampton(1734), as recorded in his *Die Sammlung Auserlesenuner Materien zum Bau des Reichs Gottes zwischen 1730 und 1760*, in *Erbauungszeitschriften als Kommunikationsmedium des Pietismus; Verlag der Franckeschen Stiftungen Halle* (Tübingen: Max Niemeyer Verlag, 2006.), 196.

ungen] must first of all be supported, as it were, by the other means of grace, especially if something remains of our old nature, something that is a cause for suffering and pain.

3.3 The Panoply of Christ-like Virtues in the Body of Christ among Those Sealed through the Holy Spirit

Consider this, my friend, if you are experiencing the strongest sensations of grace and love, and you did not have this distinguishing seal within yourself, then it could be said, *I am yet truly representative of what God describes in His Word as his children.* I nevertheless have within me what God says in His godly Word about those who belong to Him, who have been relieved of their sins in His blood. If that is so, what then would remain of the assurance of the grace of God?

(61) Even if I had the strongest affections, the sweetest assurance of particular times of saving grace, yet I did not notice within myself any change of heart and mind through the Holy Spirit; if I did not notice that the Holy Spirit had truly granted to me the new birth experience [wiedergeboren], that I had become a new creation, that the world and sin had been put out of sight for me, that I now hungered and thirsted for nothing more than for God and His grace and for the blood of my Lord and Savior Jesus Christ. I say, if I had none of these things, I could not truly say that I am with God in grace.[4]

Hence, I also say, although the affections penetrate the heart affectively and are very precious, and are incomparable in view of the loveliness of other things, a person may not consider him or herself better than anyone else because of these affections. Instead, one must be assured through other operations of grace if that person does not want to suffer the shipwreck of one's faith.

Further, by this seal or means of assurance of grace by the Holy Spirit I must remember that it cannot be said that perchance the souls who have arrived at assurance through such affections of their standing in grace are also extraordinarily precious to the Lord Jesus. No, it is better to look upon this more as signs of weakness that God had to take such visible measures

---

4. This statement reflects the author's version of what it means to embody the Body of Christ in history as one communion sealed by the Holy Spirit in the blood of the crucified Christ, which envisions Pentecost fulfilled for the new humanity in Christ.

for them to come to their place in the Father's house, since, through their unbelief, (62) the other kinds of sealing through the Word and the sacraments had been resisted.

It is important to recall from our Easter faith, that, if God grants to you such a notable sealing through a blessed, powerful affection of His grace, He takes you, as it were, to the meal of the Easter Lamb. Consider how bitter was the salt that went with that meal, otherwise it would not offer you much use. Whoever has experience and gives attention to the ways of God concerning what the Holy Spirit pledges to undertake with such souls will generally see that where the Holy Spirit offers such sweet refreshments and affections for the certification of their standing in grace, much bitter salt will also follow thereafter. And that happens out of the great mercy of God! For the Easter Lamb would not be for us the right taste and nourishment if it had not been prepared with the right salt, so that thereby its true power might be received which was intended for our souls [or inner lives].

I have brought up this topic especially for the sake of many *who appear among the children of God in large numbers in these times,* as well as among the crowd of those who are seeking what is best for themselves within the Christendom of this present age.[5] For many, the eucharist is taken for granted, or only lightly esteemed. If we were to recall what it meant for the Jews facing the ardor of the exodus from Egypt, its meaning would also be greater for us in our precarious state of faith. If the Holy Spirit directs us to the biblical truth concerning this vital means of grace, He will make clear to us that there is something much more important than merely finding personal affection and refreshment from this holy meal we eat in the presence of God. (63) Our great God and the esteemed Holy Spirit provide you with His grace so that He makes available to you, in power, through this meal, an entire range of precious gifts from His promises which are fitted for our lives in Christ.

3.4 The Quest for Authenticity as Christians

Here is what we do. Take hold with both hands. Position yourself in prayer, hold on with earnest supplication, until the Holy Spirit, who discerns what is best for your circumstances, imprints deeply within your heart His seal. Delight yourself with this. Give thanks to your God and Savior for it. One

---

5. This is a critique of the elite class of European Christendom in that day of its demise. Here he reflects the critique of Spener of the civil estate in *Pia Desideria* (1675), Part One. John Tappert, ed, *Pia Desideria*, Philadelphia: Fortress, 1964.

among many will so pay attention to this that he will not at all want to be brought to this point before his feet are firmly set on the rock that is Jesus Christ, and until he attains such a powerful discernment of holy affection [Empfindung].[6]

I have personally observed this occurrence among many souls [persons!], among whom the Holy Spirit was Himself powerfully demonstrated. He has made it completely clear from His Word.[7] The Holy Spirit has gifted them with powerful holy affections with their use of the sacrament as well, that it might become authentically [wahrhaftig] distinctive in a way unlike anything they have known in the external world, because God's Spirit is working and living within them.

For many of you, there is a deep desire to go more deeply into this seal of our faith. You want to know and to feel His Presence. It is not enough to worship God without coming to terms with our inner lives, and to recognize without doubt that His seal is what the Holy Spirit wants to press upon their hearts, long darkened through all kinds of unnecessary doubt which we make for ourselves. What remains for such souls is to completely and simply abandon [überlassen] themselves to the working of the Holy Spirit, so that He can undertake with you that which is commensurate with His wisdom. I have found it necessary to remember this.

With regard to holy affections, for which the Holy Spirit secures and seals many persons, it is important that those persons through whom God channels this precious seal should not think that they have become privileged as possessors of this gift before others have received it, thereby leaving others with the sense of being slighted thereby. Ah no! That would be a nasty sign! The more that grace works in the soul, the lesser does the soul

---

6. Here is the sense of discernment as distinct from affection. Note the extent to which Steinmetz describes the features of the encounter with the Holy Spirit based in the Teschen revival-context, where revival was occurring for the first time in Protestant tradition. He is careful to identify these exercises in the Spirit as adiaphora, and not even as the primary evidences of the Spirit's salvific work in confirming to the heart the atoning work of Christ on the cross, which is based in the proclamation of Word and sacrament in Lutheran tradition. But, as the title of his addresses makes clear, these religious exercises are not the standard liturgy of the Word; they are being presented within the apostolic context of Pentecost renewed. This is mystic-based Pentecost revival in a Lutheran context, occurring in a moment of time before there were any categories or nomenclature to name it for what it is. Again, the parallels with Jonathan Edwards's accounts of revival, occurring at the same time a hemisphere away, are impressive.

7. Notice that it is not the preacher who has made it clear under the Spirit's anointing! Steinmetz is not speaking here as preacher in charge but as witness to the sovereign activity of the Holy Spirit functioning in a revival setting.

become. That is an unmistakable word, a firm foundation in our religion. The greater, the more glorious; or, is it not that the more noble the grace that indwells a person is, the smaller that person becomes.

Grace has the power, the miraculous power, which makes you courageous as those on God's side of the struggle for faith, to hold yourselves against the powers of death and the devil. However, on the other side, that which is extraordinary can also bend us lower in our station in life, to become humble before God and others. For, the more grace one receives, the less attention one has and the more unworthy that one is regarded.[8]

So it goes with this means of grace, so that it is quite necessary to note that persons are not to think that those who came before others had something special. Ah, no! If the enemy could ever bring a person to that place, one would soon see that the grace was becoming constricted. One would soon notice what kind of sharp discipline by the Holy Spirit would result, whereby a person would be assisted and advised. Now follows, a very important and necessary question, yes, I well might say, one of the most important matters on (65) this subject, namely, by what means[9] then may one be able to recognize whether one really has partaken of the sealing with the Holy Spirit?

There is deception in this matter. It is the greatest misfortune which one can encounter in time and in eternity. Whoever has only a love for his soul will probably now pray heartily to God so that He might confer grace. To speak about this matter correctly and simply is our goal, because it is not a matter which belongs only to the intelligent but rather to the simplest. *Since they want to become blessed, they must know what is good, as do all the most learned. On the contrary, the most learned one has no precedence before the simplest child of God.*

There is no distinction in the presence of Jesus. The intelligent and the simple must learn to recognize whether or not he can now be certain of his salvation, and whether that which he holds for certainty of salvation is also what is found in the ground of his heart [Herzensgrund].[10]

---

8. This formula reflects Luther's focus on the humility which is prerequisite to address God in a theology of the cross as opposed to the hubris implicit in its opposite, a theology of glory.

9. The author uses "wherefrom" (Woraus).

10. The theme of Herzensgrund resonates with Steinmetz's younger contemporary, the master teacher and hymnist of all Pietists, Gerhard Tersteegen (1697-1769), whose anthropology finds God's dwelling place in homo sapiens to be the Seelengrund. See Tersteegen, "True Godliness," in Samuel Jackson (tr), *Spiritual Crumbs from the Master's Table* (1837) reprinted (Kessinger Publishing, 2009).

But, my God! What kind of an incoherent jabber is it if a person proceeds in such a fashion until his death bed, or if a man comes before the day of judgment, as it appears in Matthew 7:21-23,[11] and thinks he will become blessed but finds himself thereafter deceived?

I beseech you for the sake of God, think about this. Can what is astonishing be true, can one really suggest anything more frightful than for a man who thought, I will now hear the judgment from God, come, you blessed of the Lord, and inherit the kingdom, and (66) the voice of God is directed against him, "Go out, you accursed one, into eternal destruction." Therefore, let us now guard ourselves against such a great wretchedness, and so ask God, for me and for you, that He might give grace for me and for you concerning this matter upon which the whole of eternity comes to rest, how you and I might stand once before the judgment of God. My Savior grants mercy to me and you and now lets me yet enjoy the perch of grace He has offered, that through this declaration many souls may be saved from the depths of their destruction and their misery.

Before I provide my answer to our question, I intend to remind you beforehand, for the sake of the persons for whom it is necessary, that this question must be regarded as being most meaningful. Is that not so? Our entire Christianity consists mostly of persons who entertain such false hopes of their salvation, bringing forth their conclusions based on their own reasoning, as though it came through a dream. Perchance they may also be drawing their conclusions from one worthy motive or another, drawing their conclusions within their own souls that they will surely be saved and blessed. Sometimes such deceived souls may disentangle themselves from their shadowy errors, so it is then highly necessary that a person examine herself based on certain principles from God's Word, from which he can be certain whether or not he has ground for hope.

To this day there are certainly those who have really encountered some aspects of grace and (67) have probably come to some measure of sealing through the Lord Jesus, but then by and by they returned back into the ways of this world. Such persons are likely to suffer regretfully if they are led to self examination either outwardly by others or inwardly through the Holy Spirit. If they are led through this disposition to acknowledge their setback due to their deviation, it would not be [a fatal lapse]. That is because they applied themselves according to their first, sweet, pleasing disposition of grace, and likewise, out of the knowledge which they accu-

---

11. "Not everyone who says unto me, Lord, Lord, shall enter the kingdom of heaven" Matthew 7:21a.

mulated from the images, so to speak, which they hold in their minds of all kinds of grace-filled thoughts.

To restore such persons from their distress and lead them back to their first, true way, it is certainly necessary to explain this question, and to await the reply. *I speak here not so much as a matter of principle, but rather for the sake of God's children*, who have their seal and hold on until the grace. Do you ask, why? A child of the light must occasionally walk in the darkness, which comes from the prophet Micah 7:7, and also Isaiah 50:10:

> Therefore I will look unto the Lord; I will wait for the God of my salvation. My God will hear me.

> Who is among you who fears the Lord, who obeys the voice of his servant, who walks in darkness and has no light? Let him trust in the name of the Lord, and stay upon his God.

God also occasionally lets it happen for His beloved ones that they come into dark hours. They cannot, so to speak, see their seal. The beloved David complained in the Psalm, "For the enemy has persecuted my soul; he has smitten my life down to the ground; he has made me to dwell in darkness, as those that have been long dead." (Psalm 143:10). Who are the dead in this world? They are the unconverted population.[12]

Concerning them, David says that the certainty of his standing in grace was, God, let it be so, so that for him it occasionally came with courage, as it is even for the unconverted men in the world, so that he could only slightly notice that he was truly converted and *was a child of God*, as an unconverted person. Ah, how good it is, if a person experiences the right sign and, as it were, receives a staff from the Word of God, thereby to assist in being grounded upon it in such turbulent hours of Anfechtung [despair] and darkness.

I have therefore said this to awaken your souls to attention. From this, you could probably notice that, although people may have a moment in the most blessed assurance, and be changed, so to speak, in the light of God, and their seal illumed them, as it were, in their eyes, even though it was morning, or perhaps it could be in darkness. Have you not seen this or that example of what we are describing here? How many a time has someone

---

12. Here the author puts his revival concerns in a globalized context, indicating the motive for entering this arena is the larger outcome of the revival in the Habsburg lands, where "pious and persecuted minorities had to achieve quick results or go under," and it happened, "thanks to revivals instituted and conducted by children." David Hempton, *Methodism, Empire of the Spirit* (New Haven: Yale, 2008), 46

walked in great joy, perhaps for more than a year, and yet they come upon darkness? That can happen to you! So now, give attention, O friend, pray for you and for me, that this presentation may truly be blessed.

(69) The answer, overall, which I must give to the preceding question, consists in this: If one would become rightly convinced that the hope and assurance which a person has of his salvation, may be a sealing of the Holy Spirit on which one could depend, you must consider these criteria:

> See whether the sealing which you now believe to have, is of the nature and manner which has all the characteristics which a true sealing with the Holy Spirit needs to have.

> Give attention to whether the assurance of the grace of God, of the forgiveness of sins, and eternal salvation which you believe to have, is also bearing fruit, which indicates the right sign for the sealing with the Holy Spirit.

We now arrive at two sub-points. If you intend to know whether the sealing with the Holy Spirit is of the right kind and character, whether it has the properties which a right sealing with the Holy Spirit must have to make it a sealing with the Holy Spirit, then consider these three markers to discern whether the sealing is authentic:

1. The right sealing of the Holy Spirit for the forgiveness of sins and for blessedness [Seligkeit] is so firmly grounded that it can also withstand the strongest challenges. Indeed, the more often one tests God's Word in all circumstances, the clearer and brighter it becomes for you. (70) The person here is conducting a test by placing himself before God and thinking, "My God, how am I hereby arriving at certainty? Through what sort of method?"

2. If he has the right assurance, he will soon be convinced that he has received this redemption through the way of true repentance and conversion, and not through a dream. He is not in a dream taking his to that end, as are those poor souls who always think they are somehow blessed, but who know nothing of true repentance, or the way of a true and living faith, which is indeed the only way and order whereby one may become sealed with the Holy Spirit. Notice, whenever one tests his assurance before God he stands so that he comes to a point on the

way[13] to a true conversion. This is a place of deep surrender and meekness on the way to a feeling of his condemned condition and mortal misery, through faith in his bloody Savior Jesus Christ. This gives him a beautiful marker that he is rightly sealed, that the matter is right with him and with God.

3. Ask and search a person further concerning the condition of grace in which the believer stands, and you will find he also has it confirmed unto himself on what he grounds this assurance, and what evidence he has for it. Thus he will verify that everything which is in the Word of God concerning the believer's standing in grace is confirmed, and he has taken this seal upon himself.[14]

By contrast, the person who has a self-made hope either knows nothing about that hope or he has one which knows either no ground or one which contains no sure content. That however is not to be found among true children of God.[15] (71)

And so it goes through all features of this sealing. Hence, I say, that the supreme feature of the act of sealing, upon which a person can surrender himself, is this: It is that which is grounded, and it is not something which is presumptuous, or selfish, nor illusory, which a person has made for himself. The Holy Spirit creates no dreams, He makes no fantasies, nor does He work that which is "ungrounded" into the heart. And why? It is because ours is a truthful God. What He administers, what He creates, that is what constitutes a true "ground" upon which certainty with God rests.[16]

---

13. The reference to "the way" into salvation is congruent with the apostolic church emphasis upon catechesis which was conducted under the heading of "The Doctrine of the Two Ways." See discussion in Gregory Dix, *The Shape of the Liturgy* (London, 1950), chapter one. This use of "the Way" to describe authentic Christianity also shows influence from Reformed Pietism, with its emphasis on covenant based salvation history in which each believer is defined on the basis of their faithfulness in negotiating the steps toward full closure with Christ through the covenant of grace. The leading eighteenth-century contemporary theologian who addresses this issue is Friedrich Adolph Lampe (1683-1729), in *Die Geheimnis des Gnadenbundes* (6 volumes).

14. This is comparable to the rite of confirmation in the Anglican and Lutheran traditions, which Steinmetz is here relocating to a revival context.

15. This appeal shows another connection of Steinmetz's addresses to the children prayer and prophecy revival in Silesia of 1707-8.

16. On the concept of Seelengrund (ground of the soul) in Pietism, and especially in Gerhard Tersteegen (1697-1763), see Dietrich Meyer, "Cognitio Dei Experimentalis oder "Erfahrungstheologie" bei Gottfried Arnold, Gerhard Tersteegen, und Nikolaus Ludwig

The second kind of sealing and blessed salvation by the grace of God, if it is to be godly, is this: it also endures in the face of want and death, amid strife and despair. The one who has only made room for a good hope has received nothing that is abiding in his blessedness and by the forgiveness of sins. He only makes room for it in a minimal degree. That person will discover nothing different from himself than do those miserable persons who are without faith.

By contrast, we note what the Holy Spirit has wrought in such a one who remains standing in dire need and the fear of death. Yes, and I will also add this: there remains not only misery and death for the one who is not sealed. That one also remains incapable of resisting amid the dire threats of the most severe forms of temptations and despair [Anfechtungen].[17] Such a state contradicts the condition befitting a true Christian.[18] The sweet affections of grace are withdrawn, but the confidence in God and in Jesus, and the love for his Lord Jesus cannot be seized by the devil. Many endure hard times of Anfechtungen, whereby our inner person is somewhat darkened in its faith, but this is not the case here.

A Christian who (72) is stabilized by his standing in grace holds firmly in such moments as long as necessary until his seal shines forth more splendidly. Then it will be seen that such persons, though fallen into deep Anfechtung, and appearing to be in a period of doubt within their condition of grace, are more confident than they were before the onset of grace. They have suffered no injury, and their seal cannot be taken away from them by the devil, amid all their trials of faith. No, the Holy Spirit has only cushioned them, so that they are not stripped of their seal, into which they had become smelted.[19] They are imprinted with the image of the Savior much more excellently.[20]

---

von Zinzendorf," in Dietrich Meyer und Udo Sträter, *Zur Rezeption mystischer Traditionen im Protestantismus des 16. Bis 19. Jahrhunderts.* (Köln: Rheinland-Verlag GmbH, 2002), 223-240. One interpreter says of Tersteegen, "as a Bible expositor in the context of a class meeting or revival meeting, he has probably never had an equal." - W.R. Ward, *Christianity under the Ancient Regime, 1648-1789* (Cambridge, 1999), "New Approaches to European History Series", 129.

17. Here again is Luther's term for the temptations of the devil in one's life.

18. Here the author makes reference to the title of the great classic of Christian devotion, read by all Pietists, *The True Christianity of Johann Arndt*, in six volumes (1605).

19. The term here, "durchgeschmolzen," is an archaic term depicting the casting of iron in a furnace, which reflects the technology current in Steinmetz's day.

20. Here we discern one more feature of Steinmetz's description of what Wesleyans call the state of sanctified grace. In this rendition, the believer is now embossed with the very image of her Savior, which is a kind of Pietist version of the honorable Catholic canon of

However, when a person is wavering in their faith, today he has it and tomorrow he has nothing, since there is not yet peace at hand and cannot imagine that he really bears the seal.[21] Ah, no! The Spirit of God is an eternal Spirit. What He works is what is abiding. That persists against all the implements[22] of hell. As the works of God can stand against everything, so must God's seal.

Permit me to offer a sign here by which one can notice that the assurance which one has of their standing in grace through the Holy Spirit, is growing and increasing. I lead out with that primarily for the sake of those who appear to have already received their seal at one time but have not preserved it. They have not paid attention to the words we read in Revelation 3:11: "I am coming quickly; hold fast what you have, in order that you may take your crown."

(73) Ah, beloved friends! May it be the case that if the assurance of grace is genuine it will not be lost, but rather increase, remain grounded, and become ever more powerful in your inward life? That is how it proceeds with the operations of the grace of the Holy Spirit. They are like a stream which, at the beginning, consists only of a small trickle, but gradually, the longer it flows, it becomes ever greater until it finally flows into the great global ocean.[23] Hence, it proceeds with the operations of God's grace, which flow from the correct source, from the pure Word and the Holy Spirit, so that the longer it continues, the stronger and more powerful it becomes. Every day this person receives more assurance. He must pass through many Anfechtungen, with each being a victory at those points where the operation of the Holy Spirit is advancing, leaving the person with an ever stronger awareness of the sealing of the Spirit.

However, we can also observe reversals as well as advances occurring along these lines of personal faith. For example, years ago I met a person who had that which was so excellent in his heart, and now he notices it hardly at all. That is a sad sign! A person showing these tendencies may

---

the stigmata of Christ, the bearing of the wounds of the crucified Lord, on the bodies of the saints, as was canonically assigned to St. Francis of Assisi.

21. This last clause may suggest that, to the author, there are instances where one might actually be a bearer of the seal but their external circumstances are not then allowing them to acknowledge it, which is at best a low degree of faithfulness to Christ.

22. The term used here, Pforten, is an archaic term, not found in the unabridged German/ English dictionaries, including Cassells.

23. This correlation of the points of the soul with the world suggest the impetus for Christian globalization which is implicit in Steinmetz's larger concern is guiding the revival which began among the children in Silesia 132.

presently experience a loss of capacity to be awakened to faith by the Lord Jesus, to draw power and life from His wounds,[24] and so will either suffocate, or cease to draw life from His death. It is for the sake of such souls that I have determined to explain this yet further.

Many times have I counseled with persons who, in the beginning of their sealing had been seized by doubts and sighed, "Ah, God! How will it be for me some day on my deathbed? How will I endure that? Therefore, such a deathbed terror often pierces the heart because they have not yet taken care to (74) withstand the final struggle. However, I have certainly taken care to warn many souls how the Holy Spirit is fully prepared to take this doubt from them and completely free them from this fear, so that they could affirm, even in the middle of the hour of death, that their seal remained undisturbed upon the heart.

In order to discern whether one's experience of the sealing of the Holy Spirit and the assurance of His Spirit is the real thing, it is also important to give attention to its power, fruit and operation, which is applicable for each of us. I can recognize a tree by its fruit. A good tree is known by its fruit. The tree, which God has planted in my heart must also bear godly fruit. Also, the sealing through the Holy Spirit must also be revealed royally in godly fruit. That is no dead work, which a person pledges to do in his thoughts and phantasies about the assurance of his blessedness. No!

The sealing by which one receives his standing in grace and his salvation through the Holy Spirit and which can be relinquished by a person at the point of need and death, is an overall powerful seal.

Permit me to mention here only three chief operations by which a person can discern the difference between a valid and well-grounded sealing and one which only feigns to be genuine but is actually a self-initiated impression or dream state, as many have reported.

(75) First, we may observe here, if assurance constitutes a true sealing

---

24. This locating the point of identity with Christ's death through participation in His blood is a theme Steinmetz shares with his colleague, Count Nicholas von Zinzendorf, through whom there even developed a "blood and wounds" cult among the Moravians at Herrnhaag (which Zinzendorf made has new base of operations after the Saxon government closed down the revival at Herrnhut and expelled the Count. Ward notes that in its extreme form, this piety led to an enthusiastic "time of sifting" around the adoration of the wounds, occurring as a subliminal diversion from dealing with the growing financial desperation of the Herrnhaag Moravian community. The result was the collapse of that community and the undermining of its international mission under Zinzendorf. Ward, *Christianity Under the Ancien Regime*, 122.

by the Holy Spirit, on which one can rely, it makes the heart of a person courageous and bold to act on their faith, but also, second, willing to let it alone and to suffer what the Savior has suffered, but also, third, it is accompanied by power [from the Holy Spirit], so that everything which one could do to hinder it is little by little overcome.

3.5 Biblical Evidences for Childlikeness as the Highest Expression of Sealing by the Holy Spirit

What is happening that is of primal importance in this operation of the Holy Spirit is that it enables a person with indisputable conviction to recognize one basic truth, the mystery of entering into the life of a child of God. *The most childlike*[25] *[Einfältig] person* is the one who can comprehend most completely what it means to find reconciliation in Jesus' blood. He learns to recognize what he has in his Savior, for a merciful, loving God, and how completely hearty the Lord Jesus is disposed toward him. For he has felt what kind of a cursed, damnable, and sinful man he has been, and yet, he also now knows that God has granted to him out of grace forgiveness for all his sins, that his Savior has released and freed him from all his sin. He knows too that God wants to grant him nothing but unending goodness and that He will grant it.

If a person believes all this from the heart, that his God and Savior desires nothing more from him than what is perfectly good and wholesome, that shall He not make him be lustful, but rather, willing in suffering? Shall He not stretch forth both hands to take suffering upon Himself, even as one might stretch forth his hands as a worthy means of help and mercy?. (76) Therefore, you are to follow naturally[26] after this, as soon as you arrive at a true place of sealing in His grace [Gnadenstand].

Then, it cannot be otherwise. The *child of God*[27] then becomes courageous, as our dear Luther was wont to say.[28] It is his heart's joy if he can

---

25. *Einfältig*: which also can mean direct, uncomplicated, simple or unassuming.

26. Here "nature" is used not in the Enlightenment sense as that which corresponds to an externally harmonious universe, but is use with reference to what is natural for a child of God in responding to the love of the heavenly Father and His beloved Son, Jesus Emanuel.

27. Literally, just the pronoun "er" (he), but we are reading this in the context of his Pentecost theme.

28. See Martin Luther, *Weimar Ausgabe* 4, No. 4367, Letter to Lauterbach, February 26, 1539, under the theme of "Children Have Unquestioning Faith" as cited in Ewald M. Plass, ed. *What Luther Says: An Anthology* (St. Louis Concordia, 1959), Volume 1: 142.

only do what God wants. Suffering can be what his God and Savior intend to have.[29] With the assurance of the forgiveness of sins, there flows also such a power of God into the heart that a person has the capacity for faithful praxis [Vermögen], even if takes you toward suffering.[30] As Paul states in Romans 8, there is that which seeks to hinder us from overcoming in fulfilling that which our God would enable us to do. I intend to make this clear for you. The assurance of forgiveness of sins and the blessed salvation is a real balm of heaven, a real anointing of the Holy Spirit. O my God, if that flows through our hearts, what kind of godly power does a person receive which he did not previously have, under the reign of the law? Accordingly, if I now consider how good it is with our Lord Jesus, how merciful my Father in heaven has been to me, how my God and Savior heartily longed for my salvation and blessedness, that results in my joy in Jesus.

As soon as a Christian, in the joy of faith, sinks into the wounds of his God and Savior, Jesus Christ, should he not find power therein, so that he can stand against everything which prejudice wants to direct against him?

God has born witness to this in more than one place in His Word, so that true faith, that is, the assurance through the Holy Spirit, might have such a victorious power.[31] I have read to you the words from I John 5:4-5:

> Everything which is born of God overcomes the world; and this is the victory that has overcome The world, our faith. And who is the one who has overcome the world, but he who believes that Jesus is the Son of God.

This already has appeared in Isaiah 33:21, where the prophet declares that "no resident" of the New Jerusalem, "will say, I am weak, for the people who dwell there will be forgiven their iniquities." The text in Zachariah 12:8 is also noteworthy in this regard, where it is spoken, "In that day the Lord will defend the inhabitants of Jerusalem, and the one who is feeble among them in that day will be like David." So shall it also be, when the soul comes to the Lord Jesus, as to the free, open well, against all sins and uncleanness.

From this, you can now see what kind of a suffering deception that would be if our Christians were always dragging around their weaknesses

---

29. "leiden kann, was sein Gott und Heiland haben will."

30. It should be recalled that this is written in the context of a suffering church of refugees who had lost home and church and often loved ones, only to be regathered in the context of revival.

31. For Steinmetz, it appears that this empowerment by the Holy Spirit is a phase beyond faith, which is related to the forgiveness of sins through the blood of Christ.

and yet they consider themselves thereby to be holy. This is your condition so long as you have not been converted to the Lord Jesus, so long as you remain under the dominion of the devil and proceed in your sins, so long as you grate under the law when it comes near, but you do not make room for grace, so that you could one day come to the sealing through the Holy Spirit and find grace in the blood of Jesus, so long as you are not only weak (78) but rather incompetent in all good works.

Had you sought pardon in the wounds of Jesus, you would not make room for complaints, inasmuch as is evident in the witness of David. David was a small boy and yet dared to confront a great giant. From where did he come? He said, "I do not come to you on my own strength, but in the Name of the Lord." And so it is for a true Christian, who knows and also says, "I live in God, in Jesus, and Jesus lives in me." Or, as Paul said, in Galatians 2:20: "It is no longer I who live, but Christ who lives within me." And from the ground he rises up against Goliath. He feared no longer, for Jesus had sealed him through His Spirit, and through this gracious sealing, power to overcome was communicated to him.

However, so long as a man remains a slave to his lusts and inordinate desires, remaining with the lust of the eye, the lust of the flesh, and an arrogant nature, he remains mastered by these things. He lies under their weight like a poor bound servant. And yet he thinks that perchance he could become blessed, or, if he gets far enough, he does something good and thinks that from this he has escaped hell and even has a confidence of the forgiveness of sins, coming from merely one instance of forgiveness for sins. Ah, that would be a horrible deception!

Whoever has the seal in his heart willingly desists from evil, seeks after the good, and bears his cross patiently when assaulted, so that (1) he has power to triumph and to overcome. Life does not continue however (79) without struggle and temptations. A Christian is buffeted by the devil, the world and the flesh. He is provoked to lust, pride, unbelief, timidity and the like. But one has power that can conquer, and lust for battle that is willing for that to be done. One would rather render body and life for the sake of the Lord Jesus before choosing to forfeit the great grace of God.

(2) The other fruit which is now necessary for us to follow is an inward, childlike and heartfelt love for God and Jesus, and for all who belong to God and our Lord. For, if people do not have love for Jesus, by whom then are they to be informed that He wants to free us from death and hell? And to forgive us gratuitously from all sin? And to accept us as His child and with His inheritance, because He wants to grant us nothing less than joy

and blessedness. Would I not have love for such a God and Savior? Indeed, one can then say without contradiction with Peter that, before all mankind and all angels, "Lord Jesus, You know that I have love for You, although not as I should, nor as You are worthy. Hence, You know Lord Jesus that I have wanted to love You and to demonstrate my love for You through my life better than to offend You."

Therefore, whoever arrives at the experience of sealing, unconditionally loves all persons who are born of the Lord Jesus, that is, all true children of God. That person also loves all people upon earth because they are redeemed with the blood of Christ. However, since he still (80) marks the sprinkling of the blood of Christ for the children of God, and knows they even stand in the blood of the Savior, as he, that they have one God as their Bridegroom, and only one kind of wounds for their salvation, one heaven for their eternal dwelling place and blessedness, so they cannot do anything else than to love them from his heart. Concerning whoever may be coldhearted against the children of God, or who would continue vexing or tormenting them, having hatred and enmity toward them, that person should not in any way think that he could ever be assured of his soul's blessedness or of any standing in grace. That stands with clear words in Scripture (I John 3:14): "We know that we have come from death into life. For we love the brethren (the children of God)."[32]

My task now is to set before you the third fruit, from which one can notice that the assurance of the forgiveness of sins is an assured sealing, and an inner lifting of praise. There is an example of this in the blessed David, in Psalm 103, which is a chief source of material[33] on the sealing

---

32. With these numerous references to the children of God as the blessed ones of God, we can infer that Steinmetz, living out of the splendor of the witness of the children in the revival which had awakened his Silesian homeland, and more, that he discerns with them the hand of God's mission for humanity as a whole, now to be made known to the larger world, in the midst of its brokenness. Ergo, the only faithful response to the witness of the children is for it to be born globally as the sine qua non for the existence of Christianity in such a shattered world as he and his comrades in faith had known.—See Steinmetz, 5,4, "Sealed for the World to Receive," 95–97.

33. The phrase "der Materie von der Versiegelung durch den heiligen Geist" (the material concerning the sealing with the Holy Spirit) is a clear parallel to the title of Steinmetz's major *Gathering of Material for the Building of the Kingdom of God on Earth* in his day. See Rainer Lächele, *Die Sammlung auserlesener Materialen zum Bes Reichs Gottes: zwischen 1730 und 1760*, which was his guide to mapping the effects of Protestantism's first revival as it morphed from a local occurrence to assume the stature of an awakening presaging a globalized Christianity in the early modern era.

through the Holy Spirit, in which you have a notable example of one who knew with assurance of his standing in grace. "Bless the Lord, o my soul, and all that is within me, bless His holy Name. Bless the Lord, o my soul, and forget not all His benefits, who pardons all your iniquities, who heals all your diseases" (Psalm 103:2-3). How often the beloved David repeats these words of praise: praise, praise, praise the Lord my soul, and (81) forget not all He has done. He rings this praise into the soul of a man or woman, who is now assured of blessed salvation, who does not have an imaginary [or, self made] assurance but one which is sealed through the Holy Spirit!

If you desire nothing more in this life than to [identify with] those who suffer and are gladly ready to suffer for Christ, you may find yourselves identifying with the sorrowful and here reach the furthest level, though still insufficient, in exalting your God and your love for your Savior which is beyond any other experience in ministry. That realization frequently bends a soul down to the earth, even as Paul said of himself, (Philippians 1:10-23). "I hope that I might be in no kind of shame, but rather that with real joy and real encouragement, Christ will yet be highly praised in my body, whether it be through life or through death. For Christ is my life, and death is my gain. But if I am to live on in the flesh, this will mean fruitful labor for me, and I do not know which to choose. But I am hard pressed from both directions, having the desire to depart and be with Christ."[34] If it should also mean death for me, if I am also to be a sacrifice for Christ, that would be fine, but only insofar as his Jesus would be glorified thereby.

Beloved, I implore you all for the sake of God and your blessed salvation, prove yourself wholly by testing your heart before the Lord to see what you have now experienced of His sealing. Is there a beginning in your heart? I hope (82) there will be many now here before the Lord who will give the witness by the utterance of their conscience [Gewissen]:[35] "Yes, Lord Jesus, you know that [the sealing] is in me, certainly not to a high degree, yet is there truly by your grace, in me, an unworthy sinner."

As the Lord intends I want to show you more extensively, in the next address, what your responsibility is with regard to this. May I also lay before your hearts these words, "Do not grieve the Holy Spirit, in whom you were

---

34. This is Steinmetz's rendition of verses 20-23, reflecting the verbage of the Luther translation of this text.

35. Here is the earliest expression of a revival sermon's appeal for audible heart response to the message of salvation. It was the moment of the "shout" in the early camp meetings.

sealed, with whom you were sealed unto the day of Jesus Christ" (Ephesians 4:30).

Now, go forth in the Name of Jesus Christ, and notice what you have heard about the sign, about whether you are truly sealed by God, and are therefore God's children.

Has it been imprinted within your heart so that when the dark hours come at some future time, you will know on whom you should depend? Perhaps God intends to lead you yet into hard testings, temptations [Anfechtungen], and hours of tribulation, so that every feeling that you now have will pass away. However, at such a time as that the devil will still not be able to lay hold of you and you will still be able to have love for your Lord Jesus, to be and remain His until the grave. In brief, you would still prefer to leave your own life rather than the Lord Jesus. Notice that you now have a sign that enables you to able to stand fast against the devil and all unbelief. However, there will also probably be many who belong to this [faith] who, now read, have been able to recognize that they are still unable to be assured of any blessedness for themselves, if they were candid about the condition of their lives.

(83) After this, there will also be some among us, who have attained insight [eingesehen] during this presentation and have also recognized that they are wretched in the standing of grace. Ah, should not many in our midst come to acknowledge that, "in the Name of the Lord Jesus, it is true that I do not yet have this [certainty of grace]?" Ah, my Savior, as you search through us to discern those who are without assurance of your grace, may each of us be candid about our condition before the Lord.

With both of these kinds of persons [the faithful and the unfaithful], I must yet offer a word of advice. Given the condition of many, what I find useful is to appeal to your conscience. You are not yet ready to come before God with a humility of heart concerning your sin. You have felt miserable about your condition, and the Spirit of the Lord is calling you out of your mortal sin, but your lust for this world still remains too precious for you, and so you have not left room for the Holy Spirit. If you have felt His prompting, you would know your condition before the Lord is desperate. If you would only open your eyes! You certainly are aware that your situation is dire. Do you want to continue in such deception? What will it help you if you have trusted for 20 or 30 years and thought all would go well with you? If you now were to stand before the gates of eternity and the judgment of God, and it then will not be true what you have imagined about your salvation, will you not sigh and cry out in desperation that you will not be permitted to be saved?

Read from the seventh chapter of Matthew (84) as well as the first part of the twenty fifth chapter, concerning the foolish and the wise virgins. Those who were foolish went forth with the wise but their hearts were not formed rightly before God. They did not leave room for the Holy Spirit, so that He might have quickened their hearts to be filled with the oil of faith. Therefore, when they readied themselves, the door was closed to them. They cried out, open the door, and the heard with horror the voice which said, "I do not know you." So will it also be with you, if you let the hour of grace pass you by.

I beseech you today before the face of God, and Jesus Christ, for whom God may awaken His heart, who of you want to turn yourselves toward Jesus' bloody wounds, and ask Him, that He might not only open your eyes to recognize your sins, but also grant you the power to sink into prayer and supplication, until you find grace. God will not allow any among you to be lost, even though you have already fallen in your sins, and so have done injury to your bloody, crucified Savior.

If even today you might only come, to be awakened to your mortal condition, and cast yourself at the feet of your Immanuel, and in this moment [Augenblick] begin to take refuge in Him, surrendering to Him your heart, so that He will lead you out, that you might surely be convinced of your standing in grace.

I have said all this, knowing that the seal of the forgiveness for sins already lies under the treasure of God, procured by Christ's sufferings, (85) which is also intended for you who have not yet been able to approach it in your unconverted, fleshly, hypocritical, and miserable condition. But it remains there, in the Word of God.

Do you want to bring your heart to Jesus, to allow Him room in your inward life [Inwendigen], then it will be impressed upon your heart and soul, and your Savior will grant it unto you. Being certain that He also died on the cross for you, would you prefer to proceed with this world as it is, in doubt and uncertainty, rather than become certain of such a great assurance? Authenticate yourself before God! No, not for the sake of your own life, for the sake of your salvation, allow yourself to become awakened, even today, if you are yet scorning the grace of God. Whatever befalls you would have slain you in your conscience beyond this point.

Listen, my friends, if you would only know what God has intended for you with the thought that you would lift your hand now and praise Him for it! God has revealed it to you out of His grace, that He can and will help you. For, so long as you have not believed, God has not been able to help you. Since all this has now been opened in your heart, since you have begun to be aware that you are a condemned human, a sinner, your blood slain Savior has stretched forth His hand, and draws near to your heart, that He might assist you.

Now, O soul, because of what you observe in your inner life, a work of grace through your Savior, so may you now be brought into confidence. But do not think that because I am such a horrible man, Jesus will not accept me. No, my friend, make rather this conclusion, that because God has begun to work in my heart, in me, an old sinner, I nevertheless intend to shelter it. I intend to go to my Savior, to weep and to pray until He will say "be comforted, my son (or my daughter), your sins are forgiven. Only take risk in the Name of the Lord Jesus. You should bring your garb with joy, whether you now make the beginning today with tears. It should happen soon, or else in the right moment, that you might experience it, that your heart might be moved by grace, and from grace might he give you forgiveness for all your sins and give everything pertaining to salvation and blessedness.

The Fourth Pentecost Edification

Community

4.1 Sealing as the Identity of the Christian Community

We have two main questions remaining from our text in Ephesians 4:30. From this point we can see that the entire Ephesians community became sealed with the Holy Spirit. Paul addresses them collectively. "Do not deceive the Holy Spirit, whereby you have been sealed (Ephesians 4:30), Paul expressly says to them. Through which Christ you also have heard the Word of truth, namely, the gospel of your salvation, through which you also have since believed, and you have been sealed with the Holy Spirit of the promise.

If one looks within our present-day Christian community, the promise of the sealing with the Holy Spirit has become a completely unknown matter. If you were to enter the little abodes of those who have been really awakened through the Word of God from their mortal death, and have made a start toward realizing a rightly fashioned Christendom, you would find within those dwelling places hardly any who know from living experience what the sealing with the Holy Spirit is. It had been made known to all among the first Christians, when they became faithful to (88) experience and acquire it. That fact prompted me to advance this strategic question: What would be the cause of the fact that even among those who actually have come to an awakening and to the mortification of their sins, this sealing with the Holy Spirit is something which has seldom occurred—and will it not soon be attained to the delight of this great, godly, heavenly and boundless sealing with the Holy Spirit?[1]

It is certainly a matter of significance which we have to consider under heartfelt groaning, whether we will not somehow find the traces of this drawing near among us? It may be that many persons will become alerted by the exploration of this question among us, and, at least, may increasingly be brought onto the path of considering what might be the reason for this spiritual awakening which has been occurring in this locality, and even ask the question of why they too could not become part of this sealing of the Holy Spirit? It is a question of whether they have also become awakened from the death of sin [Sündentode] and were no longer continuing in an illusion concerning eternity. There has certainly been hardly any mention made of this important matter among others.

So long as one is a worldly-minded person,[2] that is, one who remains unconverted, who still lives in the lust and love for the world in arrogance, self-love, the lust of the eye, the lust of the flesh and a haughty life, then that one cannot discern the Holy Spirit. Then the question becomes how does it proceed among awakened persons, for whom one really notices and hopes for what is better? They are and intend to no longer be of the world, (89) and likewise it is seldom evident that such persons can say with joyfulness of heart, "I certainly now know that my Savior has truly died on the cross for me and has gone to heaven, so that all my sins are forgiven and, if I would die today, even my soul would be located at His right hand."

Consider this: all who are obstructed by doubt are possibly standing in dispositions which hinder the progress of grace in their lives. It is probably not possible to enumerate all the possible hindrances which prevent this or that soul from attaining the sealing of the Holy Spirit. Some may be held back from coming too soon and easily to the sealing. This is because God

---

1. His question suggests this anticipated, even eschatological, event will have borderless implications, indicating the convergence of personal awakenings through the sealing of the Holy Spirit with a global movement of grace hastening the fulfillment of the missio Dei (God's saving mission with humanity through the redemption that is in Christ).

2. Here the term Weltmensch denotes a carnal and not a globally informed person. Steinmetz references the term "world" in these two different senses, and it is important to distinguish them in his thought: the former usage is that which requires saving grace, the latter usage is an expression of how the world is viewed in light of saving grace. For treatment of his understanding of the global person as opposed to a worldly person, see Part Three, Chapter Four on Christian Globalization.

works in a hidden manner with this or that person.³ He perceives among some persons that which bodes well for the future [kunftig], and is probably discerning that He must make the pearl of great price a bit more difficult to reach, lest that person might stray in a prodigal or wasteful manner if they laid hold of their sealing too easily or quickly.

However, God seems to want to proceed differently for other persons. There are also those who must have more than one kind of experience to rally themselves toward this goal of the Spirit's empowerment. They are the kind who think they could not even have desired the sealing with the Holy Spirit without first becoming skillful and grounded in the basic aspects of Christianity.⁴ Under such conditions it would be unlikely if they ever received the sealing with the Holy Spirit.⁵ Among others, it is the preoccupation with the body or the dispositions of the self which procures this work of grace, meaning that God's Spirit is being put to the test and is required to provide more evidence for its validity before they can be brought to a salutary assurance. (90)

Then there are those who by nature are prone to melancholy. Their bodies and souls are out of sorts from nature, so that everything is a difficult challenge, with a propensity for melancholy. This requires many ways for the Holy Spirit to be operative in revelation for them to be convinced, which is not likely to occur in most instances.

For yet others, there are also personal conditions which must be met, which cannot be made in public, which would require a person to make their decision for faith based on an undisclosed gamble they are confronting.

Perhaps each one here needs to take responsibility to consult with the experienced children and servants of God about his concerns, when they cannot yet come to terms about their condition nor can they make the proper use of the means of grace on behalf of their salvation.

---

3. This is an implicit doctrine of prevenient grace, which is explicitly found in Arminian theology.

4. Christentum is Christianity, whereas Christenheit is Christendom: the former denotes the true faith; the latter the cultural embodiment of that faith, as in European Constantinian: one faith embodied in one empire.

5. The implication here is that such persons are making their quest for reason into a stumbling block to faith, reminiscent of Paul's reference to the Greeks in I Corinthians 1:22–23.

4.2 Hindrances to Sealing with the Holy Spirit in Community

I am now constrained to bring up a few of the most general *hindrances* to faith, from which each one needs to make applications that are relevant to their own situation. I here identify just two classes of hindrances, as follows:

First, there are many persons whom God has awakened who grant complete and unreserved room for the Holy Spirit in their lives. They permit themselves to be brought by the Spirit into a true uprightness and faithfulness, leading to a genuine earnestness for the Lord. They have acted out of a sense of the truth of the matter, so that they might be saved. They preferred to leave aside substance and goods and let everything go before they would want to permit their poor selves [souls] to be lost.

Second, the other kind of persons probably do become awakened and convinced that their situation could not remain as it was. Instead, they must become different persons. However, matters do not get resolved for these persons, and there is no genuine earnestness for the faith on their part. They are not ready to leave all in this world, but they want to remain inwardly steady, faithful to the good awakenings, movements and sensibilities in their hearts.

Now, we intend to investigate both kinds of persons, to understand from what sort of (91) origins each of these two kinds of persons [souls] have proceeded. There are those who not only prevail upon God's Word, becoming awakened from death unto life, but they also desire to come to a due thirst for earnestness, so that their many complaints had to continually be trod under their feet; however, they also knew that they understood virtually nothing about the sealing with the Holy Spirit, and so they in truth could not say they had become partakers of this great eternal benefit.

Permit me to address the case described above, as follows: I will explain the matter with few words, for simplicity is best for bringing light on the subject. It is of overall greater importance that, among the awakened and the sincere persons [souls] for whom there is an earnestness, which is for the sake of their salvation, there is a large number of them who do not enter into the sealing for the Holy Spirit. These same persons are often able to pretend, because they formerly wanted to perceive, have and do too much.

I do not say this is a mistake in Christianity for a person to want to comprehend, have and do too much. No, that would be a false statement.

For a true Christian is like a hungry and thirsty child who is never satisfied. To speak of such a Christian, this is one who never has enough, who keeps on longing for an ever-greater measure of faith, love, patience, hope, and remorse, among others. I say, however, that before such a one becomes a partaker of the sealing with the Holy Spirit, before one ventures to receive the seal of assurance through the Holy Spirit, many pretend too much.

I intend to make all this more clear by God's grace, and go through it point by point, and (92) to try to explain it by means of the most common, paschal[6] and forthcoming examples.

1) Persons (souls) whom God has truly awakened through His Word, for whom there is also true earnestness in their Christianity, are sometimes not able to enter into the sealing through the Holy Spirit because they carry out their preparation so that they want to experience entirely too much before they have even presumed to have the seal, which is the assurance through the Holy Spirit. For example, there are seals which come from God's Word, which, if a person should desire the seal of the forgiveness of sins, to desire to receive this from the grace of God and the forgiveness of their sins, he must first recognize and feel himself to be a mortal sinner, according to Romans 4:5. This is one who has and comprehends nothing except what is deserved through an eternal judgment and damnation. Concerning this, he must enter into a godly sorrow. This works a repentance, which no one can regret.

Moreover, such a person deserves that he can obtain a general aversion to all sins, if they want to come to true repentance, on which that one also can receive the forgiveness of sins. These are pure truths but often they are misunderstood. They want to have this state, if they have heard of it, and always in the highest degree. God not only lets them recognize this, and also lets them feel that they are mortal sinners, but they do not feel its meaning sufficiently, that they are mortal sinners. They do not reflect long and deeply enough on its meaning. They want to feel it with the pain of thousands of stripes, but since they do not have that level of intensity, their fallback is invariably, "I have (93) it but I do not have it yet."

And so it goes with godly sorrow. God grants it to each soul and gives it in its necessary measure, because, as evidenced by the biblical reference in which it belonged also to David, who soaked his bed the entire night with his tears, while the answers to his supplications were not yet at hand. So, a penitent one [the soul] may think it is not yet as it should be, no matter

---

6. Meaning "Easter-like" [östersten] events

whether that one has already truly been repentant for their sins. You too may already be truly sorry for your sins, and making penance for them, for grieving and offending your God.

It is likewise with the remaining parts of this discussion. God allows a person to succeed in repentance insofar as it takes him to the point of true earnestness wherein one prefers to lose his own life than to sin, because remorse has not yet been truly felt. There is a deficiency in this stance before God. With each sin one begins to lament and say, "Ah, I have as yet felt no true remorse and hatred for these sins." That is exactly what I mean in saying that candid persons want too much to feel their sin, not only as mortal sinners, not only to have a truly godly sorrow and a right minded remorse toward sin, but also, just because they do not perceive this sorrow with appropriate lament and come to true remorse for all their sins they regard what they do feel as being for naught in God's eyes. However, in this situation, the Holy Spirit, as I have already indicated, would prefer us to bring the matter through a gentle, steady impulse of grace than with such harshness and intensity. The Holy Spirit's tug is much too excellent (94) to proceed in such a blatant and haughty way, if it truly comes to the heart of the matter.[7]

2) The person who has come to true honesty in their Christianity but has not attained to the sealing of the Holy Spirit, demonstrates that before he ventures to accept it, he wants to possess too much.... Perhaps a person hears of someone telling another about quite extraordinary gifts of grace and benefits which came from his Savior. Similarly, this second person might fall thereafter and then you think, "I have not yet had that happen!" Are you therefore going to cast off your hope as it were at some moment? If hereafter the Holy Spirit comes, and offers, so to speak, the Seal to the soul, he then begins working on the sealing, when did he receive it and perceive it, saying, "I heard about this from this or that one, and thereby have hindered the Spirit, so that He could not imprint His sign upon me." Dear brother, who then has known you on this and that time or place? You are known by the Word of the living God. Indeed, perhaps God can manifest Himself at some time to this one and to that one. That is not even always necessary or wise.

---

7. At this point, Steinmetz's pastoral counsel resembles that of his near contemporary, Gerhard Tersteegen, whose hymns and addresses speak of a gentle inworking of grace to effect conversion. See Meyer, "Cognitio Die Experimentalis oder "Erfahrungstheologie" in Meyer, *Zur Receptionen mysterischen Traditionen*, 223–240.

So it was for the apostle Thomas, who thought, "If I do not see and feel it, then I cannot believe it." The Lord Jesus freely did that wonder of love to Thomas, but (95) must we not long for that from the Lord Jesus, so that He may make it so with us also, for one must turn away from his general ways of walking and sink into Jesus' blood, to hold himself still before grace and let this also be worked out within him, what and how as He will. Honest souls attain this by this other point, that, before they want to attempt this, to accept the sealing of the Holy Spirit, they first want to have the highest power in Christianity. For example, they see among many there is a great gift for prayer, among others, a great joy in witnessing, even if it should cost death and life, they would perceive through this or that gift, which they did not yet have, and thereby hinder the continuous inworking of the Holy Spirit in their heart, until God's Spirit could no longer come with His goal and purpose among them.

3) There are also those who still want to do many things [in advance of becoming sealed]. *They also no longer want to become children and youth but prefer to do manly deeds and they are not yet agreeable with being new born,* since they supposed they were only to lay on their mother's bosom as infants, should they now permit themselves to be fully born of the second birth, since they already want to do great things? They hesitate if they do not handle themselves as skillful men of status. If they come in battle, it is premature, for they continue to flail around with many sins which beset them. Certainly the power of the Lord Jesus is only for those who receive the victory.

Their sins must still be plaguing them. Thereby consider this: with me is likely nothing to be done. How would I yet be able to manage all of this only for myself so I could then be sealed with the Holy Spirit? My condition is much too miserably fragile. No, the Lord Jesus alone can withstand the misery. He intends to help the miserable. Yes, He intends to better their condition. He intends to make miserably poor children stronger and grounded and set in the position that they can receive the powers of the youth and, in turn, of the adult men in their Christianity.[8]

---

8. Christianity here references the church as Body of Christ, following Paul's metaphor for church in I Corinthians 12. Here this Body is presented as the community of the second Adam (Christ), as in Romans 5. Here is the first explicit appeal to the recapitulation theme found in the apostolic father, Irenaeus, bishop of Lyons in the second century AD. It is built on the Adam/Christ typology, whereby the first Adam's life of disobedience is typologically revisited in the obedient walk of the second Adam (Christ incarnate), progressively setting a bound humanity free of the curse of Adam as they pass through the developmental stages of human life, consummated in the resurrection of the body. This is the historical approach

Therefore, only await the appointed time.⁹ Flee the enemy fervently and, being spurred on, the Holy Spirit will therefore help you become assured that you will become lord over sin and you can overcome it.

4.3 When Awakening Shapes the Community of Faith

Further, I will touch here on one other aspect regarding how a Christian is not sealed until he comes into an overcoming state. My previous explanation of this was that so much was understood through overcoming in the context of awakenings, that we would conclude that there is to be no standing still with respect to them. For example, if God moves you in your heart, you respond with repentance, you change and become another person. You must transfer/proceed in the struggle of prayer until an actual change now takes place through the Holy Spirit working in you. Further, if it is the Holy Spirit who initiates this change, leading you by faith, and giving grace so that the seed of the gospel falls into your heart and begins to reign and move there in the powers of faith. Then appears the world, and Satan, and your own heart, and these proceed to try to deny this. (97) Since you must remain in the struggle of prayer, until you come into real faith, it is only then that you arrive at the confidence of a child, before your Lord Jesus. Then the Holy Spirit also commences to propel you into holiness, with earnestness. He then instructs you that you must revoke all sin, which acts in opposition to your flesh.¹⁰

---

to redemption that is revisited in the federal (covenant) theology of Cocceius in the mid seventeenth century, whose work had influence in Lutheran Pietist as well as Reformed Pietist circles in the early eighteenth century in Europe. Implicit here is the breadth dimension of the new birth in Christ, which embraces the renewal of the new humanity on a global scale— a theological basis for a global Christianity. Note: for Steinmetz, this breadth dimension complements the dimension of a depth relationship with the Head of the community, located in our sharing in the crucified blood of Christ, shed as atonement for our sins. This view is congruent with Luther's theology of the cross also, for whom the breadth dimension was represented by the flow of the "overflowing love for neighbor" (quellende Liebe) as the fountain spilling over from faith in the promise of the Word into love for those for whom Christ died, enabled by the Holy Spirit.

9. The notion of kairos time was recovered in Irenaeus, and later Cocceius, as well, being the moment when God breaks into our time to release us from another point of attachment to the curse of the first Adam.

10. Here the author clearly breaks from Luther's stance of simul iustus et peccator: that the Christian is by the gospel simultaneously just and a sinner, because now faith is empowered by the sealing of the Holy Spirit in your heart to make you an overcomer, pressing toward the holiness which renounces all sin, without which no one will see God. Compare this position with that of John Wesley on Christian perfection, since Wesley was brought to

When many Christians begin to hear that this kind of overcoming is needed, they do not correctly comprehend its meaning. When they occasionally feel a sinful impulse within themselves, they think, "Ah, Lord, I can no longer expect to receive the merit of Jesus since I still feel sinful desires in my heart." Have you spoken that in your own dear human strength, that you are no longer capable of feeling any sinful impulse? No, it is necessary that you step into the struggle and cling to it, until you conquer and prevail, so that you would no longer be lord over yourself,[11] but that you would continue the struggle even to your grave. It is a question of whether you are going to continue steady in the grace of God and thereby you must hold on until, ever lifted higher, until you receive power to overcome these enemies one after the other.[12]

Behold, my dear friends, if you now are thinking, "so long as I only feel a tug of sin, the seal does not belong to me," so then it is ever a hindrance. For, if the Holy Spirit wants to impress the seal upon you, you hold your hand against it, saying, "no, the seal does not yet belong to me." (98) The Lord does not impress this upon you with power, but only when you remain in stillness.[13]

Here I will remind you of a few points. It may be asked, whence, or from what source does this proceed for upright persons (souls), so that before they allow themselves to be sealed through the Holy Spirit, they sense all too much, they have all too much, and they want all too much.

---

the assurance of his faith in pardon and perfection through the Steinmetz-influenced Christian David, preaching in Herrnhut. W.R. Ward and Richard P. Heitzenrater, *The Bicentennial Edition of the Works of John Wesley* (Nashville, TN: Abingdon, 1984 to Current Date), I, *Journal and Diaries, (1735-1738)*, 270-274.

11. This is the antithesis of the childlike spirit within the true Christian.

12. Here is noted Steinmetz's prevailing emphasis on the overcoming quality of Christian perfection, with its emphasis on the will (in a position which Nordmann calls voluntaristic dualism, based in Luther although made explicit in the cosmology of Jakob Böhme. (See Nordmann, *Im Widerstreit von Mystik und Föderalismus*, 155-163). This contrasts with the more passive mysticism of Tersteegen, for whom the key to oneness with God is a stepwise, childlike release from the struggle of the will into the pervasive Presence of God (akin to Nordmann's model of a mysticism which is speculatively monistic. See Nordmann, op. cit., 148-155). Wesley would have aspects of both emphases in his eclectic approach to spirituality, though ultimately he favors the latter. See "The Plain Account of Christian Perfection" in *The Works of John Wesley*, Volume XI, 366-446. See page 369 for Wesley's English rendition of a Tersteegen Hymn on this theme.

13. At this critical point of the God relationship, Steinmetz defers to Tersteegen's position over that of the voluntaristic dualists. God ultimately acts upon us in His grace with tender love and not brute force.

This comes most of all out of a kind of uncertainty. The entire process is not yet known and revealed to them, so that most of all they are thinking that God may extend to them no grace, not the forgiveness of sins, not the Holy Spirit, and not eternal life because of these concerns.

For example, God grants them the forgiveness of sins because they had been distressed and afflicted about this. They did not want sin to triumph over them any longer. They were true and candid about this because they no longer wanted sin, death and the devil to triumph over them. Ah, no, I cannot say that all at once, God forgives sins for the sake of His grace. That would be saying too much, since faith is actually the chief means which is provided by our side for the attainment of the forgiveness of sins. I certainly receive pardon through faith, as the means, or the hand, as through the hand of a beggar, but it is received not for the sake of faith, but rather for the sake of the Lord Jesus Christ. Therefore, I can through faith receive the forgiveness of sins, because my bloody Jesus has earned that. If you grieve yourself to death, (99) even after that you will receive no forgiveness of sins, if the Lord Jesus has not earned this for you. No tears, no bloody perspiration has earned your pardon, since he perspired blood for your sins on the Mount of Olives, so that he complained, "My God, my soul is distressed unto death." Behold, soul, that was the sorrow whereby the forgiveness of your sins, the grace of God, and eternal life, have been merited. On this ground you now must build, and do not think that, if I had only prayed so much, had so much wine, or such an amount of sorrow, I would receive forgiveness."

4.4 Entering the Blood of Jesus as the Core Which Forms Community

No, all of that is completely false. You do not rest your trust on the right foundation. There you are confusing the forgiveness of sins, the ground of our salvation, with the means. Do not put the means first. Does the beggar earn his gift with the gift of the crumbs in his hand, which You have given to him? Ah, no! However, if he does not stretch out his crumby hand, he could certainly not receive anything from you. You O Lord give this to him gratuitously, although, he must stretch out his crumby hand as the means for receiving the gift. So do likewise. Learn to build all your blessedness, your grace, and your life alone within the blood of Jesus, on which your hope is fixed.

As for the other side of this matter, all sorrow for sin, faith, prayer, the battle against sin, the use of all the means of grace— you cannot give all this to yourself, rather, it is the Holy Spirit who says, take and use this. The Holy Spirit grants to you so much to afflict you – so much may afflict you in God's Name, but He gives you just so much, as will be necessary (100) for you.

The Holy Spirit grants just so much grace of faith for you, so much as is needed. Had you first of all a small hand, like a small child's hand, and stretched this out, until it entered into the blood of Jesus, you would receive the forgiveness of sins, according to the Holy Spirit, who will show grace to you.

Likewise, the Holy Spirit grants you just so much grace for the just battle against sin. Therefore, make use of it and do not let it lie in a sweat rag. Then, you will give to God out of sheer mercy what will be needful. That you must observe well.

Dear friend, the Holy Spirit is a bestowed gift. The sealing through the Holy Spirit is also a bestowed gift. Heaven and blessed salvation is an earned gift. It lies open to all. Jesus has earned it. You are permitted [that salvation] only bowed, as a poor sinner, hungry and thirsty, coming only with the most childlike and the simplest trust and heart, because everything is already prepared there.

So, this is the voice of the upright messenger, "Come, you persons (souls)! Everything is ready." That is the word which the King of kings commends as He prepares the wedding feast for His Son, so that the entire world might be invited to it.[14]

Go forth and say, "Come, then, for all is prepared. Everything is to be found in the treasures of God. We are only permitted to participate gratuitously. But it therefore also becomes more dreadful in our judgment at the last day, if we do not come. Come, all is prepared, your Jesus wants to have nothing other than your poor heart, your godless heart. (101) Come as sinners, come as godless, come, as those condemned, come, whoever you are; you are not in a position to make yourself better. Lay yourself in the bloody arms of Jesus, come, and receive His salvation. Only through the Spirit. Come and take only what you have already gained through the Lord Jesus Christ; come, stretch your hands out after His righteousness, which endures forever. That gift should enable you to share in everything, all heaven should be yours, which Jesus has gained for you.

Ah, beloved friend [soul], come yet, may the corruption of this world not be of more account to you than are the valuable treasures of our Lord Jesus Christ.[15] How will we one day account for ourselves before

---

14. Here the term "world" (Welt) is used in the positive sense of those who, precious to God, are invited despite their unfaithfulness, to the wedding feast of His Son. Here is also the context for viewing the world as the field for the harvest, e.g. for a global Christianity.

15. See Matthew 13:45-6.

God? Dear Savior, let my heart be awakened to yours, that we may all be brought into blessed meditation.

However, would it now not be possible that God could grant the sealing to such persons, who have formerly wanted to have, find and do too much [according to their own agendas?] Why may they not come to know the love of God now? Under these present circumstances, may He not provide this for them? I answer, "No, no, He cannot give this. The person herself first needs to let go and depart from all those things of the past which had been a hindrance. This is also the cause why the Holy Spirit leaves so many sincere souls proceeding alone [on their life's journey]. He may let them continue for several years, as has often occurred. Ten or twenty years may have elapsed for some, yet nothing has changed for them? And why?

First of all, God does not coerce His gifts upon persons, not, if the person keeps saying, "No! No! I cannot yet accept this; I am not yet in (102) the position to do this, I am not yet sufficiently repentant, I am not yet pure, holy, earnest, or sincere enough, which would go against God's way of ordering things."

There are also those who see themselves as pernicious or obnoxious whenever they had been confronted with the sealing. They would think they had to merit it, for example, if they were sincere about following Jesus. They would first have to leave everything in this world, except for that which the Holy Spirit had provided them. No, it is not that you should necessarily dispose of everything you have to be able to receive saving grace; rather, you are not to place your confidence in your own melancholy when it becomes so obtrusive. Neither ought you place your trust in your own faith, when it seemed so strong; you must not place your trust on your own strengths, prayers, singing, powers of endurance, and the like. For that builds your house on the false ground, which the devil can also subvert.

If you are resembling any of these ways of thinking, you must place your trust simply in the blood, death, and merit of Christ Himself. Everything else, viewed as means, as preparations, as gifts of grace which one has received, must remain only as resources which could be taken into the service of the Lord Jesus. One could not accept anything from the Lord Jesus if you did not already have sorrow, that is, if you did not feel your sins. Hence, you should ask of the Lord Jesus, (103) not that you would merit something through this human trait, but you must have faith that you only have one hand, for the other is joined to Jesus. Hence, you need to wage war on these powers of yours, to struggle against the sins which make you mischievous or petulant, that they not become mixed with your service to the Lord, lest you become separated again from Him and thrown back into the world.

4.5 The Sins that Cling

Now I intend to address another kind of person [in the community], for whom your conscience may tell you that if they remain as they were they would never be blessed in salvation. No one ever comes into a real and genuine earnestness in their Christianity because they cling to this or to that sin, which they would not consider putting aside. Therefore, they do not arrive at the point of true uprightness, to a true joy and peace in their conscience. Instead, they go along with seeking all sorts of favorable exercises, and often become awakened to wage war on many kinds of rowdy or deviant persons in their conscience, they pray well, and yet they remain as they were.

Here we find why it is not difficult to discern why such persons cannot attain to a right sealing with the Holy Spirit. It is because most men of this sort harden themselves by their frequent objections against the operations of grace of the Holy Spirit, and they are almost always lacking in any feeling or passion for the things of the Spirit. In brief, their souls occasionally seem to be working their way loose from any vital sense of the faith, which makes them seem dry and insipid in their inner heart convictions. (104) Among honest persons, as we have previously noted, it is apparent they have not received the sealing because they previously had exhibited far too much spiritual zeal and too much desperate need to be busy in their religion, yet without any desire for spiritual sensitivity.

With the help of God's grace, it may be possible to make comprehensible the problem being addressed here. I say, if the people who are intelligent would see that it is not right or sufficient for them to come to a sense of certainty in Christianity and yet desire no sealing, this occurs because there is a deficiency in their desire for feeling and sensibility, or affection [Empfinden]. They hear that all people, and not just one, were permitted to feel a great measure of sorrow [Traurigkeit], and they lay hold of that and then are only at peace with awakenings to the least possible degree.[16] They had hardly begun to feel their misery for sin when it was thought they had

---

16. This describes the position of the Lutheran Orthodox theologians and pastors who had been among the foremost critiques of the children's revival as well as the major revival in the Teschen parish thereafter. See discussion in the contextual chapters of this study.

a sufficient measure of sorrow for sin and of grace and that it was not necessary for the congregation to continue with prayer.

Ah, Lord Jesus! Ah, dear Savior! Let me not be deceived, but give me the right measure of recognition and sorrow over my sins, give me my apportioned measure of tears, which could melt [zerschmelzen] and dissolve [zerfliessen] my hardened soul, so you are even able to picture it in your hand, as it grows. Behold, such cold souls do not pray, neither do they stand near to those who are praying, since they see this as being a much too affectionate display of religious feeling.[17] For, if God comes occasionally, and the Holy Spirit (105) works a chill in them, because of their sins, so they beat down their thought, go out, set their eyes rigidly on other matters, and why? It makes them too sad. O, that is a bad thing, dear man, so long as you make it so. So, you will never again come near to the sealing with the Holy Spirit, because you do not make room for the Holy Spirit! The Holy Spirit finds it necessary, that He gives you a greater measure of sorrow. Your heart is very hard, it must be melted down it must become tender [weich] in the Hand of your Savior, when what He is forming should be brought to fullness, and you want nothing of it.

Therefore, He has had to do away with you, because you are so disagreeable. You shrink from and put to shame those persons and think, "if I see you so sorrowful, they will think, then I am the greater sinner." Poor worm! Then you are not that?! Do not your heart and conscience tell you that? Whoever does not believe this and does not want other men to come to this discovery, that one may be an abominable sinner, who does not yet have the beginning of a right knowledge of himself.

Even so it goes with the other sectors of Christianity [in our day]. We have heard in the discussion above that a person must come to an aversion and remorse for all sins, so that this remorse might not remain so pervasive throughout his time, but rather could probably be overcome in an earnest abnegation of the heart and a fleeing before sin. If now such persons hear and yet hardly one or another of their great sins begin to buckle, then they

---

17. Steinmetz's discussion here bears striking resemblance to Jonathan Edwards's description of those divided over displays of religious affection in his Northampton, Massachusetts Congregational worship, where the Great Awakening erupted in North America in the decade after Steinmetz's revival at Teschen, Silesia. Steinmetz followed the progress of the revival at Northampton, as recorded in his chronicle, *Die Sammlung auserlesene Materien*, 304 and 363-4, and Ward, *Protestant Evangelical Awakening*, 268), as recorded in Steinmetz's chronicle of the international awakening in his day. (See chapter following chapter on the chronicle and its impact.)

think they now have the proper aversion in the face of all sinners. (106) The sign that God has declared in His Word as a marker of a true repentance is what they do not want to know, and also, that a general and earnest aversion for it is required, when one prefers to give up his life than to continue sinning while he is knowing, willing and resolving against His God.

As we find with the dear Joseph, here was one who preferred to let his life be in mortal danger than to do something evil and to provoke his God in heaven (Genesis 39:9).[18]

As we proceed, we note here, it is also the case with such poor men that they want to have much too little when they hear that faith the size of a mere grain of mustard is worthy and acceptable before God. Likewise, if the grace of God in Christ could only be extended out to a child's hand, the forgiveness of sins, life and blessed salvation are surely conveyed in such an act. They hold to this faith without guile, in the simplest thoughts of their Savior and of faith. It is not a matter of bowing a knee and saying, "Ah, my God! Grant me yet true faith," and "Ah, dear God, let me not be deceived, let me not be at peace with anything that is the way of all flesh. I do not prescribe for you what you are to give unto me, except, grant me a true faith through the Holy Spirit, as the Spirit of faith. They do not do that, but they are at peace when their intent is to follow a path of possession like unto a robbery.

With the third section I make the matter more clear. It happens among such impure minds because they do not want to do anything which they probably (107) should and could do, and likewise they do too much of what they should not do, therefore these want to do too little before they can come to the assurance through the Holy Spirit. From this it follows that a person who wants to have God's grace, the Holy Spirit and the sealing certainly must use the means of grace, whereby God words faith in us, namely God's Word, which he must observe diligently unless it is not possible to desire faith.

However, many persons will not remain with that Word more than a quarter of an hour. That is because it is dangerous to them: because it causes repentance after no more than a quarter of an hour! Unless they choose to turn to it, study it, pray, and exercise themselves in it they can freely come to no saving grace, any more than I can become healthy unless I

---

18. Genesis 39:9: Joseph to Pharaoh's wife when she tempted him to adultery: "There is no one greater in this house than I, and he has withheld nothing from me except you, because you are his wife. How then could I do this great evil, and sin against God?"

take the medicine the doctor prescribes for me. Even so, prayer is a royal means of grace whereby a person can come to access the entire breadth of God's grace, even like the orator skillfully arranges his work. No! That can happen only through earnestness.

If people do not want to take the effort, and desire to pray, they can harass and work themselves to pieces, but take not a moment for prayer, and then how would such souls think they would somehow arrive at the sealing of the Holy Spirit?

Hence, there is a chief hindrance that prevents such poor souls from ever arriving at the sealing, and that is because they will not use the means God has provided! Yet, many others probably use the means well, and they too do not find themselves turning in the right direction. There are (108) people who visit every service of worship, never gladly neglecting a sermon, yet they remain as they are: when they have heard it, would they then receive the sealing of the Holy Spirit? No, that is only the means.

If you leave the means standing where it is, and do not make use of it that is like having a glass of medicine brought from the pharmacy, and then is set down and not used. So, take up the Word of God, fasten yourself to it, so to speak, in the vessel of your retentive memory, then you let it take its course. You do not need for your soul to be aroused by it, and to be simply meditating means you can even restrain yourself in the battle against sin for awhile. Hence, it can freely come to naught for you. That is especially so for a chief offense, which such souls certainly do not want in the struggle against the lust of the eye, the lust of the flesh, and an arrogant spirit. Only the overcomer is crowned. If sincere souls receive a smidgen of power, they turn toward it faithfully, but our foul Christians do not do this in this age in which we are living. Ah, they feel many sins still raging within them, and much impurity which arises within them. They feel haughty, carnal desires continuing to come over them, and yet they take no time to address these things, to give themselves to struggle and prayer against these things, and to long to flee unto God, until they would be overwhelmed by the power of the blood of Jesus, and therefore there is nothing to constrain them from being overpowered, as cattle to the slaughter, and they cannot become sealed (109) through the Holy Spirit.

For that is and remains ever certain: so long as sin has its free reign over a person, so long cannot that person come into the sealing with the Holy Spirit. I do not say, so long as a sinner feels that he is unrighteous, for the person also freely sealed through the Holy Spirit, certainly feels sin. He is stimulated and enticed by the world and his own flesh. However, I am saying, so long as a person allows one sin to reign, he may be coarse before the world –these may be secret lusts—or hidden carnal longings, if he gives them their reign, and so he is overcome. And that is the way it lies with the greater part of our populace. The perverted advance and are openly glorified, and even chatter about assurance of the forgiveness of sins, and it is evident how the prevailing sins stick fast, in the free reign of inordinate greed and lusts, in the reigning concern for the belly, in the reigning arrogance, in the reigning sensual pleasures, lacking bridle and reins, and then thinking, they have forgiveness.

For such persons, it is idle deception. For they do not want to do what they could and should do through God's grace. They want the power, the good feelings, and the grace, which the Holy Spirit offers, but not so they could be turned toward a true uprightness. Do you ask then, why it is that such persons are not sealed? I answer, if one sin yet reigns in me, and I am thereby a slave unto it, being found within me, so then must He even seal for me this sin? Can then God do this? How would you (110), if you also only had one evil hand, and the doctor healed it for you with the filth which is still within it, would there be peace for that physician? Therefore, would we be at peace with the God in heaven, and with the Holy Spirit, if He were asked to heal our hearts, gave us the gracious assurance and sealing of His Holy Spirit, if He, so to say, closed up our heart, gave us the gracious assurance and sealing of His grace, and the devil had his regiment yet in our heart. He cannot do that. It is against God's essential nature, and consequently is against his order. Christ and Belial do not agree with one another. If you want to notice this, what could yet be profitable for you in this simple presentation? Make use of this, to learn to know rightly your state of affairs.[19]

19. In this section, Steinmetz has exercised what Wesleyans would later call the office of an exhorter, done after the sermon in the camp meetings, in which the appeal to salvation is made to individuals who are under conviction from the gospel message. It continued as they came forward for prayer, at the place later known in the American context as the "mourners' bench," where the important ministry of bringing to closure the redemptive work of the new birth, as well as the baptism of the Holy Spirit, a later phrase, which is prefigured with Steinmetz's frequent reference to the "sealing of the Holy Spirit," as the point of personal appropriation by the Spirit-convicted sinner of the infilling of the Holy Spirit to take residence in the reborn soul (or person), in effecting the new creation in Christ ("And he who sits on the throne said, 'Behold, I am making all things new...'" Revelation 21:5). As Ward has documented, the revival based in Teschen, which also spread through the hinterland and towns of Silesia, reflected this mode of "bush meeting" evangelism later characteristic of the second Great Awakening on the North American frontier, under the leadership of the itinerant preachers of Methodism, the United Brethren in Christ, and the

There may be persons, or readers of this message, who do know now have assurance, who would withdraw into themselves to come to terms with their standing before God. Now their inner self has been laid open before God, and that person falls down before Him in tears. He asks God if He would ascertain this for him from His Word, as with a mirror. He would inquire whether he would be among the firstborn, or the last, among those who have been examined; also, whether he has sought for too much recognition, acquisitions, accomplishments to become a child of God, or too little. The latter group is probably the more numerous n our time. When a peson wants to place too much attention on his circumstances, he is also likely to rush through self examination and be satisfied with only a meager repentance. He was satisfied as long as he felt some flash of faith, or perceived some slight change in the quality of his living, however slight or inneffectual. They are at pease, whether or not they feel like it, so that they, like slaves, can remain at ease while continuing to attend to their pet sinful attractions. Such a moment of truth says much about our common parliance. It says much about our conscience within us, whether we have wanted too much too little, thereby hindering the sealing which goes forth. These folk want to approach God with little preparation for what it means to stand in His Presence, so that God would likely choose to remove any of the fruit of the vineyard from some, and bestow the sealing of His Spirit upon those seeking to build their lives solely upon the reconciling blood of the Lord Jesus Christ. In the hymn, If God is for me, then I go forth, verse three, actually refers to a sealing, and expresses this with beauty and grace:

> The ground on which I right myself,
> In Christ and in His blood,
> That makes it that I find The eternal only true good.
> For me and for my life
> There is nothing upon this earth:
> What Christ has given me,
> That is Love which has all worth.

Therefore, beloved friends, notice perchance, you still have so much confidence in your mourning, regarding those gifts and powers you have, that it would not be good to trust in them. Therefore go forth today, and learn, like a small, forelorn and unworthy sinner, to ground your hope on

---

Evangelical Association, as well as the later non-denominational evangelistic meetings of Charles Finney, of New Light Presbyterian pedigree.

Jesus and upon His blood, and pray with supplication that, out of the fullness of Jesus Christ, God might move to create so much grace, as your need requires, so that you may soon arrive at the standpoint of sealing; however, you remaining persons, who probably will become convinced (112), that you have wanted too little to be sensible of His Presence. Notice yet where there may be the reign of this or of that sin, notice too the power of unfaith, so go forth, cast yourself down before God so long as needed, until you too truly carry the victory over this. You will experience how blessed and sweet you become as you are overwhelmed with the grace of God.

THE FIFTH PENTECOST EDIFICATION

Sealing and the Globalization of Christianity

5.1 Community Lives Between Deception and Hope for the Future

There remains one chief point from our text to be explained, with a question to be answered: How these persons are in relationship, who have become partakers of this royal blessing of the sealing with the Holy Spirit, for the sake of the blood-stained merit of Christ, and what must they avoid especially from the standpoint of God's grace through the Holy Spirit, when that great grace will appear one day before the judgment seat of God which should not then appear as such a great peril.

The text shows us what should be the answer to this question; namely, that a Christian who has partaken of the sealing with the Holy Spirit, must certainly take care not to grieve the Holy Spirit of God with which he is sealed. Notice what the Holy Spirit has given for us to discern, through Paul. If [114] it is by the Holy Spirit that it is said we should not be deceived, this is more than a statement from a mere man. The Holy Spirit is the most simple and authentic Being among us, as true God, along with Father and Son. Yet, we would not discern Him simply as the Being who is steadfastly and unalterably with us, with the capacity to enliven us with joy or cast us down in sorrow. No, the greater reality here is for us to observe how Scripture makes known the entire character and disposition of the Holy Spirit.

What does the apostle mean here? Throughout Scripture, such a magnificent One as the Holy Spirit is imparted to us to bear witness to a person who becomes grieved as the one for whom He is grieved. For example, one who is a king on earth may pledge to bear witness to another if he has been offended by that other person. An example would be parents who bear witness against the conduct of their children. What is happening there? Such considerations do not supersede the larger issue, namely that in the Bible the entire nature and disposition of the Holy is made known

Parents who are grieved by their children not only discipline them, but also, if he finds no improvement among them, he disinherits them, and lets them (115) be deprived of all the goodness and excellence they could receive from him. The apostle intends to say as much: "You persons who once partook of the great grace of sealing through the Holy Spirit, declare yourself yet right before this great, eternal and unending God. Take care, lest you provoke Him to turn Himself from you." (See I Samuel 16:14, and 28:15-16), and to withdraw Himself from your heart, for His grace and His comfort have been allowed to be plundered, to burden you instead with His curse, wrath, and punishment, to cast you out as rebels and disobedient ones from the kingdom of grace, and to burden you with those kinds of punishment which are given to fiends and rebels against God. They did not permit grace, love and benefits to move them to obedience, which He had wanted them to observe.

That is the general understanding of this Word, which is also explained in Isaiah 63:9-10:

> In all their affliction He was afflicted, And the angel of His presence saved them. In His love and in His mercy He redeemed them. And He lifted them and carried them, all the days of old. But they rebelled and grieved His Holy Spirit; Therefore, He turned Himself to become their enemy. He fought against them.

As a regent toward his subjects, when they did not rightly obey him, He punished with harsh discipline, so the Holy Spirit bore witness to His sealed ones, if they grieved Him.

Hence, it is necessary that true Christians guard themselves carefully if they have become partakers of the great grace of the sealing with the Holy Spirit. Without doubt, would not a heart open to learning [lehrbegieriges] desire to know what is the source of the grieving of the Holy Spirit and then advance so far so as to be fit to remove that enemy of His love, which is the place where grace resides, as well as trust and joy? That enemy threatens to replace these operations of the Spirit with death, the curse, damnation, strife and an absence of grace, indeed a judgment to eternal death.

A few hours would not be too long to speak in depth on why it happens that the Holy Spirit could become grieved. But to speak of it briefly, we can say that the Holy Spirit is grieved through everything a person does and fails to do which oppose the provisions found within the godly Word, and also all that which contradicts the witness of that person's *conscience*. In the meantime, I intend to conduct a special entreaty or brief on the matter and show how a person [soul] is led stepwise downward by Satan, and could be placed by him within the most unfortunate condition, thus being the source of what grieves the Holy Spirit. When this occurs, He fully withdraws Himself from that person, thereby consigning that one to the condemnation and judgment of God to eternal damnation. Such a one then longs futilely for an opening to find the redemption of his soul.

5.2 Pentecost Delayed: The Problem and Its Resolution

Notice, therefore, the onset of the grieving among those who had been sealed with the Holy Spirit takes place when they begin to become careless with regard to the disciplines of the Holy Spirit, including a disregard for the penalties of disobedience of His admonitions. If they again depart from the grace of growth, they do not remain attentive to that which the Holy Spirit is working in them after enticing them somewhat to the Word of God, and to prayer. (117) When such persons then begin to think that there is really not so much at stake in being told they are destroying themselves in all kinds of external, visible things—when that happens, surely Satan is well impersonating himself as the defender of their souls against these charges. For the devil gives due attention to all the regulations they are to follow, and seeks them, time after time, to draw them away from the discipline and regimen of grace prescribed by the Holy Spirit.[1]

Parents and schoolmasters overall become grieved when children who once had been on the cutting edge of obedience and attentiveness to grace thereafter begin to be volatile and cease observing the best admonitions which the Holy Spirit selected for their souls. He had selected these for their well-being, that they might become the site for the erection of His

---

1. This may be one of the author's most insightful pastoral insights into the motives of those resisting the directives of the Holy Spirit, that may be regarded as timeless insights applicable in general to contexts of spiritual revitalization amid human resistance, now as then.

temple, thereby grieving Him, whom He also sealed. They have now allowed themselves to be brought down by the flesh and blood, Satan and the world, so that they no longer take sufficient notice of His Word and his holy disciplines. The Holy Spirit also certainly notices that the most convenient path is that of perversity. Thus, the devil begins with such persons [souls], and if they do not notice what he is about, their consciences certainly fall even further, until they descend into the greatest offenses against the Holy Spirit.[2]

As the Holy Spirit is now grieved by the aforesaid masses, the outcome is the return of those persons [souls] to disobedience, and inattentiveness to the movement of grace—O, then (118) the Holy Spirit is only grieved all the more, if persons permit themselves to be brought by such inattention to the Holy Spirit into all kinds of disorders. For example, many a one who has stumbled amid ridicule and was ready to speak frankly, in the power, then became overpowered, because that one did not give attention to the movements of grace from the Holy Spirit. So it goes with other occasions when the person who gives little attention or neglect to prayer lets himself be led astray by unnecessary words and actions, even if they were not too coarse or evil.

The most expensive loss for such disobedience to the discipline of the Holy Spirit is that those persons do not remain alert to every moment of the Spirit's movement of grace. Ah, how soon will they then be brought to that place where they set themselves up against humble obedience, declaring [aussprechen] this or that unnecessary word regarding this or that unnecessary action, even without the use of coarse language. This is then a very painful grieving [empfindliche Betrübung] of the Holy Spirit, when He must take notice of this in my soul, which interferes with His work.

We find something of interest in joining these thoughts to the text in Ephesians. In the 29th verse, the apostle permits no idle talk, not only nothing filthy, but also no unhelpful babble from your mouth. What is at stake here concerns the grieving of the Holy Spirit. Someone comes out with clearly useless gestures and unnecessary words, and yet they say they

---

2. Steinmetz's focus on the grieving of the Holy Spirit provides a pneumatic interpretation of character formation in the context of early revival communities, as represented here by Teschen, and this could profitably be compared with other models of faith formation which do not rely on the direct intervention of the Holy Spirit to actualize effective structures of ministry such as the Anglican and Reformed models of catechesis completed in the context of ministry. Compare the discussion of Wesley's appeal to catechesis in his "Character of a Methodist", *The Works of John Wesley*, Vol VIII (Zondervan ed.) 340-347.

mean nothing ill by all that. (119) Is that then useful? Is it beneficial to the soul?[3]

Ah, might all who read these words and recall they who were to be the temple of the Holy Spirit may they truly feel the seal, and notice this well! O, what might you experience in your heart as a holy disclosure of the Spirit? From where does it come, my beloved friends, that many times all affections of the Holy Spirit seem to have departed from your hearts? Have not unnecessary words flowed from your mouths? Have not things become woven into your actions which are to be reckoned among the stupidities of your life? That is already another matter which also has its own dangers for the soul.

The persons who are already beginning to babble, with foul jargon coming from their mouths, are by their actions acknowledging that they have offended the Holy Spirit, leading to His departure from their hearts, which is to demolish the temple of God's Holy Spirit, Who had set Himself up in their hearts.

If you have not yet called this to mind, as Paul seems to have noticed was the case with the blessed, sealed congregation at Ephesus, then you remain in sheer inattentiveness to the work of God in this latter time. Then the devil will again become powerful in their souls as the nefarious spirit who returns to his evil abode. And it remains for these unfortunate persons that, if they are not soon converted anew [wieder umkehren], the discipline of the Holy Spirit will soon withdraw from them, and, against their

---

3. Take note here that the author is dealing with far more than adiaphora, or scrupulous attention to minutiae, instead of addressing the big issues of the Christian life. Here is the point of the matter: if what is being affirmed, that the Holy Spirit transforms sinners into holy vessels sealed in His Spirit, who bear witness to the atoning blood of Christ, then, the very point in the universe where heaven and earth are joined has now become the life and witness of the reborn believer. Hence, replicating this sealing work in the masses of fallen humanity becomes for Steinmetz the vehicle for growing in critical mass a new humanity which would be for his day the theological equivalence of what the Temple of Jerusalem was for Israel and the new Israel of Paul the apostle. Just as the details of the temple were crucial for the well being of Israel as a covenant people of God, so it is with these new temples springing forth in the midst of revival. Recall, it was a revival that stemmed from an awakening of children, who, for Steinmetz, gave birth to a latter day Pentecost and are the embodiment of the true heirs of the Kingdom, taking their place of destiny in a new post Christendom age arising from the war devastated landscape of eighteenth century Europe. For further reading on the prophetic promise of the Hebrew Temple being the place where the "new heaven and new earth meet," see N.T. Wright, *Paul: A Biography* (New York: Harper One, 2018), 403.

better conscience (120) what those things He has ready for them from God's Word, which now will not be revealed to them.

Whenever someone has descended to this level, the Holy Spirit withdraws. No more than doves can abide in stench and dung, with such demonic filth and such outbreaks of such abominable sins, can He live and inhabit in such persons [souls] any longer. Although the pure and Holy Spirit would still gladly abide in such persons, the reality is that they have destroyed His temple and home which He has built in their hearts, and so it is necessary for Him to withdraw from them to be able to maintain His holiness [Heiligkeit].[4]

This is the last step, whereby the Holy Spirit can be driven from your heart, although He had formerly been your dearest and most trustworthy friend, who had lived, moved, defended, quickened, and comforted you and had done everything which only the Holy Spirit could have contributed to your blessed salvation.

And may we not forget that persons not only grieve the Holy Spirit through indecent behavior toward Him. They also cause this grief when they indecently testify to Him in the community with whom He is dwelling [thereby preventing the full reign of the Spirit in that community]. We [as a community] also testify falsely against those in whom the Holy Spirit dwells whenever we treat them badly, deride them, and condemn or slander them for that which is spoken with reference to the Holy Spirit. It is not the persons but the Holy Spirit and His work who is ultimately being assailed by these condemning statements.

The Holy Spirit is also grieved when (121) there are those who act inappropriately against His instruments and servants, or when someone does not want to acknowledge what the Holy Spirit is doing or working in or through His instruments. We have an obvious example of this in Acts 5, where we find the story of an oppressed pair of parents who were so glad they had been sealed with the Holy Spirit, namely, Ananias and Sapphira. These unblessed people let themselves be led astray by their evil hearts so that they began to turn away from the discipline of the Holy Spirit and also to capitulate to their rebellious flesh and blood. They certainly did not want this to be noticed by the other Christians, so they found a hypocrit-

---

4. Steinmetz views holiness as inherent within the Holy Spirit and not the human with whom the Holy Spirit longs to dwell. At this point he may have retained some measure of Luther's simul iustus et peccator, although Steinmetz has gone further in positing the durability of the Spirit's indwelling of the sealed soul than is found in Luther. Compare Luther, "Two Kinds of Righteousness" (1519), in Dillenberger, 86-96.

ical way to cover their deed, which also happens in our day when persons are in the habit of concealing something they have done.

Recall the basis for their offense. Since Christians of that same time carried their possessions together in their association or fellowship, the poorest among them could enjoy something of that substance under the ministry of Peter. When Peter asked them, "is that everything?" they lied. They had held something back in secret avarice, but they wanted the same time to pass as Christians who were living as were the other pious believers, and so had placed their substance in the common coffer. Since now they had lied to Peter, they also lied to the Holy Spirit, because Peter was a vessel in whom the Holy Spirit dwelt. From that moment there resulted a frightful fall by which the two of them died a sudden death. It was a horrible example of all those hypocrites who (122) no longer want to be obedient to the Holy Spirit, and yet have contrived with lies and so to take cover under an appearnace of godliness, hiding what had been a previous evil deed which was brought forth anew within their hearts. Ah, my God! how much of that deception is there among our present day Christians.

5.3 Avoiding the Pitfall of Ananias and Sapphira

It is almost modish among our current so-called Christians that, when they are presented in light of the children of God, or God's servants,[5] they try to present themselves as more pious than they really are. It has almost become a general observation that the devil has been brought into the world to induce men to stumble, as did Ananis and Sapphira, with airs or bearing that do not reflect who they really are at heart. Ah, unfortunate souls! They will encounter the blow that Ananias and Sapphira confronted.

Is this not so, beloved friends? I appeal to your conscience, have there not been many a one among you who have made this choice? I plead with you, read once more the fifth chapter of Acts, and consider whether your souls could yet be preserved in the face of this deception, and be saved from it.

There are however yet other matters whereby people are wont to grieve the Holy Spirit, not only by deceitfully laying hold of His Person while hid-

---

5. Here again is our theme of the children of God, appearing here to denote the highest court of appeal in Christian virtue to which faithful believers are to be accountable, as before God Himself. See Matthew 18 1-4.

ing their selfish affections, but also by misrepresenting His Person and His guidance wrongly go about their dealings with other persons. For example, if such persons who have already once , and then allow Satan to agitate them again to deceive other apparently good and upright Christians, how is this not a more grievous example for all time, that persons who once had something of God's excellence have allowed themselves to be led away from the savior by the devil, (123) and probably would thereafter become the tools of the devil themselves, for the destruction of other persons? Ah, my God, how is the Holy Spirit grieved by this, and the temple of God destroyed? What kind of horrible curse do such men unleash upon themselves? They become such persons, eternally, and must bear this heavy burden sufficiently.

There is found in I Corinthians 3:17 a noteworthy word, of which I could here remind your souls.[6] "If anyone destroys the temple of God (that means a soul, who has once become the temple of God) God will destroy him." God will destroy such a person in eternal judgment if he does not seek the salvation of his poor soul in the blood of Jesus, during his time of grace here on earth.

May I remind us of something from the mouth of the Savior as found in Matthew 18, where our Savior placed a small innocent child in His midst among His disciples, and spoke with them according to these words: "You must convert, and become like this one, if you would want to enter into the kingdom of heaven." He then added these noteworthy words in verse six: "but whoever causes one of these little ones who believe in Me to stumble, it is better for him that a heavy millstone be hung around his neck, and that he be drowned in the depth of the sea." What does Jesus intend to say to us with these words? Who annoys a child? That means, who is the one whom Jesus loves, whom evil would lead astray with words and works? for him it would be better that a millstone...etc. Ah, there is inexpressibly much to be of importance if one is a little child, in which the Holy Spirit began His work through baptism, which then another misleads to something evil, and hindering the work of the Holy Spirit. O, you parents, for the sake of God, notice this which you have around you each day, your chil-

---

6. "If anyone destroys the temple of God, God will destroy him, for the temple of God is holy, and that is what you are" (I Cor. 3:17). What a word in a day when mass warfare had recently visited Europe in the Thirty Years War (1618-1648), and its long aftershocks, as well as in a day as this, with millions of fetuses aborted and terrorism taking its rampant toll worldwide.

dren. Ah, dear God, what would this or that man likely have for a curse upon him, who has provoked this or that child, and hindered so that the Spirit of God and His work of grace has not continued to operate? We consider those little ones, whose conscience was assaulted, who continue yet unto this day with meekness within them, seeking with tears the grace which is in the blood of Jesus Christ, before the judgment of wrath which has been pronounced here, concerning also the spread and breakthrough [ausbricht] of that grace,[7] and before they experience what is called the grieving of the Holy Spirit, even towards other men.[8]

That is a short version of what I need to bring forth, concerning how and by what means the Holy Spirit is grieved, not only in view of His Person, but also for those others.

You persons [souls], who are not yet sealed with the Holy Spirit, will probably still notice, I believe and also hope, that you will have perceived and felt *within your inward parts*[9] something sensible and affective, through my presentation. I have identfied these issues as warnings to be heeded with carefulness; especially with regard to your souls which have been sealed for you with the Holy Spirit (125) and where you have found grace in the blood of Jesus Christ. May you choose to become diligent in these matters, so that daily you may open your hearts more and more to the leading of the Holy Spirit, and that you may become attentive to allow each of the impulses of His grace to take their course in your life, without the suppres-sion of any of His promptings as you go forward, lest you grieve Him who is devoted to you.

For only when you are careful in these matters will you be protected from the remaining outbreaks of evil which will beset you. If you are not careful, they will return and overtake you in a short while, so that the Holy

---

7. A poetic reference to his theme of the telos of the work of grace which began with the children's revival in Silesia: the birthing of the vision for a globalized Christianity, understood as the triumph of the children of God in history, since the judgment of the accuser is complemented by their prevailing witness unto the ends of the earth and before the seat of Christ in heaven. (See Revelation 7:9: "After this I looked and behold a great multitude that no one could number from every nation, from all tribes and people, and languages, standing before the throne and before the Lamb, clothed in white robes with palm branches in their hands.")

8. By inference: "other men," denote, for Steinmetz, those for whom the gospel, which was lived out by the children, was also intended, but who were prevented from receiving that message of life due to the subversion of the evil one.

9. Here, as earlier, Steinmetz returns to the theme of the mystical heart of a person as being the core to his personhood; the term here, "Inwendigen" is used synonymously with the more frequently appearing anthropological reference in these addresses to "souls."

Spirit becomes offended in a large measure. However, I have hope for you that you will protect yourself before this occurs. O, how I wish that all of you might take notice to grasp and hold on to this faith, even those poor, unfortunate persons who have really offended the Holy Spirit after they had been sealed by Him.

Do you ask who these persons may be? Allow me to offer a brief description here:

I understand that among those persons who have grieved the Holy Spiri are those who have become inattentive and have fallen away, but who might soon become awakened by the impulses of grace and give attention to God. He is One who had already turned away from this "backslidden" person, but who has now let Himself be delighted again through this person's extraordinary shifts of attitude toward repentance unto God. Then, after receiving forgiveness for his sins in the blood of Christ, this person then consciously and with resolution again turned toward sin, or at least allowed himself to be driven with the words and works of evil.

You poor souls, who certainly might not think that your offense would really be too much for the Holy Spirit to grieve. I appeal to you, however, for the sake of God, to only consider what happened to Ananias and Sapphira, when they grieved the Holy Spirit. Remember also what we read in 2 Peter 2:21, where it says, "For it would be better for them not to have known the way of righteousness than having known it, to turn away from the holy commandment delivered to them." There were those who grieved the Holy Spirit after they had once been taken from their sinful condition through His sealing, Would it be better, had they not known the way of truth at all, so they would not have been joined to the saving knowledge and union with Jesus Christ? Certainly, such poor souls had also been lost in their sins, but their judgment would still not be so great. For if it would be more tolerable for Sodom and Gomorrha on the judgment day than for such persons, who knew the truth, received the Holy Spirit who sealed them with His grace, and yet they fell away, and grieved the Holy Spirit. Hebrews 10:26-27 still remain as noteworthy words, especially verses 28 and 29. "If anyone breaks the law of Moses, that one must die without (127) mercy, given two or three witnesses. How much severer punishment do you think he will deserve who has trampled under foot the Son of God, and has regarded as unclean the blood of the covenant by which he was sanctified, and has insulted the Spirit of grace?"

We also find an important example in I Moses (Genesis) 6:3, where the Holy Spirit gives the chief reason why the entire first world was designated to perish in their sins. The people of that time no longer wanted to let themselves be punished by my Spirit, or as the text says, "My Spirit cannot rule among them." This is a clear example of how God has already punished such men in this world, when they received the Holy Spirit and then grieved Him again and did not want themselves to be ruled any longer by Him. That says it for us, you poor unfortunate souls. You have to expect that.

However, when God spares you, even in your lifetime, then think only for a moment of your deathbed. What comfort do you have then, when you, in desperate need, wish you could now trust Him as you Comforter, in that hour of death?[10] There can be no one else for you to trust. If you grieve the Holy Spirit now, then you forsake forever all assurance that you could have on your deathbed, and you will go with shudders into eternity. Ah, for the sake of God, come to your senses yet, which convinces you that you have grieved the Holy Spirit after receiving grace from Him, (128) and after He has begun to work within you. May you even now urge that on, to flee to Him, and seek grace anew in the bloody wounds of Jesus Christ.

I know that the devil usually tried to hold persons back from a genuine conversion when he perusuades them not to return to Jesus by saying it would not be possible for them in their circumstances, their age, or their locations to come to a true and basic change of mind. That is however a terrible deception of the devil whereby he seeks nothing other than to gain time to destabilize their hearts and bring them into eternal perdition. For the enemy of our souls makes the case that the Holy Spirit either cannot or will not help in those places and times. Astonishingly, both of those objections are a slander against the Holy Spirit. Ought one conclude that the holy, true God should not be powerful enough to stand by us in all circumstances, places and times?

Do not therefore let yourself by sidetracked by the devil, but only bow before your Redeemer, Jesus, who has gifts to be received, yes, even for the faithless persons who have fallen again and departed from His Presence.

---

10. This is an allusion to the first question of the German Reformed Heidelberg Catechism (1563), which had been introduced into Brandenburg (the home district for Halle, where Francke taught and directed the great Pietist outreach center) with the transfer of Reformed population from the Palatinate during the incursions there from the Bourbon monarchs of the seventeenth century. Question one of the Heidelberger asks, "What is your only comfort in life and in death? Answer: That I belong to my faithful Savior Jesus Christ." See The Heidelberg Catechism with Commentary (Philadelphia, United Church Press, 1963), 17.

Observe this, and go to the cross of the Lord Jesus, praying and weeping so long as necessary until the blood of Jesus and also the water from His side floods your hearts, until you make room for the Holy Spirit to flow through your inward life. (129) Whoever will honestly intend to do this will truly receive Him, even if you had even been among those who have grieved Him.

Allow me a closing word here. It is for you who truly have never experienced a genuine conversion of your heart through the Holy Spirit, and consequently have received no sealing with the Holy Spirit in the blood of Christ. You remain in your sins, your self-assurance, and in your hypocrisy, and you are also convinced that you have grieved the Holy Spirit. Do you ask, what then? We may assume all is well until we reach that point when we know we really do not know or trust Him, and so are truly guilty before Him. Do you claim to have Him but you have not often felt Him in your heart? Has He not often convinced you in your heart that He must become otherwise than He has been with you, that you need to find a reckoning [geraten] with the blood of Jesus Christ? Has not the Holy Spirit been *held out before you from your childhood onward?* Nevertheless, have you not also thrust Him away from yourself? Have you not closed your heart to the Holy Spirit? Have you not hindered Him from making the working of His grace to become an attainment for you, as your end purpose in life? And have you not grieved Him by all of this?

O, the poor beggar is grieved if he is turned away empty from our door. Likewise, should not the Holy Spirit also be grieved in such a fashion if He is not given a hearing? Granted. However, to the man who reads this statement and does not want to be reminded that the Holy Spirit once impinged powerfully upon his heart, I say, 'you are still baptized, and that you cannot deny.' (130) In baptism you have been imparted with the Holy Spirit, and He had been poured out upon you. Then, you grieved Him in your fragile youth, and He had to withdraw Himself from your heart.[11]

Therefore, you cannot excuse yourself, saying you have never known any special movement of grace from the Holy Spirit. So have you also grieved the Holy Spirit. And if you remain and continue in this, what, then, can you expect, you unfortunate soul? Can you really believe, and hope, that He will somehow make you blessedly redeemed if you continue to

---

11. Here he aligns with the Lutheran and Anglican views of confirmation as an infilling of the Holy Spirit, which requires accountability on behalf of the one baptized to be retained. The implication is that in baptism the Holy Spirit's sealing of the believer in Christ's atoning death on Calvary is sacramentally received.

grieve Him as you now are, throughout your entire life? O, no more! Seek, through a true conversion to Jesus, that He could delight Himself through your entire life. The devil indeed has 100 cords whereby he binds a man, and 1000 ramparts whereby he guards the palace of the heart from having access to God. For many that may be why they think they have not been able to have contact with the Holy Spirit, an idea which Satan maintains, saying to us: it would not be possible. There is no truth to that claim. It is a lie and a slander against the Holy Spirit.

5.4 Sealed for the World to Receive

Jesus is available to all persons, if they only want His sealing. For Christ has acquired this sealing for all humankind so they may able to receive the Holy Spirit for the true alteration of their hearts. It is true that Christ has died for all mankind, and it is also true for all mankind that they can be brought to Jesus and become blessed. On the other hand, He holds off Satan and makes it possible that, if they are truly converted, they would no longer be able to enjoy the lusts and joys of this world because they have discovered (131) that the joy of God is unendingly greater and more blessed than the joys of the world. For so high as the heaven is above the earth, so widely better are the joys of the Holy Spirit than those of the world.

The devil holds many souls captive when he brings his thoughts into their hearts, deceiving them with the thought that it was not yet time for them to become converted. They reason, if that moment had come, the Holy Spirit would be working so powerfully within them, that He could not be resisted. My God, what is that for abominable and irrational thinking? If the moment had not yet arrived, God would also be accused by the fact that He wanted to have you lying in the power of Satan for an extended time. Could you believe that of God, who gave His Son Jesus Christ for you? Is it possible that God has not spared his only begotten Son, for your sake, that He might let you lie for even an hour bound in the cords of Satan?

Now, now is the accepted time, says the Holy Spirit, the moment that you have been awaiting. The moment when God is ready for that purpose. His fatherly arms are day and night outstretched, as God says in Isaiah 65:2, "I spread out my hands all day long to a rebellious people, who walk in the way which is not good, following their own thoughts." For what purpose does God give you His Word? Why then does God work so convincingly in your soul? Why does God bring you into such opportunities, such places, and such circumstances where He can work within you, i.e., engage you at the most inward level of your being? What does it mean to abandon yourself to God, as such a source of wisdom that He does nothing without purpose. (132) Therefore, leave no room in your lives for such astonishing intellectual slander of God which is not infrequent in our time.

It would be an unfortunate conversion if one wanted to coerce someone for some unknown purpose. How would that seem to you? Would it be considered a work of grace if a king wanted to lead one into his royal palace with chains and bands, and would that likely be considered as a work of grace? It would be such an unregenerate action if the Holy Spirit forced or bound with chains to get us into the palace, or the Kingdom of God. You would find no blessedness in such an action if you must be forcibly converted like that. And therefore it is a great travesty if one waited on such a movement, which a person would not be able to withstand.[12]

The Holy Spirit has not promised to show such special grace to every person, but He longs in His Word for all persons to take note, first, of the knocking of the Holy Spirit and, second, to give attention to all movements of the heart, and, when that occurs, to open the heart of a dispirited

---

12. This appears as an implicit critique of high Calvinism. Given his context, it is more likely, that Steinmetz is hinting at the spiritual route to a globalized Christianity, as opposed to a political or military route, such as that which Roman authorities had authorized in the various medieval military crusades against the enemies of the faith as well as at the forcible conversion of pre Christian medieval people groups such as Wends (Poles), not to speak of the Jesuit endorsed advances of the Austrian Hapsburg forces against Lutheran lands like Silesia in the Counter-Reformation. With such a historical context, it is a revolutionary idea to chart a course of extending the Kingdom of God through the spiritual liberation of oppressed persons (then termed souls) of all nationalities through the preaching of the theology of the cross linked to the Pentecostal sealing of those freed from the law, sin, and death, with the indwelling life and discipline of the Holy Spirit, which is positioned to confront a decadent social order called Christendom with the agape love of God. This describes the program of a Pietist-based Protestant revivalism whose course Steinmetz will chart in his magnus opus, the "Gathering of Diverse Materials for the Building of the Kingdom of God," which will next be examined as a sequel to the revival under Steinmetz at Teschen (from ca 1719 to 1730, then transferred to new fields in the German, Dutch, Scandinavian and Anglo/American kingdoms, and colonial regions to the West, a mega revival which was itself the fruit of the simple but urgent and powerful Silesian children's revival of 1707-8. By the way, Methodism is an important chapter in that larger narrative, initially linked as it was to Steinmetz via the ministry of Christian David at Herrnhut.

humanity and disclose Himself to all to all so He may come and reconvene the Last Supper [Abendmahl] with them.[13]

5.5 The Closing Prayer of Steinmetz

May the faithful Jesus have mercy upon each person whom God has created, so that no one might think [of rejecting God's Spirit] along the lines which have here been mentioned. Now, beloved friend [soul], you have also been moved in this time, through the Spirit of God in your heart, and so, abandon yourself to Him, with the resolve that now, from this day onward, the Lord your God shall have your heart and soul, and, He replies, I will become and remain yours, both in time and eternity. Yes, my Lord Jesus, that is what You would work within us, for the sake of Your eternal and heartfelt love. Amen.

---

13. The account of the Pentecost sealing of the Holy Spirit began with the great work of the Father establishing His righteousness among a Satan-bound humanity through the love exchange of His crucified Son, Jesus Immanuel, whereby His Holy Spirit seals Himself, in Jesus' blood, on the hearts of those who have met Christ at the cross, thereby conveying His forgiveness and resurrection life to empower them to live and bear witness in blessed salvation as children of God, whose holiness is now illuminated in excellence throughout all the earth.

PART THREE

"A Little Child Shall Lead Them"

In overview, Steinmetz's Pentecost Addresses had a regenerative historical outcome, based upon a spontaneous and authentic revival among children at prayer in Silesia (1707–8) and transferred to Teschen in the next two decades, where the revival became full blown. The outcome of this revival is measured in (1) an impetus for a globalizing Christianity, and (2) a commitment to a twofold soteriology which became the core of the evangelistic message of the Wesleys.

How extraordinary it was that the first occurrence of awakening in Protestant history occurred in the context of children caught in war-torn eastern Europe who would become its herald. This was in fact what happened. Amid oppression by Roman Catholic authorities of Lutherans (e.g. Protestants, for Lutherans were the only legal option beyond Catholicism in that locale and era), were found young schoolchildren who would not accept this outcome. In 1707, the children of Sprottau, in the forestland of upper Silesia, began meeting two to three times daily on their own, in a field outside the village. This spontaneous activity had the intent to pray for the salvation, peace, and restoration of their churches where they could freely worship their Christ whom they dearly loved. They recited Psalms, sang hymns and prayed with prophetic zeal. With deep reverence they either fell on their knees or lay prostrate as they worshipped, seeking Christ's forgiveness for their sins and those of their nation. They encountered resistance from many adults, including clergy. Their care for their parents, even those who resisted their acts, did not prevent them from climbing out of windows to meet for their prayers. Observers gradually began to conclude that this event was indeed a work of God. Even civil authorities who were summoned to restrain and punish them would lay down their whips and let the children pass. Their perseverance and phenomenal growth in numbers led this initiative to become a game changer in interrupting the long legacy of warfare in their society.

The setting for the Silesian revival is found within the narrative of this initial awakening among the children, accompanied by an awareness of the extant conditions in Protestant Christendom of that time. It was internally challenged by institutional conflict between the forces of Protestant Orthodoxy and Pietism, and it was externally challenged by the onslaught of the Counter Reformation, allied to the geopolitical forces of the Hapsburg Empire with its capital in Vienna. Those forces had successfully and brutally established its hegemony over large swaths of churches which had embraced the evangelical faith of Luther in the wake of the Protestant Reformation. The revival occurred in the midst of this turmoil, which forced it to be relocated to other regions across Europe and the globe in the decades of the 1730s and 1740s.

It is also our contention that, in addition to the geopolitical implications, the children's revival also gained stature by being interpreted in light of competing intellectual explanations of Christian faith in the early modern era.

Chapter 1

EUROPEAN CHRISTENDOM IS AWAKENED TO THE WORLD

1.1 Introduction

Our purpose is the genesis of a vision for Christian globalization since the Protestant Reformation, viewed as the interface of the passion of Christ with a recovery of Pentecost in an oppressed humanity. This interface represents a joining of a depth with a breadth dimension within the pathos of human response to tragedy.

The apostolic theme of Pentecost finds correlation with the biblical mandate for the global missio Dei of Christianity in Pentecost (Acts 2). The earliest signs of revival in Protestant tradition appeared amid the devastation of war associated with the Counter Reformation in Eastern Europe during the early eighteenth century. Since the birth of Christendom in the Constantinian settlement of the fourth century, Pentecost had been observed primarily as a liturgical date within the church calendar of Christendom, as later reconfigured into the era of Protestant Orthodoxy. However, the preacher of this incipient revival, Johann Adam Steinmetz, gave primary focus to the theme of Pentecost to identify the moment of history before which he then stood. The location is a refugee congregation in Teschen, Silesia,[1] a province located at the conjunction of present day Poland, Czech Republic, and Germany.

---

1. As well as in the German provinces of Salzburg and Austria, where Lutherans were now being liquidated by warring Catholic princes allied to Jesuit priests.

Ministering to a community of displaced Saxons, Poles, Czechs, and Hungarians, his massive congregation numbered between 40,000 and 70,000 adherents, making it likely the first "megachurch." The awakening there occurred in the context of a ministry team serving with Steinmetz, who were conducting simultaneous preaching in three languages. The theme of the preaching is reflected in the series of Steinmetz' *Addresses on Pentecost*,[2] reproduced in this volume in English translation and perhaps the earliest addresses devoted to this theme in the context of revival in evangelical Protestantism. This document has been presented in annotated form with the intention of reconstructing a picture of how the Pentecost message was initially presented in this context.

The revival first appeared as an event of spiritual and prophetic power and depth among a large community of desperate orphans from the war devastated Lutheran parishes of Silesia. The first phase of revival, which emerged within that context in 1707–1708, was also the initiation of a concern for the globalization of the Christian message, beginning with the coming together of Germans, Poles, Bohemians, Czechs, Moravians, and Hungarians under the influence of revival. This event occurred after the passion of the children, accompanied by protracted prayer and prophecy. Their spiritual exercises were drawn from their familiarity with Luther's small catechism, with the prominence of its theology of the cross. These exercises continued fervently for eight months before the arrival of a Swedish army to stabilize the area, an event the children believed was in response to their prayers. The events preceding and following this remarkable occurrence are examined in Swensson's *Kinderbeten: The Silesian Prayer and Prophecy Revival*. The contrasting reports of its outcome, also contained in the Swensson study, represent a sustained analysis of this first revival in Protestantism. They represent a critical assessment of the data by a Lutheran church leader in Silesia, Caspar Neumann, who was no friend of Pietism or of revival, and an appreciative assessment by a Lutheran theologian from Giessen, turned radical Pietist, Johann Wilhelm Petersen.[3]

The latter interpreted this event within the framework of God breaking

---

2. Johann Adam Steinmetz, *Der Versiegelung der Glaubigen mit dem heiligen Geist in einigen Pfingsterbauungstunden*. Or *Concerning the Sealing of Believers with the Holy Spirit: Five Lessons in Pentecost Edification (ca 1720–30)*, here the 1857 Brönner edition. This primitive volume on the theme of Pentecost as revival was based on his sermons from the early 1730s and published in that era. The present author located an edition from the Cincinnati Historical Society Archives in 2006.

3. The Radical Pietists, phase two within the larger movement of evangelical Pietism, represent a domain which has more recently become the subject of critical research, largely

spiritual strongholds through the power of the prayers and prophesies of the children, noting that "Pentecost has not been fulfilled fully because the youth had not prophesied,"[4] a reference to Peter's Pentecost sermon (Acts 2:16ff), concerning the great and fearful day of the Lord" preceding Christ's return in Judgment, which Peter related to "your young men and daughters prophesying".

For Petersen, that apocalyptic event would then usher in God's universal reign in Christ, which, in his reading, would open the door to the restoration of all things in Christ" (the so-called apokatastaseos panton, the "Wiederbringung aller Dinge"). Such a reading of Pentecost was timely at the transition from the seventeenth into the early eighteenth century, capping an epoch when human warfare of biblical proportions (in the Thirty Years War) had devastated Europe like never before.

However, in the ensuing revival under the preaching of Steinmetz at the Grace Church in Teschen, a direct outcome of the Kinderbeten awakening over the succeeding two decades, Pentecost is interpreted to signal the onset of a global revival. Here was a theme further explored and documented in the chronicles of Steinmetz, who has been identified as the catalyst for monitoring this revival through neighboring Moravia and Saxony, including the Moravian base at Herrnhut. From there it extended, to western Europe, the global Moravian diaspora, and Methodism, as well as through radical Pietist-based expressions of revival based in the German Wetterau district, which also became launching points for transatlantic

---

through the work of Hans Schneider and his circle at Marburg. His major study, *German Radical Pietism* (2007), has been translated into English and now appears in our Asbury Theological Seminary Series on Pietist and Wesleyan Studies. This study includes figures whose ministries were set apart from the state churches. Their leading representatives include the radical Pietist historian Gottfried Arnold, and the forenamed Gerhard Tersteegen. A large part of what sets radical *Pietists* apart from the earlier radical *Reformers* of the Protestant Reformation is their deep involvement in recovering late medieval German mystical theology as a basis for recovery of a genuine Christianity apart from the Christendom model, unlike the Anabaptists/Mennonites, who organized believers churches intending to restore a primitive church pattern of discipleship. The major difference between them and church Pietists was the radicals' unwillingness to permit their ardent devotion to the mystical literature from overpowering their commitment to remaining politically correct as ministers within the official church bodies of that time." J.S. O'Malley, "Pietism and Wesleyanism: Setting the Stage for a Theological Discussion," *Wesleyan Theological Journal*, 53:1 (Spring 2018): 56-78.

4. *Die Macht der Kinder in der Letzten Zeit, auf Veranlassung der Kleinen Prediger/ oder der Betenden Kinder in Schlesien/aus der Heiligen Schrifft Vorgestellt von Johann Wilhelm Petersen* (Frankfurt und Leipzig. In Verlegung Samuel Heil und Johann Gottfr. Liebezeits, 1709; cited in Swensson, 79.

revivalism in the eighteenth century. Steinmetz was the first to chronicle for German-speaking Europe the extension of revival to New England in the days of Jonathan Edwards—all of which is to say the Pentecost to which the prayers of the children pointed has changed from heralding an apocalyptic event to being an event opening the path to all humanity being reached for the gospel. Steinmetz articulates this new theme in his Pentecost addresses, and he acted on that premise by conducting, along with his "bush preachers" born of the Teschen revival, evangelistic forays into neighboring Moravia, Poland and Saxony, spreading that revival far and wide.

Among those participating in that extension of the revival included Christian David (1692–1751), who was instrumental in its powerful entry into the Herrnhut community of the Moravians, in Germany. When John Wesley visited Herrnhut in autumn 1738, following his Aldersgate conversion (and Aldersgate was one point in that movement of revival which had begun at Teschen and and thereafter transferred to the Moravians at Herrnhut), he was powerfully drawn to David's message of a twofold gospel, signified in the disciples' journey from Calvary to Pentecost, and now made available to all through the gift of the Spirit—a message which David had internalized through his spiritual mentor, Steinmetz, under whose ministry he was confirmed in the faith being proclaimed in the Grace Church.

David also made clear to Wesley that this journey was also from pardoning to sanctifying grace, as a journey to full salvation in Christ, by the sealing (alias baptism) of His Spirit, which was being widely disseminated in the revival Steinmetz had launched, as now articulated by David. We know the subsequent history of this twofold doctrine of saving grace in the annals of primitive Methodist preaching. It was being disseminated through a diversity of revival voices on the European continent, including the radical German Philadelphians, Hochman von Hochenau, Rock and the Inspirationists, and churchmen like Lampe and the Otterbeins, and the unsectarian Tersteegen, to name some of the most preeminent voices of this awakening. It was through these voices that the transatlantic revivalism born of Pietism would occur, under the theme of the manifestation of Pentecost.

In several places where the revival spread, children were involved in praying and prophesying as an impetus for its breakthrough. This was particularly evident in Herrnhut, where the awakening among children there was the last and determinative step in enabling it to break through there (called the Durchbruch by the Halle Pietists), in 1727.

1.2 Biblical Context

The New Testament is replete with references to children as emblematic of the new humanity envisioned for a world in travail by the Triune God of Christian faith. Jesus is first worshipped by a child, John the Baptist, who leaped in his mother's womb when he received the angelic message concerning the coming nativity of the Lord. The second person to worship the child Jesus was the elderly Simeon who had been "led by the Holy Spirit" to come daily to the Temple to meet the Messiah until he saw with his eyes the child Jesus, whom he declared was the "Light to the Gentiles."

In Matthew's account, following his transfiguration, Jesus is approached by the disciples with the questions, "Who is the greatest in the Kingdom of heaven?" And consonant with His parabolic style of proclamation, He places a child in the midst of them, declaring, "Truly I say to you, unless you turn and become like children, you will never enter the kingdom of heaven" and "Whoever humbles himself like this child, he is the greatest in the kingdom of heaven," and "whoever receives one such child in my name, receives me; but whoever causes one of these little ones who believe in me to sin, it would be better for him to have a great millstone fastened round his neck, and to be drowned in the depth of the sea" (Matthew 18:2-5).

The natural condition of fallen humanity is the converse of that imagery. We will not be continuously converted from a willful sense of autonomy and self-serving parochialism. There are whole tracts of our lives we keep aloof from the penetration of the Spirit of God, and that worldview militates against the apostolic mandate that the Jesus movement was to have the world God created, in all its dimensions, as its frame of reference in making disciples for the Christ and His Kingdom.

The power of the Christian past for the transformation of this world and its humanity into the children of God, which is also the fruition of the new birth in Jesus Christ, was encapsulated in the apostolic Christian community with the event of Pentecost. It is the locus of the transfer of empowerment from the ascended Christ to the company of witnesses to the decisive work of human salvation in Jesus' death on the cross. The Holy Spirit was at work in history before that event, but He, the ascended Christ, was not here, after His ascension, not until Pentecost, when His Spirit's baptism, to use Lukan language, puts us on God's line, and not on their own line of vision for the world. That is the line of demarcation, from ministry from our own human perspective, to confronting the world with the gospel of Christ. The disciples' constant questions and His repeated attempts to address them are now resolved in understanding[5] that also equips them to be the children of God in mission to the world. That company is also dignified in Peter's Pentecost address with his declaration that "in the last days it shall be ... that I will pour out my Spirit on all flesh, and your sons and your daughters shall prophesy" and it shall be that "whoever calls on the name of the Lord shall be saved."

It is noteworthy that those for whom Christ would die are identified in John's gospel in the words of the high priest Caiaphas, who declared to the Pharisees who were upset by the signs of Jesus that "you do not understand that it is expedient for you that one man should die for the people, and that the whole nation should not perish, and not for the nation only, but to gather into one the children of God who are scattered over the earth (or abroad)."[6] It was "from that day" that they "took counsel how to put him to death."[7] This "gathering into one" of the scattered children of God was now occurring, with Pentecost.

Steinmetz develops his Pentecost addresses under the biblical theme of Ephesians 4:30, "And do not grieve the Holy Spirit by whom you are sealed unto the day of redemption." Paul builds his case on the "foundation of the apostles and the prophets" so that "you may be strengthened with might through His Spirit in the inner man, ... that Christ may dwell in your hearts through faith, and that you, being rooted and grounded in love, may have power to comprehend with all the saints what is the breadth and length and height and depth, to know the love of Christ which surpasses knowledge, that you may be filled with all the fullness of God" (Ephesians 2:20, 16-19).

The indwelling of Christ through faith and the grounding in love references the depth dimension of the God-human relationship in Christ, while the "power to comprehend with all the saints what is the breadth [as well as the depth] of the love of God" references the breadth dimension which is the global mission of Christianity, beyond the restrictions of all institutional expressions of Christendom.

Children fulfill their vocation in relation to parent in the God relationship, who address Him as "abba" (Romans 8:16), signifying the child's intimate access and fellowship with God as paradigmatic for faithful worship in praise, adoration, and intercession on behalf of all for whom Christ has died. The children whose prayers launched Protestantism's first revival

5. John 14:26.
6. John 12:49-52.
7. John 12:53.

would make intercession for the lost of their Silesian homeland as the singular outcome of their adoration unto God. The biblical basis for summoning humans to approach all of life as coram Deo is to share our Lord's ministry of intercession on behalf of the humanity for whom He died and for whom He now intercedes from His heavenly session as Head of the Body of the new humanity.

Pentecost comes after a profound encounter with the passion of the cross, as found in the disciples' journey from the grief of Calvary to the wonder of the resurrection and ascension, all seen as preliminary for the expectant waiting for the Spirit in Acts 1 and 2. This pattern is replicated in the history of the first revival in Protestantism: the Silesian children suffered as children who as war refugees and orphans, prayed and sang as angels of light who would become signs of the new humanity in the generations to come as the revival unfolds from their passion.

1.3 The Roots of Awakening: The Struggle for the Survival of the Reformation

Steinmetz's addresses were to have a transformative outcome, building as they were upon a spontaneous and authentic revival among children [1707-8] that was transferred to Teschen in the following two decades. That outcome would be measured in terms of (1) an impetus for a globalizing Christianity, and (2) a commitment to a twofold soteriology which became the core of the evangelistic message of the Wesleys. It is our task in Part Three to demonstrate how these outcomes came to pass, given the historical framework in which they occurred. It is a narrative which has not been constructed in full, because we did not have access to the sources which enable this case to be made.

The initial setting for this revival is found in the narrative of the children's revival itself, accompanied by an awareness of the extant condition in Protestant Christendom of that time, through which it occurred. It was internally challenged by institutional conflict between the forces of Protestant Orthodoxy and Pietism, and it was externally challenged the onslaught of the Counter Reformation, allied to the geopolitical forces of the Hapsburg Empire with its capital in Vienna. Those forces had successfully and brutally established their hegemony over large swaths of churches which had embraced the evangelical faith of Luther in the wake of the Protestant Reformation. The revival occurred in the midst of this turmoil, which forced it to be relocated to other regions across Europe and the globe in the decades of the 1730s and 1740s.

Here we transfer our attention to the time and place for the genesis of the vision for Christian globalization within post-Reformation European Christendom, and this takes us to the early eighteenth century and to an eastern providence of the Holy Roman Empire, Silesia. This was a dark hour for the legacy of the Protestant Reformation, which was hanging by a thread amid the robust Roman Catholic strategies known to them as the Catholic Reformation, and, to the Protestants, as the Counter-Reformation. We here find ourselves two hundred years past the Reformation. Amid the context of social dislocation in the decade after 1700, due to warfare accompanied by religious persecution, the recovery of the apostolic theme of Pentecost finds renewed correlation with the biblical mandate for the global missio Dei (Acts 2).

It was in that location that the earliest signs of revival in Protestant tradition appeared amid the devastation of war associated with the Counter Reformation in Eastern Europe during that era, capping an epoch when human warfare of biblical proportions, in the Thirty Years War, and its aftermath, had devastated Europe like never before. It is important to grasp the major parties at odds in this struggle, since each would present different interpretations of the revival which would break out in the midst of their struggle for European domination.

Let us begin here with an acknowledgement that our use of the term revival follows the research of the noted British historian W.R. Ward[8] in distinguishing it from the term renewal, which refers to the spiritual refreshment and undergirding of existing parish structures. However, revival first occurred where the structures of organized Christendom have been displaced, usually through warfare, leaving a population destitute of organized religion. For example, Pietism in Germany was a renewal movement from the seventeenth century, based upon the preaching of the new birth in Christ (John 3) as the basis for Christian identity, but implemented through heartfelt observance of the means of grace, and personal praxis of the faith as nurtured in "colleges" or conventicles of piety (the collegia pietatis), to use the language of Philip Jacob Spener in his manual for Pietist renewal of church and society. The model for Pietist renewal is famously based in the work of August Hermann Francke at the Prussian University of Halle, whose orphanage, printing center, and coeducational

---

8. W. Reginald Ward, *The Protestant Evangelical Awakening* (Oxford, 1992).

educational system provided the basis for renewal of all aspects of Prussian society and the inauguration of evangelical missions beyond the German Empire.

By contrast, the war-torn and uprooted situation in Silesia at the dawn of the eighteenth century describes the context where revival first occurred, a place where nothing remained to be renewed. It was an event without precedence, at least in the history of Protestantism, with the possible exception of the breakout of the "child prophets" during the struggle for survival of the French Huguenots after the revocation of the edict of toleration for Protestants (the Edict of Nantes) by the Bourbon monarchy in seventeenth century France. Before our word "revival" was introduced, the term "awakening" was used in German (die "Erweckung") to denote a supernatural breakthrough of saving grace into apparently hopeless human tragedy where there could be no plausible explanation for its occurrence. That is really the converse of "renewal," which suggests improving the status quo. Awakening would signify the faith language for the rebirth of a religious community, by the breakthrough of a sovereign move of the Holy Spirit.

1.4 The Revival Associated with the Children at Prayer [Kinderbeten]

With reference to the place of its occurrence, Silesia was an ancient nation tucked between Saxony and Prussia (west), Poland (northeast), Bohemia and Moravia (southwest), and Austria and Hungary (south). Silesia had existed under the uninterrupted dominance of neighboring states, continuing even to the present day, and was influenced by the incursion of external religious eruptions (such as the late medieval Hussite movement from Bohemia and the Lutherans from Saxony).

At the end of the Thirty Years War (1648) only three principalities in Silesia remained Protestant, according to the principle of cuius regio, that is, whoever is the prince is the one who decides the religion where limited rights of worship had a tenuous existence. The balance of power in Europe between the nations was precarious in 1701, when the War of Spanish Succession began. Northern principalities in the Holy Roman Empire, allied with Sweden, Holland, and England, formed the Protestant block, while the southern Catholic nations of southern Europe, under the flag of the Hapsburg Catholic regime in Vienna, formed the Roman Catholic block. Then came an hour of crisis in 1707 when a mobilized army of

10,000 soldiers under Karl XII of Sweden was preparing for war against the Hapsburg Emperor Joseph I, already embroiled with warfare against other nations. The children's revival which occurred in this milieu brought together the polar extremes of the world of European royalty and that of the Silesian children, oppressed by the loss of homes and parishes. It occurred almost concurrent with the invasion of Silesia by the Swedish King Karl XII and an army, who made direct contact with these children.

The larger geopolitical background to this extraordinary event is located within the international complexities of the War of the Spanish Succession (1701–1714), which then involved the major European powers. The summer of 1707 was a time of high tension among the emissaries of these nations. The main flash point was contention over the Spanish crown between the Bourbon kings in France and Austrian/Spanish branches of the Hapsburg dynasty. Fresh from victories over Russia and Poland, Karl XII had been enroute through Silesia. He had become aware of the legal provision in the Treaty of Westphalia (which had ended the Thirty Years War) allowing the King of Sweden the privilege of negotiating for the Protestants in Silesia if there was a treaty violation on the exercise of the rights of free worship.[9]

The king promptly demanded return of the seized Protestant churches in Silesia, to which the Emperor Joseph I unexpectedly conceded. The emperor was shocked that the Swedish king would risk his army defending the religious rights of the oppressed Silesian Protestants against the powerful Catholic Hapsburgs. Being under duress from war on several fronts, Joseph agreed to grant the request, in return for assurance he could continue to occupy Silesia.[10] There is also evidence that Karl was motivated by a desire to uphold the proud legacy of his predecessor, King Gustavus Adolphus, who gave his life defending the religious rights of Protestants on the European continent.[11]

As Eric Swensson indicates in his definitive study, the Silesian children's prayer revival is not an unsubstantiated event but a "mass movement with a nation of eyewitnesses."[12] Both of us acknowledge our debt to

---

9. Swensson, 27.

10. Data for this political confrontation is found in Norbert Conrads, *Die Durchführung der Altranstädter Konvention in Schlesien* (Wien: Bohlau Verlag Köln, 1971, 16, cited in Swensson, 28.

11. Ibid.

12. Swensson, xiii.

W. Reginald Ward, a late British Methodist historian, whose history of the Protestant Evangelical Awakening first made this event known to Anglo Americans. This overview of the events reflects the research Swensson completed in the Halle Archives in Germany, and reflects the present author's conversations with him.

The awakening of the children began in forested mountains in Silesia at an undisclosed date in 1707, when the children of this war-torn nation spontaneously gathered for prayer, reading Scripture and singing hymns. They would assemble two or three times daily, usually morning, noon and afternoon, to pray for peace, including religious freedom, in their homeland. It soon spread throughout the nation, including the towns and cities. They began to follow a pattern of walking quietly two by two to a site where their worship was held, with the children lying prone on their faces in prayer.[13] Adults in the vicinity would stop their activities to observe the children with reverence. This launched a revival, not a renewal of existing congregations, because parish life had been utterly destroyed and the members were scattered, many as refugees in adjacent Saxony.

These spontaneous prayer gatherings of the children resulted in an awakening which erupted repeatedly in Protestant areas of Silesia and in other nations throughout the continent over the next several decades, with the peak of intensity and activity in the 1730s and 1740s in Western Germany and Holland. Subsequent expressions of that revival typically were either initiated or accompanied by revival among children. This impetus led to the reorganization of the Moravian Church, as a consequence of the Herrnhut children's revival in 1727. It also occurred within the context of an anticipation of the imminence of the last times of the church on earth. This expectation was expressed by its early interpreter, Johann Wilhelm Petersen, who also noted that it was preceded by the prayer movement of the child prophets of the Cevannes in the struggle of the oppressed Huguenots in mid seventeenth century France. Swensson notes the orderly yet spontaneous character of the children's revival, lacking in paternal ecclesial control or interference, despite subsequent input from the structured outreach ministries of the Halle institutions in Germany which accompanied its development.[14]

This revival, first manifest among children, marked the first major occurrence resulting in the growth of an informal, evangelical Protestant network concerned with disseminating and promoting this phenomenon

---

13. Swensson, 32.
14. Swensson, 34.

as a genuine movement of spiritual awakening. It was unlike any known human-initiated movement of ecclesial renewal that had appeared in work of the Pietist theologians, particularly in it operating outside the parameters of official Christendom in either its evangelical (Protestant) or Catholic expressions. Initial responses to the children's revival were contained in official Protestant church publications of the day.[15] Reports in English also appeared as early as 1708 in England and in 1709 in Boston.[16] The remarkable, divine nature of this phenomenon is underscored in the title of the first English report, which shows there is no terminology to define it except to say it was an "Account of Extraordinary Pious Motions and Devout Exercises" observed in Silesian children.[17] Historiography on this event has advanced rapidly in the decade since a volume by Dietrich Meyer appeared in 2008, which has had the effect of underscoring the uniqueness of the children's revival as not being a replication of the prayers of the invading Swedish soldiers, who did not enter the Gebirge, a region where the children were initially based.[18]

An appreciation of the response to the revival from various quarters of Christendom and beyond requires some orientation to the religious parties of the day, often linked to rival universities which served as theological centers within Protestantism in the Holy Roman Empire and adjacent lands under imperial Hapsburg dominion.

1.5 The Theological Foundation for the Children's Revival in the Reformation Encounter with the Cross

When probing is done into the theological basis and readiness of these young children to be susceptible to an awakening of religion, the first thing observed is that they were living without parental and pastoral

---

15. These included the European *Fama* (an early chronicle of public events), the *Grundliche Nachrichten* (a more interpretive account with eyewitness reports and some transcriptions of prayers thought to be from the children), and the *Acta Publica* (a larger version of the *Nachrichten* that included documents concerning the Altranstädter Convention, which had enabled an interim in the Hapsburg Catholic invasion of Silesia, due to Swedish intervention). Other documents on the revival are discussed in Swensson, xvii, including Petersen's *Die Macht der Kinder*, which is examined in this study.

16. Praise out of the *Mouths of Babes: or a Particular Account of Some Extraordinary Pious Motions and Devout Exercises. Observed of Late in Many Children in Silesia* (Downing, 1708), and a version published by Increase Mather in Boston, 1709.

17. Ibid.

18. Swensson, xxii.

supervision due to wartime conditions. They were also surviving within a culturally isolated subsistence within the mountains and bush country of lower Silesia.[19] Having said that, our inquiry needs also to acknowledge that "the" event, the Kinderbeten, occurred after the passion (e.g. suffering) of children. At a tender age, they only had recourse (in addition to the inspiration of the Holy Spirit) to what they had memorized from Luther's small catechism, with the prominence of its theology of the cross. They had also learned to sing from memory the hymns of the Lutheran reformation, and they had access to the German (Luther) Bible. All this is to say that their protracted prayers and prophecy, and the regularized spiritual exercises they followed, was the pattern of Lutheran home worship, where the Protestant faith had surreptitiously been kept aflame during the decades of repression under the Hapsburg regimen of forced recatholicization of Silesians (beginning in the early seventeenth century). These exercises continued fervently for eight months between late 1707 and early 1708, before the arrival of the Swedes stabilized the area for the time being, an event which to the children was answered prayer.

Being schooled in Lutheran catechesis, the orphans would have memorized these words from the small catechism:

> I believe that God has made me and all creatures; that He has given me my body and soul, eyes, ears, and all my limbs, my reason, and all my senses, and still preserves them;...that He provides me richly and daily with all that I need to support this body and life, protects me from all danger, and guards me and preserves me from all evil; and all this out of pure, fatherly, divine goodness and mercy, without any merit or worthiness in me; for all which I owe it to Him to thank, praise, serve, and obey Him. This is most certainly true.

> I believe that Jesus Christ, true God, begotten of the Father from eternity, and also true man, born of the Virgin Mary, is my Lord, who has redeemed me, a lost and condemned creature, purchased and won [delivered] me from all sins, from death, and from the power of the devil, not with gold or silver, but with His holy, precious blood and with His innocent suffering and death, in order that I may be [wholly] His own, and live under Him in His kingdom, and serve Him in everlasting righteousness, innocence, and

---

19. Swensson, 33.

blessedness, even as He is risen from the dead, lives and reigns to all eternity.[20]

Luther had discovered through the German mystics that God receives us "as we are," without having attained merit to stand in His Presence, since on the cross there is a "blessed exchange" between Christ, who is "full of grace, life and salvation," and me a sinner, "full of sins, death, and damnation." That is because "faith" (or trust, fiducia) comes between these two [Christ and myself], "and then sins, death and damnation will be Christ's, while grace, life and salvation will be ours."[21] At the moment when the Word, who is Jesus Christ in the flesh, whom we receive by faith, "imparts its qualities to the soul, '[it is just as] the heated iron glows like fire [on the blacksmith's forge] because of the union of the fire with it."[22] This means our existence is grounded in the promise of God, which comes from the preaching of the message of the cross (Romans 1:16–17).

The message of this new man imaged in the cross is not a word to humanity in general, but always it comes only to that one who takes responsibility for hearing and believing this incredible promise as from God Himself. This promise which constitutes our humanity is available only to those who hear in such a way that they do not remain deaf.[23] It is a Word which only comes to the one who, while in anguish that the commands of the law are always beyond my reach, is able to lay hold on this blessed promise through the inspiration of the Holy Spirit, which breaks through the command and annuls its judgment and curse upon me (Romans 7:13).

In brief, it is through the passion (suffering) of Christ on the cross, as I with agony see Him wrapped in my sins and made a curse for me, that I am no longer overwhelmed with my own sins, and look upon them now, not in myself, but in Him. He promises to meet us in the cross in this way, says Luther, and not to trust that promise is to "remain wrapped in our

---

20. Martin Luther, The Small Catechism, Articles 1 and 4, in Philip Schaff, ed., *The Creeds of Christendom*, Volume I, 74-78.

21. Martin Luther, Freedom of a Christian, in John Dillenberger, ed., *Martin Luther*, (New York: Doubleday, 1961), 33.

22. Ibid., 60.

23. Luther's sermon on Mark 7:31-7, the healing of the deaf man. Luther, WA 36:493–95, cited in Oswald Bayer, *Martin Luther's Theology; A Contemporary Interpretation* (Grand Rapides, Eerdmanns, 2008), 106.

sins," is to take Christ completely away . . . and "to make him utterly unprofitable to me."[24]

It is on this foundation that Luther developed the two propositions defining the identity of the Christian: (1) a Christian is a perfectly free lord over all, subject to none, and (2) a Christian is a perfectly dutiful servant of all, subject to all.

Based on the love exchange between Christ and the sinner on the cross, the first proposition is validated; based on his concept of the "overflow of faith into love of neighbor" (quellende Liebe), the second proposition is validated: the purpose of Christ's redemptive passion on the cross is not validated until we who are in Christ by faith are so caught up by a love beyond ourselves that is overflowing toward our neighbor without measure...then the goal of our redemption is realized in faith active in love.

This was the line of preaching under which the Silesian orphans had been reared, which was straight from Luther, as filtered through his catechism. They were reciting the catechism from memory, and the incredible strength from confessing this "love exchange" and receiving its blessing is what buoyed their spirits as they entered into a season of protracted intercession and prophecy for the whole church, and theirs in particular. In their faithfulness to Christ they entered into His favor, and their earnest prayer for release from their bondage was, in their souls, a prayer answered when, after eight months of perilous and persistent prayer, a friendly army of Swedish Protestants broke through into Silesia and made a safe zone for them and their surviving family members to find peace and freedom to worship, under a treaty signed by the warring parties which also included the personal intervention of the great Pietist leader from Halle, August Hermann Francke.

With extensive resources from his Pietist base in Halle, Francke forged an agreement with the combatants that a ring of Jesus churches could now be built to accommodate the thousands of Silesian refugees to this conflict, as well as those from neighboring nations. He then provided manpower and materials to construct a huge edifice at Teschen to seat 6000 refugees in worship, which ended up as an overflow congregation of an estimated 70,000 members.[25]

1.6 The Crisis of Faith Provoked by the Revival: The

---

24. Luther, Lectures on Galatians, in Dillenberger, 135, 137.

25. This was according to the records of Steinmetz, as cited in Ward, *Protestant Evangelical Awakening*, 73.

Struggle for the Completion of the Reformation, Encompassing Polarized Tensions in Protestantism

When we encounter the tragedies which befell the generations of Protestants who followed in the wake of Luther and his co-reformers, we are struck with the magnitude of the vision he had for what might occur through the recovery of the Bible and his living proclamation to "let God be God" in the midst of an idolatrous generation. It was a generation in which humanity was downtrodden by corrupted powers functioning in the name but not the power of authentic religion. His breakthrough in declaring afresh the Pauline theme of a theology of the cross had the potential of remaking the structure of church and society as then constituted. However, the momentum slowed and was diverted along the lines of entrenched economic and political interests which prevailed over the potential for a full reformation of Christendom in his day.

The light seemed to grow only more dim during the seventeenth century, with the outbreak of the Thirty Years War and its aftermath, whereby the contrast between an authentic Christianity and a demoralized and virtually shattered Christendom seemed to become increasingly apparent. In the latter half of that century, after the tenuous Peace of Westphalia (1648) unsuccessfully attempted vainly to reset the pattern of "cuius regio" for administering church and society within an unstable corpus Christianum, we enter a period when genuine expressions of religious vitality shifted from organized Christendom to undercurrents of mystical spirituality which mostly, and covertly, nurtured souls seeking direction for life. Recent research has documented that the fifteenth century saw the emergence of a plethora of mystical literature, without precedent in Christian history, which primarily nurtured a despondent laity, in an age of clerical corruption and lack of spiritual focus.[26]

It is not uncommon to find within history those times when great vision is revealed, holding redemptive potential for the future of humanity, which are nevertheless followed by darkness and despair. The shadow that hovers seems more forbidding than the status quo which preceded the vision. Such a season may also be a time for hopeful waiting, with attentiveness until a generation arises who aspire to live in accordance with the visiothat was given. This was the pattern evident in God's dealings with

Abraham after his arrival in Canaan with the covenant promise, when he

---

26. W.R. Ward, *Early Evangelicalism*, 13–15.

Abraham after his arrival in Canaan with the covenant promise, when he says to God "Behold, you have left me no offspring, and a slave born in my house will be my heir."[27] In such times, the driving issue for a civilization is to know that the promises of God are trustworthy. In this post Reformation era there was the draw of a new wave of intense mystical writers who appeared after the demise of the period of hope engendered by the great Reformers.

The era of *Protestant Orthodoxy*, between the mid-sixteenth to the latter seventeenth century witnessed the rise of the entrenched religious systems built on the policy of "cuius regio, eiuius religio" ("whose region, his religion"). This version of "orthodoxy", not to be confused with either apostolic Christianity or Eastern Orthodoxy, was accompanied by a growing intellectualizing of the faith of the Reformers. The driving center for the Protestant tradition shifted from the parish and the pulpit to the academy and the doctrinal systems now designed to shift the center of the Reformation proclamation of a living God from praxis to a human fashioned theory. It was an attempt to communicate the faith of the Reformers through an intellectual assent to truth in place of awakening faith through the living proclamation of the Word of God with the witness of the Holy Spirit.[28] In that arrangement, the consensus of the church as the communio sanctorum (communion of saints), and in coordination with benevolent civil authority, such as the princes in Germany or the town council in the Swiss cantons, would provide the modus operandi for the reformation of Christendom to occur. The era of Protestant Orthodoxy was a shift from a God-centered to an academia-centered delivery system of the Reformation faith.

However, the era of Orthodoxy, from ca 1550 to 1650, was becoming a time of yearning for spiritual renewal among the laity, a push back against the fashionable style of reverting to writing and delivering homilies in Latin to dispirited congregations and to the polemical defense of confessional orthodoxy as the highest priority, rather than attending to the praxis of faith by the laity. It was also the era when the growing interest in reading late medieval mystical theology, the legacy of the "devotio moderna,"[29]

---

27. Genesis 15: 3.
28. This shift became apparent in Melanchthon's Loci Communes of 1521 (Luther's successor at Wittenberg), from an exclusive emphasis upon *fiducia* (trust) to *assensus* (assent to doctrinal truth) as the locus of faith, a pattern which Scharlemann has called the dual approach to knowledge, in Protestant Orthodoxy. See Robert Scharlemann, *Thomas Aquinas and John Gerhard* (New Haven: Yale, 1964, chapter one).
29. These writers included Tauler, Ruysbroek, Suso and others.

became apparent. This literature awakened yearning for a personal access to God, accompanied by personal spiritual reflection and by a speculative attempt to find God in cosmology informed by the recovery of the Bible.

The standard account of the events had previously been the Lutheran Orthodox report of Caspar Neumann,[30] who attempted to delegitimize the authenticity of the revival. Swensson was the first contemporary interpreter to opt for its authenticity, as against those who regarded it as copying the prayer exercises of the Swedish troops,[31] viewing it as the outcome of the children's disciplined habits of prayer. Such prayer meetings were common among the Silesian Protestants after being uprooted from their homes and parishes due to the war.[32] However, the typical meetings consisted of adults in much smaller groups.

In minimizing the significance of the children's revival, Neumann was likely motivated by the coercion from the Hapsburg overlords who had closed most of the Silesian parishes and removed their clergy, and who could likely complete their elimination of Protestants to the extent that had been done in neighboring Bohemia or Moravia.[33] With the closing of Protestant schools many children were forced to attend Catholic schools, families were required to attend Mass, and the Luther Bible was banned.[34]

In some localities families with children were forced to reconvert to Catholicism or their belongings would be seized.[35] As director of the Lutheran parishes in Breslau (Silesia), Naumann was imposing his Lutheran Orthodoxy upon a nation which, while embracing the Protestant Reformation, had asserted an independent spirit, with openness to renewal and especially to a mystical spirituality that harkened back to their indigenous reformer, Caspar Schwenkfeld, who still had his supporters in Silesia.[36]

The rise of evangelical Pietism in the seventeenth century, the major expres-

---

30. Caspar Neumann, *Unvorgreifliches Gutachten* (Breslau, 1708).

31. Even Ward takes this view, although he otherwise affirms its authenticity. See Ward, *Christianity under the Ancien Regime*, 1648–1789 (Cambridge, 1999), 94-95.

32. Herbert Patzelt, *Geschichte der Evangelischen Kirche in Österreichisch-Schlesien* (Dülmen: Laumann-Verlag, 1989, chapter one, note 42, cited in Swensson, xxv).

33. Swensson reports 1200 churches were closed, xxv.

34. In some localities families were forced for reconvert to Catholicism lest their belongings be seized. Swensson, 14–15.

35. Ibid., 15

36. The spiritual ethos in Silesia has been called a "Melanchthonian" (meaning irenic) Lutheranism.—Schott, "Der Pietismus in Schlesien," Meyer, Schott, and Schwarz, *Über Schlesien Hinaus: Zur Kirchengeschichte in Mitteleuropa, Festgabe für Herbert Patzelt zum 80. Geburtstag*, 129.

sion of the renewal of spirituality in post Reformation Protestantism, occurred under the influence of this surge of mystical literature upon its luminaries, Johann Arndt, the herald of Pietism with his *True Christianity* and Philip Jacob Spener, with his program for renewal based on the collegia pietatis, in the *Pia Desideria*.[37] They were able to restrain their immersion in mystical literature as sources of personal and ecclesial renewal by their steadfast commitment to pastoral ministry within the official church structures of Christendom, namely the Lutheran state churches in the Holy Roman Empire of the German Nation. There were also those whose personal investment made them willing to put that interest ahead of retaining loyalty to official church structures. This conflict of interest resulted in a schism within the membership of Spener's Frankfurt conventicle, which may be viewed as a point of origin for a sub movement within the Pietist movement known as the German radical Pietists, now spinning off from the Pietist movement of renewal within the parishes of European Protestantism.[38]

When the first revival in Protestantism occurred in Silesia in 1707, viewed as a breakthrough of God amid turmoil from warfare, its first interpreters included both radical and church Pietists. The reading of that event as such a breakthrough occurrence was found in both of these interpreters. However, these two types of Pietism represent distinctly different ways of understanding the meaning and significance of that revival for the future of Christianity. From the standpoint of this study, both interpretations were pointing the way toward a post Christendom view of Christianity, which would have a global rather than a distinctly European frame of reference. However, the position of each had distinctively different implications for how a genuine globalization of the faith would occur.

Being church renewalists, Pietists such as Spener, Francke, and Freylinghuysen, Francke's heir apparent at Halle, looked for renewal to occur within the established structures of state church parishes and its liturgy. Their hope was that the long range result of shoring up preaching, catechesis, as well as worship and sacraments, and even extending church

---

37. And also through pastors in the Reformed tradition, particularly Labadie, Untereyck and Lampe. See F. Ernest Stoeffler, *The Rise of Evangelical Pietism* (Amsterdam: Brill, 1966) and *German Pietism in the Eighteenth Century* (Amsterdam: Brill, 1973).

38. The major study here is Hans Schneider, *German Radical Pietism*, Tr. Gerald McDonald, (Metuchen, New Jersey: Scarecrow, 2007).

mission abroad would usher in an era of greater times for the church on earth, now reconstituted and cleansed of its corruptions infested during the struggles based in the politics of Protestant Orthodoxy. However, the radicals cut themselves free from official ecclesial restraints to envision an imminent apocalyptic crisis including Christ's return in judgment and in restoration of his kingdom on earth. This outlook has been categorized as an ascent of millennialism, especially with reference to the heightened interest in the immediate recovery of the Philadelphia community of brotherly love (Revelation 3) as espoused by Jane Leade and the Philadelphians. His visions would find their major expression in the Philadelphian communities formed high among German radical Pietists in the early eighteenth century.

The Pietist quest—both church and radical—for a fresh encounter with God had dimensions of depth as well as breadth. Depth in the God encounter would find expression in a breadth of vision for the global extension of the evangelical Protestant faith. This quest was pursued through a season of intellectual grounding for a newly found urgency to pursue an evangelical Protestant vision of a global mission for Christianity. Its motivation would not be human initiative but rather a participation in God's redemptive plan for the new humanity, redeemed in Christ (the missio Dei). One sign of this new dimension of embodiment of the Body of Christ was the recovery of the apostolic proclamation of Pentecost.[39]

Each of the three perspectives on the children's revival, Protestant Orthodoxy, the Catholics, and the Pietists, brought their sociocultural as well as theological concerns to bear upon their interpretation of the event. For example, in minimizing the significance of the children's revival, Neumann, representing the position of Protestant Orthodoxy, was likely motivated by the coercion from the Hapsburg overlords who had closed most of the Silesian parishes and removed their clergy, and who could likely complete their elimination of Protestants to the extent that had been done in neighboring Bohemia or Moravia. With the closing of Protestant schools many children were forced to attend Catholic schools, families were required to attend Mass, and the Luther Bible was banned. In some localities families with children were forced to reconvert to Catholicism or their belongings would be seized. As director of the Lutheran parishes in Breslau (Silesia), Neumann was imposing his Lutheran Orthodoxy upon a nation which, while embracing the Protestant Reformation, had asserted

---

39. See Peter's sermon on that occasion, Acts 2:14–36.

an independent spirit, with openness to renewal and especially to a mystical spirituality that harkened back to their indigenous reformer, Caspar Schwenkfeld, who still had his supporters in Silesia.[40]

The children's revival also appeared amid the background of a Pietist ethos which had spilled over into quasi revivalism, as evident from their bush preaching and worship not unlike that of the "barn burners" among the German immigrants in colonial Pennsylvania, featuring protracted repentance under fervent preaching, replete with prophetic and apocalyptic preaching. This was a feature in progress among Pietists in Silesia almost two generations before the rise of Methodism in England.[41] A leading pastor in this genre was the Lutheran Johann Christian Schwedler, who later became a catalyst for the great revival in Silesia, attracting many Schwenkfelders to his preaching, and whose hymn, "Ask ye what great thing I know" (1741) is still found in the United Methodist hymnal.[42] In short, in that era of the Counter-Reformation, the shift was from parish based ministry to small group and family based worship.

The director of the many faceted Halle University project for personal and social renewal, the Lutheran-trained Pietist theologian, August Hermann Francke (d. 1727), opened the door to globalization beyond European Christendom with his multifold program of outreach based upon a vision of universal regeneration of humanity, which is to be distinguished from the doctrine of universal restoration of all things found in the more radical Pietist voices of the Petersens. Francke's focus was on world change, without limits, to bring the gospel to all humans in all cultures. This is distinct from the hope for better times for the church which was articulated exclusively within the Christendom model by the de facto founder of Lutheran Pietism, Philip Jacob Spener, who had shifted the focus in Lutheranism from Luther's justification by faith to regeneration (the new birth) and renewal (the equivalence of sanctification for

---

40. The spiritual ethos in Silesia has been called a "Melanchthonian" (meaning irenic) Lutheranism.—Schott, "Der Pietismus in Schlesien," Meyer, Schott, and Schwarz, *ÜberSchlesien Hinaus: Zur Kirchengeschichte in Mitteleuropa, Festgabe für Herbert Patzelt zum 80. Geburtstag*, 129.

41. Some of these (barn preachers) were also known as the "Inspired" *(die Inspiriirten)*, the name of a prominent movement of radical Pietists in the Rhineland more than a generation later (the 1730s).

42. Johann C. Schwedler (1741), "Ask ye what great thing I know," in *United Methodist Hymnal* (Nashville: United Methodist Publishing House, 1989), 163; see also, Horst Weigelt, The Schwenkfelders in Silesia (tr. Peter Erb), (Pennsbrg, Pa: The Schwenkfelder Library), 132, cited in Swensson, 13.

Wesleyans). Much of Francke's outreach was enabled by the extraordinary network of converted lay persons at all levels of society. He relied heavily on his connections with pious Silesian nobles who supported the Halle ministries, which included his orphan house, coeducational schools, publishing house and Bible institute as well as the university with its theological faculty.

Francke replicated the Halle campus at various sites in Silesia, making it a strategic center for his global reform plan.[43] Three of his nobles who formed his inner circle in Silesia were Halle graduates. Francke also served on the council which drew up the peace resolutions of the Altranstrādter Convention, enabling freedom of worship within a war free zone where refugees could settle. There was a string of refugee churches established along that line, with the center being the city of Teschen. Francke provided funds for the building of the emergency churches along that line, called the Grace churches. In Silesia Francke arranged a "secret council" of these nobles who included a well-placed purchasing agent and missionary to Breslau who had political connections in Prussia (Berlin) and with Tzar Peter II of Russia, and was responsible for supplying a secret warehouse of Bibles and tracts to Protestants in Hungary, on behalf of the Halle world mission.[44]

The contemporary observers of the children's revival, in the accounts found in Swensson's study, provide essential data for the course of the revival and how it developed over time. Johann Anastasius Frelinghuysen, Francke's designated successor and a Pietist editor of an influential Lutheran hymnal discerned that the revival at its inception was a work of God, a "spiritual breakthrough wrought of God."[45] A concise version of the data from those observers is supplied here, to provide context for our study of their role in the inception of a globalized view of evangelical Christianity in the modern era.

Intercessory prayers from pastors serving in the remaining Protestant principalities had been raised for three years before the event began, "not without the greatest disgrace and persecution."[46] Another pastor's interces-

---

43. Johannes Wallmann, *Der Pietismus* (Vandenhoeck und Ruprecht, 2005). 1-3f cited in Swensson, 16.

44. Swensson, 17.

45. Schott, *Pietismus in Schlesien*, 139.

46. Pastor Friedrich Opfergelt to A.H. Francke, 7 February, 1704, in Witschke, "Urkunden zur Geschichte des Pietismus in Schlesien," *Jahrbuch des Vereins für Schlesische Kirchengeschichte*, 79–81. (tr by Swensson, 23).

sion featured lament: "Our Lord and Father, I am wounded . . . I am dust and ashes . . . be not angry with me that I still speak more . . . .You know that we . . . with many thousands . . . still request our places."[47] The children, having memorized their Small Catechism from Luther, garnered strength in claiming their baptism, whereby "the new man shall come forth daily and rise up, cleansed and righteous, to live forever in God's presence."[48]

For those who thought the children were imitating the praying Swedish soldiers, it should be noted that those forces represented a grand army of uniformed troops, singing psalms and hymns from the Lutheran hymnal in morning and evening prayer, with great pomp and circumstance. By contrast, the children had learned to pray in the rustic camp worship of the refugee communities in Silesia.

The children's prayers were for God's mercy upon them, for revival, and for them to become God's messengers.[49] Significant for the importance of children being the focus is one note on the revival appearing in the *Grundliche Nachrichten* saying that it began on the liturgical day called Holy Innocents' Day, the day Herod ordered the children to be killed in order to kill the Messiah.[50]

The records on the revival indicate that the children began in the mountains and the revival swept over five principalities in five days.[51] When their gatherings were not tolerated in their towns the children quietly left for the fields where they continued to pray. They sang, read scripture and fell on their knees in prayer, but all in orderly fashion. Soon their trek grew in many places to three to four thousand people. Bystanders watched reverently, with tears in their eyes. They could be heard singing a quarter mile away. Their pattern was often to sing seven hymns at a time, with each hymn interspersed with prayer. They also read prayers from Johann Arndt's *Paradies Gärtlein*. They were heard to pray for God to give back to them their churches. It was not fiery preaching but quiet worship. Some reports conveyed supernatural wonders, like their prayer books turning into incandescent light and doves flying around them within reach. A greater wonder was how mischievous children could pray on and on with such reverence.[52]

47. Printed in *Grundliche Nachrichten*, 7. (tr. By Swensson, 24).
48. Martin Luther, "The Small Catechism," in *The Book of Concord: The Confessions of the Evangelical Lutheran Church*, 349.
49. Swensson, 33.
50. Neumann, *Grundliche Nachrichten*, cited in Swensson, 31-32.
51. Swensson, xxii.
52. This is a summary of observations from the Grundliche Nachrichten, tr. By Swensson, 33–36.

With reference to the reactions to the children, even the Lutheran Orthodox church inspector Caspar Neumann conceded it was from God,[53] although, as an Enlightenment thinker, he had no interest in acknowledging it to be a supernatural event. Several of the Protestant clergy opposed the event, often from fear that it would incite further oppression against Protestants by the forces of the Counter-Reformation. Hence, Neumann ordered that the prayers be continued only inside the churches. The revival continued over eight months, with the largest phase of it being after Christmas 1707.

Freylinghuysen, the Lutheran Pietist interpreter, also colleague of Francke's, critiqued Neumann's report as not being sincere in supporting the children, and Frelinghuysen went further to say the prayers were functioning to awaken people to the "supernatural battle of good and evil."[54] Further, it was Frelinghuysen who went so far as to liken the Kinderbeten to Pentecost, seeing it as a sign of the coming fulfillment of the ages: "the work itself is a great sign and wonder of our time."[55]

From this perspective we may discern historical context for the revival is the movement of German Pietism, which gained traction in the Lutheran and Reformed sectors of European Protestantism in the late seventeenth century. The renewal initially sought by Spener in his Frankfurt parish ministry, which was cut short with the disbanding of his conventicles, would make its unexpected and deepest manifestation in the Silesian revival launched by praying and prophesying child orphan. During this era, a move toward globalization among the Halle Pietists under the leadership of Francke was the Danish/Halle project to launch a Pietist-based mission to India in the first two decades of the eighteenth century, which bore significant fruit. A parallel Pietist renewal was also occurring in the Reformed provinces of the German Wetterau district which was concurrent with that of Spener among the Lutherans.

As for the Pentecost connection, this was the unanimous reading of the events of the Kinderbeten from the Pietist responses, and it varied according to the versions of the church Pietists, like Frelinghuysen, and the radical Pietists, like the Petersens. When we come to Steinmetz, who arrived in Silesia in 1715,[56] the theme of Pentecost is again appropriated, although this time it will

---

53. Neumann was also a known student of science and philosophy, whose writings were commended by Leibniz. Ward, *Protestant Evangelical Awakening*, 68-69.

54. Swensson, 55.

55. Frelinghuysen, Johann Anastasius, *Verschiedenen Prüfungen*, (N.B., printed May 1, 1708, anonymously, author and publishing house undisclosed, Swensson, 52 (my translation).

56. In 1715 Steinmetz at 26 moved from his phase as a student in the Saxon University of Leipzig, where he attained a personal appropriation of justifying grace and was confirmed in his call to ministry in his native Silesia by accepting a pastoral appointment in the village of Molwitz. He would then be called as pastor in Töppliwoda, and from there, to Teschen (1719), a major

function as a personal Pentecost to be sought by every sinner confronted with the gospel in the context of revival, also in the context of the sealing with the Holy Spirit, for the assurance of the forgiveness of sins and blessedness in salvation (sanctification).[57]

The Catholics latched onto the reports of the revival as supporting their suspicion that Lutherans were thereby violating the terms of the Treaty of Westphalia by holding conventicles, and so found ground to press for their final elimination from Silesia.

The Pietists saw the revival as part of salvation history, as a process of continuous divine intervention, following the federal (or covenantal) understanding of that term.[58] They reflected Spener's outlook of hoping for better times for the church, as distinct from Lutheran Orthodoxy, which continued Luther's imminent apocalyptic interpretation of the end time. In his *Prüfung*, Frelinghuysen as Pietist took issue with Neumann's mixed review of the revival, suggesting the revival should just "run its course" until things returned to normal. However, by identifying the revival as a regenerative work of the Holy Spirit and also a renewal of the apostolic theme of Pentecost, Frelinghuysen viewed it as a "great sign and wonder of our time."[59]

As a radical Pietist, Petersen took the most supportive view of the revival, declaring that although, as we shall discover, his estimation of the "wonder" of the event is undermined by his beliefs concerning what was to be its ultimate outcome in the history of salvation. He likened the prayer of these children to a "holy fire", using the language of Pentecost, and saying that:

> If the prayer of all the saints were like that of the children in Silesia, and if many congregations would begin to come together under the open sky, there would be a good in-breaking . . . . The prayers are not about one or the other community; rather . . . the prayers of all the holy ones on earth will be emitted together before the golden altar and the golden censer and coals of holy fire . . . as the prayer kindled by the holy fire and through Christ Jesus proving that his mighty power will not fall without effect upon the earth.[60]

The power of the children is a testimony to the rest of the church on earth that "he that overcomes and keeps my works to the end, to him will I give power over the nations" (Revelation 2:26).[61] This power is reflected in the fact

---

Catholic city in Silesia which also retained the only extant Protestant congregation. Renner, 39-41, and 50.

57. Part 2, First Lesson, Section 6, 36.
58. Part 3, Chapter 2.2.
59. Frelinghuysen, *Prüfung*, 37 (106), Swensson, 64 (my translation).
60. From *Die Macht der Kinder*, 16 .7.
61. Ibid 27.

that, though not without sin, children lead less complicated and more focused lives. They also resemble martyrs in the way they were treated and persecuted.[62] There is a certain globalization theme at work here in the inference that "if everyone would pray like the children prayed, it would break the power of the enemies of God."[63]

---

62. Ibid, section 2.
63. Swensson, 78.

Chapter 2

"These are not drunken as you suppose": The Children's Revival as a Renewal of Pentecost Confronts the Intellectual World of Pre-Revival European Protestantism

On the first Pentecost, after the signs and wonders had appeared to the gathered international assembly of Jews, the initial response was wonder and apprehension. "All were amazed and perplexed, saying to one another, what does this mean? But others mocking said, 'They are filled with new wine'" (Acts 2:12).

The interpreters of the children's revival, with their divergent perspectives on the event, reflected the range of responses given by the Jews gathered at Jerusalem on the first Pentecost. Those who were offended, declaring it to be contrived and frivolous, were the representatives of Protestant Orthodoxy, even resembling those who mocked the assembled disciples with the charge of drunkenness (Acts 2:13b). But those who were sympathetic with what they saw and heard, contended for its authenticity. These were the Pietists. Then there were others among the sympathizers who even linked it to the apostolic miracle of Pentecost.

The Pietist quest—both church and radical—was for a fresh encounter with God, which had dimensions of depth as well as breadth: depth in the God encounter would find expression in a breadth of vision for the global extension of the evangelical Protestant faith. This quest was pursued through a season of intellectual grounding for a newly found urgency to pursue an evangelical Protestant vision of a global mission for Christianity. Its motivation would not be human initiative but rather a participation in God's redemptive plan for the new humanity, redeemed in Christ (the missio Dei). Those who most clearly linked the event of the children's revival with Pentecost came from the ranks of the radical Pietists, and from the writings of two of their representatives, Johann Wilhelm and Johanna Eleonora Petersen, whose engagement with the new intellectual world of the early seventeenth century is a moment for us to grasp in this chapter.

The motives for Johann Wilhelm Petersen's decision to identify with the extraordinary events of the children's revival are discerned within his struggle between two of the most important intellectual worldviews in circulation in the early eighteenth century on the continent of Europe, which has been referred to as the "strife between the mystics and the federalists." Understanding the issues at stake here provides a template for negotiating our way through these rival worldviews then competing for a hearing in early seventeenth century Europe. It was a day when the old structures of Christendom, now in shambles after the disaster that was the Thirty Years War and its legacy, and could not be restored to their prewar stability. Each of these two options offered a distinctive approach to defining and implementing a new social order for the post-Christendom age, at least in eastern Europe, where the old social structures had now disappeared, in the first decade of the eighteenth century. The first interpreters of the events comprising the Silesian children's revival approached their task from the perspectives that came from an engagement with these rival intellectual worldviews of their day, through which they were seeking to find a way forward in interpreting this data and what it meant from a global perspective. These persons and their theological perspectives are introduced in the section that follows.

The differences between these two schools of thought also strike to the heart of what is needed in focusing the issues of the meaning and significance of that revival, also with implications for contemporary Christian globalization. Mystics represent the depth dimension of a Christian spirituality engaged in globalization and federalists denote its breadth dimension. It is significant that the concern for depth in the God-human relationship also spawned a parallel concern for the issues of breadth, of extending that faith community throughout humanity.

In Johannine, and also Pietist, terms, the new birth presented to Nicodemus by Jesus (John 3) was the mark of personal regeneration through the same Holy Spirit who then prevents the early Jesus movement from digging a homeland in Judea, but to go to the uttermost parts of the earth as a people without a mortal homeland. Matthew attests to the latter in the Great Commission passage of Matthew 28, but John offers a similar breadth perspective in Jesus' prayer for His disciples, "I do not pray for these only, but also for those who believe in me through their word, that they may all be one, even as Thou, Father, art in me, and I in Thee, that they may also be in us, so that the world may believe that Thou has sent me" (John 17: 20-21).

In one sense, Petersen favored extending this breadth dimension of the Christian gospel to its ultimate parameters, the universe as a whole, as implicit in his restoration of all things doctrine. And yet, he leaves that option in God's hands to fulfill, by virtue of the purging fires of the last judgment as the avenue for destroying and recreating the human race together with everything else. It is not a call for revival and personal regeneration to be replicated throughout all humankind by human initiative. The children's revival was to him a harbinger of the latter day events which would trigger this scenario of God intervening to effect the Wiederbringung (restoration of all things).

2. 1 The Composition of That World Which Produced Two Ways Forward

The children's revival has been presented as a historical event of consequence. Two possibilities surfaced in the wake of that event, both featuring an appeal to the fulfillment of the apostolic promises of Pentecost. The first option was an announcement from 1708 of Christ's imminent return in judgment and followed by the restoration of all things, signifying an end to history as we know it. The second option held the promise of a global movement of spiritual awakening based upon a two-stage presentation of soteriology to be presented to every creature on earth, appearing as the building of the Kingdom of God on this earth. This chapter concerns the first option, which was heralded with evangelistic zeal by the prominent Lutheran turned radical Pietist couple, the Petersens. The second option was a delayed response, first heralded by in the decade of the 1720s by Johann Adam Steinmetz in his Pentecost sermons preached at the megacenter of the first revival in Protestantism, the Grace Church in Teschen, Silesia.

The extent to which it became the impetus for a wide, even global movement of awakening in large part depended upon how its life-giving power was received and channeled within the network of communication which had then been forged through Pietist influence in state church Lutheranism. This network was the product of that contingent of renewalists within the geopolitical world of a European Christendom reeling from a century of massive religion-induced warfare. The polemical spirit which prevailed had congealed into controversy between two divergent factions: the Orthodox Protestants on the one side and the Pietists on the other. The latter in turn were divided between the church Pietists and those radicals who had given up attaining their goals through the official bodies of Christendom. Note too that the conversation between these disputed parties in Lutheranism was occurring in the midst of a deep vein of mystical literature which was gaining wide appeal in Protestant Europe in the early eighteenth century.

The intellectual grounding for radical Pietism can be located in the body of German mystical theology which antedates the Reformation and as we have noted rose to a remarkable crescendo of influence among rank and file Protestants as well as Catholics in the post-Reformation era (through 1700). This fact calls for some explanation, in view of the usual bias against mysticism. In the century preceding the Reformation, a major avalanche of books was published by Christian mystical authors.[1] The reasons for the wide popularity of this literature can be identified by considering the historical context.

With the steep decline in the fortunes of Rome from the era of the "Great Schism" of the papacy in the fourteenth century Europe, and the decline of scholasticism, many lay persons in the Protestant churches turned to the stream of mystical literature to address the great questions of theodicy in an increasingly resistant culture. In brief, they were despairing of finding pastoral answers to difficult theological questions from Catholic scholastic sources, and so turned to the great well of mystical theology with its roots in medieval Jewish Cabbalism and alchemy. Since the writings of Paracelsus in the sixteenth century, there was unleashed into popular European culture a new paradigm for understanding science and religion in a spiritual harmony which was attested by findings in early modern science.

These writers enabled the literate to own alternate views of theology radically different from the prevailing hierarchical systems of Roman Catholicism as well as Protestant Orthodoxy, being systems which put God at the end of a long syllogism. Aristotelian thinking had become dominant in the age of Protestant Orthodoxy, and similarly among Catholics.[2]

1. See W.R. Ward, *Early Evangelicalism; A Global Intellectual History*, 1670–1789 (Cambridge: University Press, 2006), 24.
2. Ward, 8.

Militating against this trend was a deep thirst for finding personal relationship with God apart from the mediating structures of medieval Catholicism, and, after the Reformation, apart the scholastic filters of Protestant Orthodoxy as well. Literature from Tauler to Kempis resourced that market and became more broadly accessible to a ready public after the advent of movable type in the fifteenth century. The intellectual grounding for radical Pietism can be located in this body of German mystical theology.

The reasons for the wide popularity of this literature can be identified by considering the historical context of its appearance, with the demise of Protestantism in wide swaths of central Europe under the aegis of a resurgent Hapsburg imperial form of Catholicism. This debacle would also prepare the way for the surge of the secularist outlook of the Enlightenment philosophers, and especially the Kantian reduction of religion to a universal categorical imperative, as the epitome of the German Aufklärung.

Here is what is at stake for us in this chapter. There was an important intellectual argument being developed to support the revival which forms the background to the work of Steinmetz and his Pentecost Addresses. It proceeds as follows.

The revival would be built upon the children's spontaneous prayer and intercessory ministry, as biblically grounded in their proclamation of the small catechism's theology of the cross. As the addresses of Steinmetz make clear, when the awakening was extended through Silesia to Teschen, the city where the Catholic authorities had their base, it ignited an even greater awakening in the megachurch of the Protestant refugees there, That, in turn, triggered the conversion of many nominal Protestants, and some Catholics, to a living evangelical Christianity. This awakening also marked the opening of a renewed controversy between the rival wings of the Orthodox and the Pietist interpreters of the Protestant faith, who were then waging a mortal struggle for the soul of Protestantism, as then constituted in the form of European Christendom.

For seventeenth century Protestants, John Arndt's *True Christianity* had a huge reception among that deep vein of people who had become alienated from the faith. Even Spener, the most loyal of orthodox Lutheran Pietists, was, in the words of Ward, "never able to lose touch with such sources of spiritual vitality as the radical underworld possessed or to escape the reproaches of the unyielding orthodox that what Arndt proposed would lead to schism."[3] This literature found its greatest appeal

3. Ward, 8

within Protestantism among the radical Pietists of the German Rhineland provinces. It quickly became the driving force behind the first conventicle Spener introduced within his Frankfurt parish, and so led to the schisms from Protestant Orthodoxy by the sects of the radical Pietists.

The seventeenth century radical Pietists entered without hesitation into the questions posed by the mystical theologians regarding how a saving relationship with God in Christ can be appropriated apart from the ecclesial apparatus of the day. Their quest was aided by the decision to jettison any allegiance to worship in the state churches, whose theologians were ever intensifying their appeals to scholastic dogma as the sum total of the knowledge of God and humans.

However, the radicals' response was itself divided on how best to explain a personal grounding in the salvation wrought by Christ, viewed in intellectual terms. There were those mystics who maintained there were two opposing and penutimately unresolvable realities governing time and space, and then there were those like Petersen, for whom reality was reducible to a single principle.

Johann Wilhelm Petersen intended to draw from federalism as a basis for making sense of events like the children's revival, but he and especially his wife were also deeply influenced by "enthusiasm," a euphemism for those who placed priority upon unmediated, direct inspiration from the Holy Spirit as the basis for faith and praxis.[4] Petersen had previously left the Lutheran Church, when, with his wife Johanna Eleonora Petersen, he was awakened to the rising Pietist movement in the 1670s through contacts with elements of Spener's conventicle in Frankfurt who were moving into what is called "chiliasm", or the belief in an imminent return of Christ to establish His promised millennial kingdom.[5] These more "radical" Pietists crossed the line from Christian orthodoxy to heterodoxy, by the norms of the official Protestant standard of belief, the Augsburg Confession. In their appeal to the direct inspiration of the Holy Spirit the Petersens were influenced by Rosamunde von Asseburg,[6] as a representative of that position.

---

4. This line of thinking had made itself felt in the days of the Protestant Reformation, in revolutionary spiritualists like Thomas Muntzer as well as quietistic or contemplatic mystics like Caspar Schwenkfeld, who broke with Luther by preferring a spiritual mode of communion to the habitual use of the external eucharist.

5. The belief in the imminent return of Christ to establish a millennial kingdom as found in Revelation 20 (chiliasm refers to the Latin spelling for the number 1,000). They gained contact with this thought through Schultz, a member of Spener's conventicle (or collegial fellowship group) who would lead it into schism from Spener's parish due to their radical apocalyptic beliefs which contradicted the osition of the Augsburg Confession of the Lutheran Church.

Petersen, who then was serving as a private tutor for his livelihood, developed his own version of this millennial doctrine by concluding, reputedly through the influence of the Holy Spirit, that not only was Christ coming for a millennial reign on earth, but also, he would complete the fullness of salvation for all humanity by a "universal restoration of all things" ("Wiederbringung aller Dinge"), which is based on the concept of the apokatastaseos panton from the Greek text of Romans 8.[7]

With this decision, Petersen shifted from his belief in the orthodox Christian view of eschatology, which teaches a judgment both to heaven and to hell in the final judgment at the end of history, to a position favoring the universal restoration of all persons and things, as a result of the eschaton.[8] He initially hoped to hold his views on chiliasm in tension with Lutheran beliefs consistent with the position of the Lutheran Augsburg Confession, that is, federal theology prevailed over orthodox Biblicism for him.

2.2 Petersen and the Appeal to Restorationism

In a classic study of the seventeenth century intellectual schools of federalism and mysticism, Nordmann notes that Petersen shifted from his belief in the orthodox Christian view of eschatology, which teaches a judgment both to heaven and to hell in the final judgment at the end of history, to a position favoring the universal restoration of all persons and things, as a result of the eschaton.[9] He initially hoped to hold his views on chiliasm in tension with Lutheran beliefs consistent with the position of the Lutheran Augsburg Confession, but at this point direct inspiration prevailed over orthodox Biblicism for Petersen.

The motives for Petersen's decision are probed in Nordmann's study of Petersen amid the "strife between the mystics and the federalists,"[10] which provides a template for negotiating these rival world views competing for a hearing in early seventeenth century Europe. It was a day when the old structures of Christendom, now in shambles after the disaster that was the

---

6. For a discussion of her, see Douglas Shantz, *An Introduction to German Pietism: Protestant Renewal at the Dawn of Modern Europe* (Baltimore: Johns Hopkins University Press, 2013).

7. See Walter Nordmann, "Im Streit von Mystik und Föderalismus: Geschichtliche Grundlagen der Eschatologie bei idem Pietistischen Ehepaar Petersen, in *Zeitschrift für Kirchengeschichte* (1930), 147.

8. Ibid.

9. Ibid., 147.

10. Ibid.

Thirty Years War and its legacy, and could not be restored to their prewar stability. Each of these two options offered a distinctive approach to defining and implementing a new social order for the post-Christendom age, at least in eastern Europe, where the old social structures had now disappeared, in the first decade of the eighteenth century. Petersen's interpretation of the events comprising the Silesian children's revival approached his task from the perspectives that came from an engagement with these rival intellectual worldviews of their day, through which they were seeking to find a way forward in interpreting this data and what it meant from a global perspective. These persons and their theological perspectives are introduced in the following discussion.

When Johann Wilhelm Petersen first championed his reading of the children's revival as being a Pentecost sign, for him, it was a sign of the gathering of all humanity for the approaching Day of Judgment, which would then result in God's enactment of the restoration of all humanity into His eternal Kingdom. He found himself explaining this resolution of the human drama of redemption (call theodicy) as an argument against a prevalent form of mystical theology, popularly espoused by a German cobbler, Jacob Böhme (1575–1624).

2.3 The Voluntary, Dualistic Mysticism of Jacob Böhme

Böhme resonated with Luther and interpreted his thought along the lines of the "torment of nature," which came from Böhme's experiments in early chemistry, then known as alchemy. Petersen reacted strongly against the dualism implicit in Böhme's theodicy by an appeal to the unified purposes of God for humanity and all creation. From that angle, he found himself espousing his view, appealing to Romans 8:18-25, of a coming universal restoration of all things, in Christ, through the Pentecostal indwelling of the Holy Spirit. From that perspective he was espousing a universal over a dualist interpretation of history.

Nordmann refers to the intellectual position to which Böhme ascribed as a dualistic, voluntaristic form of mysticism,[11] signifying that there are two rival forces at war in the cosmos, which are given the labels of the forces of light and darkness, good and evil. As an alchemist, working from nature as well as grace, Böhme sought to uphold Luther's dialectic of a hidden God of majesty and a revealed God of crucified grace, He based

---

11. Nordmann, "Der Seitenarm der dualistische-voluntaristischen Mystik," 155.

that dualism in the spiritual struggle of two contrasting principles, God's love and His wrath.[12] These two forms of God's action were now being reflected in seven "nature spirits"[13] which lose their original harmony in God once enmeshed within an originally harmoniously created world now under the influence of Lucifer. This signifies a cosmic struggle between love and wrath which are reflected as strife within nature and history.[14]

The dualistic voluntarist type, as represented by Böhme, is reflected in his mystical writings which caught the attention of religious seekers across the Continent and in England during the early decades of the seventeenth century. He was also influenced by Luther's law/gospel dialectic,[15] that humans only relate to God, biblically, through the mediation of the law (God's commands to guide humanity in its fallen condition) and the gospel (God's promises to all located in the substitutionary death of Christ upon the cross).

In paradoxical form, Luther had found that Scripture makes room for God to work through the instrument of the law, sin and death, and even the devil, to reveal His wrath toward unfaithful humans—not out of hatred of what He created but redemptively so that unfaithful humans would be redirected from their own self-sufficient ways to look to God as the sole source of their lives. Further, only on the ground of that self-discovery can a human properly be directed to the promise of Christ, that He alone is the God for us as our sin bearer. The freedom of the gospel comes only after a person accepts for himself that his unfaithful life has been crucified with Christ and he is now strengthened through the love of God who has died for his, to allow that love to now flow through his to the others in his life. Serving them in love is serving Christ Himself.[16] Luther would distinguish here between the alien and proper roles of Christ.[17] So long as we continue in this fallen world we live by the paradox of the cross, which both calls us to death to self and to life for the neighbor.

Böhme was impacted by the inevitability of living within that duality, and he extended its influence to the world of nature as well as Scripture.[18] His investigation of basic chemical properties, as manifest in fire, water,

12. Ward, *Early Evangelicalism*, 22.
13. Ibid.
14. Ibid.
15. See Jaroslav Pelikan, *From Luther to Kierkegaard; A Study in the History of Theology* (St Louis: Concordia, 1950).
16. Luther, "Freedom of a Christian," in Dillenberger, 74.
17. Luther, "Two Kinds of Righteousness" (1519) in Dillenberger, 86-96.
18. Ward, *Early Evangelicalism: A Global Intellectual History, 1670-1789* (Cambridge, 2006), 12 and 17.

and air, led him to discover there the struggle between opposing forces in nature, such as fire vs water, salt vs sweetness, darkness vs light, et al, and went so far as to catalogue trinities of chemical substances which conveyed one or the other of the forces of enmity versus harmony.[19] Hence, the struggle within humanity of unfaith vs faith is paralleled in comparable struggles in nature and in the cosmos, indicating that in all dimensions of reality the theodicy of good and and evil continues unabated throughout the history of humanity, with the final resolution only coming on the other side of history and the cosmos as now constituted.

Although many tracked with Böhme's system as a reflection of the way they encountered life in fallen human history, the inevitable tendency was for those inclined to mysticism to gravitate toward the opposing option, given the deep human desire for an elusive harmony and peace to become realized in this life.[20] Nordmann refers to this as the "dissolving tendencies of mysticism" (die auflösenden Wirkungen der Mystik). This tendency also shifted from a focus on willing to a focus on being, which is also regarded as "pure" mysticism.[21] Hence, the voluntarist view of mysticism has been suppressed under the other variety. Nevertheless, Böhme advances a voluntarist view of the Holy Spirit, which was likely mediated to him from Luther and the Reformation. From this angle, overcoming disorder through God's order via global revival is not a possibility within history.

Obviously, the dualist view could not lead to a hope for global tranquility under the reign of the gospel. For Böhme that would mean that "even Lucifer would someday become an angel",[22] which to him would be absurd. While Petersen was affirming revival through a spiritually monistic frame of reference, Böhme replied that a picture of aesthetic unity through metaphysical monism left him cold.[23] The great juxtaposition which he perceived in all of nature and history is translated at the end of history as a final division, not unity, through which God fulfills judgment. His view is that all development involves struggle between opposing

---

19. Ibid., 22

20. Nordmann, 156.

21. Nordmann observes that all mystics show some degree of both types of mysticism, although one or the other tends to predominate. Nordmann refers to this as the 'dissolving tendencies' of mysticism (die auflösenden Wirkungen der Mystik), 158-59.

22. Heinrich Bornkamm, *Luther und Böhme* (Bonn: 1925, 159), cited in Nordmann, 156.

23. "Die aesthetische Einheitstendenz des mystischen Monismus läst ihn kalt, den grossen Gegensatz, den er überall entdeckt, dessen Problemen er mit blütendem Herzen nachgeht, beträgt er auch aud den Abschluss der Geschichte." Nordmann, 157.

forces. The particularities of this development remain obscure in his thinking, since he wants to avoid reducing this struggle to some conceptual meaning.[24] It is enduring to the end without understanding the struggle that counts. In the end, many of Böhme's disciples migrated over to monistic mysticism, finding unity more satisfying than division as the outcome of history.[25]

Petersen arrived at his interpretation of the children's revival as a result of his growing disillusionment with the conflict between these two opposing schools of Christian mystical theology distinctive to his day.[26] The one places emphasis on the will to track with a supernatural order of reality consisting of two opposing forces contending for dominance, while the other prefers to envision a unified worldview, akin to Neo-Platonism as discerned through a Spirit-guided process of supernatural cognition. In brief, to be aware of the world, in early seventeenth century religious thought, meant seeing it through one of these two prisms—that is, if one were intent on discovering the God of the universe apart from the standard Aristotelian scholasticism accepted by the official Catholic and Orthodox Protestant systems, then under much duress, and which gave definition to Christendom as then constituted. How one resolved these issues determined what was the actual shape of "world" to which the Christian gospel is directed, in that era when the global dimension of revival first gained its traction. This is to say, the theology of salvation history and community, which is the prime emphasis of monistic mysticism, are thereby immediately revealed in an act of restoration.[27] However, such optimism is denied in Luther and Böhme.

Like Luther, Böhme made use of the dreaded human condition which Luther had called Anfechtung.[28] He was not satisfied with a monistic designation for evil in the sense of Neo-Platonism, which defines evil as the privation of ultimate being. Instead of doubling back into metaphysics, he sees evil as a real, active force, incapable of being ordered by a moral assessment approach to the meaning of evil. This means that Böhme has to assign some level of reality to evil as well.[29] Dualism controls his understanding of salvation history.[30] In his view, human life in history is an

24. Ibid., 158.
25. Ibid., 159.
26. Ibid., 148–163.
27. Nordmann, 158–159.
28. See Paul Althaus, *The Theology of Martin Luther* (Philadelphia: Fortress, 1966), 33–34.
29. Nordmann, 156-7; for comparison with Luther, see Bayer, *Martin Luther's Theology*, 96-213

uncommunal, not a communal, existence, with ultimate stability coming only on the other side of divine judgment. History advances amid duality which tracks with the way life really seems to be, and visions of metaphysical monism seem annoyingly artificial to him. History might better be described as the great juxtaposition.[31] This kind of mystical discernment occurs not with glibness nor joy, but with pathos.

For Böhme, God fulfills His final judgment through division, not unity.[32] Hence, he does not attempt any conceptual resolution of the struggle inherent in this dualism. The particularities of this eschatology are less important because Böhme is cautious in trying to impose conceptual meaning upon this struggle. He does not join blessedness to the knowledge of Christianity nor to one's relationship to Christian faith. Even heathen Jews and Greeks can be blessed even if they have not come to know Christ in the flesh, if only they would stand steadfast in the second principle, light, and have earnestly sought after God.[33]

Parenthetically, it might be noted that Böhme affirmed a modified deism.[34] After the millennium, the earth will be destroyed by a fire from within. In the final judgment, a separation occurs, and from then there is only light and darkness. The blessed then become the androgynous ones (a reference to a new humanity which replaces sexual distinctions), living under the scepter of Christ, and a perfect harmony between spirit and nature reigns at last. However, the force of evil remains forever excluded from the transfiguration of nature. With this view, the restoration of all things doctrine (Wiederbringung aller Dinge) is not what comes into focus for Böhme.[35]

2.4 The Appeal of Federalism

In his disdain for the irresolution and dualistic struggle in Böhme, Petersen opted for a linear view of salvation history leading to a unitary outcome at its terminal point.[36] He wanted to view the renewal of Pentecost, as represented in the children's revival, as the identity of that

30. Ibid.
31. Im Gericht vollzieht.""Nicht eine letzte Einheit schliesst sie ab, sondern eine letzte, absolute Scheidung, die Gott in Gericht vollzieht." Bornkamm, 295, in Nordmann, 157.
32. Nordmann, 155-156
33. Ibid.
34. Ibid. 158.
35. Böhme goes so far as to say that "even heathen Jews and Greeks can be blessed if they have not come to know Christ in the flesh, if only they would stand steadfast in the second principle, light, and have earnestly sought after God." Nordmann, 157.
36. Nordmann, 16.

telos. He reflected the position of a former Lutheran theologian who remained intent on earnestly tracking key events in the mundane world of daily life from the standpoint of the struggles of his age. He was interested in tracing the course of salvation within world history throughout time and space, to discern the majesty of the God of the universe at work as creator and redeemer of the universe.

His reading of Johann Reitz's *History of the Reborn*[37] sparked his interest in the federalist school of thought then developing in Holland and the German Rhineland. It was based on the thought of the Dutch Reformed theologian Johannes Cocceius (d. 1603–1669).[38] With him the foundation is provided for a new theological school based in the study of "salvation history," to which Petersen indirectly appealed as an intellectual basis for making sense of events like the children's revival.[39] Cocceius's influence served to counter the pervasive influence of Aristotelian scholasticism in the universities of the day, Catholic and Protestant alike. Recall that this was the era of Protestant Orthodoxy, which was focused on defending Protestant confessions against the resurgent Catholicism advanced by Rome and linked to the powerful Hapsburg Emperors of the Holy Roman Empire, and their Jesuit allies.[40]

For Pietists like Petersen, the breadth dimension of the God/human encounter is expressed in the federal theology of Cocceius. Cocceius contended that theological study should be based in the content of Scripture, in which revelation of divine truth is communicated in covenantal form to humanity. Here foedus (Latin for "covenant") is the focus of theology, alongside regnum, or the emphasis on the rule of God in history. In this view, God's covenant community has the building of the kingdom of God as its goal. Cocceius was opting for a historical rather than an ontological approach to theology, which gave rise to the important emphasis on "salvation history" in biblical and theological studies. Federalism came to be understood as the vehicle intending to connecting one's witness for Christ with the larger world. It was also regarded as the "actual domain of eschatology."[41] In mystical writers of a speculative nature, like Böhme and his

---

37. Johann Heirich Reitz, *Historie der Wiedergebohrenen...* 5th ed., (Berleburg, 1724), cited in Ward, *Early Evangelicalism*, 58.

38. Johannes Cocceius, *Opera omnia* (Amstelod, 1701–1706), 12 Bände.

39. Reflecting Irenaeus, Cocceius relied on the typological experience of Christ as the second Adam. Nordmann, 164.

40. The deeper meaning of the federalist school and its implications for the history of Christianity is found in Gottlob Schrenk, *Gottesreich und Bund im Äkteren Protsetantismus vornehmlich bei Johannes Cocceius* (Giessen: Brunnen Verlag, 1985).

41. Nordmann, 164.

successors, eschatology only appears as a universal expression of the breadth of God's redemptive purpose, rather than opting for a historical and geographical destiny in this world.[42]

Cocceius also appeals to patristic and medieval theologians to ground his interpretation of salvation history. Reminiscent of Irenaeus, the second century opponent of Gnosticism, Cocceius makes use of typology as his method of interpreting Scripture to explain the difference between the historical dispensations of Adam and Christ, in the divine economy of salvation history.[43] Cocceius' stages of redemptive history were articulated within the framework of this salvation history, which also represented a shift away from any dependence upon philosophy (i.e, Aristotle) to establish its meaning. His system represented "an attempt to develop a comprehensive view of redemption based on a biblical foundation" of God's self-revelation.[44] The extension of the covenant of the Kingdom of Christ to become "a light to the Gentiles," to use Simeon's imagery, constitutes the concern for breadth which lays claim to the planet earth as the true scope of the redemption wrought by Christ on Calvary's hill. To view this comprehensive event as "salvation history" is synonymous with viewing the Bible as a great "symphony", or an edifice of flawless symmetry.[45]

The possibility of tracking the spread of revival by observing how the Spirit of God works through one people group after another in reaching the ends of the earth for Christ was given a historical grounding in Cocceius' "salvation history" (heilsgeschichtlich) method of tracing the unfolding of God's covenant of grace through time and space, resulting in extending of the kingdom of God on earth. According to Cocceius the kingdom of grace, originating in the Old Testament, is developed in the New Testament through a rhythmic series of events consisting of seven periods, indicating how Christ has extended His reign to its fulfillment. The first period begins with the ascension to the destruction of the Jewish Kingdom, the third period begins with the Constantinian age, as the era of the millennium (or the apocalypse), extending to the rule of Louis the Bavarian, which indicates that Cocceius considered that era now completed. The fifth period, representing the Reformation, reflects a degree of liberation from the shackles of medieval serfdom. The sixth period is the era of the Thirty Years War, a judgment of purification over the people of God.

42. Ibid, 165.
43. Nordmann, 165. See Romans 5.
44. Ibid.
45. Ibid.

In the seventh period, the consummation of history occurs, with the sign of the seven trumpets. A general conversion of the population now occurs and to be sure, in the nearer future.[46]

Schrenk observed that, although Cocceius was cautious in interpreting the future, he did not shrink from a calculation of the drastic change that would occur.[47] At the close of the seven periods comes the eschatological event, which forms the Kingdom of Glory. Then Christ transfers the Kingdom to the Father. Cocceius does not give a detailed description of the Kingdom of Glory, and he makes no mention of a restoration of all things.[48]

Petersen's restoration doctrine departs from the historical approach to theology of the federal (covenant) theologians in that the latter focuses soteriology on the events in the gospel narratives. At this point, Petersen substituted his premillennial universal restoration theory to account for how fulfillment would come for the global promise implicit in Pentecost. This was the event which brought the gospel of Christ to "Jews from every nation under heaven" in fulfillment of the promise of Joel, "I will pour out my Spirit upon all flesh (Acts 2:17 and Joel 2:28-32). Petersen's doctrine is more closely related to biblical eschatological thought than is the more speculative approach of mystical theology.

In line with the federalists since Cocceius, Petersen finds here evidence of a stepwise economy of God's revelation in history, based on a typological reading of the biblical text concerning the life of Christ on earth (e.g., the fall was precipitated by a tree, and so its reversal must occur through the instrument of another tree, Calvary's cross).[49] However, Irenaeus did not advocate universal restoration as the outcome of Christ's work of recapitulation of the human race in Adam.

Consequently, Petersen looked further in patristic sources as support for a restoration of all things position. He found favorable evidence in Origen at the point of his appeal to a spiritual reading of the biblical text which would be trans-historical, following Origen's tripartite reading of the biblical text. This reading proceeds from literal to moral to spiritual/allegorical levels of exegesis, corresponding to the levels of body, mind and spirit of which human anthropology is constituted. With Origen, we find

---

46. Ibid., 45-46.
47. C G. Schrenk, *Gottes Reich und Bund im älteren Protestantismus*, (Gutersloh, 1923), **234-5**.
48. Cocceius' treatment of these last age developments is found in his *Praefatio zu den pera des J. Coccejus*, I, 1-48, cited in Schrenk, 231.
49. Irenaeus, *Against Heresies*, in Hugh Kerr, *Readings in Christian Thought*, 27-35.

an underlying Neo Platonic theme concerning the process whereby the multiplicity of the world comes forth as a stream of life flowing back to its source.[50]

Petersen also noted that Cocceius drew from a medieval as well as a patristic source. Irenaeus' developmental view of salvation based on typology was also accelerated in the economic view of the Trinity developed by the thirteenth century Calabrian monk, Joachim of Fiore (1135–1202), and especially his critique of the church as the economy of the Son which will soon be superseded by the economy of the Holy Spirit. Here it is important to note that, for Joachim, this coming age of the Spirit features God's calling of children to embody humanity in the fullness of the imago Dei: "Then He will choose the children in the age of the bearers of the Spirit (Geistesträger),"[51] which, conversely, is also the age of the growing increase of knowledge (wisdom).[52]

There are biblical references Petersen finds which suggest that "small and dumb (unmutig) bearers of the Spirit" will prevail in the coming age of the Spirit, which is the final expression of a global Christianity. These include Jesus' prayer, "I thank Thee Father, Lord of heaven and earth, that Thou hast hidden these things from the wise and understanding and revealed them to babes" (Matthew 11:25), as well as the adoration of Psalm 8:1, "O Lord, our Lord, how majestic is Thy name in all the earth! Thou whose glory above the heavens is chanted by the mouth of babes and infants." Petersen was making this case in the face of what he called "the remarkable Silesian prayer children" from 1707–1708, indicating that he was not speaking in abstract terms but that this actual historical event was a sign of the approaching consummation of history.[53]

The possibility of tracking the spread of revival by observing how the Spirit of God works through one people group after another in reaching the ends of the earth for Christ was given a historical grounding in Cocceius' "salvation history" (heilsgeschichtlich) method of tracing the

---

50. The following sources in Origen, as an early representative of Christian mystical theology, are noted in Nordmann (148-9), as follows: "Mysterium 1.3.7 and Mysterium 2.12.1–5".

51. Walter Nordmann, "Im Widerstreit von Mystik und Föderalismus: Geschichtliche Grundlagen der Eschatologie bei dem pietistischen Ehepaar Petersen," in *Zeitschrift für Kirchengeschichte* (1930), 148.

52. Nordmann (150) notes Petersen's reference to Joachim of Fiore in predicting a coming revival of children to be the harbingers of the great Age of the Spirit which would launch the final third age of history. Petersen also related that event to the children's revival in Silesia in **1707-08**.

53. Sources in Petersen as cited in Nordmann, n.16.

unfolding of God's covenant of grace through time and space, resulting in extending of the kingdom of God on earth. However, while Petersen made use of Cocceius' historical developmental approach to the reading of Scripture, he also objected to Cocceuis' relegation of the millennium to a past age. Cocceius does not give a detailed description of the Kingdom of Glory, and he makes no mention of a restoration of all things.[54]

This promising theological system unfortunately became subject to a change of focus from covenant to contract, which means the biblical narrative of redemption shifted from a covenant, reflecting the mystery of God's grace to a contract fixed by God for making rational choices of commitment without appeal to grace or an encounter with the living God at all. Interpreters of Cocceius have also noted that the development of this "salvation history" theological system, in spite of its shift from philosophy in defining faith, was itself susceptible to becoming submitted to philosophical influence.[55]

When Petersen reached this stage with Cocceius, he found another thinker who served as a bridge between Cocceius and Petersen's quest to find justification for his notion of universal restoration as the ultimate meaning of Pentecost. Pierre Poiret (1646–1719), was a Huguenot turned radical Pietist, who would also prepare a way for Petersen's restoration theme. Poiret had gathered the most comprehensive collection of mystical writings from medieval Catholic as well as Protestant sources, thereby greatly accelerating the growing consumption of mystical literature in seventeenth century Europe.[56] What Poiret provided Petersen was a revised version of Cocceius' plan of salvation history which replaced the biblical theme of covenant with a mystical-spiritualist theme of "Divine Economy" (oikonomia).[57]

This shift inverts Irenaeus' historical use of that term into a series of advancing spiritual realms. His *L'oeconomie Divine* treats this theme from the church fathers to the end of history, a spiritual theodicy of the universal being and activity of God in His encounter with humanity.[58] Poiret organizes world history into seven ages whereby two diverging ways are

---

54. Johann Wilhelm Petersen, *Mysterium Apokatastaseos, order das Geheimnis der Wiederbringung aller Dinge Band* 1, (Berlin, 1700), 2, 96.

55 Cocceius, summarized in Nordmann, 164.

56. Nordmann, 166.

57. Pierre Poiret, "L'oeconomie divine ou Systeme universel et demontre des ourvres et des desseins de Dieu en verles hommes" (Amsterdam, 1687).

58. Ibid. English translation: *The Divine Economy: Or, an Universal System of the Works and Purposes of God Towards Men, Demonstrated* (London: R. Bonwicke), 1713.

posited for the salvation of humanity: one through the inward call and the other through the means of external verbal expression. In the age of Christ's appearance, the primitive community of believers lived by three laws of purity, consisting of "exclusion of the unconverted, of self-desire, and of worldly wisdom."[59] These laws were soon disobediently overthrown, and thereafter theology based on pneumatic revelation was co-opted by worldly philosophy as the main focus. To Poiret, this shift signified that the church in all its historical expressions had devolved into Babylon.[60]

In the final (seventh) age, the outpouring of the Spirit will occur, which follows the unraveling of the "sects" and especially of the "Ordo Eccesiasticus" (Christendom as it then existed).[61] In the seventh period Christ returns in bodily form, launching the millennial reign. Unlike Petersen, Poiret had taught that, following the thousand year reign, the general resurrection occurs, "partly to life and partly to damnation", without a restoration of all things.[62]

What is extraordinary about Poiret's schema of redemption is his attempt to read the biblical narrative based on mystical spiritualism and not salvation history, which had been the norm from Irenaeus to Cocceius, the founder of the federal school of Reformed theology. He deviates from federalism both in method and outcome. Here is how it worked: For Cocceius, the outcome of salvation history is defined by eschatology and its meaning is defined by typological exegesis. For Poiret, there is a threefold distinction of historical, typological, and prophetic senses of the biblical text.[63] In the history of Christian thought, this may be the first instance where mysticism, which is inherently trans-historical, breaks through into eschatology.[64] However, Poiret's reading of the biblical text replaces the central motif of covenant as a historical event of God-human encounter with his concept of the divine economy, in which oikonomia, a term which Irenaeus had used in a historical sense to refute gnostic docetism, now is redefined as a trans-historical concept pointing toward spiritual aeons transcending and directing the outcome of mundane human history.

59. Pierre Poiret, *Mysterium Apokatastaseos,* Band I, 308, cited in Nordmann, 173.
60. Here Poiret reflects the influence of the spiritualist prophetess, Bourignon.
61. Cf Nordmann, 174.
62. Nordmann, 153.
63. Poiret in Nordmann, 154. Nordmann attributes this appeal to eschatology by Poiret to his conformity to the pneumatological theory of return he learned in the mystical theology of Bourignon.
64. Nordmann, 166-168.

Poiret expresses his mystical spiritualism by means of three core Christian themes of creation, fall and redemption, all interpreted through a doctrine of the Holy Spirit reflecting his distinction between an internal and an external reading of the account of salvation history. His description of the biblical narrative appears to be not greatly dissimilar to that of Cocceius. However, Poiret's distinction reflects basic opposition to the Cocceian understanding of what it means to be a Christian.[65] Whereas Cocceius relies on a historical, typological exegesis, reminiscent of Irenaeus, Poiret appeals to a mystical and prophetic approach to biblical exegesis. He deviates from the core of mysticism with his appeal to eschatology, but he does so by reference to an overarching "divine economy" which is given a trans-historical, mystical-spiritualist interpretation.[66] Divine Economy, not covenant, is the central feature of development in salvation history. In addition, the focal point for the divine economy is not the historical narrative of scripture but an "interim period after death, where God cleanses us from sin in the purging fire."[67] The latter view contrasts with the cruciform theology of Cocceius.

The extent of Petersen's dependency on Poiret appears minimal in the sense that he only sparsely cites Poiret's work, but his central focus on the restoration of all things (Wiederbringung aller Dinge) reflects Poiret's mystical-spiritualist tradition of the divine economy issuing in a cataclysmic fire of judgment which would lead not to the annihilation but to the spiritual restoration of humanity and all creation.[68] Poiret's line of thought is also congruent with Petersen's outlook that revival in the church would come through the ministry of children. Petersen's schema has the course of history leading from the "young" age marked by purity to the spiritual return of Christ to restore that primeval age in the post-fallen, "venerable" (meaning senile) age of humanity, which is called the sixth age."[69]

It was from this perspective that Petersen interprets the data of the children's revival as a renewal of Pentecost. It is a sign of the proximity of the return of Christ and the unleashing of the end time redemptive events that embody the coming age of the Holy Spirit when the purging fire will complete the restoration of all humanity. The expectation is not for global

---

65. Ibid., 166–167
66. Ibid., 154f, attributes this use of eschatology in Poiret to the influence from the mystical thought of Bourignon.
67. Poiret, in Nordmann, 155.
68. Nordmann, 168.
69. Nordmann, 175

revival in ongoing historical terms which would fulfill the promise of Pentecost to all nations that is represented by the children's revival.

It was in response to Böhme, with whom he was in correspondence, that Petersen turned toward the restorationist position, which would affirm a monistic cosmology. It would reflect his thought concerning the "restoration of all things." Obviously, the dualist view could not lead to a hope for global tranquility under the reign of the gospel. For Böhme that would mean that "even Lucifer would someday become an angel",[70] which to him would be absurd.

There was also an English figure who played a formative role in Petersen's intent to move from a dualist to a monistic form of mysticism. Jane Leade, who is known as the founder of the Philadelphian movement (from whom the city of Philadelphia, Pennsylvania, would be named) based his thought on an eschatological interpretation of Revelation 3:8-10. "I have loved you because you have kept my word and have not denied my name, and I will keep you from the hour of trial which is coming on the whole world."[71] Also, "He who conquers, I will write on him the name of my God and the city of my God, the New Jerusalem which comes down from God out of heaven" (Revelation 3:12a).

This movement mainly took root among radical Pietists in the Rhineland of Germany,[72] Through this eschatological community, symbolized by the church of Philadelphia in Revelation 3, he envisioned duality being finally overcome by brotherly love in an unpartisan eschatological community living in the love of Jesus. Here, the forces of torment become overcome in a final resolution. Philadelphian societies in Germany and Pennsylvania in the seventeenth century gave expression to such an eschatological community within history, which suggests a realist eschatology and "a prospect for a monistic outcome of the events of this world in a "restoration of all things" (Wiederbringung).[73] He also continued to make use of the imagery of Böhme.[74] It has been claimed that the Petersens

---

70. Heinrich Bornkamm, *Luther und Böhme* (Bonn: 1925, 159), cited in Nordmann, 156-7.

71. Ibid., 69-70.

72. Especially under the leading of Heinrich Horche of Herborn, who produced the Marburg Bible under Philadelphian influence, and Gottfried Arnold, author of the first modern work of church history, which adopts an "unpartisan" view of the church and its history. See Arnold, *Die Unparteiische Kirche und Ketzer Historie.*

73. William Penn invited Philadelphians to his colony (Pennsylvania) after 1685, and the city of Philadelphia bears the name of this group, which settled in nearby Germantown.

74. This includes the language of the heavenly Sophia and the androgynous man who results in her union with a heretofore fragmented post Adamic humanity. See discussion in

adopted their restorationist doctrine from their reading of Leade, in German translation, but others, notably Marcus Matthias, have demonstrated that they never identified with the Philadelphian Societies in Germany.[75] Nordmann notes that there issued from Leade's influence a conceptual line of millennialism, purgatory, and the restoration, which were worked out in greater detail by Petersen, and that this reworking of the data continued into the eighteenth century, with "the Inspirationists with their focus on private revelations."[76] It is significant that, in spite of his strong criticism of the official Church of England of his day, Leade, like Böhme in the Lutheran Church, avoided separation, maintaining a kind of "fellowship" (Gemeinschaft), a leaven in the official church.

Under the guidance of spiritual writers like Poiret and Leade, Petersen has now left behind biblical covenantal thought. He is not interested in the covenantal schemes which distinguish between two kinds of covenants, that of works and that of grace. His focus is not the contrast between the unrighteous and the righteous, but upon an organic development through law. Along those lines, Petersen bypasses true covenantal thinking. It is not a matter of God and humans exchanging relationships, as in Luther's theology of the cross. Instead, he allows one economy to end and another to break out in its place, building on what has been completed, and he does so by appeal to God's general act of final restoration of all things.

In critique of Petersen's view, Nordmann notes that, before this point of consummation, there is nothing of redemptive significance to be noted in his view of history.[77] Petersen's concern for a conclusive resolution of all imperfections in history enables him to slight the details, the false starts and ambiguities of real history writing. This makes Petersen more interested in tracing general lines of development than focusing in depth on each historical era and its empirical detail. In proto-Hegelian fashion, Petersen sees "each historical era is in the light of the other." It seems correct to conclude that his monist outlook puts an end to attempts to find correlation between the acts of God and of humans, which means that questions per-

---

Nordmann, 156–57.

75. Markus Matthias, *Johann Wilhelm und Johanna Eleonora Petersen, Eine Biographie bis zur Amtsenthebung* (Vandenhoeck und Ruprecht, 1992), 187.

76. Nordmann, 160. Petersen also relied on the thought of John Pordage, an editor of Böhme and an important associate of Leade in the British Philadelphians, through whom he developed the details of his three doctrinal themes: Christology, ecclesiology, and eschatology.

77. Nordmann, 174–5.

taining to the judgment and the resurrection of the dead transition into the domain of kingdom thought and cannot be addressed on earth.[78]

Petersen's plan of salvation, the lens through which he read the data of the children's revival, the first revival in Protestantism, represented an attempted amalgamation of themes from the mystical theology of his day with the movement of federalist thought, which was becoming influential in biblical, systematic, and pastoral theology in the early decades of the eighteenth century. His line of interpretation also represented the first major theological exposition of the meaning and implications of revival for the future of Christianity, now viewed from a global, non-Christendom perspective.

Based upon his assessment of this data we may conclude that Petersen was prepared to read the data of the children's revival from the standpoint of the "unfolding of the economy which goes back to the gracious will of God." [79] Here is how he explained this process: "The Restorer has given testimony from His Father to the First Born and then to his kin, that even before the sin either of angels or of men had occurred, there was already a Physician, a Healer of sin that would be there, who could reconcile, mediate, and bring everything to righteousness."[80] Only in that Economy is there the possibility of deliverance for humanity and all creatures, in the one and unrepeatable sacrifice of Christ.[81] In a statement which reflects an elaboration of Luther's theology of the cross, Petersen declares, "everything exists in Christ."[82] Further, Petersen declares Christ "has seen and allows us to see His wisdom preeminently within the ordering of His aeons in His entire royal Kingdom throughout the passage of time and the bringing forth of things in such determined and appointed times."[83] When Christ has fulfilled all the economies for which He was sent, He submitted all things to the Father upon His ascension He submitted all things to the Father, so that God may be all in all."[84]

What is significant about Petersen's treatment of the biblical text "from eternity to eternity", in developing his Wiederbringung theme, is his super-

78. This is the conclusion drawn by Nordmann.
79. Nordmann, 171.
80. Petersen, *Mystereum*, 1. 22.
81. Ibid., 1, 99.
82. Compare this statement with Luther's theology of the cross (See Luther, "Freedom of a Christian," in Dillenberger, 55.)
83. Petersen, *Mysterium*, 1, 99.
84. Petersen, Zeugnis der Wahrheit von der Wiederbringung aller Dinge wieder einen Retrolapsarianern . . . (an undocumented source in the personal possession of Walter Nordmann, 173.

imposing over the biblical themes of sin and redemption an alternative and conflicting methodology of "secret and discovery" or the unfolding of the economies which is for him a stepwise uncovering of godly secrets.[85]

He bases the superiority of this interpretation upon an appeal to immediate inspiration of the Holy Spirit. "A word of my power is higher and reaches further than the other" since it is called a "revelation of the Spirit."[86] His position is based on the claim of growth in understanding that appears in humanity according to the image of God, in this "mature" age, which finds support in the words of Christ, "Since the age was yet young, I am no longer reliant upon it, like one nurtured by children who also cannot comprehend anything beyond a child's level of understanding. However, with those who have come of age it is a far different matter, until they all enter into my mature age and discover for themselves all my treasures of wisdom."[87] Here Petersen has reversed his position of exalting the wisdom of children which occurred in his response to the children's revival, and in his volume, *Die Macht der Kinder* (*The Power of Children*). Now he is saying the closer the last age is approached, the greater will be the discoveries of knowledge.[88]

The flaw in this thinking is that he attributes this rising level of knowledge to his own spiritual insight into the "higher" meaning of the biblical text, based on his theory of divine economies. This contrasts with Friedrich Adolph Lampe, the leading German Reformed Pietist theologian of the early eighteenth century, for whom the rise in godly knowledge in this age is attributed to discoveries in science and in biblical interpretation, but not by appealing to a higher extra-canonical theory like Petersen's *Wiederbringung aller Dinge*.[89]

Petersen's reworking of the schema of the covenants which is basic to Cocceius' federalism consists of redefining covenant as economy.[90] Covenant inherently requires two parties (God and humans), and so maintains the Reformation focus on the exchange in relationship between God and humans based on the mystery of the cross. The abrogation of a

---

85. Nordmann, 174.

86. Johann Wilhelm Petersen, *Von einigen Öffnungen des Geistes durch den Geist der Weissagung von dem bevorstehenden Gerichte, und danach folgenden Reiche des Herren, und endlichen Neumachung aller Dinge* . . . (Marburg, 1715), 275.

87. *Offenbarung*, 317.

88. Ibid., 533, and 276.

89. Fiedrich Adolph Lampe, *Geheimnis des Gnadenbundes* (1727). See discussion of Lampe in O'Malley, *Early German American Evangelicalism; Pietist Sources for Discipleship and Sanctification* (Lanham, MD: Scarecrow, 1995).

90. Following Pierre Poiret, Nordmann, 163-64.

covenant relationship, which was the occasion for human sin, was a real disruption in the divine ordering of history but to Petersen it is relativized and made meaningless in the face of the coming restoration of all things. Economy is solely God's work in reordering his creation. It leaves little room for human volition in soteriology. One economy runs its course in history, followed by another, so the abrogation of God's covenant with humanity, which is so consequential in Cocceius' thought, is now rendered inconsequential, since the outcome is all determined by God.[91] The major distinction within this oikonomia (economy) is between creation and redemption, which included the restoration of all things. The abyss between faith and unfaith, underscored in Luther and the Reformation heritage, has, in Nordmann's interpretation, been replaced by the new focus of "not yet" and "now" (which is also "hope" and "fulfillment."[92] Hints of this interpretation are suggested in the parable of the householder who goes to market to order the affairs of the lazy workers.

Note the striking implications of Petersen's position. If all things are predetermined there is no possibility of new beginnings.[93] By inference, revival itself becomes a meaningless event in terms of effecting the outcome of the global missio Dei. The overall management of historical periods, which he extols as God's acts, there is really nothing more than a cover enabling a deterministic system to unfold. "Nothing hastens the other, but each particular event is rendered ineffective by the succeeding event, as it is revealed.[94] By this outlook, Pentecost is not a gift to be actualized through human faithfulness to a divine mandate, but rather, it is the connecting point in the oikonomia schema between Christ's redemptive work on the cross and the turn toward God's actualizing that event throughout a universal economy effecting the entire human race. What, from Petersen's perspective, is the Christian to do in this world? Rather than participating in a great exchange of sin and grace through the work of Christ and the infilling of the Spirit, Petersen's focus upon the irrevocable divine restoration of all persons (Wiederbringung aller Dinge) conveys the inference that one ought to "strive for the quickest possible attainment of blessedness."[95]

91. Nordmann, 175.
92. Nordmann,178. In this monistic interpretation of the order of salvation, Christ is the "medum" through which occurs the event of God affirming who God is, in creation, redemption and restoration.
93. Nordmann, 170–74.
94. This is a summary of Petersen's position found in his *Das Geheimnis des Erstgebohrenen aller Creatur von Christo Jesu dem Gott-Menschen* (Frankfurt, 1711), 314/5, as cited by Nordmann, 176.

The inevitability of this fortuitous outcome, for a sinful humanity deserving punishment but instead receiving salvation, could have gone in one of two directions. One, Petersen might have sided with the Epicurean answer, eat, drink and be merry, not despite the fact that we die tomorrow, but because our death tomorrow will itself be put to death by the coming restoration of all things. Petersen, however, does not take that option. The other response to this fortuitous outcome would be the one he mercifully did take. He reasons, if the God of this universe is so intent on rescuing the errant human race at all costs, even in spite of their deserving punishment and death, then, our proper response to that abundance of grace would be let it happen and as it does, observe within yourself all the graces of the abundant life which have gratuitously come your way. Here is how Petersen verbalized such a sentiment:

This doctrine[96] incentivizes us to avoid all the lusts of this world, to purify all the blemishes of the flesh, and of the spirit, and to perfect holiness in the fear of the Lord, without which no one will see the Lord, whereby we remain preserved among all the righteous of the first and the second death, and from now on may remain blessed among the holy departed souls.[97]

Whereas Cocceius' attitude was theocentric, Petersen's was anthropocentric. The focus shifts from certainty concerning the saving acts of God in history to a celebration of blessedness that all things will be consummated in Christ, through his key doctrine of universal restoration. Petersen's motive for taking this turn of thought becomes more clear when we consider the background of his world of thought. Nordmann suspects that it may be the result of his inherently Lutheran disdain for the Reformed bias of Cocceius, as found in the emphasis on divine sovereignty and predestination.[98]

By contrast, Petersen's basic commitment to a Lutheran emphasis on the theology of the cross comes with a focus on the universality of God's love in Christ for all who embrace its promise. What underlies this distinction is the split within German mystical theology between a tradition that is speculative from the side of dualism versus that of monism. The idea of a general restoration of all things, reflecting the spiritual superficiality of a concern for merely considering the data of salvation, can only be advanced through the influence of speculative mysticism. Petersen, like

---

95. Petersen, *Mysterium Apokatastaseos*, 1. 3, 25, cited in Nordmann, 179.
96. i.e., the Wiederbringung aller Dinge.
97. Petersen, *Mysterium Apokastateoseos*, 1. 3, 25.
98. Nordmann, 180.

Arnold and others, takes from speculative mysticism its concern for the comprehensive totality of salvation, from which the original sprout of mysticism emerged. Speculative mysticism runs the constant danger of reducing salvation history to a mechanical process confined to natural law and to turn the saving acts of God into a cosmic rhythm with definite intervals.[99] Speculative mysticism removes the Christian concept of sin in spite of giving the appearance of acknowledging it. Consequently, it seeks to mitigate the virtual opposition between the world and the kingdom of God into the notion of a development from imperfection to perfection, while it attaches itself to this world in the past and the future, including other worlds and aeons.[100]

If Petersen's interpretation of the children's revival, using this approach, had remained the final word, there would have been no place for the spread of a globalized Christianity, built on revival, over the face of the earth. But that is what in fact occurred. Hence, the other Pentecost interpretation of the Kinderbeten, that of Steinmetz, will prove to be the enduring and relevant model for us to probe, especially in light of the subsequent history of global evangelicalism, and this includes the Wesleyan tradition, with its achievements for the Kingdom of God in its first two hundred years.

Steinmetz's closing prayer in his Pentecost Addresses offers a counter to the Petersen option that we have examined:

> May the faithful Jesus have mercy upon each person whom God has created, so that no one might think [of rejecting God's Spirit] along the lines which have here been mentioned. Now, beloved friend [soul], you have also been moved in this time, through the Spirit of God in your heart, and so, abandon yourself to Him, with the resolve that now, from this day onward, the Lord your God shall have your heart and soul, and, He replies, I will become and] remain hers, and his, both in time and eternity. Yes, my Lord Jesus, that is what you would work within us, for the sake of Your eternal and heartfelt love. Amen.

---

99. This paragraph is a summary of the major themes of Petersen's restoration theology which is presented in Nordmann's historical discussion contrasting mysticism and federalism. Ibid., 171-183.

100. This is largely in the work of W. R. Ward, particularly his *Protestant Evangelical Awakening*, 79, 81, 88, 90, 92, 98, 116, 146, 163, 178, 258, 275, 286, 297.

2.5 Steinmetz and Revival: The Linkage of Pentecost to the Cross

How ironical it appears that the man through whom the first revival in Protestantism occurred has been accorded scarcely a footnote in the general histories of Christianity. His name does not even appear in Herzog's definitive nineteenth century *Real Encyclopedia*. Only in recent studies of the history of modern evangelicalism do we find occasional references to him.[101] He is overlooked by most studies in the history and thought of Pietism, as well. All this is to say, we have our work defined for this chapter: making the case for the "stone mason", by which he was known by his contemporaries, as a play on his surname.

The main study of his life appears in a nineteenth century German monograph by L. Renner, which provides the fullest account of his life in its historical context, and in another from the National Socialist era of the 1930s, by Ernst Schubert of Friedrich Wilhelms University in Berlin.[102] In identifying him as the John the Baptist for the history of revival in Protestant tradition, we present him here from a fresh perspective which draws from the surviving historical data.

Steinmetz definitively embodies each of the features of the present study. He is formed and educated in the third generation of Lutheran Pietism, following Spener, and then Francke, with whom he was closely associated in his formative years. However, given the occurrence of the Kinderbeten (prayer awakening of children) in his homeland of Silesia at the dawn of the eighteenth century, he pioneered in shifting from the focus in Pietism as a renewal movement within European Christendom toward the direction of a spontaneous awakening movement which bore the marks of what has come to be known as revival. It was then an innovative concept which transcended the boundaries of institutionalized religion to become a transnational and potentially global phenomenon. Finally, in naming this event, Steinmetz drew from the apostolic Christian language of Pentecost, particularly as conceived in Pauline terms. He is the first of many attempts in modern Christianity to develop a theology of revival, based in the recovery of this apostolic theme. From that perspective, his work is pioneering, and in need of discovery and study by students of Wesleyan theology and Pentecostalism, as well as the history of religion.

---

101. This is largely in the work of W. R. Ward, particularly his *Protestant Evangelical Awakening*, 79, 81, 88, 90, 92, 98, 116, 146, 163, 178, 258, 275, 286, 297.

102. See L. Renner, *Lebensbilder aus der Pietistenzeit*; Ernst Schubert, *Auslanddeuchtum und evangelische Kirche Jahrbuch 1939* (München: Christian Kaiser Verlag, 1939).

Here is an overview of his distinctiveness in light of his life and times, which offers context for the reading of his addresses on the revival of religion, first appearing here in English translation. The addresses are important for several reasons. There is the early date of origin, which is linked to the historical effectds of the children's revival of 1707-08 in Silesia, resulting in the formation of the Grace Church in Teschen. Here Pastor Steinmetz led a massive awakening, including preaching from the theme of these Pentecost addresses. This occurred in the decade from 1719-1720.

This awakening precedes the Wesleyan revival in Great Britain, as well as the First Great Awakening in America. They are connected to a location in central Europe in the bellicose aftermath of the Protestant Reformation, where the great powers were contending for control of the continent and where Christianity understood as Protestant or Catholic was being determined. Also, through the leadership of this preacher, the first network to link the continent with the religious movement which would shape Anglo American civilization was formed and identified under the larger rubric of the new humanity first announced at Pentecost. Last, and perhaps most noteworthy, it was initiated not by any prestigious theologian, churchman, or folk hero, but by unnamed and obscure children, meeting within a remote mountain setting.

The interface of each of these factors is lodged in the life of Johann Adam Steinmetz (1689–1762). He was a man of the Book in a day when it was more a source of polemicism than inspiration for living. He was committed not only to understanding the biblical text at a cognitive level, but also emphasizing its certainties from a pneumatic reading of the text.

Born in rural Silesia, then a majority German-language nation in central Europe long overlaid by the occupation of foreign powers, his father was pastor in the Lutheran parish of Brieg, where he served the diaspora Protestants in this region after the end of the destructive Thirty Years War that engulfed central Europe. He narrowly survived death on numerous occasions in his youth. His father became an admirer of Spener and he desired a sound education for his son.

In the decade following the death of his father in 1699, when Johann was ten years of age, conditions for Protestants in Silesia took a turn for the better. The Silesian children's prayer awakening began in 1707 and continued for eight months when the Swedish invasion occurred. The children's prophecies of a coming restoration of Silesian Protestantism appeared to be fulfilled with the arrival of Swedish King Karl XII with an army fresh from victory over an alliance of Poles and Russians. Given the

Hapsburg conquest of the Protestant parishes in Silesia, the devout Swedish Lutheran monarch had his troops conduct their worship and singing while on march rather than in churches. The spontaneous, Spirit-directed children's camp meetings, a term later adopted for Methodists in North America, were now held along-side those of the Swedish troops. The children's movement now swelled as thousands joined their ranks, and they emerged from the mountains to arrive in the Silesian capital of Breslau in early 1708. Revival was advancing in a spontaneous way among the Spirit led children, now joined with fervent Swedish soldiers. The children had encompassed the entire nation of Silesia in five days and "many thousands knew that through the entire summer of 1707 the children were praying everywhere, in the bush and in the streets."[103]

The ramifications were profound. Word of the children's revival swept into Germany with the publication of a report in a Protestant periodical known as the *European Fama*. Protestants in Silesia had long been accustomed to worshipping outdoors in the "bush", since the initial defeat of Protestant forces in this region back at the Battle of White Mountain in 1610. Hence, Protestant children had become well equipped for open air worship when their spontaneous movement began in the early eighteenth century.

Caspar Neumann, the Enlightenment trained Protestant leader in Breslau, being suspicious of the children's revival, now encouraged the revival-led children to find churches in which they could continue their worship, which he had placed under official watchful oversight. Before these events unfolded, the young Steinmetz, raised by his mother after his father's death, had relocated to Saxony, where he was admitted to the University of Leipzig. Steinmetz was a gifted student who sensed a call to ministry, and became consecrated to his studies. Following an interlude of wavering in his discipline, he was scorned by a fellow student who said, "If I had the talent of God you have, I could become something in the Kingdom of God." Shamed, he then became diligent to that end.[104] It was his reading of Arndt's *True Christianity*, which helped him to discover and resolve his problem with vanity, declaring that "the power of reconciliation worked at the bottom of his soul."[105]

---

103. Gerhard Eberlein, "Die schlesische Betekinder vom Jahre 1707/8," in *Evangelisches Kirchenblatt für Schlesien*. Zweite Jahrgang. Liegnitz: Druck von Oscar Heimze, 1899, 52, cited in Swensson, 42.
104. Renner, 26.
106. Ibid., 27

Leipzig had previously been a center of Orthodox Lutheran opposition to Pietism, but, with the death of Benjamin Carpzov, the leading voice of resistance, the University faculty had recently shifted over to become Pietism friendly. His theological mentor there, Professor Johannes Olearius, was a gifted Greek scholar and theologian. A major spiritual stirring occurred among the students at Leipzig during his student years, which influenced Steinmetz profoundly. He committed himself to prayer and to study, enabling his childhood piety to give way to a mature certainty in the faith and a joy in pouring out his soul before God. True to his Pietist heritage in Silesia, he now spoke of receiving the first tangible evidences of "God's grace toward him as a child of God."[106] He acquired a careful knowledge of New Testament Greek, as well as Lutheran dogmatics, and his ardor for his study attracted the notice of his professors and peers. His confidence was also lifted by news from Silesia of the effects of the children's awakening which had swept through his homeland amid oppressive Hapsburg occupation.

Steinmetz then sensed that God could have a place for him in this new day for the advance of the gospel in Silesia. This was the situation on the ground when he received his first appointment after graduation from Leipzig, going to the rural parish of Mollwitz, located near his boyhood home in Brieg where many relatives still resided. He accepted this call as a divine directive, which he confirmed after consultation with his family. He also had responsibilities for the care of his widowed mother. The congregation had heard him preach and was eager for his arrival. He was a pastor who spent himself for his people, always concerned most for their conversion and faithfulness to the power of the gospel to transform lives beyond rote religious observance.

His reputation went before him, and in 1717, at the age of twenty-eight, he was requested to move to a larger parish of 10,000 in the town of Töppliwoda,[107] where Steinmetz soon found himself immersed in the awakening which had been reverberating through Silesia since the children's revival had first swept through the nation a decade earlier. This was one of the 125 churches which had been returned to the Protestants[108] after the Treaty of Altranstädt, after some 70 years in Hapsburg "captivity."[109]

The challenge was great. Töppliwoda was an untamed congregation long separated from its Catholic traditions and now unformed in the faith. He

---

106. Ibid., 36f.
107. Ibid., 43.
108 Note: Protestants means Lutherans. One German equivalent for Protestant is "evangelisch" ("evangelical").
109. Ibid., 44.

combined selfless humility before God with courage to attack the dominion of Satan who held captive all "mouth Christians" who had not come to know the saving grace in the blood of Christ. He adapted his sermons to his context, giving emphasis to the law, to bring repentance of wayward souls before offering prematurely the consolations of the gospel. He was forthright in addressing sins and annoyances which had beset the congregation, preaching the Baptist's penitential sermons.[110]

The gravest point of confrontation he faced was with Catholic authorities, who were only reluctantly conceding the rights to the congregation proffered by the Altranstädt Treaty, was the issue of holding private conventicles outside the regular hours of worship. Here Steinmetz displayed his courage against oppressive authority as well as his pastoral care for his congregants. He had begun the practice of evening devotions in his household, which then included houseguests. Soon others wanted to be included, and, not wanting to miss an opportunity to present the gospel, he chafed at having to refuse them. From an edict passed in 1712 by the Protestant Consistory, an official body reinstated by the Treaty, such a practice was regarded as an act of holding small, illicit churches outside the approved congregation. It was an innovation which could be punished by closing down the entire ministry of a church.[111]

Consequently, after the pastor initially refused to admit those who were not part of his household, a peasant boldly protested by reminding Steinmetz that he was still the pastor and that he had foresworn to "give life and limb to the truth." Steinmetz then consulted four experienced lay members of his church, who were divided on the matter. It was such a concern to him that he became physically ill and scarcely able to preach, a condition which was lifted only when he finally resolved to make confession to an offended layperson regarding the matter.[112] The man responded to Steinmetz, "If the Lord called you to it, do it, or God will slit you."

110. Ibid., 43.
111. As Swensson notes, this regulation illustrates collusion between Orthodox Lutherans and Catholic officials who still controlled Silesia. The former feared Pietism perhaps more than their Catholic adversaries, since they were at loggerheads over what constitutes Christian identity: the new birth in Christ and lay empowerment, or mere conformity to Confessonal Lutheranism as regulated under clerical authority. This regulation was to prevent Pietism, which was to be officially renounced from every pulpit, and to outlaw all chiliasts (believers in a coming new age of history) and those who only "externally" subscribe to the Lutheran Augsburg Confession. Swensson, *Kinderbeten*, 86f.
112. Luther had removed the sacrament of penance but had reinstated the practice of general confession of sins to one another, through Christ, as part of the general priesthood of all believers.

Steinmetz did do it, and lay conventicles were now held in defiance of public authority, but not until he had a dream following that conversation in which his counselor appeared to him with the godly seal of the Holy Spirit imprinted on him.[113] Here was an early reference to the theme of his major addresses on the Pentecost sealing of the Holy Spirit as God's commissioning and granting assurance to the believer of his standing in the blood of Christ, for forgiveness and empowerment for blessed living in the Spirit.

Word of the awakening which had begun in the children's revival soom reverberated in the congregation at Töppliwoda. The Pentecost sealing of the Holy Spirit on the lives of these believers was at work. We read the following from a contemporary life story of Steinmetz regarding this work of the first meeting outside regular worship, standing open to all members of the parish:

> The first time around 40 people came in. He catechized about John 3:16, and at the conclusion he was forced to ask if anyone of those present would have heard of it in his heart. A bailiff confessed to this, who for a long time felt his misery, as he had come to the assurance of mercy, which was to our stone-mason [Steinmetz] a real heart-refreshment. In addition, during this first hour, twenty-seven souls were seized, being moved to follow their faithful teacher into his room, where after the first movement of the Spirit of God they prayed and cried for an hour before the Lord. For eight more days there were so many listeners, and in the aftermath this crowd increased even more.[114]

The groundswell of support for these meetings to be open to all in the community overcame any fears of rebuke from the authorities. The Catholic governor of the district sent commissioners to examine the case, but they did not press charges. Whenever Steinmetz was threatened with legal suits, he would respond to his critic, "Let him pray!"

Following the precedent of the Pietists in Germany, he adopted the practice of registering persons for confession and communion, which meant he could handle personal interviews with parishioners on matters of soul as part of regular pastoral duties, rather than being extracurricular. It was costly in time, however, seeing that almost 2,000 registered for the

---

113. Renner, 45

114. From the only extant biographical sketch of Steinmetz's life, taken from an obituary that appeared from his funeral in 1762, prepared by Pfarrer Stisser, the priest of the convent in Bergen, where Steinmetz served as Abbot in the years after his deportation from Silesia, and as found in the nineteenth century monograph by L. Renner, 45-46.

first communion offered after this practice was instituted.[115] This kept him in constant service from before dawn to late at night for eight days. It also had the effect of reducing the number of ecstatic encounters with those who claimed encounters with the Holy Spirit apart from participating in the ecclesial means of grace.[116]

These sessions came more as a consequence of the pastor's responsiveness to the movement of the Holy Spirit within the lives of his parishioners than as a function of the regular, sacramental ministry of the church. His subsequent Pentecost addresses indicate what he saw intrinsically occurring here: the initiative to make spiritual preparation for the sacrament was more basically a response to the sealing ministry of the Holy Spirit, to certify in the hearts of these seekers the forgiveness of sins in the blood of Christ and the blessing of the Spirit for continuous guidance of their lives in living for the Lamb of God and not for the passions of the world. [117] Through these arduous spiritual labors, Steinmetz was learning to minister more out of the power of God than from human expectations, and to become content with God's grace being facilitated, more than human issues and enmities being addressed.

It is significant that the Catholic prelate who investigated this issue amazingly refrained from relaying a negative report. It was as though his hand was stayed by the same power of God at work in these proceedings. When Steinmetz was asked about this, he responded simply, "Just let him pray."[118]

These incidents served to give Steinmetz a favorable audience in the greater Protestant community of Silesia, and presently the largest Silesian Protestant parish, the Grace Church in Teschen, contacted him to come as their senior pastor in 1720.

---

115. Renner, 46f.

116. These accounts of the movement of the Spirit in the lives of his parishioners shows remarkable resemblance to the incidents of "religious affection" reported by Jonathan Edwards at his Northampton (MA) Congregational Church, coming almost 34 years later to launch the first American Great Awakening. Steinmetz had by then established communications with Edwards to compare notes on their respective awakenings, in which it was acknowledged that the Silesian event took precedence. See Jonathan Edwards, *Treatise Concerning Religious Affections*, ed. John E. Smith (New Haven: Yale, 1959).

117. See the text of Steinmetz, *Pentecost Addresses on the Sealing with the Holy Spirit*, in this volume.

118. "The impression which can be drawn from this was adequate so that nothing further needed to be done about it, whenever Steinmetz ventured to reply, "Let him continue to pray."' Renner, 46. Translated by J. Steven O'Malley.

By this time, the center of the Silesian revival had shifted to this large congregation, and to one of the six Jesus Churches that had been erected, in accordance with the Treaty, in Hapsburg lands. Francke, spearheading the Halle institutions and their network of missional resources, had intervened to make possible the building of the four thousand seat barnlike worship center known as the Grace Church in Teschen. When it opened, forty thousand diaspora Protestants converged to form the congregation. As Ward notes, however, Francke was geared for projects of church renewal; but what he now had on his hands was revival, which was not under his control.[119]

It was this church in the diaspora community of Teschen to which the young Leipzig-trained Silesian pastor, Johann Steinmetz, was invited to come as senior pastor. Their commissioners had come to hear him preach and to interact with his members. Despite the tears from his congregation at Töppliwoda, he agreed to meet personally with the commissioners in Teschen, seeking God's leading. They even offered to hire a Polish speaking preaching assistant to work with that language group in the parish, because Steinmetz was unprepared to preach in that language.[120]

Here was the beginning of an international ministry, which would in time extend globally from this parish in Teschen. Considering the ministry team assembled to serve with Steinmetz, it appears to be a foretaste of global Christian revival in micro expression.

Ominously, before accepting this post, Steinmetz also received an anonymous letter from a clergyman who discouraged him from coming, saying there was great suffering awaiting him there. It appears this came from one of the clergy in Teschen who did not want to serve with Steinmetz. Here again a prophetic word came to Steinmetz, signifying how he was increasingly ministering in the power of the Holy Spirit, in line with his Pentecost focus. It was as follows: the warning letter arrived sealed in an envelope on which was written words not intended by the letter writer, which declared, "Fear not what you are about to suffer" (Revelation

119. Ward, *The Protestant Evangelical Awakening*, 80.
120. Ward introduces the able ministry team which was assembled to serve with Steinmetz at Teschen: "Johann Muthmann took charge of the Czech preaching, Steinmetz the German preaching and general management, Samuel Ludwig Sassadius, a graduate of Jena and an energetic catechist, was the appointee for the Polish preaching. Still more fiery were the theological assistants in the school. Georg Sarganek, Andreas Macher, and Johann Liberda were all young, active and trained at Halle in Slavonic languages; Liberda, in particular, in whom the preacher and political agitator were almost indistinguishable, was not only one of the most capable theologians Teschen ever brought forth but one of the most effective revivalists of all time." See Ward, *Protestant Evangelical Awakening*, 76.

2:10).[121] These words deeply impressed Steinmetz, who looked to the power of God. Nevertheless, the letter was a harbinger of great testing which would come to this pastor at his new post. He went to the new post prayerfully, after being richly blessed in Töppliwoda.

Great hope was placed in the possibilities of improved conditions under the terms of Altranstädt, although reality soon showed another face. The reigning Hapsburg Catholic power had no intention of honoring those terms. As soon as the pressure upon Vienna from the War of the Spanish Succession was removed, the Hapsburgs found time to resume their plan to recatholicize the Silesian population by removing as much as possible of what was left of the Altranstädt agreement with the Protestants. The main issues in the ensuing controversy between Steinmetz and the Catholic authorities in Teschen, in league with the orthodox Lutheran consistories in Silesia, will be identified here, for the purpose of providing insight into:

(1) how these issues unfolded in the city of Teschen, Silesia;

(2) how the collusion of religion and politics resulted in the suppression of revival in the nation of origin (Silesia), and how that awakening then shifted to other nations and localitiies. Here was a momentum that ignited and advnced the idea of a globalized Christianity extending beyond central Europe, under the aegis of the fulfillment of Pentecost;

(3) how the reverse of this position is seen in the solidifying of the orthodox Lutheran position on Pietism and revival, which has largely endured to the present day, and the evidence that argument mounted to develop their position;

(4) how Steinmetz may properly be identified as the key human agent in this scenario for the opening of new avenues of transmission for a proto-Wesleyan theology of salvation and evangelization to be transmitted at the higher levels of European Protestantism through the agency of his Moravian contacts.

First, we consider how the composition of Teschen and Steimetz's strategy for ministry there shaped the controversy in which Steinmet was engaged upon accepting the important post of the Grace Church, also known as the Jesus Church of Teschen.[122]

When he arrived he found that the foundation which had been laid for the church ten years ago, after the Treaty of Altranstädt authorized it to be

---

121. Renner, 49.

122. This congregation continues to serve the Teschen community, under its Polish name, under the name of the Grace Church.

planted, was never allowed to be completed by the Hapsburg authorities. and consequently, worship had occurred in a makeshift manner.

Steinmetz's first goal was to see that the building was built, as well as the school, and services were held as it was under construction. With the assistance of Francke and the Halle resources, the makeshift, plank barn-like structure was begun, although, with funding coming slowly, it was not completed until 1730, ten years later. By then, it seated 6,000, with another 3,000 able to crowd into the extended services of preaching and worship,[123] and thousands more worshipping on the surrounding grounds. Preaching occurred simultaneously in at least four languages. On one occasion, visiting Polish emigrees found a way to access the worship by climbing to the roof and removing the top planks to enter from the top. These were people famished for the gospel, and they knew it when they heard it.

Evidence of the Pentecostal sealing of the Spirit was strongly evident in the strong bond of godliness and intercession formed between the senior pastor Steinmetz and his chief associate, Muthmann.[124] Soon there were signs of awakening throughout the congregation, with people crowding into worship services featuring preaching of the Word of God.[125] Catechetical and related classes meeting in the schoolhouse flourished. One source notes that even Catholics were being attracted to the services.[126]

He began with a commitment to develop a rich love and knowledge of the Bible as God's revelation for His people, particularly as focused on the cross of Christ and communion with the blood of Jesus, as certified to the believer by the sealing of the Holy Spirit, accompanied by joy and confidence in the faith. One of Steinmetz's guidelines was always to present the whole plan of salvation in every message, so that it could be internalized by persons who had no familiarity with biblical teachings.[127] He had the gift of urgent preaching which tracked closely with his hearers, and especially with the moving of the Holy Spirit in their lives as He discerningly engaged them in his message. He was able to convey deep theological and

---

123. Ward, 74.

124. "The fellowship of the Holy Spirit and prayer became ever more closer together in the continuing ministries of these two men and advanced their common work." Renner 58. Translated by J. Steven O'Malley.

125. "There arose new living faith which confomed the people to the Word of God." ibid.

126. Renner reports that "they dared to identify themselves as Catholics." Ibid.

127. See Renner, 92-93, on the whole plan of salvation.

spiritual insights through clarity of expression and repetition of key themes, where necessary.

The 40,000 to 70,000 members[128] claimed by the Grace Church were among the persecuted Protestant minority whose lives were precarious, and yet, under their new pastor and his ministry team, they entered a joyous period of worship and praise, and growth in the knowledge and service of Christ. Classes in the newly constructed school house were led by the highly regarded teachers, Rector Jerichovius and Rector Sarganek.[129]

The context for the imperial persecution engendered by the awakening began before the awakening commenced with the Pietist initiative on its behalf. It became a major incentive for the Pietist August Hermann Francke to commit funds from his network of resources at the Halle University complex for this project. A member of his inner circle was Count Henckel, whose Oderberg estates bordered Teschen. Francke also knew the city to be a point of convergence for Poles, Czechs, and Slovaks, since each of their borders were adjacent to the city, being located just below the main mountain pass to Hungary.[130] These were also people groups which had suffered most intensely under the scourgeof the Counter-Reformation. Steinmetz also corresponded frequently with Francke, and his preaching bore resemblance to that of Halle, both in style and content, which becomes evident in his Pentecost addresses.

The controversy Pastor Steinmetz faced in the context of the revival under way at the Grace Church, and the travail which was predicted for him, both reflected the objective of the Hapsburg Catholic rulers of Silesia to undermine the Altranstädt provisions for Protestants. In addition, there was stiff opposition to any signs of Pietist influence in the congregation from the Orthodox Lutheran leadership in the Protestant consistory (governing council). Spokesmen for the old guard in the church had viewed Steinmetz and his team with suspicion from the beginning. They seemed blind to the many signs of new life in the congregation, ostensibly because they did not think Steinmetz came to his position with the support of the church elders. Apparent envy of his success soon deepened into outright enmity. They claimed his sermons did not conform to orthodox Lutheran doctrine, and that the catechetical sessions constituted conventicles, banned by Catholic law.[131]

---

128. Depending on which statistical records are used.
129. Renner, 58.
130. Ward, 73.
131. Renner, 59.

The issues Steinmetz faced with the Catholic authorities were financial, theological, and most were purely ideological. These were financial abuses: high fees were charged for Protestant pastors to be installed in their churches. Catholic priests had high incomes and avoided the tax burdens such as the Protestants carried. High fees and preapproval by the Catholic authorities were required for acts of ministry performed by Protestant clergy, including pastoral care.

Theological/ideological factors included: All Protestants who had been born Catholic must reconvert within six weeks, all other converts to Protestantism were not to be allowed to remain in the nation without resignation of their faith. All Protestants with Catholic parents or grandparents must reconvert. There was special opposition to Pietist Protestants because they objected to indecision and ignorance of the meaning of faith, which made them harder to convert to Catholicism, as well as closer to one another.

Further, anyone convicted of Pietism was denied the legal tolerance accorded to those who subscribe to the official Protestant confession of faith, the Augsburg Confession. It was difficult for Grace Church pastors to gain clearance to visit their ill members, although such restrictions did not exist for Catholics. At least, these restrictions were not as severe as in the horrid Thirty Years War (1618–1648), when all Protestants had been expelled from Teschen.[132]

Steinmetz also encountered opposition from local residents who resented his use of foreign laborers in church construction. These were Protestant Bohemians and Moravians, mostly Hussite in background, who had endured intense Catholic persecution in their homelands which were adjacent to the Teschen area.[133] He also gathered them after daily hours of labor for food and clothing, especially during harsh winter seasons, as well as for prayer and counsel. These initiatives led to awakenings in their homeland, amid the severe restrictions the Habsburg overlords had imposed upon them. This provided another channel for the spread of the revival in Silesia that was now based in the Grace Church of Teschen. The result was that whole villages in Moravia (present day Slovakia) were

---

132. These restrictions are presented in the account found in Renner, 51–53.

133. These lands were originally German speaking provinces of the Holy Roman Empire, but in the late middle ages they were populated with Slavic peoples, the Czechs and Slovaks. Likewise Silesia, originally a German speaking nation, was then slowly becoming populated with a minority of Polish speakers, who were also Slavic in background. All of these language groups were represented in the Teschen area, and provided a rich cultural diversity for the awakening occurring in the Grace Church.

awakened through their connection with the Grace Church revival. Many Protestants there were now prepared to leave their homes and migrate into German Protestant lands, particularly Upper Lusatia and Saxony to their north. Catholic authorities blamed Steinmetz for encouraging them to leave, although he was actually doing the opposite; strengthening their communities to function within their homeland.[134]

Third, the intense pressures from Hapsburg clerical authorities were aligned to the interests of anti-Pietist Orthodox Lutherans who officially represented the Protestant interests in this recatholicized Silesia. This axis also heightened the readiness for the Protestants to seek to be warmed and renewed by a recovery of their biblical faith. To that end, Steinmetz sought to maintain fidelity to the Orthodox Lutheran standards, but he did so from the perspective of his own personal encounter with the power of God in the sealing of the Holy Spirit. This was an asset upon which Steinmetz and his ministerial team built as the awakening advanced among the repressed Protestant population which was concentrated in this one large congregation under their care.

He was, after all, serving under the auspices of the Breslau Edict of 1712, whereby the Catholic authorities, in league with Orthodox Lutherans, forbade Pietism to be promoted in Silesia, and regarded it as being antithetical to the canons of the Lutheran Augsburg Confession. For that important reason, he was constrained to minister without explicitly appealing to Pietist sources or themes, although implicitly his entire ministry was strongly influenced by that ethos, now reconfigured for the purpose of promoting the awakening (revival) of true Christianity, and not merely its renewal, as it had been with Spener and Francke.

The difference between these Pietist leaders and Steinmetz was uncomplicated: the previous leaders had been ministering in a context of an undisturbed though decadent Protestant form of Christendom in Germany; however, Steinmetz was ministering in a context where that form of Christendom had been deconstructed and virtually abolished, under Hapsburg Catholic dominance. Steinmetz was planting a church where there had been one two centuries earlier, but which had been destroyed through the travail of the Thirty Years War and its Counter Reformation aftermath.

Finally, with regard to the strategic role of Steinmetz, note the importance of this last statement. The era of Steinmetz's ministry in Silesia, and

---

134. Christian David, *Servant of the Lord (Memoir)*, #11, 13.

Teschen in particular, was consequently a time to return to the beginnings: if God was to have a church based on His Word in that place, He would act to raise it up. That is precisely what was happening in revival, then understood. It is a wholly different understanding of the meaning of that common term in church parlance, from the way it was enculturated in American evangelical Christianity, particularly in the context of the second Great Awakening of the nineteenth century. Charles Finney, the influential mass evangelist in the latter awakening, made clear that we do not need to wait on God for revival to happen, because it is not a miracle but a "right use of constituted human measures [methods]" for achieving a desired outcome.[135] In Steinmetz's day, churches did not have revivals; revival happened as the breakthrough of God into desperate human conditions, and, sometimes, it used churches in the process.[136]

The plan adopted by Steinmetz and his ministry team was to instruct the congregation, uninformed by ordered sermons and youth instruction, in a love for the gospel. To facilitate this, Muthmann, Steinmetz's primary associate in ministry, set up catechetical classes with the boys, meeting with the elders on stated occasions through the week. On Sundays, following the morning services, the sermon was repeated in the afternoon by Muthmann. He also met with the large company of communicants who arrived in Teschen from distant points, on Saturday before the Sunday worship.[137] Many of these were practices which Steinmetz had tested in Töppliwoda.

Notice here that, these practices were not means to cause a revival but were ways to channel the power of God which was already being savingly manifested in the services. In fact, there were many who came to saving faith in the new birth with the sealing of the Holy Spirit before they got to Teschen, or apart from the Sunday service altogether. These were ministers living in the consecrated power of the Holy Spirit, who was working through them in sovereign ways throughout the details of their daily ministries. Prayer was continuing incessantly by the ministry team and consecrated lay members working with them.

In 1722 complaint was filed against Steinmetz with authorities in Breslau, the national capitol of Silesia, by adversarial clergy in Teschen, in

---

135. Charles Grandison Finney, *Lectures on Revivals of Religion*, ed. W. G. McLaughlin, (Boston: Harvard University Press, 1961).

136. I will leave it to the reader's judgment as to which approach would be the viable one for our present day

137. We learn of these practices from the reports compiled in Renner, 55–58, and also in Richard Kammer, *August Hermann Franckes Auslandersarbeit in Sudost Europa*, in Schubert, *Auslanddeuchtum und evangelische Kirche*, 121-203.

response to the authorities' admonition for provincial consistories to keep a watchful eye on clergy suspected of sympathy toward Pietism and who did not abstain from holding "private meetings."[138] If guilty, a heavy fine would be levied and a clergyman's expulsion could be required. Two indictments were placed against Steinmetz under this rubric, and the second indictment was supported by the Jesuit residence in Silesia. The state agency had even hired spies to monitor the activities of the suspected "Pietists."[139] Steinmetz's ministry continued under this duress.

Two members of the Protestant clergy arranged for the case against Steinmetz to be taken before the Wittenberg theology faculty for interpretation and recommendation. However, since Wittenberg was committed to the Orthodox, anti-Pietist Lutheran theological position, it was deemed preferable for the case to be transferred to a neutral theological faculty, which was neither Pietist, like Halle, nor Orthodox, like Wittenberg. Jena University was selected as meeting that criterion. Consequently, a Jewish faculty member at the latter institution, Buddeus, issued a judgment which enabled Steinmetz to be exonerated. Again, this controversy raged while awakening was continuing to stir in the larger parish of the Grace Church at Teschen.[140]

After a decade of revival under the heavy hand of Hapsburg and Orthodox Lutheran duress, authorities finally conspired to remove him from his post and shut down the awakening continuing there. When at last Steinmetz was placed under duress in a carriage transporting him out of Silesia in 1730, he could look back at a mighty work of God which had begun and now was being disseminated. This was occurring through many international visitors to Teschen over the preceding decade, as well as lay preachers who went forth from that place, and a large company of the Silesian nation, now under religious occupation, who silently looked to him as their voice of hope.

When he crossed the border into Saxony, he was aided by friends there, including Zinzendorf and leaders of the Halle mission center, two growing rivals for ascendancy in the Pietist world mission. He quickly was placed, he believed under God's direction, into key pastoral positions. Soon this

---

138. "The fiscal indictment of the administrative office in Breslau [was directed] against Steinmetz and the preachers identified with him, explicitly because of their Pietism." cited in Renner, 59.

139. Ibid.

140. A discussion of this controversy from the Orthodox Lutheran standpoint is found in Richard Kammel, "August Hermann Francke's Auslandsarbeit in Südosteuropa," in Ernst Schubert, ed., *Auslanddeutschtum und evangelische Kirche, Jahrbuch 1939* (München: Kaiser Verlag, 1939), 141–148.

led to his appointment as abbot of the Protestant church center at Kloster Bergen (the Bergen Cloister, a former Catholic monastery site) in Magdeburg, and also as superintendent of the Lutheran churches in that region.

Deeply concerned for theological education as a vehicle for revitalization of a war weary Protestant church establishment, he inaugurated projects of mass publication, public lectures, and discipleship classes for clergy and lay people alike through the campus of the Cloister.

It was from this base that, for thirty years (1732–62) he singlehandedly edited the most comprehensive gazette on the building of God's kingdom in eighteenth century Europe and America, published in German for a panGermanic readership, under the title of the *Gathering of Materials for the Building of the Kingdom of God on Earth*. It was a prime vehicle for organizing a network to effect communication across national and religious borders for advancing the movement of the Holy Spirit in the revitalization of Christianity and the salvation of humanity, beyond the bounds of his Lutheran confessional tradition, under whose leading his entire ministry had been directed.

Among the papers he compiled for free public lectures at Kloster Bergen were his Pentecost Addresses, based on his revival preaching in the days of the great Silesian awakening at Teschen, which were first translated into English for the present study.[141]

It was the first Continental initiative to reach out to leaders of the budding awakening as it reached England, Scotland, and North America, in the first third of the eighteenth century. In other words, thanks to the work of Steinmetz and his colleagues, German speaking Christians had become much more aware of what was transpiring in the Anglo world than vice versa. Our lack of awareness of these lines of development have greatly constricted our capacity to engage what the Holy Spirit has been about at the dawn of modernity in creating a new future for the Christian world mission.

In our third chapter in part three of this study, we will focus on the key theological development of that Continental awakening which offers new insight into the roots of the Wesleyan two stage approach to salvation, exceeding what has previously been exhibited. I am thankful for the important work of my colleague Laurence Wood in laying foundation for this development, from the side of Anglican/Wesleyan sources. This study

---

141. See their dates of publication found on the title page of the Pentecost Addresses, in this volume.

complements that effort by proceeding from the Continental side, and carrying the roots of that lineage to newly acknowledged and important sources of influence.

Chapter

THE PIETIST SOURCE OF THE TWO-STAGED SOTERIOLOGY IN THE WESLEYS

3.1 Steinmetz, David, and the Wesleys: A Comparison of the Themes of Pentecost and Sanctification in the Continental Revival and in the Wesleys

This chapter introduces a largely unexplored but significant discussion of the multiple uses of the Pentecost motif in relation to soteriology, and sanctification in particular, in the larger context of revival and Christian globalization, as these became manifest within post-Reformation Continental Protestantism. It is a theme which Professor Laurence Wood has broached in his studies of the *Meaning of Pentecost in Early Methodism*.[1] In a second volume, he focuses on the thought of both Wesleys, alongside that of John Fletcher, within the context of early and nineteenth century Methodism.[2] The study demonstrates the distinctive way in which each author nuances a critical theme striking to the core of the evangelistic message of the Wesleys, which also continued through nineteenth century Methodism. Previous paradigms for alternate explanations are effectively deconstructed in the course of this research.

The present volume develops a theme he also addresses in one chapter of the latter study, concerning the relationship between the Wesleys and

---

1. Laurence W. Wood, *The Meaning of Pentecost in Early Methodism: Rediscovering John Fletcher as John Wesley's Vindicator and Designated Successor*, in J. Steven O'Malley, The Pietist and Wesleyan Study Series, (Lanham, MD: The Scarecrow Press, 2002).

2. Laurence Wood, *Pentecost and Sanctification in the Writings of John Wesley and Charles Wesley, with a Proposal for Today* (Lexington, KY: Emeth Press, 2018), in The Study of World Christian Revitalization Movements in Pietist/Wesleyan Studies, J. Steven O'Malley, ed.

the Pentecost impulse within the continental revival which antedated Methodism, also a concern of the present study.

3.2 The Role of Christian David in the Dissemination of Steinmetz's Theology of Pentecost

The link to Wesley in our continental discussion is through the Moravian evangelist, Christian David (1690–1751). He was a native of Bohemia, born in the aftermath of its devastation and conquest by the Viennese Hapsburg empire in the early seventeenth century.[3] After the Thirty Years War, there was rigid repression of Protestants in the twin states of Moravia and Bohemia. Some hope was restored after Swedish king Charles XII entered Silesia in 1708. Through the protection he provided, some 7,000 Protestant peasants, many having Hussite background,[4] were yearning for freedom of worship in their native Bohemia and Moravia.[5] The founding of a preaching station in Upper Silesia at Teschen under Francke's leadership enabled "evangelical" (i.e., Protestant) literature from Halle to be funneled into Moravia and Bohemia. Others managed to escape from Moravia to Teschen and were converted by Steinmetz's preaching after his arrival there in 1720.[6] These contacts with the revival at Teschen helped stabilize the Protestants in the adjacent lands of Moravia and Bohemia, who had been under great duress from Catholic forces. Carpenters and stone masons from villages in neighboring Moravia were hired to construct the large Grace Church and school in Teschen as a center for refugees from four adjacent nations, living under repressive Hapsburg conditions. The

---

3. This occupation began after the defeat of the Protestant forces by the Hapsburgs in the Battle of White Mountain (1610), and conditions only became more desperate during the protracted Thirty Years' War, which began with a Hapsburg attack on Protestant leaders in Prague (1618–48).

4. John Hus was executed by the Catholic Council of Constance (1415) for his Four Articles, criticizing worship and cultural conditions in his day. His followers, the Hussites, went underground, with some splitting into a more violent, apocalyptic sect known as the Taborites and, in the aftermath of the religious wars, many found refuge in the neighboring province of Moravia to the east of Bohemia. These two states, originally of Germanic population, were colonized by Slavs in the late medieval era, the Czechs in Bohemia and the Slovaks in Moravia. They had early organized as the Unitas Fratrem, of the Unity of the Brethren, and their great leader in the seventeenth century, when they existed as an underground movement, was the brilliant educator, Jon Comenius, a graduate of Herborn Academy in Nassau, where Philip William Otterbein was also educated before embarking as a missionary to the German Reformed in North America.

5. Ward, *Protestant Evangelical Awakening* (PEA), 78.

6. Ward, PEA, 79.

revival spread underground from Silesia into the villages in Moravia and Bohemia, which was rigidly resisted by the Hapsburg governments in these states.[7]

After the Jesuits were successful in expelling the Protestants from Teschen by 1730, along with their preacher, Steinmetz, Protestants hiding in the Silesian hills began to conduct excursions into the city to help beleaguered Protestants there, and Silesian children arose again to restart their prayer meetings, which had been the beginning of the revival there, twenty three years earlier.[8]

When these signs of awakening were stirring in the region, Christian David found himself among those residents of Moravia who came north into Upper Lusatia seeking work and a residence in the German lands.[9] He was joined by other German-speaking Bohemians and Moravians,[10] who were dodging imperial Catholic oppression.

Born in the Moravian village of Senftleben, Christian David, a carpenter, would lead the first contingent of these ethnic migrants from Moravia to Berthelsdorf, the estate of Zinzendorf in Upper Lusatia (Germany) in 1722.[11] David's parents were Catholics of Czech and German background. By all measures he was a bright and gifted, although largely uneducated. Ward speaks of him as a man of "pronounced independence of mind," and, given his migratory nature, he carried bitter memories of the Hapsburg imperial attempts to recatholicize Moravia and Bohemia, which, amidst the migratory nature of his carpentry trade, gave him a propensity for "sampling alternatives to his parents' Catholicism."[12] He had considered becoming a Jew but did not. While apprenticing to be a carpenter in 1713 at the home of an elderly Protestant, he had once found a Bible hidden under a roof. Reading it, tears came to his eyes and he resolved to become a Protestant after finish-

---

7. Moravians and Bohemians also assisted in the reconstruction of Zinzendorf's estate at Herrnhut, in Upper Lusatia, which was north of Moravia, where he invited them to relocate to become a Moravian religious colony under his direction.

8. Ward, PEA, 81.

9. The name Herrnhut means "The Lord's abode, or watch" and was a sign that this was a community of expectant prayer

10. Most of the inhabitants of Moravia and Bohemia were Czech speakers.

11. Ward, PEA, 121.

12. Ward, PEA, 125.

ing his apprenticeship.[13] He taught himself to write from a printed book, and the Bible was his favorite book.[14]

When he arrived in the German lands, he met his first Protestants while in Berlin and Görlitz in 1717, where he had gone for carpentry jobs. In Berlin he attended his first communion, but "what he had sought to find there he did not find," and, in addition, he saw to his great sorrow that "a person could not even act earnestly according to Christian teaching free and unhindered without experiencing great ridicule."[15] In Görlitz, a town on the Silesian border, he met some notable revival leaders of the pioneering Silesian revival, including Schwedler and Rothe, whose focus was then upon helping beleaguered Protestants to escape from that Hapsburg controlled land.

David also received pastoral care during his physical illness at Niederwiesa, a Lutheran congregation on the Silesian border served by a Spirit-anointed and warmhearted evangelical (Lutheran) pastor, Johann Christian Schwedler.[16] He had gifts as a hymn writer and also as an effective revival pastor in his refugee congregation located on the border of Saxony with Silesia. Schwedler reportedly preached nine hour sermons to a congregation with many Silesian refugees who were fleeing their homeland. People listened often in spiritual rapture, with his great theme being Christ, the crucified Lamb of God. He regularly visited the bedfast David, when he became ill with a severe fever, and led him to experience conversion through the saving power of the gospel of Christ.[17] Following this conversion, David recovered from his illness, but recorded that he continued to struggle with moving from "being justified" to "having the full assurance of faith."[18] He went on his way, strengthened in body and soul, but still with many unanswered questions of faith.

In his illness he promised God if he lived he would return to share his Protestant faith with his countrymen in Moravia, God willing. This was a promise he kept.

13. Vernon H. Nelson, ed., *Christian David, Servant of the Lord; The Archives of the Moravian Church,* Publication 11 (Bethlehem, PA: 1962), par. 5, 9.
14. Ibid., par. 2, 10.
15. Ibid., par. 3, 10.
16. One of Schwedler's hymns is found in the United Methodist Hymnal, "What is that great thing I know, what delights and stirs me so, whose the Name I glory in, Jesus Christ, the Crucified." Johann C. Schwedler (1741), "Ask Ye What Great Thing I Know" in The United Methodist Hymnal (Nashville: United Methodist Publishing House, 1989), 163.
17. David's conversion under Schwedler is reported in his dairy, and also in Ward, PEA, 90.
18. Ward and Heitzenrater, *Journal and Diaries, I,* 274.

Ward observed that it was Schwedler who "converted Christian David," and also that he was thereafter "confirmed in the faith by Steinmetz at Teschen."[19] This confirmation would have occurred after 1720, while he resided in nearby Görlitz on the Silesian border, since that was the time of the beginning of Steinmetz's ministry at Teschen with the awakening accompanying it. This act of confirmation may have been realized over a succession of visits which he made with Steinmetz, which are recorded in his memoirs, reaching their completion by 1725, in a definitive meeting with Steinmetz on questions of soteriology.[20]

In his visit to Teschen in 1722, David found the revival in progress there in the large Grace Church, with preaching occurring simultaneously in German, Polish, and other languages. David's dairy reports that the congregation consisted of 30,000 Poles and 40,000 German speakers. This awakening continued through 1730, when his ministry there was terminated. Steinmetz's colleagues, Thomas Muthmann and Saddadius, were declared to be goodhearted though unconverted Wittenbergers.[21]

While visiting Steinmetz in Silesia, David shared with him his intent to deliver his fellow Moravian nationals from the Habsburg repression, but Steinmetz cautioned him not to bring refugees from Moravia until there was a place of shelter for them.[22] After his first meeting with Steinmetz his host took pains to open a passage for David to escape Jesuit authorities in Silesia and reach the German border at Görlitz, where David was handed over into the hands of the mystic, Melchior Scheffer.[23]

3.3 Christian David's Narrative as Recorded in John Wesley's Journal

David would provide John Wesley a firsthand report of the events in faith formation from his early life, as recorded by Wesley in his *Journal*.[24] Wesley

19. Ward, PEA, 90.
20. David's confirmation in his new faith was sealed over the course of multiple visits with Steinmetz at Teschen in the early 1720s, culminating in 1725. David, *Memoir*, 17 and John Wesley, *Journal and Diaries*, I: 271ff.
21. This indicates they graduated from a University which was Orthodox Lutheran and anti-Pietist. *David, Memoir*, par. 7, page 11.
22. Renner, 59 56.
23. Melchior Scheffer was then pastor at Görlitz, the hometown of Jakob Böhme, and, together with Schwedler and Steinmetz, they became a trio singled out by the Jesuits for persecution based on the charge they were opening illegal conventicles in the church, by encouraging fellowship among those sealed in the Spirit (as well as baptized as Lutheran Protestants) unto salvation in Christ. See Ward, *Protestant Evangelical Awakening*, 116.
24. Wesley, *Journal and Diaries*, 2, 273–5.

relayed that he had an opportunity of spending several hours with Christian David," and "the substance of what he spoke, I immediately after wrote down, as follows."

He then proceeds to record how David had first become so disenchanted with both the Catholics and the Lutherans in Moravia that "I loathed the very name of Christ, and "in this temper I wandered through many countries seeking rest, but finding none." It was with Jews he met that he became convinced from the Old Testament that Jesus was the Christ. He still could not find peace of soul, nor success in repentance in overcoming sin.

Christian David explained to John Wesley that it was after leaving the Lutheran parish where he had resided in Berlin, followed by a tour in a voluntary army of the Prussian army, that he returened to his trade as a carpenter, relocating to Görlitz, on the Silesian border in Saxony. It was there during the period of his life-threatening illness that he was visited daily on his sickbed for 20 weeks by Pastor Schwedler of the local parish.

John Wesley would later record in his *Journal* the following words from David about Schwedler: "From him [Schwedler] it was that the gospel of Christ first came with power in my soul." "Neither say I then that the 'being justified' is widely different from the having 'full assurance of faith'" (Romans 3:24).[25] "I remembered not that our Lord told his apostles before his death, 'Ye are clean'; whereas it was not till many days after it that they were fully assured, by the Holy Ghost then received [at Pentecost], of their reconciliation to God through his blood."

He summarizes this to mean, "The difference between these fruits of the Spirit was as yet hid from me; so that I was hardly and slowly convinced I had the one, because I had not the other."[26]

3.4 Early Guidance from Steinmetz

The years between his initial embrace of evangelical Protestant faith, through the influence of Schwedler at Görlitz (1717) and his completion of that journey under the guidance of Steinmetz in Silesia was the turbulent era of the early years of Zinzendorf's community named Herrnhut (the Lord's watch). Zinzendorf's attitude toward the awakening in Teschen, which had then reached as far as the Protestants in Austrian Salzburg, was, as Ward puts it, "ambivalent."[27] Like David, Zinzendorf had

25. Wesley, *Journal and Diaries* (August 10, 1738), 273-4.
26. Ibid., 274.
27. Ward, PEA, 116.

also been closely connected with Steinmetz, in addition to the "Pietist nobility" which supported Protestant interests in beleaguered Silesia.[28]

The condition Steinmetz gave to David for bringing from Moravia would be met when Count Zinzendorf purchased the Berthelsdorf estate from his grandmother and appointed the Silesian revival leader Richard Rothe to that Philadelphian-oriented parish. Count Zinzendorf, hearing of David, sent Rothe of the Berthelsdorf parish to Görlitz to meet David, and convey the Count's invitation for him to "Let as many as will of your friends come to hither [e.g, to Berthelsdorf where the Herrnhut community would be planted], and I will give them land to build on, and Christ will do the rest."[29] David accepted the invitation and in two years the number of settlers reached 150.[30]

3.5 David's First Migrants Reach Herrnhut

The first handful of refugees David brought from three German speaking Hussite refugee communities in Moravia was a historic event: in Zinzendorf's absence, David was directed by the estate manager, Heitz, to settle them at an unsettled area at the far end of the Berthelsdorf estate. Here David began building for them their first home in 1722, which would become the first house in the future famous Moravian center of Herrnhut.[31]

As Ward notes, this act "provided the spiritual guarantees for which Steinmetz had been looking."[32] In other words, David was seeking to comply with Steinmetz's intent to monitor the Protestant exodus from Silesia. David learned from the circle of revival leaders in Silesia headed by Steinmetz where to go in Moravia to bring out emigrants because Steinmetz had just returned to Teschen from a preaching tour in Moravia, with the result that many were converted, and thus readied for this migration.[33]

---

28. Zinzendorf's "meddling" with Silesian Protestantism also made him suspected by the Jesuits, who controlled Hapsburg religious policy in Silesia. They charged him with instilling a new "Pietist" religion into Silesia which would run counter to the religious settlement (Westphalia) where religious borders were redrawn European religious borders in Europe after the Thirty Years War.
29. *Memoirs of Christian David*. Cf. on invitation to CD to Berthelsdorf. *Memoirs of Christian David*, par. 13, "From about Pentecost 1722, ...", 14.
30. John Wesley, *Journal and Diaries 2*, 275.
31. John Wesley, *Journal and Diaries 2*, 275.
32. Ward, PEA, 124.
33. Ward, 124.

In the religious formation of Zinzendorf's new community of Herrnhut, there was initially a dearth of influence from the spiritual leadership of Steinmetz, the lead preacher and pastor of the original awakening in Teschen, who would give birth to revivals and elsewhere in the diverse region surrounding Silesia. Lacking that influence, the first migrants to Herrnhut who arrived under David's direction became divided in religious beliefs between the Reformed-leaning settlers and those among the early Herrnhut settlers who were orthodox Lutherans, led by Rothe and Count Zinzendorf.

3.6 Division Over Religion in Herrnhut

Less than half of the original Herrnhuters were Moravians, and they were themselves divided into two main groups: a Lutheran party, led by the Neisser family, which supported Zinzendorf, (who was committed to the traditional Moravian Unity of the Brethren church order within an inter church context) and an anti-church group, led by David, who at first sought to separate themselves from the Lutheran parish.[34] To avoid separatism, Zinzendorf imposed a constitution on the community forming a church structure. The old brethren office of lay elder was revived and David was elected by lot to be one of the twelve elders, then one of the four senior elders. However, David abruptly moved out of the village, built his own hut and despaired because he had helped bring so many to Herrnhut only to have them made Lutherans, and since they also were not converted in the revival, they were "doubly children of hell."[35]

This erratic moment was accompanied by David's subsequent disillusionment with a Calvinist, Johann Georg Heitz, the estate manager at Herrnhut[36] who insisted on the Calvinist theme of election. David feared that it would discourage settlers at Herrnhut from taking comfort in the promise of the gospel. That fear was shared by large numbers of the original settlers. Our source for these events is John Wesley's *Journal* entries from his visit with Christian David in Herrnhut, where David reported how he had contracted an intimate acquaintance with a Calvinist," who "brought me over to his opinions concerning election and reprobation,"

---

34. Ward, 126.
35. The Herrnhut Diary, May-August 1727, printed in *Zinzendorf und die Herrnhuter Brüder*, ed. H C Hahn and H. Reichel (Hamburg, 1977), 95-108; cited in Ward, PEA, 126.
36. Heitz, from the Reformed community in Zürich, had been brought to Herrnhut by Zinzendorf to manage his estate. John Wesley, *Journal and Diaries I*, 276. This event occurs between 1724 and 1725.

and "by me were most of our brethren brought over to the same opinions." Reflecting this period of religious division in Herrnhut, David stated, "we were in great straits, and many were dejected." David concluded, "it may be that we are not of election."[37]

Consequently, Zinzendorf urged Steinmetz to "go to a neighboring minister, Pastor Steinmetz, and talk with him fully on that head, whether Christ died for all." This he did, and he reports further, "God fully convinced me of that important truth." Consequently, after reporting back to Zinzendorf, the Count "desired we might all meet together, and consider these things thoroughly."[38]

In the course of seeking Steinmetz's counsel on this key theological stumbling block, the results led to David completing his assurance of salvation in terms of Steinmetz's two stage approach to salvation. This is evident in the results of the meeting with Zinzendorf in Herrnhut, when the Count called a three day conference which brought closure to this theological crisis and positioned the community toward an expectancy for awakening, which would come, in God's time, from its origin in Silesia to Herrnhut.[39]

It is apparent that the agenda of that important meeting went far beyond the one question that had been broached, because, as David continues to relate to Wesley, the following: "We met at the house, and parted not for three days." Their focus was to "open the Scriptures and consider the account which is given therein of the whole economy of God with man, from the creation to the consummation of all things, and by the blessing of God we came all to one mind on that fundamental point."[40]

It is noteworthy that David later chose to explain his personal faith development with John Wesley during Wesley's visit to Herrnhut more than a decade later, in 1738. The contention over whether Christ had died for all or only for the elect, had led David to seek the counsel of Steinmetz at Teschen. The assurance he received about the universality of Christ's atonement and his death on Calvary, as sealed in the heart of the believer by the Holy Spirit based on Pentecost, had its origin in the preaching of Steinmetz at the Grace Church in Teschen.

---

37. Ibid., 274.
38. Ibid, 275f
39. Zinzendorf refers to this conference as occurring at Berthelsdorf (his estate adjoining Herrnhut), 1725. David, *Memoir*, 7, 19.
40. John Wesley, *Journal and Diaries 2*, 276.

Notice that the focus on "the whole economy of God" which David also conveyed to John Wesley would be inclusive of the two-state approach to salvation which Steinmetz had featured in his Pentecost sermons from which the Teschen awakening had sprung to life. When John Wesley in August 1738 entered a Journal reference to David's expression "the whole counsel of God," these were the exact words that Steinmetz used to convey to David the message of the Pentecost "sealing of the Holy Spirit." These were also the same words David had used to explain to Zinzendorf at Herrnhut in 1725 what he had learned from Steinmetz in the revival at Teschen, concerning God's will for the full salvation of all people, that enabled Herrnhut to become host to the spread of the awakening from Teschen in 1738, which occurred under the arrival of preachers sent by Steinmetz at Teschen in Silesia. These words referenced Steinmetz's message of full salvation through the sealing of the Holy Spirit. According to Steinmetz's biographer, Brönner, this phrase expressed Steinmetz's intent, "orally and in print," to set forth his project for the "whole counsel of God and His blessedness" that he might "confer the entire garment of salvation" that refers to the "truly converted person."

David's conference with Zinzendorf after his return from his meeting with Steinmetz was followed by an incursion of Jesuits (who were the coercive arm of the Hapsburg government on religious policy in Vienna) probing into the thought of the Herrnhut community. They were suspicious of the connections between Herrnhut and the work of revival in Silesia where the awakening had occurred which they had opposed, especially since Herrnhut was suspected of becoming a separatist sect from the Berthelsdorf Lutheran parish to which it belonged.

The imperial Commissioners who were sent to Herrnhut sent a report to the Emperor in Vienna, the capital of the Holy Roman Empire of the German Nation, which reported to that court these declarations touching on the matter of the "whole economy of God" in salvation:

> Point 3: whosover they are who are being sprinkled by the blood of Christ and sanctified through faith, we receive as brethren, although at some points they may differ from us. And
>
> Point 4: Therefore we have no cause to form any congregation separate from this, especially seeing we both use that liberty which Christ has purchased for us, and so often experience the power of the doctrine that is taught there.[41]

---

41. W. R. Ward in his editor's footnote in Wesley's *Journal and Diaries 2* states this "document formed a sort of constitution for the settlement at Herrnhut, there being as yet no constitution of the Moravian Church." *Extract of the Public Instrument Signed at Herrnhut,*

Christian David also related to John Wesley how the concern for the Pentecost sealing with the Holy Spirit following justification was the critical feature needed among those with whom he was serving in ministry.

Prior to David's trip to confer with Steinmetz, Zinzendorf's Herrnhut community had also been teetering on collapse over the division on religion among the members. The stabilization in doctrine and mission purpose issuing from the joint meeting with Zinzendorf after his return helped position the community to adopt a stance of expectation that awakening was needed and would come to Herrnhut, in God's timing.

Eventually, and unexpectedly, Herrnhut found itself being stirred into new life by the arrival of the first stirrings of revival from the awakening in Silesia under Steinmetz's lead. His associates, Schwedler and Liberda, arrived in Berthelsdorf and began preaching revival in Herrnhut in 1727. The revival inspired acts of reconciliation between the separated groups in Herrnhut, and David was too drawn into this momentum from revival.

This turmoil might have been the end of Herrnhut, but, with revival not far away in neighboring Silesia, preachers, like Liberda, from Steinmetz's team in Teschen, and Schwedler, came to Herrnhut and preached reconciliation among their divisions.[42] A great peace came over the community as they experience an initial input from the Pentecost revival which was then at its peak under Steinmetz's leading in Silesia.

3.7 The Onset of Awakening in Herrnhut

Zinzendorf who was seeking to avoid separatism at all costs placed emphasis upon the early Hussite practice of ministry through lay offices. Given the new sensitivity toward the coming revival put them on a "cloud of grace" which hallowed their community.[43] Bible classes were begun by Christian David, followed by all-night prayer meetings.

August, 1729 cited by John Wesley, *Journal and Diaries 2*, 276-7 and n11. Note: the liberty purchased is an allusion to the experience of the Pentecost sealing (Versiegelung) of the Holy Spirit which imparts assurance of forgiveness and also blessedness (Seligkeit) as the gift of joyful holiness for time and eternity. This was the substance of Steinmetz's preaching in the revival which began in Silesia and spread to Moravia, Bohemia, and Saxony, including Herrnhut. See the title of the Pentecost addresses found in Part Two above. The citation from this document demonstrates the influence of Steinmetz's twofold soteriology in the Herrnuhut community at that time.

42. Ward, PEA, 125.

43. Eric Beyreuther, *Zinzendorf und die sich alllhier beisamen finden*, (Marburg, 1959), 206-207, cited in Ward, 127.

Then, the one remaining thing needed was supplied, which was the rise of an intense spirit of prayer among the children of the community. This was a feature in the apostolic Pentecost and was replicated in Silesia to launch the first Protestant revival.

Aware that the Silesian awakening had been launched by the children's revival of 1707-08, David now interceded for an awakening among the children in Herrnhut, as the one missing factor in a manifestation of revival in Herrnhut. As Petersen had made clear in his *Die Macht der Kinder*, this was the missing feature in the manifestation of Pentecost in Christianity since the time of the first Pentecost, and its arrival in Silesia was the spring for the great revival there.[44]

Came it did. It was triggered by the personal crisis of eleven-year old Susannne Kühnel, who was moved at his mother's death by his deep peace in the Lord as he passed. Susanne's distress was now compounded by a personal conversion struggle, which lasted three days and nights, and lay upon the whole community, until he awakened his father with the words, "Father, now I am a child of God. Now I know how it was and will still be with my mother."[45]

Three other girls reported having a parallel experience, and they all came to faith in the same evening. After hearing of this occurrence, Zinzendorf sought out the girls and prayed with them upon his knees. The entire community now came out weeping and singing, and the Herrnhut diary recorded this event in light of the great Silesian revival twenty years earlier.[46]

Through these initiatives, the awakening—by then, the English word revival was also being used to describe the event—had reached Herrnhut, amid its disorders. David was then functioning as an active agent for its advance as it had begun in Silesia and had now spread into Herrnhut and beyond. The entire community joined together for communion, with tears and songs of praise., as "On 23 August [1727] such an impulse of prayer came upon the boys and girls that it was not possible to bear them without heartfelt emotion."[47] This account from the *Daily Journal* of Herrnhut, dated August 23, 1727, speaks to the heart of this event:

---

44. See Part 3 chapter 2.2 above.
45. Ward. *Ancien Regime*, 115.
46. Ward, PEA, 127.
47. Erich Beyreuther inzendorf und die sich allhier beisammen finden (Marburg, 1959), 151f., 155.

Such an impulse of prayer came upon the boys and the girls that it was not possible to hear them without heartfelt emotion, and through Susanne Kühnel an extraordinary movement arose in their assembly which became daily more true and serious .... There was to be heard on August 29 from 10 at night until one in the morning a heartrending praying and singing by the girls of Berthelsdorf and Herrnhut on the Hutberg. At the same time the boys were at prayer in other places. So powerful a spirit prevailed among the children as is beyond words to express.[48]

3.8 Progress in the Moravian World Mission through David

Christian David would become Zinzendorf's most freewheeling preacher among the Moravians. His goal was to build upon his initial discovery of saving grace through his first encounter with Schwedler and now find certainty of faith and an assurance of salvation, which the traditional rules of the Unity of the Brethren were unable to offer him.

While David was honing his theological formation, Zinzendorf was also undergoing his own pilgrimage to faith as director of the Herrnhut project. When he had married into the house of Ebersdorf, he had become influenced by the commanding persona of his wife's grandmother, the countess von Ebersdorf, a member of the inner circle of counselors to Spener as well as Francke at Halle. He was also a champion of the Philadelphian version of Christian community, modeled after Revelation 3,[49] which he effectively implemented within his small estate of Ebersdorf. Its model of Philadelphian love, freed from sect or party, remained Zinzendorf's ideal which he now unsuccessfully hoped to introduce into Herrnhut. He then turned to a German edition of the history of the Bohemian and Moravian brethren and read it to the community. This action had resulted in the adoption of the rules of the ancient order of the Unity of the Brethren, as his preferred vehicle for instituting his ideal of a Philadelphian community.[50]

Viewed in the context of the revival which had reached Herrnhut, Christian David now found himself energized to participate anew in the community project. He began leading Bible classes for men and all night

---

48. Herrnhut Diary, cited in Ward in his translation, 127.
49. See the discussion of Philadelphianism in Part 3, chapter 2.2 above.
50. As was noted in the previous chapter, Philadelphian, rooted in the thought of Jane Leade, had also been influential on the thought of Gottfried Arnold, in his major historical study (*Die Unparteiische Kirche und Ketzer Historie*).

prayer meetings were launched. From David's perspective, the incentive for participating in these spiritual exercises was to hasten the arrival of a full fledged awakening in Herrnhut.

Among David's major achievements in this awakening was his intervention among the thousands of Protestant exiles forced out of Salzburg, Austria, in the 1720s by Hapsburg coercion, heading north into German lands. He intercepted a large group en route to Nürnberg in Germany from Salzburg, presenting them with the message of salvation in Christ (with the sealing in the power of the Holy Spirit), as well as distributing hundreds of Zinzendorf's edition of the Bible. Most of these copies were soon confiscated by Catholic authorities in Nürnberg.[51]

In the midst of this busy traveling ministry, David formed an unusual arrangement with his wife, Anna Elisabeth Ludwig, whom he met while staying with Schwedler in Görlitz: he had poor health and he traveled frequently, therefore, he remained in that town with their five children and he set his staff to travel as God led him. He preceded him in death, after a protracted illness, in 1745.[52]

After the era of division and disillusionment in Herrnhut during the early 1720s, it was the children's prayer revival at Herrnhut which overcame that community's threat of dissolution in 1727 and led to its acceptance of the oversight Zinzendorf had instituted.

3.9 The Close of the Revival in Teschen and Tensions between Halle and Herrnhut

Two other events highlight the interlude between the conversion and sanctification of Christian David and the arrival of John Wesley as a visitor to Herrnhut over a decade later. When the Hapsburg Emperor succeeded in closing down the revival and ministry at the Grace Church at Teschen in 1730, there were soon charges brought by the same Emperor against Zinzendorf and the Herrnhut community for proselytizing among his Catholic subjects, such as the Salzburgers. This threat was averted when the Saxon state government drew up a plan for the Salzburger Lutherans who had entered their territory to swear allegiance to the (Lutheran) Augsburg Confession, which was protected by the peace treaty between the two sides. More important, Zinzendorf, the accused cause of this disruption, was banned by Saxon state authorities in Dresden from ever return-

---

51. Ibid.
52. Nelson, ed., Christian David, *Servant of the Lord*; The Archives of the Moravian Church, Publication 11 (Bethlehem, PA: 1962), par. 5, 11.

ing to Herrnhut.[53] The community at Herrnhut thereafter came under the authority of the adjacent Lutheran parish of Berthelsdorf.

Going forward, Zinzendorf then relocated his community from Herrnhut in eastern Germany to Marienborn, in a Lutheran state of the Rhineland Valley of western Germany.[54] This left David at Herrnhut without Zinzendorf's presence there. The 1730s was also the decade where Christian David served with Zinzendorf, from his new base at Marienborn, in extending the mission of the Unitas Fratrem (their official name) throughout the world. They did so by planting tropes, or institutionalized movements within established Lutheran, Reformed or Anglican state churches, which in theory would not be another church confession but rather a representation of a coming Philadelphian community of love.

A second consequential development during this interlude occurred on the global scene. The most important conflict within the history of revival included alternate views of its ultimate purpose. The practitioners of "renewal" at Halle, represented by Francke, and the practitioners of "revival", based in Silesia (Steinmetz) and Herrnhut (Zinzendorf) represented those two different perspectives.[55] In a day where conversions are made instantaneously, especially in American Protestant history, it needs to be understood that, then, making a Christian was not a short term affair. For Halle, it involved a conversion experience which was to result in a lifetime of renewal service within the official channels of a God given Christendom; for Herrnhut, they were impatient for the end time to come, and so renewal was replaced by revival, meaning, a Christian could be made in three days or less, through an emotional experience of conversion.

Note this was really not a rational choice to be made; rather, it was determined by historical conditions. In European Protestantism, revival began where there were Protestant minorities in Hapsburg Catholic lands, which could only have a future if revival leaders acted quickly before the public officials shut them down. There was no leisurely time for church renewal, or, for that matter, neither was there any intact Protestant church left to renew when the wars finished. That, you see, is how we got revival in

---

53. Ward, PEA, 132.

54. Zinzendorf's original vision was Philadelphian in nature, based on the model of community found at his grandmother's estate in Berthelsdorf, which followed a sect by that name, whose goal was to realize on earth the kingdom of peace envisioned in the Church of Philadelphia, in Revelation 3. This was a radical Pietist movement which called all the "elect" of God to leave their existing churches in order to achieve this ulitimate fulfillment for humanity.

55. Ward, PEA, 133.

Protestantism. Do we wish for those conditions again? Or is that too high a price to pay for God to act redemptively in our time?

The final straw in the tensions that developed between Halle and Herrnhut in the 1730s had to do with the fate of August Spangenberg. Here it was Steinmetz, but not Christian David, who gets squeezed in the middle of this dispute. The short account of this has Zinzendorf promoting a young member of his community, a Halle graduate named August Spangenberg, to a position on the Halle theological faculty (1731) when he still had favor with his alma mater. Soon Zinzendorf was encouraging Spangenberg to introduce fringe and separatist protocol at Halle, like the uses of love feasts and foot washing, which, Halle thought, could easily devolve into elitist separatism dividing the church. Spangenberg, identified with that effort, wanted to limit the sacraments to the reborn. This led to widespread critique of Zinzendorf as well as Spangenberg at Halle, as demeaning the unity of the church under the terms of the Peace of Westphalia, which governed Christendom in Europe at that time. The controversy resulted in Spangenberg's dismissal from Halle in 1733, and he then joins Zinzendorf in ministry with Moravians in the new world, including his interviews with the unstable John Wesley en route to Georgia.

Zinzendorf had procured two church positions for Steinmetz after the latter was expelled from Teschen, as places of continued service in the spread of the gospel in revival. Both David and Zinzendorf had admired Steinmetz's heroic work in revival at Teschen amid opposition, and wanted to see him receive a new position in a more favorable setting. After appointment to a Lutheran parish,[56] he became abbot of Kloster Bergen in Brandenburg.[57] Steinmetz and Zinzendorf remained in frequent correspondence, making it easy for the latter to impatiently and urgently ask Steinmetz to come to the aid of the defrocked Spangenberg. Interestingly, Steinmetz chose to criticize Spangenberg lightly, as well as Zinzendorf himself, for acting in a schismatic way, hindering the unity of the church, which were the same charges made against him by the Orthodox Lutheran

---

56. The place was Neustadt an der Asch.

57. Catholic monasteries were closed in the Protestant lands during the Reformation, and they sometimes were turned into educational retreat centers for clergy or laity. Steinmetz found this office a place where he could network for the advancement of the revival that began in Silesia to global dimensions.

and Catholic front in Teschen.[58] It was a comment that reflected an irreparable rupture between Halle and Herrnhut.

3.10 David's Later International Mission Ventures Featuring Steinmetz's Two-Staged Approach to Salvation

Before and after Wesley's visit to Herrnhut in 1738, Christian David undertook major missions on behalf of the globalizing of the evangelical mission of the Moravians. He became the "first planter" of the "private bands", akin to the one that Wesley had joined in England, founded by Peter Böhler.[59] After the eruption of revival in Switzerland under the lead of Samuel Lutz ca. 1727, David was engaged in that work as well. In 1729 he traveled to Riga, Latvia, and to Reval (present day Tallinn, Estonia) for a year, earning his living by manual labor, and winning many souls to Christ. One, a widow of a German general whose forces had occupied this region, was converted to Christ and agreed to turn his estate over to the Moravians for their mission center in the Baltic.[60]

Awakening continued to spread under David's leadership in the 1730s, to the time of Wesley's visit to Herrnhut in 1738. Soon after Wesley's visit, David departs for yet another Nordic mission, taking him to Livonia (present Latvia). Here, Christian converts were organized into classes and choirs, and by 1742, the Moravian records indicate they had 14,000 members in the Baltic region alone.[61]

The careful reader of Christian David's *Memoir* will observe that he gave special focus to the years of his extensive evangelistic tours in northern Europe and Greenland. It can also be observed in these journal entries the

---

58. Ward, 141. There was an anti-Methodist reference in Steinmetz's criticism of Zinzendorf, when he said "The Brethren taught sanctification along the lines of Wesley and so were guilty of sheep stealing." This has to do with Moravians putting their converts in private bands, as Wesley did with his classes, which, to Steinmetz, meant they functioned de facto as new churches. Steinmetz could not have made such a statement in 1733 if he wanted to, because there were no Methodist classes until 1739 at Bristol. Hence, what we have here is a later redaction in the record, since all later Orthodox Lutherans spoke negatively of the Methodists as divisive sectarians We must note that Steinmetz never saw a model of a Methodist class with its rules for working within the Anglican parish system, and he never objected to Spener's use of a conventicle in his parish at Frankfurt.

59. W.R. Ward and Richard P. Heitzenrater, The Bicentennial Edition of the Works of John Wesley (Nashville, TN: Abingdon, 1984ff), I, *Journal and Diaries*, (1735-1738), 270.

60. Ward, 149. The German nobility favored Christianitiy over the pagan gods of the Estonian culture, thereby weakening the latter in advance of David's arrival.

61. Ward, 151.

extent to which he placed primary focus upon the two state approach to salvation which he had acquired from Johann Adam Steinmetz, over the years of the latter's mentoring of his life and ministry. David gave credit to Steinmetz for his role in that regard on more than one occasion. Furthermore, this bonded relationship was acknowledged by Count Zinzendorf, as editor of David's Memoirs. On one occasion he wrote that "love and friendship has always prevailed between Christian David and the Inspector and later Abbot Steinmetz."[62] He explained their relationship in this manner: "All other servants of God in Silesia, however, could not stand him (Christian David)," but "Abbot Steinmetz was a great light among these people. He could love and honor a man even though he did not agree with his principles."[63]

In his last recorded letter to Zinzendorf, from 1751, David recalls 28 years ago (which is the time when Zinzendorf sent him to Steinmetz for the confirmation of his faith) when he received "the gift of the Spirit" who "has instructed me in my ignorance, strengthened me in my weakness, kept and comforted me." He expresses to Zinzendorf his now longstanding devotion to the world mission of the cross and Pentecost, and he wishes for Zinzendorf to prepare a plan of mission for him similar to his last 28 years. His words are presented in their original form:

> Dearest Papa! Now is the acceptable time, the day of salvation. God has reconciled the world unto himself, not imputing our trespasses unto us, but the grace of God that brings salvation chastises us for all our ungodliness . . . . My heart is completely willing to keep all his commandments, . . . to do my carpentering or to be his messenger. But this I cannot know except through the congregation,[64] even as the angels and the churches themselves. But John[65] was the mediator. And so long as I also have the congre-

---

62. Zinzendorf, *Christian David, Servant of the Lord*, 13.

63. Here Zinzendorf alludes to David was opposed by Steinmetz for taking people out of their country (ibid. 14), since, at that time David was "prejudiced against the Lutheran religion and practice and believed it a worse form of church life than any other." To Steinmetz, such zeal for migration out of Silesia meant that "...they would transfer themselves from their blessed condition under the cross to a miserable form of constitutionalized church, which had the name of living, but was dead." Ibid.

64. Congregation has two points of reference: Revelation 3, which speaks of the Philadelphian church of brotherly love, whose lampstand remains bright, among the other six, and also the Grace Church, a 70,000 member congregation in Teschen, Silesia, where David was confirmed in the faith through the Pentecost sealing of the Holy Spirit, and for whom Steinmetz was, in David's words, "the soul of the undertaking." *Memoir of Christian David*, 12.

65. John refers first to the evangelist, author of Revelation, through whom Jesus medi-

gation and its angels upon whom the Spirit rests and by whom I have enjoyed the gift of the Spirit these 28 years.[66] All my life I have not known how to begin anything on my own account. The Savior has brought me to your house and made me your assistant, and I cannot depart from this or else you would have to cast me away. I do not wish for anything except what is the will of the Savior and the congregation. [67]

David recorded in his *Memoir* from 1717 his first apparent encounter with Steinmetz.[68] Subsequently he met Steinmetz at the Grace Church in Teschen after Steinmetz became the senior minister in 1720.[69] David exclaimed:

> #9. It is easy to imagine what a sight it is to observe 70,000 people flocking together once a week to one house and remaining in continual activity from early morning through the day and night until the following morning. What inspector Steinmetz's share in it was can be seen from the incumbencies at Stassfurth, Hof, and Saalfeld. The result is known. Inspector Steinmetz was therefore the soul of the undertaking.[70]

David's ecclesiology and soteriology merge in his images of "the congregation," which historically was the Teschen Grace Church but also signified, as the launch point of the awakening which was sweeping Europe and beyond,[71] from 1730–1760, the community of the Lamb and those sealed in the Holy Spirit unto salvation and sanctification in the blood (Pentecost). The Personalia of David by Zinzendorf also describes how ten years after the children's revival began nearby in Silesia, conditions were favorable for revival in Teschen, where Steinmetz was now serving as senior

---

ated the witness of the Holy Spirit to effect the first awakening in Protestantism, or, second, to John who was Johann Adam Steinmetz, through whom the Spirit was sealed unto the Lamb in the life of Christian David. See how this theme is developed in his next sentence above.

66. The reference to 28 years takes us to 1723, the year of David's decisive theological encounter with Steinmetz, which led him finally to comprehend the "whole economy of God" (Wesley, *Journal* 2, 275) regarding salvation.

67. This congregation, the Grace Church, literally birthed the thousands of converts to the faith who went forth from Teschen into the surrounding lands and unto the uttermost parts of the earth, especially when we consider the link between Teschen and Herrnhut, Bristol (England), Northampton (Massachusetts), and all points beyond. Letter 25, January 3, 1751.

68. *Memoir* (#6), 11.

69. Renner, 54.

70. Zinzendorf, *The Personalia of the Late Christian David*, #9, in *Memoir*, 12.

71. The initial framework here was 1730 to 1760, the years of Steinmetz's Chronicle of the Building of the Kingdom of God.

pastor, presiding over Lutheran associates who were "goodhearted, unconverted Wittenbergers[72] who probably never before had given any thought to the new birth and conversion."

According to their principles they should have acted against him [Steinmetz as leader of the revival],

> but the wise conduct and divine character of Insp. [inspector] Steinmetz in his office kept the two men [Muthmann and Sassadius] constantly loyal ... and guided them into all the activdays pertained to the extension of the Kingdom of the Savior.[73]

Throughout his *Memoir*, David refers, as did Steinmetz, to the fellowship of the reborn, wherever they are manifest in his extensive mission, as the "children of God," which has both an apostolic, biblical foundation[74] and also a historical reference to the Silesian children's revival. The revival had been interpreted by Petersen in his classic study of that occurrence, as an apostolic Pentecost event because of its prominent inclusion of children (Acts 2:39).[75] For example, when David left Teschen and preached in Moravia in 1727, his theme in introducing the order of salvation was to appeal to Romans 8:18 concerning "the marks of God's children."[76]

David speaks with humility and candor when he admits, God declares the greatest is the brotherly love of the brethren, wherein all are called children of God, "although I have not been too peaceful and can only make a small claim to the promise."[77]

In his imagery of the two stage soteriology, David envisions the congregation of believers as having a foundation in the cross and blood of Christ and an "upper part of the structure," to "purification and sanctification both of the body and the spirit, and to the fruit of faith, hope and love."[78] He opens this discussion observing that God always brings his help at his own time, just as now. For he knows the right time, when he can give his

---

72. Wittenberg, Luther's ministry location, had become the defender of Orthodox Lutheranism by 1700, standing firmly against the new birth "excesses" of Halle and the Pietist movement.

73. *Memoir of Christian David, Servant of the Lord,* #7, 11.

74. See Part Three chapter two above.

75. "For the promise is to you and to your children, and to all who are far away, everyone whom the Lord our God may call."

76. *Memoir of Christian David,* November, 1727, #3C, 35. Here he discussed the marks of the children: "For all who are led by the Spirit are made Sons of God." (Romans 8:18).

77. Ibid, 47.

78. Ibid, #9 January 18, 1733 at Augsburg (Germany), 45.

little children—to whom sometimes it seems very long—help at his own time, just as now.

In his letter from Livonia [later, Latvia] in 1740, David distinguishes between the pardoning and regenerating features of the two stages of salvation:

> As many of us as walk in the light will have our feet that are covered with dust cleansed with the blood of Jesus. The Savior's cause is doing well and is spreading constantly . . . . But there are some who have obtained grace to enter the holy of holies by the blood of Jesus . . . . My calling and that of my brethren is to point souls to the serpent that was lifted up. Thus the hearts of poor souls will be cleansed by faith, the warriors' hearts however in the faith.[79]

In his letter to Abbot Steinmetz from July, 1741, David addresses him as

> my dear old father and brother," and asks, 'But what should I, according to your wish, say about myself, how I stand with the Lamb? . . . in the blood of the Lamb, who is my Mediator [justification] and surety [sealing of the Holy Spirit], it becomes clear to me that I am the reward of his cross, of his effort and labor.

For David, the Pentecost sealing of the Holy Spirit clearly has its globalizing implications.

> The blood of the Son of God, that great worldwide ocean of grace, is swelling up in the countries of the West. There is ebb and tide—it returns to the Orient where it had its origin, and it runs its circular course through the lands of the North. There are old beams and trees floating along which are thrown up on the shore here and there, in Greenland, Norway, Lapland, Finland, and even in the Polar Sea, as far as the Orient to the Magi who were guided by the star to seek and find Jesus. Now the star, the blood of Jesus, and the tide of grace, is returning again and again with those and for those who do not wish to be saved by any other means solely than by the blood of Jesus. Give us the bright morning star! Day and night uttereth speech . . . hid from the heat thereof (Psalm 19:3-7 [English translation 2-6]. Now this is Jesus Christ, the Son of Righteousness, in his bleeding for us.[80]

79. Ibid, #17, April 30, 1740, 52–53.

80. Ibid, To Lieutenant General von Campenhausen at Orvelle in Livonia, January 1743, 59–60.

Zinzendorf as editor of David's *Memoir* has accentuated those sections that uplift the theme of Christ's atonement as the basis for the worldwide mission of the gospel. David complements that theme with his inclusion of the second focal point in that salvation, the Pentecost sealing of the Holy Spirit, a dimension which is featured in David's account of his ministry as reported to John Wesley at Herrnhut in 1738. A representative segment of that account is included here:

> In the meantime[81] we found that a great remiss of behavior had crept in among us. Observing this terrible abuse of preaching Christ for us, we began to insist more than ever of Christ living in us. All our exhortations and preaching turned on this. . . . Our constant inquiries were, 'Is Christ formed in you? Have you a new heart? Is your soul renewed in the image of God? Is the whole body of sin destroyed in you? Are you fully assured,[82] beyond all doubt or fear, that you are a child of God? In what manner and in what moment did you receive that full assurance? If a man could not answer all these questions, we judged he had no true faith.

He further explained, "I plainly perceived that this full assurance was a distinct gift from justifying faith, and often not given until long after it; and that justification does not imply that sin should not *stir* in us, but only that it should not *conquer*." Finally, he concluded, "For many years I had had the forgiveness of sins, and a measure of the peace of God, but I had not till now that witness of His Spirit which shuts out all doubts and fear."[83] This emphasis finally came home to the community in Herrnhut, he reported:

> At my return to Herrnhut I found it difficult to make my brethren sensible of this, or to persuade them not to insist on the assurance of faith as a necessary qualification for receiving the Lord's Supper . . . . This we urge as the principal thing which, if we rightly believe, Christ will surely be 'formed in us'.[84]

These, then, are the significant developments in the ministry of Christian David in the decade between his conversion and his encounter with John Wesley.

---

81. This was dated after David's return to Herrnhut from a trip to Moravia, cited in John Wesley, *Journal* 2, (10 August 1738), 179.
82. The German here would be Versicherung (assurance), which was Steinmetz's term for the sealing of the Holy Spirit in his Pentecost sermons (supra).
83. Ibid, 280.
84. Ibid., 281.

3.11 John Wesley meets Christian David at Herrnhut (August, 1738)

In the fall of 1738, during a season of preaching at Herrnhut, John Wesley appeared, as a visitor fresh from his Aldersgate conversion in England. Wesley came by way of Halle, where the mission of the Pietist renewal center there was now being directed by the son of the late August Hermann Francke, and from there he proceeded to Herrnhut. The outcome was the formation of diasporic Moravian communities in England, Georgia, Pennsylvania, Lapland, Estonia, Central America, Greenland (David went there in person!) and numerous other global points, as a forerunner of a globalized evangelical Christianity.[85]

Wesley reports that on four occasions he heard sermons from Christian David. Three times David chose the subject of those who are "weak in the faith", that is, justified in Christ but without the "indwelling of the holy Ghost." He described the state in which the apostles were living from the crucifixion of their Lord until the descent of the Holy Spirit at Pentecost as a time when they "had faith" but "were not properly converted" and "had not new hearts nor received the gift of the Holy Ghost."[86] It was the fourth sermon, "concerning the ground of our faith," which made the deepest impression on the newly-converted Wesley. Unlike the "penitential struggle" (Busskampf) which Francke of Halle had set forth as a condition for justification, David insisted that "the right foundation is not *your* contrition, . . . not *your* righteousness, . . . nothing that is wrought *in you* by the Holy Ghost; but it is something without you, viz., the righteousness and blood of Christ." "So shall you be cleansed from all sin . . . being renewed day by day in righteousness and all true holiness."[87]

Two days later Wesley spent several hours with Christian David, whose preaching was having great influence on the Moravian Brethren as well as Wesley, with its emphasis on the great objective work of Christ combined, notes Ward, with a "pietistic sense of his indwelling", through the gift of the Holy Ghost (Acts 2:38).[88] In conversation with Wesley, David related how he (David) had been a seeker in Moravia, and, after leaving his Roman Catholic and Lutheran roots, he began to search for evidence that the New Testament prophecies had been fulfilled. He began to realize that "'being justified' is widely different from the having the 'full assurance of faith'

---

85. Within the German Holy Roman Empire, according to the Peace of Westphalia (1648), there could exist only three confessions within Christendom: Catholic, Lutheran and Reformed. All others were to be prosecuted.
86. Ward and Heitzenrater, *Journal and Diaries*, I, 271.
87. Ward and Heitzenrater, *Journal and Diaries*, I, 272.
88. Ward and Heitezenrater, *Journal and Diaries*, I, 273, n.98, also 271, n.90.

3.12 Wesley, David and Steinmetz Seen in Tandem

An important link which this study has discovered between the Pentecost and sanctification theme of David, conveyed to Wesley, and that of Steinmetz, David's spiritual mentor, is the volume of addresses delivered by Steinmetz on "The Sealing of Believers with the Holy Spirit, in some edificatory Pentecost meetings based on Ephesians 4:30."[89] These were delivered by Steinmetz (and published posthumously) after is expulsion from Teschen in 1730, and had been delivered at the Closter of Bergen where Steinmetz served as Abbot and as superintendent of the Lutheran consistory there. They reflected the message he delivered in his sermons preached during the revival at Teschen. This evidence substantiates the claim made by Martin Schmidt that "it was this preaching that prepared John Wesley for conversion and . . . he owed more to David than to anyone, Peter Böhler only excepted."[90] Much later in his ministry, Wesley would be drawn to the Pentecost interpretation of sanctification presented by John Fletcher, but then he was revisiting a theme to which he had earlier been exposed in his encounter with Christian David at Herrnhut, in August of 1738.

Here is the first comparative inquiry into the subsequent preaching of John and Charles Wesley, in consultation with John Fletcher, the Swiss immigrant turned Anglican rector who became their colleague in the English revival, with that of Steinmetz in his Pentecost addresses. Our intent here is to illumine the similarities and differences between the revival preaching in Silesia, where revival first occurred in Protestantism, and the later Methodist revival in England and North America.

The preaching of Steinmetz is presented in this study as featuring the Pentecost sealing of the Holy Spirit which was the seminal theme informing the unfolding of the first revival in Protestantism, occuring in the wake of the Silesian children's revival and was communicated, via Christian David, to John Wesley and the early Methodists, through whom this revival was extended to England and beyond.

---

89. Johann Adam Steinmetz, *von der Versiegelung der Glaubigen mit dem heiligen Geist. In einigen Pfingst-Erbauungsstunden aus Epheser 4, 30* (Frankfurt/Main: Brönner, 1857, third edition), 131 pages; first published ca. 1720 while pastor at Teschen. The influence between Steinmetz and David was reciprocal: the latter aided his mentor when under charges of sedition by the Silesian Catholic authorities were made against Steinmetz, David sent, with little response, official affidavits from Herrnhut to the Hapsburg church offices in Vienna petitioning them to live up to the toleration requirements of the Altranstad Convention, which had provided a basis for a renewal of Protestant preaching in Silesia. *Christian David, Servant of the Lord* (Memoir), #10, 13.

90. Martin Schmidt, *John Wesley*, cited in Ward and Heitzenrater, *Journal and Diaries*, I, 273.

Wood has demonstrated that John Fletcher, John Wesley's later colleague in the revival in England, shows in his letters to Charles Wesley that "his own theology of Pentecost was a clear expression of what John Wesley had learned from Christian David and had incorporated into his early sermons and what Charles Wesley had incorporated into his hymns."[91] Further, Fletcher confided in this correspondence with Charles that he believed the "dispensation of the Holy Spirit . . . to be the grand characteristic of Christian perfection, and connected with the promise of the Father" and that "those who were baptized and sealed with the Holy Spirit on the day of Pentecost were in the state of Christian perfection as distinguished from the faith of babes, or carnal believers, which the apostles had before the day of Pentecost."[92] It is apparent that Charles was sympathetic to the idea of a future Pentecost since it was a highlight of their ongoing conversation. They concluded, "We await a day of Pentecost but we do not pay enough attention to it."[93]

By comparison, Steinmetz did not tie Pentecost with a coming age of the Spirit in any Joachite sense. For him, the sealing of Pentecost occurs as we allow the blood of Jesus to complete its work in us "to be cleansed from all unrighteousness" in the atoning blood. To the extent that the child of God accepts that "sealing" by faith made ecstatic in love, received as the act of God's sealing Presence in the Holy Spirit, is it made personally effectual. This act of sealing is aligned with the apostolic promise which was realized among believers at Pentecost, and was also manifested in the entire Christian community at Ephesus (as Steinmetz notes in his addresses on Ephesians 4:30, "do not grieve the Holy Spirit into which you were sealed)."

However, Steinmetz's basic conviction was that all this occurs through the work of the cross (Luther's *theologica crucis*), completed on behalf of the sins of the whole world, and as witnessed by the apostles. For Luther, this was the passive righteousness of faith based on *Christus in nobis*, to which the Augsburg Confession bore witness. However, with Steinmetz there is a shift at this point.

There is this difference. For Luther, the focal point was the transfer of grace to the sinner when faith enables his to lay hold of the gift of righteousness in Christ (which Luther called the *fröhliche Wechsel*, the blessed exchange, whereby he may now live as no longer an unworthy beggar, out

---

91. Wood, *Pentecost and Sanctification*, 208.

92. Fletcher also confided that this was an event yet to come for him in the future. He stated he would die a disciple of John if he did not receive the baptism of the Holy Spirit, citing only the eleven year old Hannah Richardson as an example of such. Wood 208-9.

93. Wood, *Pentecost and Sanctification*, 209.

of that life rather than his own, as pure gift, in order to serve others, in the overflow of that love which has been received.[94]

For Steinmetz, however, the focal point has instead been shifted to the point in which one has moved in the ordo salutis with the apostles beyond the mount of Calvary, and has found grace at the point where the apostles were gathered again as they had been in their last meal with their Lord before His passion, but now including the host of witnesses from all parts of Judaism, on the day of Pentecost, whereby I am invited to join with the apostles in bearing witness to the redemptive work of the Holy Spirit. That ministry is to seal my heart and soul in the assurance that the virtue of the blood of Christ is now available for me in this new hour of the Holy Spirit's coming in fulfillment of Christ's promise to the apostles after His resurrection and before His ascension. It is to live from the joyful discovery that this promise is now not offered to me from the perspective of my brokenness and condemnation before the law, but rather from the discovery that, I am no longer standing alone before the cross. In this dispensation, I am now filled and transformed by the love of God through the indwelling Holy Spirit, whose Presence is the seal that I am His in His atoning power, through receiving the gift of His shed blood as applied to my broken life,[95] and to live out of that in blessedness and holiness.[96]

Steinmetz signals a shift from Luther's position which had remained with that life imputed to me in Christ. It is now viewed externally as that moment when the Father has shifted from being the God of the law to the God of the gospel, toward the wholly new dispensation of Pentecost.

The difference between Luther and Steinmetz appears to be located at the point where Luther had insisted that we go from the scourge of death, and hell to the paradoxical declaration that I, nevertheless, in all my corruptibility, nevertheless behold myself through Christ as freed in that mortal condition from being a worthy culprit of damnation to being, for the sake of His obedience unto death, a channel of His love for my neighbor (it is always a gift perceived only in the paradoxical logic of faith). For Steinmetz, I am now moved from that point of view at Calvary to that of the joy of the promise not only conferred but sealed and hence empirically received at Pentecost.

---

94. Luther, "Freedom of the Christian," (Dillenberger), 74.
95. See the section where the mystical Presence of the blood of Christ is first experienced with efficacy in the event of Pentecost—see Part,Two, Pentecost Addresses, First Pentecost Lesson, Section 4, Fourth Lesson, Secion 1 (above).
96. Ibid, 7.

The other main point to be made here is, apart from this shift from Calvary to Pentecost in Steinmetz, there would not have been provided a theological basis enabling the birth of revival as theological foundation for Christian globalization. From its beginning with God's awakening of a people in bondage in the aftermath of the Counter-Reformation struggles of Protestant Orthodoxy, the revival spilled over the borders of Silesia into all surrounding lands and beyond within a decade of its manifestation.

This was a theology for a moment in history, It was also a moment when thinking shifted from parish renewal, in a now debilitated Christendom, to global awakening across one border after another, and then one continent after another, as the larger implication of Christian life under the sealing of the Holy Spirit became manifest with the accompanying mandate of Pentecost, sealing the mandate of the witness of the Holy Spirit to that the forgiving and reconciling work of the cross. In the words of Peter's Pentecost sermon (Acts 2:39), "For the promise is for you and your children, and for all who are far off, as many as the Lord our God shall call to Himself." and, in Paul, the message of Pentecost for the church at Ephesus, so sealed, is not to "grieve the Holy Spirit in which you were sealed," but to be faithful in this new vocation.

3.13 Steinmetz's Means for Implementing This New Pentecost Vision of the Redeemed and Globalized Life of the New Humanity in Christ

Steinmetz developed the Pentecost theme to mean that the sealing of the Holy Spirit is conveyed as the means which the Holy Spirit may use to bring the efficacy of saving grace into the believer's life of faith, which are threefold: the testimony of the Scripture, the sacraments of baptism and the Lord's Supper, and, third, there is the internal sensibility to the direct sealing of the Spirit within the soul of the believer apart from the external means of grace.[97] In his perception, these three occur in different combinations for different persons.

In his emphasis on these three means Steinmetz was affirming that there is not a general sealing available to humankind, since it is not efficacious as long as there is any sin remaining within the person who claims redemption in Christ. What made sealing authentic for him is the revival

---

97. See Steinmetz, Pentecost Addresses (on three marks of sealing with the Holy Spirit, in Pentecost Addresses, Second Lesson, Section One.) This moment of grace is most appropriately located in the moment when catechization has brought one to confirmation of the gift of Calvary new sealed for me in the Holy Spirit.

or "Erweckung" context in which it has occurred. The assurance conferred in that event became the measure of the efficacy of the act of sealing. Christian David gained the "Versicherung" (a noun which can be translated as either assurance or confirmation) in relation to the sealing, when he heard Steinmetz preach at Teschen, and he was also receiving the gift of Pentecost, e.g., that which was the experience of the apostles at Pentecost, who also received the signs (Siegel, or seals) along with the wonders, although evidence has not been found of the "flaming tongues of fire" at Teschen.

The precise subject to which the sign points is the shed blood of Christ on the cross, or, in theological terms, the great Christian mystery of the atonement, to which David had first been exposed in Schwedler's preaching on the cross at Niederwiesa, before he traveled on to Teschen and encountered Steinmetz's focus on sealing and blessedness in the Holy Spirit at Pentecost.[98] Now the pardon of all his sins, which was promised to him by the preaching of Schwedler in the midst of David's dire illness, and which was the power message behind the revival which swept through Silesia on the heels of the children's revival was now confirmed upon David.

This was the message which David brought with him when he returned from Silesia to Herrnhut. It not only impacted Wesley on his itinerary there in 1738, but had also been the spark which also initiated Erweckung (revival) at Herrnhut in 1727. The life of that community was revitalized in an awakening triggered by a children's revival as in Silesia, occurring in a low point in its history. The internal tensions which seemed irreparable concerned disagreement over whether revival should be encouraged there, as in Silesia (David's position), or whether the focus should be upon

98. In his letter to Abbot Steinmetz in July, 1741, David looks back on his initial encounter with the two stage approach to salvation he learned from him during the time of his visit with him during the great Teschen (Silesia) revival, and reports as follows: "Now, my dear old father and brother, this is what I can report of the Brethren. But what should I, according to your wish, say about myself, how I stand with the Lamb? I am a poor sinner, my Savior knows that well, but one that has found grace....but in the blood of the Lamb, who bears the sins of the whole world, who already from the beginning as it were, was slain, who is my Mediator and Surety [sealer in the Holy Spirit], and yesterday, today and in all eternity will be and remain my all, and it becomes clear to me that I am the reward of His cross, ...and that with faith I should come every day, and this with confidence, just as I am."- Christian David, *Servant of the Lord (Memoir)*, #19, 55. In September, 1741, David writes again to Steinmetz, "What is your attitude toward our brother Zinzendorf? That he is a servant that is sealed with the blood of the Lamb, a poor sinner who has nothing but grace and in all eternity deserves nothing else."*Memoir* #19, 57.

Zinzendorf's initial commitment to reconstitute the ancient order of Unity from the early Hussite Brethren.

Zinzendorf had experimented with revivalism as the means of extending the mission of the renewed Moravian Brethren in the world. However, before the awakening came which would prove formative for the community in 1727, Zinzendorf had been prone to vacillate on the subject. The reason for this may be traced to his infatuation with the Philadelphian model which had first enamored his grandmother as the model for his estate of Hennersdorf. It sought to realize the Philadelphian idea (Revelation 3) of an unpartisan fellowship of all comrades in Christ. On the other hand, he had officially committed himself to reconstitute the ancient Unity of the Brethren, according to their canons for an apostolic community. Then again, he thought he had found his model for revival within the large "inspirationist" revival which erupted in the Reformed territories of the Wetterau (Rhineland). It was emerging as an influential sect under the leadership of Johann Friedrich Rock (born, 1668). Being radical Pietists, Inspirationists rejected working within established churches of Christendom altogether and so had a marginalized influence on the mainline church bodies in Europe. In his day, Rock was seeking places to expand this work, leading Zinzendorf to invite him to observe the community at Herrnhut. After a short visit, Rock outright rejected what he observed of its worship life, declaring to Zinzendorf that it was devoid of the Holy Spirit.

By contrast with these options, the revival which came from Silesia through the influence of Steinmetz and Christian David advanced across borders as both men, and many of their lay associates, preached in the awakening that reached Herrnhut, as well as in neighboring Bohemia and Moravia, and the adjacent German states. These initiatives were received as spontaneous expressions of a fresh ministry of the Holy Spirit. The effects on Herrnhut were to equip and transform the community (especially as seen in the deep involvement of the children in Herrnhut) in ways that also detracted from Zinzendorf's ability to continue his original community, with its grounding in the Unitas Fratrem of the ancient traditions of the Hussite brethren. The Saxon government, which had lordship over Herrnhut and was compromised in its Protestantism by its obligations to the Hapsburg Emperor, could not tolerate that community after it had become swept with revivalism, which the Saxon regime perceived threatened the stability of imperial Christendom (in the Holy Roman Empire). Consequently, Zinzendorf was forced to leave Herrnhut and relocate his community elsewhere after 1730, the year of Steinmetz's expulsion from

Teschen. The new home for the Moravians then became Marienborn in the Rhineland (Wetterau) district of Western Germany. It was from that base that the bulk of Moravian global mission activity was developed in the 1740s and beyond, including the missional work of Christian David.

After the departure of Zinzendorf from Herrnhut, the remaining community easily accommodated itself to function as a Lutheran parish (the official church of Saxony) without little trace of revivalism. Marienborn itself endured the travail of religious excess in the form of the "blood and wounds" (of "time of sifting") controversy, which did not involve David, but resulted in financial ruin under Zinzendorf's overextension of his resources in the global outreach of the Brethren. When bankruptcy forced Marienborn's closing in the 1740s,[99] the buildings were purchased and maintained for a season as the headquarters of the Inspirationist revivalist sect, which by that time had grown at least as large as had the Moravians in the provinces of the Hapsburg Empire.[100]

---

99. In 1738 Zinzendorf was expelled from Herrnhut by the Saxon government for resisting anti conventicle decrees and relocated to Marienborn in the Wetterau, where the relocated Moravian community continued its global outreach until the financial collapse of that center (under the duress of internal conflict called the "time of sifting") in 1753, when it was taken over by the Society of the Inspired who continued the revival which had its beginnings in Silesia into the nineteenth century. See Ward, *Protestant Evangelical Awakening*, 130.

100. When the Inspirationists began to lose their prophetic voices, after the first generation of this movement, it declined in membership, although officially surviving through exodus to Iowa in the nineteenth century, where it remains in altered form under the name of the Amana Community (from which the later Amana frigerators had their origin), 161-174.

101. August Hermann Francke (d. 1727) was the leader of the great Pietist renewal center at the University of Halle, who was trained at the university of Leipzig, as a follower of the work of Philip Jacob Spener (his Pia Desideria was the manifesto for church renewal which launched Pietism within the Lutheran churches when it was published in 1675 founded by the new Prussian government in the hope of creating a viable option to the decadent Ortho-dox Lutheran and Reformed universities which had maintained their status quo since the days of the Reformation two centuries earlier. His practical focus led to the formation of the first coeducational schools in Europe, open to all classes and supported by revenue from spiritually renewed parishes which received new pastoral leadership from graduates of the theological school at Halle. Here was launched the first world mission center for evangelical Protestantism to be taken to the world, and the first mass printing press for Bibles and Christian literature, which resulted in the distribution of over two millions copies of the Luther Bible in the early decades of the eighteenth century. The first Protestant missionaries to India, for example, were Halle graduates in the first decade of the eighteenth century. It was that energy which led to Francke's incursion into the church crisis in Silesia, where Pietist renewal was for the first time transformed, under the influence of the Holy Spirit (the children's revival) into a new phenomenon of God called an

Notice the pattern here: revival which began in one locale (Silesia) would develop through the instrumentality of diverse persons and ecclesial traditions, including the Moravians and the American Great Awakenings, including the Methodists, United Brethren in Christ, and Evangelicals, among others, who would each have their moment in the sun, in specific times and places, as the center of that revival, until its cutting edge moved in the twentieth and twenty first centuries into the Global South.

The complex relationship of Zinzendorf to the development of the revival based in Silesia is also compounded by his apparently impulsive reaction against the theology of conversion developed by Francke,[101] which had been influential in resourcing the primitive revival in Teschen and had also been replicated in many facets of the Halle mission for the renewal of European Christendom and extending its influence globally.[102] Zinzendorf objected to Francke's focus on a "legalistic" approach to penitential remorse under the law, called the Busskampf (penitential struggle), as the initial step in conversion, leading to the Durchbruch ("breakthrough") of the power of the gospel to bring peace of soul. For Zinzendorf, it is preferable to look only to the love of the Lamb of God as the incentive for conversion, simulating Jesus' question to Peter, "Do you love me? Feed my sheep . . . " (John 121:15-17).[103] For Zinzendorf, if one only feels Jesus love for you and your for Him at that moment, that is sufficient to your becoming joined to the Lamb of God at the point of His blood sacrifice for your sins. In short, it was an affective exaggeration of Luther's understanding of the "blessed exchange" which constitutes the evangelical experience of justification by faith.

Steinmetz had experienced Zinzendorf as his advocate in the Silesian revival and later through Zinzendorf's assistance in new ministry posts for Steinmetz in Germany in the period after his expulsion from Silesia in

---

Erweckung (awakening), later popularized by the term revival.

102. Halle missionaries were the first to enter India, a century before William Carey and the Baptists. Through Francke's work with the King of Denmark as the support base for that initiative. They were also influential on the rise of the mission arm of the Church of England, the Society for the Propagation of Christian Knowledge, which was modeled in part on Halle, through the influence of William Boehm. See Ward, *Protestant Evangelical Awakening*, 302–310.

103. Count Nicholas Von Zinzendorf, "Concerning Saving Faith," from Nine Public Lectures (1746), Peter Erb, Ed. Piestists: Selected Writings (New York: Paulist Press, 1983), 314.

1730. He then maintained a fifteen year correspondence with Zinzendorf. The substance of much of the later correspondence between them concerned his disagreement with Zinzendorf's rendition of the new birth in terms of subjective feeling (Gefühl) of the passion and love of Christ, devoid of the repentance based in the conviction of the law.[104] Steinmetz rejected Zinzendorf's approach, as taking too lightly the need for fallen humans to experience the forgiveness and removal of sin through the cross, by the Holy Spirit's sealing of that work, among all who would be sealed in His blood, This action produces the condition of Seligkeit, the blessedness of new life in Christ as the basis for the fulfillment of Pentecost.[105]

This goal is articulated here not in terms of a collective goal for humanity through transcendent design, but as a provision of grace empowered by the Spirit so that the narrative of Pentecost may become, through personal human volition, replicated in the life of each child of God who is drawn to the promise of the Father.

Steinmetz also spent time in his later ministry in Magdeburg, Germany, taking issue with an alternate response to the first revival in Protestant tradition, the children's revival in Silesia. The position he critiques is that held by Wilhelm Petersen, who offered the first affirmation of that revival in his study, *Die Macht der Kinder*. In that account, this revival signaled the approach of a new age into which the church would be ushered as its telos or ultimate missional goal: humanity was now at the threshold of the imminent return of Christ as Judge of all mankind, as a period of salvation and expurgation of those who fall short of the kingdom of God, so that, ultimately, all may enter the final state which he called the "restoration of all things."[106] Petersen had based his expectations for that outcome in the

---

104. Steinmetz's friendly discourse and disagreement with Zinzendorf on the matter of the "Wundenlitenei" (the litany of the wounds of Christ) was the point of contention, which came to a head in the period after Steinmetz's dismissal from Teschen and service as abbot in the Cloister Bergen, from 1736 and continuing through that decade, involving his personal visit to Herrnhut to confer with Zinzendorf on the matter in 1739. Renner, 104–109. Steinmetz refers to this as a fanatical excess of devotion not grounded in Scripture, likening it to the attraction of bees to honey to the point of self-destruction, which he calls the "Art von Bienen," the manner of bees. Renner, 107.

105 Renner, 18, and Steinmetz, Pentecost Addresses, Third Lesson, Section 2, "A Panoply of Virtues Among Those Sealed."

106. "Der Wiederbringung aller Dinge", see Nordmann, 166–172; Steinmetz addressed these issues during his tenure as abbot at Cloister Bergen in Magdeburg. Renner, 97–99. Here he is responding to correspondence from the "pious Count of Cassel" who speaks favorably of this doctrine as conforming with the position of Halle Pietism, which it was not. Steinmetz responds that it is unbiblical (e.g., Mark 9:43–48 and I Corintnhians

children's revival, which provided his paradigm for the ultimate design of human destiny in a world governed by a benevolent God. Hence, it was a kind of harbinger of the dawning age of the Enlightenment, in which old patterns of a decadent and ignorant humanity would recede from visibility. From this optimistic outlook all unpleasant issues of heaven and hell, regeneration and reprobation, would be superseded by the final triumph of divine mercy, through the power of the Spirit's intercession.

It is intriguing that both Petersen and Steinmetz looked upon the children's revival with kindred spirits: they saw the children as the embodiment of those who will enter the Kingdom of God. The difference lay in how this is quantified and what of God gets expunged in the process. To be specific, Petersen was a soft kind of universalist (since there is still place for a temporal purgatory for fallen humans). Steinmetz was, as Luther, faithful to Augustine's cosmology: there are two communities of humans under God's watch, and the one which is blessed is separated from the other as a mass of perdition, because they rightly ordered the ends of the caritas, to be directed toward God and not the creature.

Petersen developed his account of human destiny under God through a personal and intellectual grappling with the two main conflicting schools of German mystical theology which reached a crescendo from the fifteenth through the seventeenth centuries, and drawing from that discussion he arrived at his benevolent view of human destiny under God. It is a discussion that he opens in an age of Protestant Orthodoxy, when the controversies over this mystical theology were having a far reaching impact at the grassroots level of Protestant Orthodoxy in the seventeenth and early eighteenth centuries.

In the future restoration doctrine we find Petersen's way of correcting what he perceived to be the oppressive influence of Jacob Böhme's German mystical theology, which Walter Nordmann called a dualistic, voluntaristic mystical theology, in favor of what that author called a speculative monistic interpretation of mystical theology. What we discover here is the depth to which an early modern theologian/practitioner of revival, like Petersen, was writing about the birth of modern revivals by appealing to the late medieval minds concerning the interface of spirit and nature in Western religion. It will give us more grounding in that little investigated

---

15:21–26), and also harmful to the soul, especially causing negligence in the faith and enmity toward God, in spite of His incessant mercy in Christ. It renders superfluous the difference between the godless and the faithful. At the core, it represented to Steinmetz the most incorrigible enmity of the unrepentant sinner against God and His Christ.

discussion to set forth here some of its seminal principles, as evidence for the rigor with which early revival figures were engaging the deeper intellectual issues underlying and supporting the new phenomenon appearing in the time of Petersen and Steinmetz which we now call revival.

Here is a short account of the main principles informing that discussion. Steinmetz saw that such a state of Pentecostal grace reached by the sealed believer signified a new era where the Holy Spirit will do a deeper and more extensive work of renewal regenerating the human community across national, linguistic and ecclesial barriers, than has previously occurred. This is signified by the title given to his chronicle and interpretation of the *Building of the Kingdom of God on Earth*:[107] it is not a kingdom humans build with God's paternal blessing; it is a chronicle of the work of the Holy Spirit bearing witness with the human spirit, that God's destiny for humanity is to become the children of God.

In his Pentecost addresses, we find Steinmetz giving much attention to conflating the convicting purpose of the law along with an affective engaging of the blood of Christ as the only solace for all legal accusations. The very notion of the sealing of the Holy Spirit for Steinmetz is dependent upon this twofold work of law and gospel in his version of the theology of the cross. To omit the struggle of repentance is to seek the joys and consolation of grace without any apprehension of the depth of sin and the impending threats of Satan, hell and damnation, which must be overcome in our lives before the dominion of the Spirit's sealing can be received by faith. In terms of twentieth century theology, such an outcome would be grace without the cross, or cheap grace.[108] Zinzendorf defended his position against Steinmetz's objections, considering it to be steeped in graceless legalism.[109]

The language of sealing in relation to Pentecost and sanctification was frequently used by John Fletcher, who was Wesley's defender and designated successor. Fletcher developed this theme from his Swiss Reformed heritage in the Genevan tradition within the context of the Swiss revival led by Samuel Lutz, whom both Christian David and John Fletcher knew personally. Three decades after John Wesley's encounter with Christian David at Herrnhut, who along with his students had explained to Wesley the seal-

---

107. "[das] Aufbau des reich Gottes auf Erden."
108. See Dietrich Bonhoeffer, "Cost of Discipleship" in Kerr, *Readings in Christian Thought*, 357–362.
109. Steinmetz's refutation of Zinzendorf occurs with reference to the implicit antinomianism of his "blood and wounds litany," as reflected in his correspondence with his mentor during his tenure as abbot of Cloister Bergen, in Renner, 106.

ing of the Spirit as subsequent to justification, Fletcher's *Checks to Antinomianism* were edited and approved by John and Charles Wesley.[110] His *Checks* were also officially approved by Wesley's annual conference[111] and Pentecost became a theme of Methodist preaching on the sealing of the Spirit and sanctification.

This theme of sealing in relation to Pentecost sanctification is also prevalent in Charles' hymnody, from the time when John returned to meet with his brother following his encounter with Christian David at Herrnhut, which was followed by the publication of their *Hymns and Sacred Poems* (1739), where the theme of sanctification and Pentecost are clearly joined.[112] In these hymns Charles uses the sealing theme we encountered in Steinmetz and David, in multiple places:

> 7 The promised Comforter impart,
> Open the fountain in my heart.
> There, let Him flow with springing joys,
> And into life eternal rise.
>
> 8 There let him ever, ever dwell,
> The pledge, the witness and the seal,
> I'll glory then in sins forgiven,
> In Christ my life, my love, my heaven![113]

Again, in Charles' hymn on Acts 2:17, "I will pour out my Spirit on all flesh":

> The Holy Ghost to man is given:
> Rejoice in God sent down from heaven.

---

110. "Charles Wesley was more influenced by John Fletcher," Wood, 136.

111. Thomas Coke, *A Series of Letters Addressed to the Methodist Connection* (London: A. Paris, Printer, 1810), 97, 190.

112. Wood, 56. Note here Wood's clear link of the Wesleys to David in affirming that "Inspired by what John Wesley learned from Christian David, John Wesley explained his own experience to his older brother according to the two stages of faith based upon the pattern of the justifying faith of the disciples before Pentecost and subsequently the disciples being "cleansed from all sin" on the disciples as a result of the outpouring of the Holy Spirit on them on the day of Pentecost...granting full assurance of faith"(46). Here Wood also notes both brothers' receptivity to this theme may be attributed to their formative experience of baptism and confirmation in the Anglican tradition, which served as the liturgical corollary for the themes of repentance and sanctification (ibid., 49).

113. Charles Wesley hymn from Acts 1:4, *Hymns and Sacred Poems*, cited in Wood, 57.

> The cleansing blood to apply,
> the heavenly life display.
> And wholly sanctify,
> *And seal us to this day* [emphasis added].[114]

In working from the "typological correspondence" between Old and New Testaments, Charles likens the Spirit's work of sealing in sanctification to circumcision in Israel:

> "The covenant old in types concealed,
> Now in the gospel is revealed . . .
>
> *The Lord his Spirit's seal applies,*
> *His people all to circumcise"* [emphasis ended].[115]

In addition to reflecting the thought of the Old Testament scholar Gerhard von Rad, this motif had a direct historical influence on Steinmetz and David through the pervasive influence in German Pietism of the federal theology[116] based in Johannes Cocceius and his successors, which first introduced this apostolic theme from Irenaeus (and later transmitted by Joachim of Fiore) to Protestant Christianity.[117]

The focus on the sealing of the Holy Spirit is a major feature of eschatology for Charles Wesley, as well, as he expresses in poetry with reference to John 14:16: "he will seal your present and eternal bliss."[118] Here we find close correlation with Steinmetz on "Overcoming as the outcome of the Spirit's sealing" in his First Pentecost Address.[119]

Steinmetz emphasized that the Holy Spirit is to be understood as the prime witness of Himself in the sealing of the believer at Pentecost, seen from the standpoint of the lack of that indispensable witness in the post Pentecost account of Acts 19:2, reporting the question Paul poses to the Corinthians, "have you received the Holy Spirit, since you believed?"[120]

---

114. "Sinners Lift Up Your Hearts," on Acts 2:17, Wood, 59.
115. Charles Wesley hymn of Acts 7:8 cited in Wood, 68.
116. From the Latin: foedus, or covenant, which birthed the concept of salvation history or Heilsgeschichte in modern Protestant theology.
117. On this, see J. Steven O'Malley, *Pilgrimage of Faith; The Legacy of the Otterbeins* (Metuchen, NJ: Scarecrow Press, 1973), Part One.
118. Wood, 65.
119. See Part Two, First Pentecost Address, Section 7.
120. Steinmetz reference to Acts 19:2, in Pentecost Lesson Two, Section 3.

Similarly, Jeremy Taylor (whose theology was part of the intellectual background of the Wesley brothers) "appeals to this passage in his exposition of the Anglican rite of confirmation as the "seal of our salvation," following the apostolic precedent of Gregory Nazianzus, who speaks of the sealing of the Holy Spirit as "a real signature, and witness, ... a sign of the Lord's dominion over us."[121] Jeremy Taylor also relates baptism, sealing, and confirmation: "in baptism we are made sons [e.g. children] of God, but we receive the witness and *testimony* of it in confirmation."[122] "Testimony" as used by Taylor is synonymous with sealing of the Holy Spirit in Steinmetz, or "full assurance of holiness" in Charles Wesley.[123]

In the line traceable from Steinmetz through David to the Wesleys (and Whitefield), there is also a common shift of focus to the future that defied the reigning apocalypticism inherent within Reformation and Protestant Orthodox theology. There is a correlation between Charles Wesley's reference to holiness as full assurance, thus signifying, "we want the Spirit of holiness to seal the heirs of heaven,"[124] and the title of Steinmetz's publication of his Pentecost addresses, which was the theme of his preaching at Teschen, through which Christian David was confirmed in faith and grounded in his own two stage understanding of salvation, which he conveyed to the Wesleys via his encounter with John Wesley.[125]

Christian David would look upon the life freed from sin through the Pentecost witness of the sealing of the Holy Spirit in the blood of Christ as a joyful suffering and endurance in the love of the Lamb, and as the function of a life of witness to the farthest extent possible in the world. It is in that spirit that he writes of the state which Wesleyans would call the sanctified life, after his arrival in Neuherrnhut, Greenland, en route from his ministry with the German immigrants in Pennsylvania in 1749: "Hallelujah, we are here now!...In Pennsylvania, the Lamb and the gracious Father and the gracious Mother" [a reference to the dual work of the cross and Pentecost] ministered to effect the sealing in the blood of Christ

---

121. Wood, 10.
122. Taylor...in Wood, 130.
123. Charles Wesley, in Wood, 13. The Wesleys' use of multiple expressions to describe Christian perfection did have its source in their reading of Taylor, as Wood notes (49), but it also may be attributed to their encounter with the sealing language of Pentecost following Calvary, which was conveyed to them by David in Herrnhut, since that was the chief expression he used to describe it, following Steinmetz. It was following that encounter that their first published hymns reflected that the prominence of that theme.
124. Charles Wesley, in Wood, 2.
125. Steinmetz, *Concerning the Sealing of the Believer with the Holy Spirit, in Several Pentecost Edification Sessions*.

through the Holy Spirit unto those who would "endure every difficulty as a blessing to the one to whom it is thus given, although to an outsider it would appear insurmountable."[126]

Closely related to the focus on the future of humanity within the Steinmetz/David/Wesleys trajectory, is the underlying theological issue concerning the difference between an incomplete and a completed state of saving grace. At one point John Wesley suggested to Fletcher to clarify that the Holy Spirit was present in the life of everyone who is justified even before one is fully sanctified, a suggestion which Fletcher incorporated in his Checks. The later John Wesley wanted it to be clearly understood that one is a babe in Christ at their justification, which suggests need for completion of the stages of adulthood and maturity.[127] While Fletcher and Charles Wesley used the term "the new birth' for Christian perfection, they allowed that all justified believers who are not fully sanctified are still children of God similarly to Steinmetz's view that the child of God is the full expression of the sealing of the Holy Spirit and that the descent of the Holy Spirit at Pentecost meant "they were fully assured" and "cleansed from all sin,"[128] although one may still be a child of God in a justified state without this fullness.

Steinmetz would differ from Fletcher and both Wesleys in locating that cleansing not in the theme of Spirit baptism per se, but exclusively in the blood of Christ, that is, in light of justification, to which the Holy Spirit now bears witness in sealing us in the blood through faith. Further, he adds that the visible verification that this sealing is from God is that it is imparted with "Seligkeit," or the blessedness and joy of the new fellowship in Christ resulting in the dominion of the Spirit in our lives.[129] In that aspect, our sealing consists of sharing in the fullness of the holiness of God, as represented in the Holy Spirit now indwelling us through His seal. We are now resourced with the fullness of His holiness as the basis for our Seligkeit, which enables us to live in dominion over sin and death. In praxis, Steinmetz's explanation of this second state of grace seems to be saying

---

126. David here describes the work of the Triune God as the message of the cross (the Lamb) together with the father and the Mother (reflecting the sealing ministry of the Holy Spirit in giving birth to the church at Pentecost) and doing so with reference to Zinzendorf 's term for the Holy Spirit as the "Mother" of believers within a perichoresis (or familial) Trinitarian model. See *Memoir (#24)*, 64–68.

127. See this discussion of Wesley's difference with Fletcher on this point, in Wood, chapters 13-14.

128. Wood, 53.

129. See the translated text of Steinmetz's volume at the beginning of Part 2 above.

that the key to its efficacy is to become ever more holy unto God not by appeal to human strength but in increasingly becoming a participant in the efficacy of Christ's shed blood, as attested to us in the seal which is imparted to us in and through the Holy Spirit as we live in light of the gift which is Pentecost.

Addendum to Chapter Three

From the Cross to Pentecost — A Theological Grid

1. A Theological Grid for Comparing Luther and the Wesleys on Cross and Kingdom with Reference to Johann Adam Steinmetz and Christian David as Their Primary Connecting Links.

These five historical figures are here compared in terms of their respective ways of expressing the following doctrinal themes: (1) the sinner and the need for the cross, (2) Pentecost and sanctification in light of the cross, and (3) the coming kingdom.

The areas of continuity and discontinuity among our five comparative voices on the cross and the kingdom established on the day of Pentecost are as follows:

(a) The Sinner and the Cross

Luther

The "Theology of the Cross" (theologia crucis) stands over against the "Theology of Glory"(theologia gloria): The former locates where faith meets God in His redemptive love in Christ, while the latter denotes the triumphal, self-justifying ways the flesh behaves toward God, out of a sense of superiority, even to God himself: "we Christians are *not* to become theologians of glory, which calls the bad good and the good bad," but rather "theologians of the cross, who say what a thing is."[1] Luther is typically dialectical here: The cross represents both law and gospel: "The law does indeed ter-

---

[1]. Thesis 21, "The Heidelbe 2 WA 41, 190f. [Weimar Ausgabe, *Luther Werke*, Weimar, 1883–2009, in 121 volumes.].

rify me more dreadfully when I hear that Christ, God's Son, had to bear it for me than it does when it is only proclaimed to me with threatenings apart from Christ and apart from this great anguish of the Son of God."[2]

The cross calls Christ to suffer both innocently and unrighteously at the same time by bearing our sins in agape love; it calls us as believers to suffer unrighteously yet joyously not as punishment for sins but by the devil and the world since they are our enemy for the sake of the Word and our faith.[3]

The action of saving grace is focused upon the point of Christ's paschal sacrifice, in which Savior and sinner intersect in the cross, which Luther called the "blessed exchange," ("fröhliche Wechsel"). Christ's righteousness is graciously exchanged for our sin (a life marked by unfaithfulness to the Word): He becomes the sinner and we become, by imputation, the righteous ones, by faith, meaning through trust (fiducia) in the promise of grace.

Steinmetz

He relies on the biblical history of redemption through Father, Son and Holy Spirit as found in the Augsburg Confession of the Lutheran Church, but his emphasis is upon encountering the crucified and resurrected Christ in the present, via proclamation, sacraments, and mystical encounter. He also laments the misuse of the redemptive work of Christ by the host of cultural Christians whom he calls "mouth" Christians only, who have never encountered Him as Living Lord, inwardly and personally, by faith.[4]

He will insist that personal access to the work of Christ on the cross comes through the inward sealing of the Holy Spirit, who bears witness to the efficacy of the shed blood of Christ for salvation.

Christian David

Christ's atoning work is the "word of reconciliation" whereby we are reconciled to God not by our works but solely by the shedding of His blood. "The right foundation is not your contrition, not your righteousness," but "it is nothing of your own, nothing that is wrought *in you* by the Holy Spirit; but it is something *without you;* viz, the righteousness and blood of Christ."[5] Like Steinmetz, his access to Christ is not historically in the events of Calvary, or in one's contrition based upon those events (even when inspired

---

2. WA 41, 190f. [Weimar Ausgabe, *Luther Werke*, Weimar, 1883-2009, in 121 volumes.]
3. WA 52, 794.
4. Steinmetz, Versiegelung, First Pentecost Address, 3a, 10.
5. Christian David, *Servant of the Lord*, 272.

by the Holy Spirit), but rather, it is inwardly, through the present working of the Holy Spirit. Also like Steinmetz, David distinguishes between what we first attempted by our own works and what was "wholly and solely by the blood of Christ."[6] He states that "your contrition" and "your grief" after hearing of Christ's atoning death are all "works of the selfsame Spirit;" nevertheless, "This is not the foundation . . . all of this is nothing to our justification." In words that Luther would affirm, he adds, "Nay it may hinder it, if you build anything upon it." True faith is nothing within wrought in you by the Holy Ghost, but it is something without you, vis. the righteousness and the blood of Christ."[7]

The Wesleys

John: Personal faith in the saving work of Christ was born in his Aldersgate discovery, based on the reading of Luther's Preface to Romans in an English Moravian meeting. He there acknowledged Christ as the sole basis for his being made righteous before the Father, through Him offering the oblation of Himself for the sin of the entire world.[8] Christ's death on the cross is the foundation in righteousness for both justification and sanctification.[9] As Cell noted, Christ's atoning death on the cross became a "burning issue" for him only after Aldersgate.[10]

Charles: Concurrent with John's Aldersgate discovery and trip to Herrnhut, Charles preached a sermon on "The Threefold State" which affirmed his belief in conversion by one and not by multiple states of faith, called being "made partakers of the divine nature...and all holiness."[11]

---

6. "The person who builds even a trifle on his own work has no sealing through the Holy Spirit, and the entire ground of his hope does not rest on the merits of Christ.....The correct sealing and assurance, which comes through the Holy Spirit...may clearly be understood as standing on the blood and merit of Jesus Christ, so that a person who comes before that cross may know, see and recognize that he is himself a sinner worthy of condemnation." *Versiegelung,* I, 3, b, 12, and c.12-13.

7. John Wesley, *Journal and Diaries I* (1735-38), Bicentennial Edition of the *Works of John Wesley,* 18:272, (August 10, 1738).

8. Kenneth Collins, *The Theology of John Wesley: Holy Love and the Shape of Grace* (Abingdon: 2007), 101.

9. John Wesley, *A Plain Account of Christian Perfection* (New York: Glane and P Sandford for the Methodist Episcopal Church, 1842).

10. Cell cited in Kenneth J. Collins, *The Scripture Way of Salvation: The Heart of John Wesley's Theology,* 80.

11. Charles Wesley, "The Three-fold State, Sermons of Charles Wesley, 139-140." Wood notes this conflation of justification and sanctification came under the influence of the English Moravians, who differed from Christian David on this point. Ibid., 57.

This is a position he would later alter, through influence upon John from David, and Steinmetz before him.

(b) Pentecost and Sanctification in Relation to the Cross

Luther

Pentecost for Luther is a liturgical event in the church calendar but it is not associated with an ordo salutis grounded in the theology of the cross, which this study has examined.

Steinmetz

Here we encounter the first occasion in the revival traditions of Protestantism to distinguish justifying from sanctifying grace, understood as Pentecostal sealing and enabling. He derives these two stages of grace from the theology of the cross. He writes as a Lutheran pastor theologian who finds opportunity, occasioned by the revival, to give renewed attention to Luther's theologia crucis. His context is an emergency (or missional) congregation launching its life and mission under the sway of a rising awakening among the masses of Protestant refugees in Silesia.

In the preface to his addresses, Steinmetz identifies Christ's redemptive work on the cross as the core soteriological theme for interpreting the meaning and intent of the awakening in Silesia which was ignited by the children's revival. He states that this theme can be outwardly known by "theoretical reason" (e.g., as it was then interpreted by Lutheran Orthodoxy and in its confessions), or by "godly wisdom." The latter phrase denotes wisdom immediately conveyed by the Holy Spirit to authentic worshippers of the crucified Jesus, which is distinct that that which is deduced through Aristotelian logic in the academy (the preferred mode of Lutheran Orthodoxy).

Basic to this task, Steinmetz shifts ground zero for understanding the evangelical experience of salvation to a point beyond the biblical narrative of Calvary, where it was in Luther, to the narrative of Pentecost (Acts 2). Only those who become assured of the promise of the gospel, in relation to the cross, occurring through the sealing of believers by the Holy Spirit on Pentecost, may be called real Christians, or the children of God.[12] This reading of Scripture is what he calls the result of godly (e.g. pneumatic) wisdom as opposed to the "natural reason" used by most orthodox or scholastic Protestants.[13] The sealing is what connects Pentecost with the cross,

---

12. Steinmetz, "The Sealing and Pentecost," Ibid., I, 4, 15–16.
13. Steinmetz, "The Sealing and Pentecost," Ibid., I, 4, 15–16.

because only through the Holy Spirit's indwelling ministry can the blood of Jesus be applied to the inner lives of the children of God.[14]

In his first Pentecost address, Steinmetz explains why the sealing which happened at Pentecost is urgently necessary for assurance of salvation. Unlike Luther, he says the gift of salvation by Christ's righteousness is not passively received in the presence of the cross; instead, it is to be urgently sought by "overcoming" one's inattentiveness to what the cross means, "which is the prerequisite for access to the sealing through the Holy Spirit."[15] However, once the Holy Spirit convinces one of corruption and a state of damnation (through the ministry of the law), one's sense of godlessness has only been compounded. At this point, Steinmetz counsels, do not give up: "You have already won the first victory. There the Holy Spirit has already conquered the evil thoughts which wanted to bind you, that you should now believe."[16] It is the work of the Spirit for preparing the heart to receive the sealing which is then to follow.

Also unlike Luther, for whom freedom from bondage comes when a person confesses that all his sin is transferred by Christ onto Himself in His atoning death on the cross; for Steinmetz, once the first victory (conviction of sin) is won by the Holy Spirit, we are encouraged to appeal to the Spirit's anointing to enable the "poor sinner" to "triumph" over "those remaining things" in the matchless blood of Christ, until, following the lead of Jacob's wrestling with the angel,[17] we pray, "I will hold on until You bless me, as an overcomer who receives the crown, the seal of the Holy Spirit Himself, the gem of blessedness and of the holy ones, not from the merit of works, but as a pure gift of grace."[18]

The focus has shifted with Steinmetz from overcoming unfaithfulness (as Luther) to overcoming ungodliness, suggesting the sanctifying quality of Pentecostal grace in which the forgiven sinner is sealed.[19] Here the Holy Spirit, in the context of Pentecost, is guiding the seeker back to Calvary so that the benefit of being cleansed by the shed blood of Christ may now be appropriated to grant personal assurance of the forgiveness of sins, and

---

14. On this, see Steinmetz, *Versiegelung*.
15. Ibid., 29.
16. Ibid.
17. A reference to Jacob wrestling with the angel, Genesis 32:24–30. Ibid.
18. Ibid.
19. Ibid. Here the Holy Spirit, in the context of Pentecost, is directing the seeker back to Calvary to appropriate inwardly and personally the power of Christ's sacred blood unto forgiveness of sins.

also to receive the Spirit's indwelling within the heart unto Seligkeit, which is translated as blessedness, or also sanctification.[20]

In his second Pentecost address Steinmetz pressed further to declare that the Holy Spirit works not only through signs of His Presence; it is also the case that the very Person of the Holy Spirit may serve as the chief seal who is imprinted within the heart of the believer,[21] along with other "ancillary" seals which usually accompany the Holy Spirit. These include the words of Scripture which are read and proclaimed, the sacraments (and especially the eucharist, but also baptism), and, third, the immediate sensations of the Holy Spirit whereby He communes with the believer directly, in prayer, dreams, and prophecies.[22] To be assured that the sealing is salvific and not temporal, he emphasizes that God brings persons to faith among His works of sealing through the Holy Spirit for those who are without guile, a childlike quality.

Viewed together, these works of sealing comprise an outpouring of the Holy Spirit. Such assurance also represents a response to Christ's work of conversion from sin to grace.[23] The focal point of that work is a personal identity with the shed blood of Jesus.

---

20 Steinmetz discusses blessedness/sanctification (Seligkeit) as the consequence of sealing in the blood of Christ unto forgiveness and righteousness by faith in his first Pentecost Address, "With the Spirit there now grows such a grounded, persevering, heaven focused assurance, that with it, one may be a child of God. Then, in an instant, a person may stand in a condition in which he will unfailingly become blessed: [blessed is from Selig, a term which includes beatification and the highest level of holiness before the Lord]… "The entire heart of God is now open with all the treasures and blessings of salvation with have been attained by our Savior Jesus And who can explain everything which flows for the blessed from the sealing through the Holy Spirit." I. 3A, 10, and I, 4, 15.

21. This reference to the immediate or direct sealing of the Holy Spirit reflects the Silesian spirituality which is based in the theology of Caspar Schwenkfeld, the spiritual reformer who disagreed with Luther about whether one may suspend use of the Lord's Supper to focus on Christ's inward presence in the Spirit directly. The Schwenkfelders continue as a denomination in Pennsylvania to the present time.

22. Steinmetz, Second lesson, Section 3, on Scripture, sacraments and the direct sensibility to the Spirit inwardly, in the use of the disciplines of meditation.

23. Speaking pastorally to those who have not found personal salvation, He advises not to conclude that God has cut Himself off from you if you have been seeking the sealing of the Holy Spirit and nothing can be discerned of His Presence in your "inner soul": Hold on! If you will only focus on discerning your God, and not your own [experiences], He will come, before you even understand it yourself, within a moment, when you are hearing, reading, or observing the Word, even when you are only slightly thinking about all of this. By a word of proclamation, a use of the holy Lord's Supper, or other means, your Jesus will unexpectedly come and apply this seal [of the Holy Spirit] to your soul, whereby your poor heart mayprofit both in time and in eternity. Do not abandon your confidence. Hasten only to weep and to pray to your God, and to your Savior. Steinmetz, Second Pentecost Address, 49.

Christian David

Reflecting the influence of Steinmetz, his mentor in the faith, David writes to him in 1741, saying, "Now, my dear old father and brother, this is what I can report to you of the Brethren. But what should I say about myself, how I stand with the Lamb?"[24] Steinmetz was alone among the Silesian leaders who remained steadfast in friendship with the mercurial Christian David, even after the latter had chosen not to follow Steinmetz's sage advice not to dispatch refugees from Silesia until there was a safe place for them across the border.

On the matter of personal salvation in Christ, it nevertheless appears David did follow his mentor's model. Like Luther, both are grounded in the cross. David declares that "there is no connection between God and the ungodly" because "they are altogether separate from each other." "There is nothing in the ungodly to join them to God." Hence, the "right foundation" is to "Go straight to Christ with all your ungodliness."[25]

David also shares Steinmetz precedent in breaking from Luther by moving to a two stage view of grace. For Luther, the theology of the cross locates the sinner precisely at the cross, before the crucified Lamb of God, by whose obedience unto death the Father is enabled to be propitiated so that the Holy Spirit can now assure that it is Christ who is carrying one's sin for which that person alone deserved eternal death. At that moment Christ, then clothed in our vile sins, is facing His Father, and not wooing those who are the intended beneficiaries of His atoning death to respond in faith. They are bowed by Anfechtung under the accusatory ministry of the law (Romans 7:5–25), for which only the death of Christ is the redemptive remedy, as validated by the promise of the Word of God (Romans 7:9–25).

By comparison, Christian David, following Steinmetz, resets the point where personal salvation through Jesus Christ occurs, to a place beyond Calvary, where the focus had remained with Luther, to the disciples at Pentecost. The scene shifts to the manifestation of the Holy Spirit with anointing upon those who had been waiting, "weak in faith."[26] The disciples had believed the message of the cross, yet remained incapacitated until the appearance of the Holy Spirit at Pentecost, where they are at last empowered as apostles, with the Holy Spirit cleansing and anointing their

---

24. Christian David letter to Steinmetz, July,1741, in Christian David, *Servant of theLord*, Letter 19, 55.

25. Christian David, fourth Pentecost sermon preached before John Wesley at Herrnhut, as reported by John Wesley, *Journal and Diaries, I*, (August 10, 1738), 270.

26. Christian David said Calvary was the place of encounter with Christ for those who were "weak in faith." Ibid, line 8, 270.

hearts to become at that moment fully assured that they are the children of God.

The Pentecost event validates Calvary, where they first became heirs of the promise, in an external event observed, but which the disciples had not yet inwardly appropriated. David distinguishes between the "intermediate state" experienced after Calvary and before Pentecost, which is described by Paul in Romans 7, which signified "they had not yet received a new, clean heart," nor "the indwelling of the Holy Spirit," which would render them "pure in heart from all self and sin."[27]

David's fourth sermon, which Wesley transcribed in his Journal, speaks of the "ground" of our faith from which this gift of Pentecostal grace proceeds. Here he speaks in the language of Steinmetz's version of the theology of the cross. The atoning work of Christ is designated as the "word of reconciliation" whereby "we are reconciled to God, not by our own works, but wholly and solely by the blood of Christ." Over against the dominant theme of Pietists in the Halle/Francke context, for whom conversion begins with a "penitential struggle" (Busskampf), preceding the "breakthrough" (Durchbruch) of grace, for David, "The right foundation for conversion is, not your contrition, not your righteousness," but rather, "it is nothing of your own, nothing that is wrought *in you* by the Holy Ghost; but it is something *without you*, viz., the righteousness and the blood of Christ."[28]

David teaches this doctrine in his letters from the Moravian mission field, as indicated in his letter from Latvia in July 1741, where he writes, "The Lamb of God is our witness at what cost we have been purchased and how much the Savior loves souls . . . . As many of us as walk in the light will have our feet covered with dust cleansed (sealed) with the blood of Jesus."[29] That is, the cross leads to sanctification, and Christus pro nobis becomes Christus in nobis; Christ for us/Christ in us.[30]

---

27. Ibid.

28. John Wesley's account of Steinmetz's preaching in *Journal and Diaries I*, Ibid. 272.

29. "A Report from Livonia, from Brother in Christ, David, in Christian David, *Servant of the Lord*, letter 17, 52f.

30. Christian David confesses in his memoir to Wesley of struggling with a proper balance between "Christ for us" (the theology of the cross), and "Christ in us" (the theology of Pentecost). The latter is to confirm the former, but the tendency he faced was an over emphasis upon the one and then the other. Christian David in Wesley, I, 273.

John Wesley

After encounters with Christian David, he learned to distinguish between a first state of justifying grace and a second state embodying the assurance of faith and the grace of sanctification as Christian perfection.[31] In response to hearing Christian David preach this message on Pentecost and sanctification on four occasions at Herrnhut, including extended conversation which followed, John Wesley expressed his agreement with David on the basic distinction between the disciples' experience of justifying faith at Calvary, where they were only "weak in faith," and the "full assurance of faith" at Pentecost.[32]

It was after his encounter with David in 1738 that Wesley introduced terminology reflecting the theme of Pentecost in his ministry, including "the baptism of the Holy Spirit," and, after a remarkable holiness revival which swept England and Ireland in 1760, he began speaking of this revival as an event resembling Pentecost, and as many persons being sanctified as were being justified.[33] Consequently, Charles Wesley and John Fletcher began using the language of the baptism of the Spirit as an expression for Christian perfection, under John's influence. This was the fullness of salvation which was then and remains now available in the preaching of the gospel. Here is reflected his instruction from David that it was at Pentecost that the apostles became "fully assured, by the Holy Spirit then received, of their reconciliation to God by [Christ's] blood."[34] The brothers differed in their emphasis on whether the experience of holiness unto perfection was primarily instantaneous in a crisis moment (John) or gradual (Charles, for whom the new birth is reserved to describe the culmination of that process).[35]

Charles Wesley

John's conversations with Christian David, as reported by his brother John, convinced Charles to change to two rather than one stage of faith.[36]

---

31. John Wesley, *Journal and Diaries* I (1735-38), Bicentennial Edition of the *Works of John Wesley*, 18:272, (August 10, 1738).

32. Wesley gives a comprehensive report of his encounter with Christian David in his entry of August 8, 1738, as found in his *Journal and Diaries (1735-38)*, in W.R. Ward and Richard Heitzenrater, eds., The Bicentennial Edition of the *Works of John Wesley* (Nashville: Abingdon Press, 1984-present), I, 273-4.

33. "A Short History of the People Called Methodists," *The Methodist Societies, History, Nature and Design*, 21:392, October 28, 1762, and Wood, 120.

34. John Wesley, *Manuscript Journal*, 1:122.

35. The view of John Tyson, in *Charles Wesley on Sanctification*, 219, and Wood, 121

36. John Wesley, *Letters I* (1721-1739), ed. Frank Baker (Oxford Clarendon Press, 1980),

Reflecting his new outlook, John wrote in his journal on October, 1738, that "although I have not yet that joy in the Holy Spirit, nor that love of God shed abroad in my heart, nor the full assurance of faith, nor the proper witness of the Holy Spirit with my Spirit that I am a child of God . . . . I nevertheless trust that I have a measure of faith and am 'accepted in the beloved'."37

After John related the details of his visit with David to his brother Charles, we find Charles using the theme of the Holy Spirit's sealing in the blood of Christ as indicative of sanctification. In his hymn, "Sinners, lift up your hearts," verses two to four include all the themes of the promise coming from the cross, the kingdom, defeat of Satan, the gift of the Spirit, the cleansing blood, and wholly sanctifying by sealing unto the day of judgment:

> Sinners, lift up your hearts
> The Promise to receive!
> Jesus himself imparts
> He comes to man to live
> The Holy Ghost to man is given;
> Rejoice in God sent down from heaven.
>
> Jesus is glorified,
> And gives the Comforter, His Spirit, to reside
> In all his members here.
> The Holy Ghost to man is given;
> Rejoice in God sent down from heaven.
> To make an end of sin,
> And Satan's work destroy,
> He brings his kingdom in,
> Peace, righteousness, and joy;
> The Holy Ghost to man is given:
> Rejoice in God sent down from heaven.
>
> The cleansing blood to apply,
> The heavenly life display,
> And wholly sanctify,
> And seal us to that day,
> The Holy Ghost to man is given:
> Rejoice in God sent down from heaven!38

25:554, June 28, 1738.

37. *Journal and Diaries II*, in the Bicentennial Works of John Wesley, 19:19 (October 14, 1738).

38. MS ACTS, MARC: MA 1977/555 (Charles Wesley Notebooks, Box 1), 21, cited in

Wood notes that the language of sealing comes from the theology of confirmation in the Anglican theologian, Jeremy Taylor.[39] It also derives from the language of Christian David, conveyed to John Wesley and then to his brother Charles, and this language of Versiegelung (sealing) comes to David directly from Johann Adam Steinmetz, whose Pentecost Addresses make liberal use of this theme, for the first time, in the context of revival.[40]

(c) The Coming Kingdom

Luther

Given his stance opposing revolutionary spiritualists like Thomas Muntzer, Luther adopted a conservative affirmation of the legitimacy of the existing offices of imperial government,[41] which he joined to an apocalyptic view of an imminent day of divine Judgment.[42] In another sense, the Kingdom has already arrived in the heart of the penitent who has trusted in the promise of Calvary; that, in the death of Christ the "wonderful exchange" has already occurred between Christ and the penitent sinner.

Steinmetz

In his *Pentecost Addresses*, he has Luther speaking anew, in the context of revival, with the evangelical admonition, "Tell Him, 'Thou, whose eyes are as a flame of fire searching my heart,...I plead nothing else.'" Rather than being self-serving by saying "I am humble," be honest: say "I am ungodly," therefore, "bring me to Him who justifies the ungodly, let thy blood be the propitiation for me.'"[43]

Representing the oppressed Protestant state church in Silesia, Steinmetz was in the forefront of supporting revival as the intent of the Spirit in bringing Erweckung (Awakening) to humanity in history, thereby overcoming the restrictive religious policies of a fading though oppressive corpus Christianum (or body of Christendom). At the same time, his intent was to work through and not contrary to the existing political order.

Wood, 62.
   39. Ibid., 49.
   40. See discussion of Steinmetz and David in this grid.
   41. As referenced in Romans 13: Government is ordained by God to be believed for conscience's sake.
   42. This position wreaked havoc in the Peasants War (1524–25) with Muntzer's conviction that the Holy Spirit was directing him to raise up the peasants in holy war against an oppressive state, believing this course would hasten the Judgment day for a reprobate state.
   43. Ibid.

Hence, he cautioned Christian David against relocating religious refugees from Catholic Silesia to Germany, as violation of sovereign borders.

Overall, Steinmetz was influenced by Spener's hope for a coming "better time for the church", as expressed in the wake of the Thirty Years' War. When the Parousia of Christ did not happen in 1700 as expected, his life of ministry in the new century was guided by a new vision of the future, set in place by the children's revival (1707-08) and its consequences, which looked to the coming Kingdom of God among those in covenant with Christ on earth (namely, those sealed by the Holy Spirit). It was in this vein that he labored three decades to collect the materials for a documentation of the building of the Kingdom of God on earth, through the extension of Erweckung (revival). More than anyone in his generation, Steinmetz documents a network of path breakers in his lifetime who were heralding the spread of the kingdom through the ministry of the Holy Spirit, tapping persons globally for the kingdom.[44]

There is an analogous relation between the personal and the corporate dimensions of this discussion. There is the Holy Spirit's building of that new order, at the personal level, within the redeemed of the Lord, through the inward sealing of the Holy Spirit as God's response to the cross. Simultaneously, the empirics of this demographic feature opens the door to visualizing an expanding, critical mass of converts to Christ through the Pentecostal sealing of the Holy Spirit, which would corroborate Spener's hope for a more glorious age of the church in the near future. It is an optimistic vision for the short term, the inverse of Luther's apocalyptic Angst.

Christian David

Following Steinmetz's lead, he is locating Pietist revivalism from its foundation in Luther's theology of the cross.[45] But then he adds this statement: "Tell Him [Christ], whose eyes are as a flame of fire searching my heart, [You] see that I am ungodly ... I plead nothing else, let Thy blood be the propitiation for me."[46] In this statement, the scene shifts for Christian David from Calvary, and also from the scene of Pentecost, to Christ's returning in judgment. David's words about Christ's eyes being as "a flame

---

44. At the same time, his intent was to work through and not contrary to the existing political order. Hence, he cautioned Christian David against re-locating religious refugees from Catholic Silesia to Germany, as violation of sovereign borders.

45. Recall that all of these voices, David, Francke, and Steinmetz are officially Pietists who are also Lutheran—and even Zinzendorf is, as indicated in his intent to maintain Herrnhut's alignment with the parish of Berthelsdorf.

46. John Wesley, line 11, 272.

of fire searching my heart," is not depicting Christ from the position of His death at Calvary, nor is it the event of the Spirit's coming at Pentecost; rather it is a direct reference to Revelation 19:11–12:

> And I saw heaven opened; and behold, a white horse, and He who sat upon it is called Faithful and True, and in righteousness he judges and wages war, and His eyes are a flame of fire, and upon His head are many diadems, and He has a name written upon Him which no one knows except Himself.

David's theme is still the theology of the cross, but here focus has shifted from Calvary, as well as from Pentecost, where the assurance of the forgiveness of sins is rendered efficacious in the sealing of the Holy Spirit. It has reached the eschatological moment of Christ appearing in final judgment. The latter is a second place where the theology of the cross is being altered by David. Our righteousness through the imputation of Christ's work on the cross has been relocated to the locus of its implementation, at Pentecost, and also, by anticipation, to the parousia when Christ's Kingdom will be established upon earth through His divine Judgment. This is the hour when the "children of God" (an appeal to the children's revival theme) are to be awakened and made ready for this prophetic future.[47]

These three themes of justification in Christian David, located in the theology of the cross at Calvary, in Pentecost sanctification, and at last, in the final judgment, find points of analogy in Steinmetz, by whom David was confirmed in the faith. David's memoirs reflect these themes as appearing after, and not before, his decisive meeting with Steinmetz.[48]

---

47. Christian David, Servant of the Lord (Memoir), "On His Journey into Bohemia and Moravia, 1727, 35: "The children of God are very much awakened because of our institutions," seen as a reference to the legacy of the children's revival. On another occasion, he says, "we have all been called children of the living God, although I have not been too peaceful and can only make a small claim to the promise, 'and they shall be called children of God.'" Ibid, "To the Congregation in Copenhagen," 1733, 47.

48. There are two possibilities of dating David's decisive encounter with Steinmetz: his Memoir first mentions encountering Steinmetz as a young refugee from Moravia, residing for five years from 1717 in Görlitz on the German/Silesian border. There, under influence from the preaching of Johann Christian Schwedler, a coworker with Steinmetz in the Silesian awakening, he experienced his first awakening to evangelical faith and also met Steinmetz. The second encounter is mentioned eight years later (1725), when he was directed by Zinzendorf to leave Herrnhut to consult with Steinmetz, then immersed in revival at Teschen. David had been thrown off balance by the prominent preaching of a Calvinist estate manager hired by Zinzendorf at Herrnhut,... who was leading some Herrnhuters to question their salvation. David talked "fully" with Steinmetz on the "head", whether Christ

John Wesley

An obvious point of continuity between Wesley and the two stage view of grace found in the German Moravian Christian David and in his spiritual mentor Steinmetz is found in Wesley's statement concerning the purpose for joining the first Methodist class which convened in Bristol during the revival there in 1739. The three rules for class members were framed by the head question: "Do you wish to be freed from your sin and to flee the wrath to come?"[49] Here the theme of the coming kingdom was celebrated by John amid concerns from the people of Bristol regarding their forsakenness in the face of an impending judgement from the returning Christ.

However, John also found space for going beyond apocalyptic judgment to a better state of the church in the future, in light of the renewal of Pentecost as the driving theme of the Methodist revival in England and beyond. He gave substance to that hope in his later sermon on The General Spread of the Gospel, which envisions a "grand Pentecost" which will become global.[50]

Here he was returning to a theme found in his early letter to his elder brother Samuel (fall, 1738), when John confided that "I now enjoy by His free mercy, the seal of the Spirit, the love of God shed abroad in my heart,

---

died for all. "I did so, and God fully convinced me of that important truth." He continues, "Not long after, the Count desired that we might all meet together, and consider these things thoroughly. We met accordingly at his house, and parted not for three days. We opened the Scriptures, and considered the account which is given therein of the whole economy of God with man, from the creation to the consummation of all things. And by the blessing of God we came all to one mind." It seems inevitable that such comprehensive discussion of the economy of God and man, in the wake of David's meeting with Steinmetz, would of necessity have included the matter of the cross and the sealing with the Holy Spirit at Pentecost, which was the main area of Steinmetz's theology which David began to emulate in his extant letters and sermons after that date, especially the four sermons Wesley heard from him at Herrnhut in 1738). Further, document providing the narrative of his theological conversation with Steinmetz, was what John Wesley transcribed, and was omitted by Zinzendorf in his memoirs of Christian David.

David reported that he and Zinzendorf found agreement on these doctrinal matters at their three day conference in 1731, although Zinzendorf omitted mention of this in his memoirs on David and also defended a one stage position in his conversations with John Wesley at London in 1741. This inconsistency in Zinzendorf is not unusual, since he was operating not as a trained theologian but as a community organizer, who could adapt his message to fit the context. These arguments represent the case for regarding Steinmetz as the main theological source for David's two stage view of saving grace.

49 John Wesley, "The General Rules," in The Book of Discipline of the United Methodist Church (Nashville: Abingdon, 1984), 50.

50. John Wesley, "The General Spread of the Gospel," *Works of John Wesley*, (Abingdon, 1985), II, *Sermons*, 34–70.

and producing joy in the Holy Spirit . . . .This witness of the Spirit I have not, but I patiently wait for it."[51]

Charles Wesley

Charles Wesley would make more use of the biblical typology which relates the personal work of the cross to the passover and exodus of Israel, while the work of Pentecost is related to their entry to Canaan, where the promises of God were fulfilled in the indwelling Spirit. In this context the theme of the sealing by the Holy Spirit, prominent in Steinmetz and Christian David, finds its place in a "concealed" mode (which is only fully "revealed" in Pentecost). These verses from Charles embody this typological theme:

> The cov'enant old in types concealed
> Now in the gospel is reveal'd;
> The gospel-cov'enant has took place,
> And saves us not by works but grace:
> The Lord his Spirit's seal applies,
> His people all to circumcise,
> And when our sins and us He parts,
> Cuts off the foreskin of our hearts.[52]

In Charles' typology, Canaan is the "sanctuary," "the abode," and "the kingdom," all signifying the perfect love for God which is the mark of the revival initiated by the coming of the Spirit in Pentecost.[53]

Hence, a parallel trajectory appears between the stirrings of revival in central Europe and among the Methodists in Britain in the early modern

---

51. John Wesley, "The General Spread of the Gospel," *Works of John Wesley*, (Abingdon, 1985), II, Sermons, 34-70.52. MS Acts, MARC, MA: 1977/555 (Charles Wesley Notebooks Box 1), 111, cited in Wood, 68. If the etymology of this motif were explored, it is probably to be found in the symbolic prophetic school of biblical typology found in Reformed Pietism, especially with the systematic theologian Johannes Cocceius (d.1669) and the federal school, with ties to Cambridge Puritanism and also German Reformed Pietism through Lampe and Otterbein. See J.S. O'Malley, *Pilgrimage of Faith, the Legacy of the Otterbeins* (Metuchen, NJ: Scarecrow, 1973).

52. MS Acts, MARC, MA: 1977/555 (Charles Wesley Notebooks Box 1), 111, cited in Wood, 68. If the etymology of this motif were explored, it is probably to be found in the symbolic prophetic school of biblical typology found in Reformed Pietism, especially with the systematic theologian Johannes Cocceius (d.1669) and the federal school, with ties to Cambridge Puritanism and also German Reformed Pietism through Lampe and Otterbein. See J.S. O'Malley, *Pilgrimage of Faith, the Legacy of the Otterbeins* (Metuchen, NJ: Scarecrow, 1973).

53. Charles Wesley, *Short Hymns of Select Passages of the Holy Scriptures* (Bristol, Farley, 1762), 1:91, cited in Wood, 75.

era. There was the Kingdom theme of the Silesian revival, whose purpose, beginning with the children, Steinmetz called the "Building of the Kingdom of God on Earth", and that was matched by the homilies and hymns of the Wesleys on behalf of the "grand Pentecost" which was coming from the "General Spread of the Gospel" on earth.[1]

1.2 Conclusion

The recovery of the Reformation theme of Luther's theology of the cross is enhanced by the discovery that this theme became the foundation from which developed the first theology of Pentecost to appear in the context of revival, within the history of Protestantism. By locating the Pentecost addresses presented by the preacher of that revival, Johann Adam Steinmetz, the theological content which informed that historic revival can now be understood, and read in the light of Luther's original doctrine of the cross. The findings of this study have also made evident the similarities between Steinmetz's addresses and the theology of Christian David, who transmitted the themes of the cross and Pentecost from Steinmetz to John Wesley and, through him, to his brother Charles, and to the larger world of the Methodist revival.

---

54. See the title of Steinmetz's account of the Silesian revival and its global extension, as well as Charles' hymn cited here and John's sermon on "The General Spread of the Gospel."

Chapter 4

Steinmetz Links the Children's Revival to Christian Globalization As the Historical Outworking of a Two-Staged Soteriology[1]

The thread we have drawn from the early stirrings of awakening in central Europe to those among the Methodists in Britain in the early modern era is linked by a common concern for tracking the rise of a globalizing Christianity. It was occurring not by imperial or even civil initiatives, in Constantinian fashion, but by the sovereign moving of the Holy Spirit upon receptive souls, beginning with orphaned children scattered by religious-inspired warfare, in a remote part of central Europe then wracked by the travail which historians politely call the "Counter Reformation." These were persons who had resorted to intercessory prayer in response to their desperate state of existence, beginning with those who were by worldly standards the least privileged in terms of the world. The pastor who discerned this inbreaking and reaped the early harvest of the revival which ensued, in his refugee congregation at Teschen, Silesia, was the first to chronicle the spread of this awakening from its initial point of origin, to many locales in Europe and in even into America by the third and fourth decades of the eighteenth century. He would publish these findings under the heading of the "gathering" of many diverse supportive documents showing the "building of the Kingdom of God on earth."[2]

---

1. This chapter addresses data drawn from: *Die Sammlung AuserleseneMaterialen zum Bau des Reich Gottes* (Magdeburg, 1745), part of a larger series of publications edited by Steinmetz that appeared under thefollowing titles: *Sammlungen zum Bau des ReichGottes* (48 volumes in 6 volumes, Leipzig, 1731–36), *Verbesserte Sammlungen des Bau des Reich Gottes* (32 issues in four volumes, Leipzig, 1733–42), and *Klosterbergische Sammlungen zumBau des Reich Gottes* (40 volumes in five volumes), Magdeburg und Leipzig, 1745-61.

2. Johann Adam Steinmetz, *Die Sammlung Auserlesene Materien zum Bau des Reich Gottes*

In this concluding chapter we will trace these lines of development of a budding trajectory which laid the spiritual foundations for the globalization of Christianity in the contemporary world. By use of the term"spiritual" we are distinguishing this initiative as a theonomous, or "Spirit initiated",and not an anthropocentric one, initiated by civil or theocratic religious authority. It is a chronicle picked up by the early Methodists, as documented in the homilies, hymns, and journals of the Wesleys on behalf of the "grand Pentecost" which John Wesley would call the "General Spread of the Gospel" on earth.

4.1 The Revival in its Silesian and Wesleyan Phases

The groundwork for this "coming out" of Protestant Christianity from Europe to the rest of the world was laid in the Protestant Reformation, and upon the theology of the cross there was superimposed by Steinmetz the first theology of Pentecost, fashioned in the heat of the first awakening in Protestantism. This expansion was facilitated by the development of the two stage approach to soteriology initiated by Steinmetz and brought to fruition in Wesleyan theology, thanks to the mediation between continental theology and the Anglo-American world achieved by early Methodist contacts with Christian David at Herrnhut. The movement from justification through the work of the cross to regeneration/sanctification through the work of Pentecost provides the platform for a message of transformation of a fallen humanity into the renewed image of God.[3]

Steinmetz has previously been interpreted mainly by Orthodox German Lutherans in the nineteenth century, like Renner, who extolled him for advancing lay theological education while avoiding radical and separatist forms of Pietism. He was also extolled in the Hitler era for extending the influence of the "Deutsch Christentum" (German Volk Christianity) in the slavic regions of Poland, Slovakia, and the Czech Republic, as well as in the German states, as preparation for a united Germany in the nineteenth cen-

---

(Magdeburg, 1745).

3. See scripture texts to support this twofold soteriology. That emphasis had been renewed in the mid-nineteenth century through the holiness movement, including the National Holiness Association for the Promotion of Holiness (1867). and related organizations, as well as the explosion of holiness denominations, largely emerging from Episcopal Methodism, and leading to the emergence of a Wesleyan-based Pentecostalism in the early twentieth century.

tury.[4] Perhaps he has been overlooked for his important role in advancing evangelical Christianity as his central contribution because his name has been unduly (and posthumously) associated with these discredited movements. So, it is our opportunity to bring him to light here through his own words in his Pentecost addresses, which reveals the heart of an evangelist akin to the ethos of later primitive Methodism, with a burden for reaching all persons, regardless of nationality, for the two state view of soteriology Wesleyans would later call "full salvation." After all, it was that "burden for souls" which drew many religious seekers from outside his Silesian homeland, including Christian David, to his preaching in the context of a massive awakening.

The gifts and graces for Steinmetz's calling to this task were evident in his early conversion at the Saxon University of Leipzig, which was his Oxford (a generation before Wesley's conversion at Oxford in England). There he studied as a foreign Silesian student committed to churchmanship in his native Lutheran church, under whom he was ordained and whose field of parishes across Protestant Europe would define the "home" boundaries for his expansive world ministry (much as Wesley served faithfully in the Church of England, though also extending beyond its sphere). At Leipzig, Steinmetz displayed his keen love for the study of the Greek text of Christianity, and here he acquired his attraction for the Pietist renewal ethos of Philip Spener, and his successor, august Hermann Francke, with whom he would remain closely associated until Francke's death in 1727.[5]

It was in Leipzig that he began a life discipline of personal intercessory prayer which would guide the course of his ministry in war-torn Silesia, amid the turbulent phases of service among religious refugees in the wake of Hapsburg oppression. In that context he gained strength to endure amid human suffering through a virulent religious oppression unknown in Wesley's eighteenth century England. Also like Wesley, he developed an extensive correspondence with other leaders and opponents of the awakening then swirling about him, as well as with needy parishioners. In addition, his preaching, while didactic, was always geared to the spiritual needs of his lay audiences. Also like Wesley, he maintained a long correspondence with Zinzendorf, and, in spite of their mutual esteem for one another, he found himself in disagreement with Zinzendorf at critical points. In brief,

---

4. See Richard Kammel, "August Hermann Franckes ausländerarbeit in Südeuropa", in Ernst Schubert, *Auslanddeutschtum und evangelische Kirche*; Jahrbuch 1939 (München: Christian Kaiser Verlag), 121–203.

5. One is here reminded of Wesley's affinity for the spiritual writings of Law, Macarius, Arndt, and many others, who would comprise his Christian Library.

Zinzendorf would not embrace the theology of Pentecost by which Steinmetz embellished Lutheran theology, rejecting the two state view of soteriology which Steinmetz shared in common with the later Wesleys.[6]

4.2 Steinmetz's Early Life as Preparatory to the Revival

Johann Adam Steinmetz was prepared for this ministry by his upbringing in Silesia. He was a youth of nineteen or twenty (1707–08) when he witnessed the children's revival. His later writings are replete with references to children as the model of the coming Kingdom of God, based on his recollection of the features of the child witnesses in Silesia. There was the purity of the children. There was their spiritual freedom amid persecution as they eked out their existence in the mountains of northern Silesia. Steinmetz remained mindful of their singular devotion to the Lamb of God based on their spontaneous worship. These exercises were drawn from the promises of the Word of God sealed in their hearts by their internalizing the small catechism, and memorizing the joyous hymns of the Lamb learned in worship, before the days of their exile. They had been nurtured in exile under the fearless devotion of generations of "bush" preachers, Lutheran pastors exiled by the Hapsburg onslaught on their parishes. These persecuted Protestants were sustained as the "evangelical"[7] Christians during the decades of their oppression.

The parents of these children had nurtured in them a love for Christ as proclaimed to them in their catechesis in the small catechism: God's law, the gospel, prayer, and worship at the Table of the Lord, which gave them access to all the riches of the gospel, whose promises they had memorized and kept to heart as they learned from the bush meeting members how to intercede for the people of God, in the simplicity of Matthew 18.

All this was internalized in their young lives, from the generations of faithful witness to intercession bequeathed to them by their bush meeting mentors whose ministry had persisted over solemn generations of persecution, when the society allowed no public and official acknowledgment of

---

6. For his part, Zinzendorf was led by Philadelphian ideals not embraced by Lutherans like Steinmetz. See Ward, 122.

7. Evangelicals was the name for Protestants to distinguish them from Catholics, during the decades of their oppression by the Hapsburg regime in Vienna. That regime had forcefully displaced the evangelical Augsburg Confession from their churches in the early part of the seventeenth century after more than a half century of nurture in the Reformation faith, going back to the generation of Luther.

any Protestant dogma. Their confession had been declared sacrosanct by the papal canons of Trent, which were now being imposed as part of a "Josephist" policy of establishing imperial hegemony empowered in an alignment with Jesuit religious zeal, marshalled to strike down all symbols of Protestant resistance to the authority of Rome as the true embodiment of Christ on earth.[8]

Then, amid all of this intimidation, the children's revival spontaneously broke forth. Its legacy empowered awakenings when people's hearts were stirred by the witness to the Lamb of God through the children, who were first viewed as an oddity, but, whose persistent and growing witness had swept over the land in the years of the revival. This event was also enabled through the political intervention afforded by the arrival in Silesia of the Swedish King Karl XII, and by the Altranstädt Convention (1707) by which he pressed the Hapsburg Emperor to grant emergency concessions (under political duress) to allow a renewal of evangelical (Protestant) worship.

The Convention had provided for the establishment of a limited number of emergency "Jesus Churches" to resource the spiritual needs of the thousands of Protestants then displaced by the forced recatholicization program. Chief among these centers was the refugee congregation gathered at Teschen.[9] To this key pastorate Steinmetz was summoned as a consecrated pastorate who had received a first rate theological education under Pietist influence at the Lutheran University of Leipzig in Germany. There he had been directed by his call to pastoral ministry to return to his beloved homeland, making himself available for ministry to the beleaguered flock of Silesian Protestants, who were seeking to rekindle their evangelical witness after decades of religious oppression. Actually, it was the renewal of Protestant worship, which the Altranstädt Convention had enabled, under the intervention of Sweden and a newfound political restraint which was imposed at least temporarily upon the Hapsburg Emperor Joseph I. The years of the resurgence of an evangelical witness were increasingly marked by enhanced efforts by the state to repress any rebirth of the Protestant spirit.

It was in that context that Steinmetz develops his new evangelical apologetic, which would join Luther's focus on Calvary to a renewal of the apostolic theme of Pentecost. The two stage view of salvation was not at that

---

8. Note the legacy of Innocent III and the legacy of the 1302 Bull *Unam Sanctum* (the one Sanctity which is the papacy), and the papal position on the church as the sole teller of doctrine (interpretation of Scripture) whose policies were now being ruthlessly enforced by the policies of the eighteenth century Jesuit missional orders.

9. Located at the southern entrance to Silesia from Moravia and Hungary.

kairos moment birthed out of some clever theological creativity by their Leipzig trained pastor. Rather, Steinmetz was articulating a witness to the faith that reflected the authenticity of the two great moments of encounter with the Word that had moved among human affairs over the previous two centuries: I refer first to the Reformation with Luther, which had laid the groundwork for a new evangelical witness to make its mark in the midst of a decadent European Christendom, dominated by an addictive and repressive theology of "glory" as distinct from a "theology of the cross," which Luther heralded.

Our narrative has shown that Steinmetz's ministry had primarily been enabled by the spontaneous event of the children's revival, which came unexpectedly and with force to empower a new generation to lay hold of a second moment from the ancient apostolic witness of Christianity, which had so long lain dormant: the event of Pentecost.

For the children, and their spiritual descendants, including Steinmetz, this was not a Montanist appeal to a shift away from Luther's Christ centered Christology, the ministry of the Word, to a subjective preoccupation with the Paraclete, as the basis for declaring the superiority of inward revelation over the external Word of God—after the fashion of Thomas Muntzer, in his infamous encounter with Luther during the destructive Peasants' Rebellion against Catholic authority (1524–25).

4.3 The Origin of the Twofold Approach to Christian Soteriology in Steinmetz

On the contrary, Steinmetz was articulating a missional theology which had a potential for recovering the global Great Commision of Jesus to the apostolic church by an apostolate empowered by the wonder of the Spirit's overwhelming anointment to become evangels of this new way of life based in the sealing of the blood of Christ shed on Calvary, even to your children, and to your children's children, who are afar to the uttermost parts of the earth (Acts 2:39).

Steinmetz's recovery of this apostolic witness becomes manifest through the Pauline lense that we shall not "grieve the Holy Spirit of God, whereby we are sealed unto the day of redemption" (Ephesians 4:30). Not to live out of the cleansing power of the shed blood of Christ in which we have been gifted in the gospel of Jesus Christ means, for Steinmetz, not to accept our enablement, by God's second great kerygmatic act of revelation in the coming of the Holy Spirit. Only on that basis are the faithful enabled to access the dual aspects of a global empowering gospel. Only there does one find the way into the two states of grace that are within the scope of God's decisive acts in Christ for the salvation of humanity.

Two implications of this insight may be discerned. First, there was the task of becoming assured of deliverance from the affliction and often domination by Satan's dominion over the souls of humans, resulting in an unfettered legacy of wars and rumors of wars which have accompanied the human project on earth since the dawn of our first parents' fall from grace, unto the present day. This signifies for Luther, and for Steinmetz who appeals to him, that the faithful must look to Christ as their deliverer by the power of His Word.[10] This concern for the demonic, implicit in Luther, is made more explicit with the Pietists, particularly with the recovery of the Fifty Spiritual Homilies of Macarius the Egyptian, which are focused on this theme.[11]

Second, there was the empowerment of the faithful with the Holy Spirit at Pentecost, which to Steinmetz references the function of the Holy Spirit in applying the shed blood of Christ, on Calvary's cross, to the sin-laden souls of this fallen humanity. The core meaning of Luther's theology of the cross signifies that, until each of us realizes that Christ is bearing our personal sins on His sacred body, and dying that these might be propitiated (atoned for) and expiated (set free) on your and my behalf, there was no clearing of the ground for God's Kingdom of grace to have dominion in our lives, and for the claim of the enemy of our souls to be forever silenced. That is what Steinmetz means by his appeal to the shed blood of Christ for us, which the church signifies in the washing of baptism.

Steinmetz preferred to use the language of sealing to represent the effect of that washing, already enacted in our baptism, but not yet made existentially real in the lives of those who confess the salvific truth of the message of the cross, but have not yet allowed its life to penetrate them.

This is the firm Christological basis for Steinmetz's theology of Pentecost, as heralded in his addresses on that subject first delivered in the great revival at Teschen (1719–1730). He was thereafter forcibly expelled by

---

11. This theme is suggested in Luther's "A Mighty Fortress," with the words, "and though this world, with devils filled, should threaten to undo us; we will not fear, for lo, his doom is sure, one little word shall fell him."

12. See especially Homily 11. It was the radical Pietist Gottfried Arnold who first translated the Macarian homilies from Greek to German in the 1720s, contemporary with the occurrence of the first awakening in Protestant history, in Silesia. That was also the decade that Macarius was translated into English and included by John Wesley in his *Christian Library* for Methodist preachers.

his theological and civil opponents in the Hapsburg regime which was still intent on silencing the Protestant witness in Silesia.

The bulk of Steinmetz's addresses is devoted to the pastoral issues of the effectual appropriation of the gift of the shed blood of Christ, signifying the righteousness of God and the gift of the Spirit which are bequeathed to the members of Christ's body who have now immersed themselves in that mystery of grace.

In one sense, this focus on the shed blood of Calvary fulfills what had been the highest expectations of Catholics of identifying with the heart of Christ's passion in their liturgy of the Mass. However, because this theme is located by Steinmetz in the context of the Holy Spirit coming at Pentecost, it is presented as an evangel taking us out of ourselves and into the world, that is, as the apostolic summons for each one to become an agent of God's reconciling grace, extending to every nation and ethos of humanity which stands apart from and against that message of reconciliation.[12]

It is because of the importance of this twofold work of grace that Steinmetz took great pains to speak to his hearers' hesitancies, encouraging them to overcome personal resistance to the salvific meaning of the cross. In these discussions, he repeatedly alluded to the narrative of the children's revival, suggesting it is only the pure in heart, whom our Lord set apart in the believing child,[13] who shall see the kingdom of heaven.

As the corollary to his focus on the gift of the shed blood, Steinmetz gave attention to what is gained as well as what is lost in the gift exchange which is the message of the cross. Our release from the old nature finds its efficacy in what Luther called the "blessed exchange": being delivered from the weight of sin, the person of faith is not left in a void or impasse, which could only be filled with worse spirits. Instead, that one is gifted with the life of Christ, who was resurrected that He might "draw all men unto himself."[14] From that angle, Steinmetz's portrayal of Pentecost is quite other than being drawn to otherworldly irrelevancies unrelated to the urgent need for an ongoing attention to the breaking down of competing principalities and powers which can erect themselves in every domain of human life.

---

13. See the Pauline text on this breakthrough act of reconciliation in Ephesians 2:12-22.

14. See Matthew 18:4-5: "Whosoever shall humble himself as this little child, the same is the greatest in the kingdom of heaven. And whoever shall receive one such child in my name shall receive me."

15. John 12:32.

4.4 Steinmetz Confronts the Restoration Theory as an Impediment to the Coming of the Kingdom of God

It is noteworthy that, amid his work with the Pentecost Addresses, Steinmetz took time to provide a pointed critique of the theory of the "Wiederbringung aller Dinge" (or, "The Restoration of all Things"). Our study encountered this theme in the context of the initial affirmative response to the children's revival given by Johann Wilhelm Petersen, the radical Pietist observer of that event. Emerging from the legacy of the late seventeenth century religious wars, he found himself confronting the dualistic system of "voluntary, speculative" mystical theology of the seventeenth century mystic and alchemist, Jacob Böhme.

Faced with Böhme's portrayal of an incessant struggle between cosmic and historical forces of good and evil in the course of nature and human history, Petersen came to an abrupt conclusion. He did so as an early interpreter of the children's revival by appealing to the apostolic theme of Pentecost. For Petersen, the revival signified that this was indeed that long delayed moment in a tortuous human history when one great overcoming divine moment will occur that forever vanquishes the perennial torment within nature and history between those opposing forces. That cessation would occur in a great moment of the Spirit's visitation to the children, and through them to that dispirited world of religious refugees then amassed in Silesia. Amid those expressions of human perdition and suffering the hand of God will be triggered to at last bring the travail of history to an abrupt end. This would occur through the fulfillment of the biblical promise that God will restore to its original created order all humanity, as well as all fallen creation, and that the reign of human disobedience will be forever replaced, not by the eternal damnation of sinners but through their divinely initiated transformation into creatures of light.[15]

Petersen had advocated this work in his evangelistic itineraries throughout Germany with his wife, Johanna Eleonora Petersen, in the early decades of the eighteenth century. However, while supporting the premise that the children's revival was indeed a manifest of the apostolic theme of Pentecost, Steinmetz was also stout in refuting this through an eschatological formula that aborts the apostolic call for extending to all the world the kingdom of God, announced in the advent of Jesus Christ. This theory of restoration would sever the church from its responsibility by relegating the

---

16. Petersen had found some ground for this thinking in a reading of texts such as Romans 8:18-23.

reclamation of a fallen world to a divine act which nullifies any human responsibility for actualizing the gospel in the world.

From this perspective, Steinmetz's incentive for devoting three decades of his life, after the revival, to developing his massive chronicle of materials for the "building of the kingdom of God on earth," may be regarded as his response to the growing popularity of the "Wiederbringung" mentality. This concern is also reflected in his critique of the emerging Enlightenment ideology in Germany (especially in Leibniz), concerning the approaching arrival of a world of orderly reason and moral beneficence, where issues of human depravity would be dissipated. From this standpoint, it is noteworthy that the recent German edition of Steinmetz's "Chronicles" provides an introduction to that pioneering study which explains that period of 1732–1760, the years covered in the Chronicle, were followed by an era in which the centers of the revival in Germany were transformed into centers for the promotion of the early Enlightenment. These centers included the University of Halle, which had been the center for the great Pietist program of personal and social renewal in the late seventeenth and early eighteenth centuries under Francke, including financial and logistical resources which his work provided for the upbuilding of the Jesus Churches in Silesia. The Grace Church in Teschen that Steinmetez pastored in the midst of the revival there was a flagship of that project.

By the latter decades of the eighteenth century, these centers jettisoned their commitment to the historic Christian confessions, for the sake of a new order enacting practical reason as the dominant religion of the continent. This lapse in faithfulness of orthodox Christianity included the Kloster Bergen where Steinmetz had conducted the last phase of his ministry.[16]

4.5 The Revival and the *Gathering*: Their Connection and Import

In this section, our focus is upon the Revival and the arrival of Steinmetz's chronicles concerning the accumulating evidences for the building by God of His global Kingdom within the history of the eighteenth century. The historical context for his work with this huge project may be observed.

17. Lächele, 94–99 documents this shift at Kloster Bergen by noting how the mission of the *Gathering* periodical which Steinmetz had edited in his lifetime, was altered to accommodate these new trends, out of a concern to be relevant to a newly enlightened and post-dogmatic era of human culture.

While he was under duress as the engaged pastor in a downtrodden Silesia, he was also caught up in an unprecedented awakening in Teschen which soon had international implications in the extent of its influence. Amid these unfolding events, he chose to prioritize active engagement with his people in the interests of the revival, which cut short time for producing published versions of his Pentecost homilies, delivered in the course of the revival. It was only after his removal from that turbulent yet productive era, in 1730, that he was permitted a season of reflection, when such academic work might be completed and extended.

This phase occurred during his tenure as the Abbot of the formerly Catholic, now evangelical Kloster Bergen in Brandenburg/Prussia, which also represented the years of his editorship of the periodical. The *Gathering* had its birth a generation earlier, based in missional concerns emanating from the Lutheran University of Leipzig in Saxony. Here Steinmetz had been equipped for his life of ministry, as a student under a new generation of Pietist-based theologians, teaching in a former citadel of anti-Pietist Lutheran Orthodoxy.[17]

This periodical was initially the brainchild of a young man named Immanuel Traugott Jerichovius (1696–1734). It was during the era of the flowering of edificatory publications emanating from the Halle-centered Pietist movement in Lutheranism. They represented a counterpoint to the heavy hand of Lutheran Orthodoxy, based after Luther's death at his old university of Wittenberg. This literature flowered in the second generation of the Pietist renewal after Spener (the progenitor of renewal in the Lutheran churches).

The renewal had spawned large numbers of published sermons and Pietist periodicals focused on godly living. This literature was divided between sources from church pastors and those from the radical, separatist groups which were spawned in the context of that renewal. Lächele notes that there was some overlap between those who were collectors of these renewal documents and publishers of journals on renewal.[18] The most prolific journalists included Johann Jacob Moser of Württemberg, who produced a periodical called *Altes und Neues aus dem Reich Gottes* (or, Old and New Things out of the Kingdom of God"), and the most influential of radical Pietist periodicals was Johann Samuel Carl's *Geistliche Fama*, produced in the small duchy of Wittgenstein-Berleberg.[19] The latter publication was

---

18. To understand the dynamics between these two competing movements within post Reformation Protestantism, see the discussion of the competing perspectives on the significance of the children's revival, found in part three of this study.

19. Lächele, 29.

influenced by the Philadelphian ethos which looked to the coming community of brotherly love which would supersede the present polemical age.[20] The project called "the gathering of choice materials" concerning the kingdom of God had its inception in the early decades of the eighteenth century in Leipzig, capitol of the German principality of Saxony, which was an era when more books were being published there than in any other place throughout the extensive German Holy Roman Empire, and Leipzig was the center of the early German Enlightenment.[21] The year of Steinmetz's death has been designated as the time of the demise of the massive of Pietist periodicals which had flourished in Germany since 1695.[22]

It was in that milieu that a new journal or chronicle was announced in Saxony in 1731, called the *Gathering of Choice Materials concerning the Building of the Kingdom of God*,[23] to be edited by Jerichovius, then a little known figure in Pietist circles. He had been closely associated with the young Zinzendorf and also with Steinmetz and his ministerial colleagues at Teschen in 1730, the year of their expulsion due to the revival which had prevailed there under Hapsburg duress.[24] Thereafter he came to Leipzig as a fervent preacher and advocate of Pietist themes of the new birth, the edifying interpretation of the Bible, and for the revival. However, as the journal was about to be launched, he unexpectedly died.

It is significant for this study that, before his death, Jerichovius, in a letter to Zinzendorf from Leipzig, announced that he was preparing to start a periodical focused on the building of the Kingdom of God. It occurred to him that he could throw the enemies of that project into confusion and also bear witness to the host of God's heavenly messengers who were the harbingers of that Kingdom.[25] His militaristic style seemed to run counter to the ideals peace which enshrined this coming Kingdom.[26]

He appears to have perceived that the task of the periodical would be to promote the Philadelphian ideals of the coming age of brotherly love, to

---

20. Ibid, 5.

21. See the role of Philadelphian thinking in the development of Petersen's radical Pietistutlook, as found in his interpretation of the children's revival; see Part 3, chapter 2.2 of this work.

22. Ibid, 18. Lächele provides a chart listing the dates of appearance of dozens of Pietist periodicals between 1695 and 1770; 34-36.

23. Ibid, 41.

24. *Die Sammlung auserlesener Materien xum Bau des Reichs Gottes*.

25. Lächele, 43.

26. This is the author's paraphrase of the German text of Jerichovius' message to Zinzendorf, found in Lächele, 47.

27. Ibid.

which Zinzendorf was committed to promoting across ecclesial lines,[27] through his "cavalier tour" of 1719/20.[28]

After the death of Jerichovius in 1734, the publication unexpectedly did not revert to another editor but to the prominent Leipzig bookseller and publisher, Samuel Benjamin Walther (1679-1754). He has been described as an infirm and anxious man, whose initial attempts to become financially successful had first brought melancholy.[29] During his student years at the University of Leipzig he came under Pietist influence, and maintained an active church life as a layman. He did not want to be a publisher but rather an interpreter for French and English students in the city. Working for a time as a medical student, he acquired an interest in the selling of academic books on diverse subjects and established himself as a bookseller in Leipzig and also in adjacent Saxon cities. He brought attention to the Pietist movement of his day, including its more radical expressions, through his work with books.[30] From that interest, he became the book seller for an informal network or society which has been likened to the formation of the Society for the Promotion of Christian Knowledge (SPCK) in London in 1698.[31] His publication work mostly featured books which facilitated access to the Bible, including classical works often neglected in his day. They were intended for an increasingly urban population confronted with many divergent voices of authority.

Walther's interest in the publication project of the *Gathering of Choice Materials (Sammlung auserleser Materialen)* consisted not in the self-promotion of its monetary aspects. He became the business dynamo behind the project by finding a new and wider market for it than the traditional ecclesial audience and thereby increase the sources of income for the Pietist periodicals which abounded in the Leipzig area.[32]

---

28. As a count, Zinzendorf was deeply influenced by the Philadelphian model of community which his grandmother had introduced into her estate at Berthelsdorf, which Jerichovius had also admired as director of the school at her estate. The latter fact is cited by Lächele, 40.

29. Ibid, 47.

30. Ibid., 51.

31. It may be noted the term radical here does not denote anarchist cultural or political views, as in the current day, but to those dedicated to a more devout adherence to the core teaching of the Christian faith, considered absent in their time.

32. Daniel L. Brunner, *Halle Pietists in England: Anthony William Boehm and the Society for the Promotion of Christian Knowledge* (Göttingen, 1993).

33. Lächele, 63.

As a result of this growth, Walther could expect more candidates for the position of editor of the *Gathering of Choice Materials*"[33] than anticipated. Steinmetz was ecstatic when he received news of this report from Walther which had come to the center of Pietist programs at the University of Halle.[34] Word came from Zinzendorf that Walther had selected Gottfried Polycarp Müller, a nearby educator in Leipzig, as Jerichovius's successor, a position which he declined from a sense of inadequacy.[35] Before his selection occurred, he had already developed plans for a periodical on the building of the Kingdom of God in association with other leaders of the revival which had occurred at Teschen.[36] They had planned to adopt the logo, "The Fellowship of the Children of God,"[37] in deference to the children's revival which had birthed these streams of awakening.

In the face of these developments, Steinmetz, who had then been relocated from Teschen to the Kloster Bergen, received support from Francke at Halle[38] to become the new editor.[39] Steinmetz would be called by his peers the "most significant and clear minded representative of the later Pietism."[40] This was so, despite the fact that he has doubtlessly become the most forgotten leader of Pietism in our time.

Steinmetz had only been in his office as abbot at Kloster Bergen for two years when he assumed the additional role of editor of the *Gathering*.[41] He had been installed in this position after a two year stint as superintendent

34. *Sammlung auserlesene Materialen*.

35. Steinmetz to Johann Ludwig Cellarius, Inspector of the Halle Orphanage, Steinmetz to Cellarius on December 12, 1734, cited in Lächele, 64.

36. Letter from Müller to Zinzendorf on August 2, 1735, Ibid.

37. "Bund der view Brüder" in Lächele, 66. These included pastors Andreas Schäffer and Andreas Rothe, who were both from the circle influenced by Zinzendorf and also products of the Silesian revival at Teschen, which Steimetz had overseen. Ibid, 66.

38. Hans Schneider, "Nicolaus Ludwig von Zinzendorf," in Martin Greschat, *Zwischen Tradition und neue Anfang: Valentin Ernst Loescher und der ausgang Lutherische Orthodoxie* (Witten, 1970), 347–372.

39. This was the son of the famous August Hermann Francke, now deceased, Gotthilf August Francke.

40. Zinzendorf, who was now at odds with the theology of new birth at Halle, with its emphasis on "penitential struggle (or Bußkampf) leading to conversion, had supported Müller for the editorship. Lächele, 66. The latter had a plan to turn the periodical into a voice embracing the sharp critique of Lutheran Orthodoxy represented by David Fassman in his "Gesprächen im Reich des Todtes," "Conversations in the Kingdom of the Dead."

41. The tribute given in his eulogy by his successor as abbot at Kloster Berge, Johann Friedrich Hahn (1710-1789), in Lächele, 68.

42. His official position was that of a prominent official in the Prussian government, as he was appointed by King Friedrich Wilhem I to become Consistorial Advisor and General Superintendent in the Principality of Magdeburg.

of the Lutheran churches at Neustadt, where his post expulsion ministry had begun. While serving at the Kloster, he expanded the building, erected a schoolhouse, and put major emphasis on developing its curriculum. Given the dire political situation in Silesia for Protestants, many Silesian refugees followed Steinmetz to Kloster Bergen, where they enrolled in its educational program.

Steinmetz began his work with the *"Gathering"* periodical in the context of a dispute between the Halle and Herrnhut (Zinzendorf) poles of the Pietist movement. As previously noted,[42] Zinzendorf had critiqued Halle for its insistence that conversion (or the new birth) should be preceded by a heartfelt penitential struggle. His temperament preferred to present the new birth as an affective response to the love of God, not marred by such Bußkampf (penitial struggle).

To complicate matters further, Zinzendorf had secured a position on the Halle faculty for one of his spiritual mentees, August Spangenberg, who presently found himself dismissed from that faculty in light of contacts with radical Pietist separatists,[43] and to the disappointment of Zinzendorf. Steinmetz's deep loyalties to Francke and his Halle mission led to a cooling of his longstanding friendship with Zinzendorf and the Moravians. Zinzendorf was also moving away from Steinmetz's commitment to the twofold soteriology of the cross and its subsequent sealing in the believer through the Holy Spirit, as reflected in his dispute with John Wesley over these issues in London in 1741.[44]

Finding himself in an "unpartisan" middle position amid these polarizing trends among the Lutheran Pietists, Steinmetz was hopeful that the launching of his periodical would enable the energy which had been spent in the Pietist movements of renewal to be redirected toward the promotion of revival in the interest of reaching the lost for Christ beyond the decadent structures of post Reformation Christendom. Mindful of his legacy with the children's revival, Steinmetz commented that his intent was to remain a child of God in the midst of these disruptions, proceeding with his editorial tasks as one transfigured by the undefiled and pure love of Jesus

---

43. See Part 3, chapter 2.

44. He sided with their exclusivist view of the eucharist which excluded unbelievers. Lächele, 80. Steinmetz also became critical of Zinzendorf's "lapse" in the "blood and wounds" ecstasy which in his view diverted of the Moravians at Marienborn. Ibid, 81.

45. See Albert Outler, *John Wesley* (Oxford, 1964), Part Three.

Immanuel.⁴⁵ In this context, he had high hopes for the great usefulness of his *Gathering* project:

> We have received the report in more than one place that God has led souls out of death into life, has strengthened others at the outset of their course, and raised up many amid adverse circumstances. He has aroused teachers as well as students, has earnestly inquired into their vocation and their Christendom . . . . These things which God wanted to manifest are made known by the initiatives of this periodical, and they have come to pass.⁴⁶

There was no question for the editor that this periodical needed to continue. He responded to the suggestions his readers in making improvements to the periodical. For example, the readers mentioned that not only written articles but also previously published reports of the working of God's grace in the transformation of human lives needed to be included in the periodical. In addition, there were calls for bringing to recognition the saving work of God in foreign lands,⁴⁷ a direct reference to the globalizing impact of the revival which had started in Silesia, and was now extending from nation to nation.

In the *Improved Gathering of Choice Materials*, the new title in 1737, these changes were implemented with the result that awakenings were described such as reports of the beginnings of Methodism in England, which were the results of correspondence between Steinmetz and John Wesley, called "A continuation of the report concerning the movement of grace . . . and the exceptional circumstances among some awakened persons."⁴⁸ He was at the forefront on the continent to report on the origins of Methodism in England, under the title, *Continuation of the Report of the Oxford Methodists in England,* since they had first become known, consisting of an announcement which, as in the beginning, rejected the pitched slanders and the opposition to them.⁴⁹

---

46. Cited in the correspondence between Steinmetz and Walbaum, in the Akten found in the *Depository of Letters from the administrative officer in Wernigeröder, Anton Heinrich Walbaum (1696-1753),* cited in Lächel, 81.

47. Gerhard Reichel, "Die Entstehung einer Zinzendorf feindlichen Partei in Halle und Wernigerode," *Zeitschrift für Kurchegeschichte 23 , 1902,* 584f, n.386.

48. Lächele, 82.

49. *Verbesserte Sammlung zum Bau des Reich Gotte*s (cited hereafter as VSAM), 15,139, 830-841, cited in Lächele, 83

50. "Fortsetzung der Nachricht von der Oxfordischen Methodisten, bestehen in einer Anzeige, der, gleich anfangs, da sie bekannt worden, gegen die ausgeschutteten Lästerungen und deren Widergang": (VSAM 16, 1740, 950-974).

This report by Steinmetz in the *Gathering* may represent the earliest announcement concerning the Methodist revival to appear on the Continent. It is presented alongside "Information on the Mission In India," described as "some breaking events occurring in the Kingdom of God."[50] Steinmetz wanted these particular reports of the "contributions to the gathering of choice materials on the building of the Kingdom of God" to be concluded with "good, edifying poems."[51] Should these be unavailable, he wanted the space to be devoted to "something useful, since much is available in this era of poetical books."[52]

It is probable that Steinmetz was unaware that John Wesley and the Methodist movement he was reporting was the work of a man brought to the message of full salvation, via the work of Christ at Calvary and its sealing at Pentecost, by Wesley's encounter with Christian David at Herrnhut, by whom he was introduced to that great theme of a twofold soteriology. David had by then been brought to salvation and confirmation of his new birth in the Pentecost preaching of Steinmetz at Teschen, which was the message he then conveyed to the young John Wesley. However, Wesley's meeting with David occurred in 1738, before the birth of the Oxford Methodist movement, at a time when Wesley was not yet involved in the revival which had begun in Silesia and would soon reach England through his instrumentality. Hence, there was probably no reason why David would have reported to Steinmetz his conversations with a young Anglican named Wesley, even though that English revival would so greatly depend on the twofold soteriology of Wesley that had its origins with Steinmetz. Neither was there any reason why Wesley would have been aware of the origins of that doctrinal position, since there is no evidence in David's conversations with Wesley, as recorded in both men's journals, of any mention of the Steinmetz and Teschen link. Hence, these connections may be the hindsight perspective provided by the research of this study, which documents the considerable degree of unrecognized indebtedness early Methodism had to those continental roots.

---

51. "Nachrichten von einigen ins Reich Gottes eingeschlägenden Begebenheiten." Aus Ost-Indien." VSAM 12, 1739, 448–457. This would have referenced the Halle based mission there, which predated William Carey by over 60 years.

52. Lächele, 82.

53. Ibid.

4.6 The Mission of the *Gathering*

The twofold view of salvation, with its focus on the Pentecost sealing with the Holy Spirit, presented by Steinmetz in his revival sermons, remained the model of his preaching in his later years as Abbot at Kloster Bergen. Alongside this development was his important work in advancing the *Gathering of Choice Materials* documenting the building of the Kingdom of God in the world, giving impetus for a new concern for a larger, and even global expansion of evangelical Christianity. He had taken on the editorship of this project after the death of its founder, Jerichovius.

As a Pietist, Jerichovius was indebted to Spener's hope for "better times" for the church, which translated into a view of salvation history (Heilsgeschichte) which looked to a coming fulfillment of biblical prophecy regarding the promised conversion of the Jews, and an improvement in the social and moral conditions of humanity through the influence of the gospel in the life of church and state. From that perspective, Jerichovius viewed the new eighteenth century, moving forth in the wake of the perilous religious wars of the preceding century, as a propitious time to focus intentionally on gathering evidence for the coming revelation of the Kingdom of God in history.[53] His focus was on practical experience and useful knowledge for a disciplined holy life rather than any preoccupation with apocalyptic speculation.

Reflecting that ethos, after 1737 Steinmetz altered his priorities in what was being gathered as evidence of this coming kingdom, to focus more on accounts of exemplary lives, through an exchange of documents among various publishers touched by the Pietist movement. One strategy he devised to facilitate this objective was the translation into German of English devotional literature, particularly from the Puritans, which would be presented in the "Improved" version of the periodical.[54] As a churchman, Steinmetz took the initiative to promote the Kingdom's coming by participating with church leaders in other nations where the revival had spread. For example, he served as a member of the Society for the Promotion of Christian Knowledge. An indication of that participation is evident in his lists of English Puritan devotional literature which he purchased for the library of the Kloster Bergen. He also translated many of these works into German and published selections from them in the issues

---

54. This outlook is to be contrasted with the nineteenth century liberal theology of the kingdom which fully replaced eschatology with human moral development, a theme which first appeared in the Enlightenment of the eighteenth century.

55. This feature appeared in 1743, Lächele, 89.

of his periodical.⁵⁵ Steinmetz worked through contacts with the Moravian August Spangenberg and his contacts with a London bookseller to locate these English sources.⁵⁶

Among those English sources, Steinmetz wrote the forward to the first German translation of Isaac Watts work, "The Redeemer and the Sanctifier," which was published at Halle in 1737, before Wesley's interactions with the soteriology of Steinmetz via Christian David at Herrnhut in 1738.⁵⁷

Steinmetz valued Watts as his source of data for the New England awakening under Jonathan Edwards.⁵⁸ In 1738 he arranged for the translation and publication of Edwards in his *Gathering of Choice Materials*;⁵⁹ along with his foreword, of Isaac Watts' London edition of Jonathan Edwards's *Narrative of the Surprising Work of God in New England*.⁶⁰ Through this linkage, the first Great Awakening in North America (1734-1735), was interfaced with the awakening movement originating in Silesia which gave impetus to his periodical. He was charting the transnational advance of the work of the Holy Spirit which hearkened back to the children's revival.

The work of Philip Doddridge, renowned Reformed author of pastoral theology and pastor of a Dissenting Church in the English provincial city of Northampton, also caught the attention of Steinmetz, as additional "choice evidence" for the Kingdom of God which had begun with the children. In 1749 he published a German translated version of Doddridge's

---

56. Hermann Beck, *Der Erbauungsliteratur der evangelischen Kirche Deutschland* (Erlangen, 1883), 179, cited in Lächele, 193.

57. The London bookseller was James Hutton. Through this contact other Pietist leaders, including Gotthilf Francke gained possession of English devotional literature. Ibid.

58. The title of the German translation with Steinmetz's foreward also reflects the twofold soteriology of Steinmetz, which was supported at Halle, given the close working relationship Steinmetz had with both Franckes: "D. Isaac Watts Versöhn Oppfer Christi, sammt den Wirkungen des heiligen Geistes," cited in Brunner, *Pietists*, 194, and Lächele, 194. Brunner notes that Watts was more readily accepted in Halle than were Wesley and Whitefield.

59. Lächele, 194.

60. Published in Madgeburg: Seidel, 1738; Steinmetz printed this work again in the Abbey, for wider circulation there, as "Faithful reports of powerful awakening and conversion among souls in a renewed Christianity in New England," the author's translation of "Glaubwürdige Nachrichten von Kräftiger Erweckung und Bekehrung vieler Seelen zur einen rechtschaffenen Christenthum in Neu England [...]," in *Closter Bergische Sammlung Nützlicher Materien zur Erbauung im Wahren Christenthum*, 3, (1745), 257-261, cited in Lächele, 196.

61. Ibid, 196.

"Sermons on the Nature and Efficacy of Grace," with a foreword by the translator, to this effect:

> Those for whom practical pastoral theology is known, who for some years have walked in the Light under the direction of the worthy Abbot Steinmetz, will read a sermon concerning the shameful and dangerous neglect of souls, which we have received from this Mr. Doddridge in England . . . . This translated work from the English cannot be read without perceiving the form of a man in whom reside the things of God.[61]

In the course of his work with these "choice materials" which was the object of his "gathering" (Sammlung), Steinmetz has set about his task with a forthright delineation of what constitutes the godly person who can be the channel of this "building" of the Kingdom of God. Steinmetz delineates the features of the godly person, who embodies authentic witness to the building of the kingdom of God. That discussion occurs in the context of Orthodox Lutheran critics of his project who are basically siding with his opponents in the Teschen revival, who had objected to his use of conventicles, promotion of the new birth, and the edificatory reading of Scripture, as deviations from orderly churchmanship, harboring sectarianism and potential division of the Protestant cause amid heightened altercations with it Hapsburg adversaries.

As for Jerichovius before him, what is central for Steinmetz is that the Kingdom comes as the reign of God, which reflects the emphasis of Spener in his *Pia Desideria*.[62] This emphasis distinguishes an imminent/earthly Kingdom from a future, transcendent one, even as there is always a tension between Jesus' parables concerning imminent events and the fullness of the Kingdom to which they point. This tension had been lost in the various utopian versions of the kingdom among the radical spiritualists of the late medieval and Reformation eras.[63] There was also the neglect of the mighty works of God in deference to the moralist interpretations of the kingdom.[64]

62. From "Foreword": to the 33. *Stuck der Theologia Pastoralis Practica* by Philip Doddridge (1749), cited in Lächel, 198. (author's translation).

63. Ibid., 104; see Spener, *Pia Desideria*, 3: "full delight in knowledge, made to be holy just as is the godly Name, through their service, His Kingdom extended, and His will brought to full fruition." (author's translation); "Völlige Vergnügung in Erkantnu / wie göttlicher Name durch ihren Dienst geheilget/ sein Reich erweitert/ und sein Wille vollbracht werde."

64. Muntzer's call for a violent inbreaking of the kingdom through his initiation of the Peasants Rebellion would qualify as such an example.

65. As embodied in the nineteenth century post-Kantian advocates of a moral rather than an eschatological view of the Kingdom of God.

Over against these polar dichotomies of the coming kingdom, Steinmetz sets his sights on establishing the kingdom through the expansion of converted or reborn men and women.[65] In that process the kingdom's presence is invariably identified by the struggle between God and the devil.[66]

Amid that struggle, the meaning of the present moment is made transparent only in light of the eschatological goal of the coming Christ to which His Spirit bears present witness. It is by this perspective that our study has found guidance in Steinmetz's Pentecost addresses. Throughout, he accentuates the need for persons to come to terms with Christ's offer of salvation through His shed blood as the Spirit seals the seeking heart in the assurance of that redemption and in the abiding blessedness of life empowered by this sealing for faithful watching and witness, unto the end of the world. And, as Steinmetz modeled in his daily ministry at Teschen and later as Abbot at Kloster Bergen, that end does not arrive by inertia but by a disciplined and incessant witness to the apostolic twofold gospel of the Cross and Pentecost to all persons of all languages and races and nations. For that witness, the church as the Body of Christ is to be perennially prepared to remain alert and engaged in finding evidence of where that kingdom is emerging.

Jerichovius, Steinmetz's predecessor as editor of the *Gathering*, spoke in metaphorical terms of the coming kingdom, saying, "with the stone and mortar, Zion will be built, and each should be in its place, according to the present economy (oikonomia)."[67] Uncomfortable for an ecumenical age, in that polemical era reflecting the Counter-Reformation, the editors of the *Gathering* harbored a view of Catholicism which was being encountered through a resurgent Habsburg Empire. In that context, they were looking for evidence of signs of a pending fall of the papacy (to them a persecuting entity) as well as the coming conversion of all Jews. Lächele interprets Jerichovius as reflecting the eschatological focus of Moser's periodical on "Old and New Things from the Kingdom of God", whereas Steinmetz gave

---

66. This was also the theme of August Herman Francke and his successor, Lange, theologians at Halle, cited in Lächele, 105.

67. Ibid. See Martin Schmidt, *Das Verständnis des Reich Gottes im Halleschen Pietismus. In Gottesreich und Menschen Reich*. Ernst Stähelin zum 80. Geburtstag. (Basel: 1969), 236-247.

68. This is Lächele's paraphrase of Jerichovius' position (5); it also reflects the symbolic prophetic interpretation of salvation history, based on Scripture and its application to world history, which had its origin in the seventeenth century Dutch theologian, Johannes Cocceius, and applied to pastoral theology in Friedrich Adolph Lampe, *Geheimnis des Gandenbundes* (6 vols, 1729) and in German Reformed Pietism. See J. S. O'Malley, *Pilgrimage of Faith: The Legacy of the Otterbeins* (Metuchen, NJ: Scarecrow, 1973).

more focus to the present rather than to the eschatological moment. He related Kingdom concerns to upbuilding what is "upright" ("rechtschaffen") and "useful" ("nutzlich") in safeguarding the present order (status quo) as the domain of God's Kingdom concern.[68]

The concern here is to highlight how Steinmetz's focus on a two-stage approach to soteriology based on Calvary and Pentecost, as found in his *Pentecost Addresses*, also needs to be factored as an influence upon his handling of the "choice materials" to be included in his personal journal and in documenting the building of the kingdom of God. The *Addresses* underscore that it was essential to his view of redemption in Christ that this twofold construct be followed for evangelism to be authentic and effectual. Here was also the formula followed by Christian David in reporting the results of his revival ministry, which reflect his mentoring under Steinmetz, and as conveyed to John Wesley in their conversations at Herrnhut.[69]

His emphasis on this twofold soteriology was grounded in his revival ministry at Teschen, which birthed his later commitment to the project of tracking the building the kingdom of God in history. Its origin can be traced to his style of ministry in Silesia, first at Töppliwoda, where he had linked the Lutheran focus on the theology of the cross with Pentecost from the outset,[70] and thereafter it is traced in his revival preaching, done in the context of the legacy of the children's revival in Silesia, which was accompanied by class and prayer meetings, reminiscent of later Methodism, and by the orderly recording of his pastoral insights gained from confession and visitations.[71]

When appointed to Teschen, the massive multinational congregation anticipated the future of revivalism and Christian globalization. Revivalism in its twofold expression was a mode of ministry that developed as evidence from prevailing circumstances, e. g. with great crowds arriving from a distance the night before, holding enthusiastic hymn singing sessions in mul-

---

69. Lächele, 107.

70. For example, in his imagery of the two stage soteriology, David envisions the congregation of believers as having a foundation in the cross and blood of Christ and an "upper part of the structure," to "purification and sanctification both of the body and the spirit, and to the fruit of faith, hope and love." *Journal of Christian David*, #17, from April 30, 1740, 52-53, see discussion in 3.3.2 above.

71. He received his call to Töppliwoda, which preceded his coming to Teschen, after a prominent Silesian nobleman was touched by a Pentecost or Whitsuntide homily Steinmetz delivered on his estate. Ward, *Protestant Evangelical Awakening*, 75.

72. Ibid, 75. He noted in his Pentecost Addresses that persons reporting ecstasies and visions must be in great need for God to use these extraordinary means instead of meeting their needs by means of his Word. See *Pentecost Addresses*, fifth address.

tiple languages. The revival first spread from Teschen beginning in 1725, when converts prayed and concluded a covenant with God following a Pentecost (called Whitsuntide) service. His ministry team functioned like circuit riders, alternating a week of public prayer meetings and pastoral care with a week of traveling to the sick, a week of rest and renewal, and a fourth week of riding to support traveling preachers.[72]

During his leadership of the revival in the Grace Church, and prior to his encounter with Christian David, the impact of that revival had begun to reach into neighboring Moravia and Bohemia, across the border from Teschen. It has been calculated that there were by 1724, some 20,000 secret Lutherans in Catholic Bohemia were seeking to escape Hapsburg oppression.[73] David, in turn, would find channels for expediting the removal of Bohemians from their homeland into neighboring Upper Lusatia and Saxony.

The arrival of the revival from Teschen into Herrnhut in 1727 had been accompanied by preaching there by Liberda from Teschen and also Schwedler, Steinmetz's Silesian colleague and fellow revival preacher. The Herrnhut revival was then expedited with David's leadership. It was triggered by an awakening among children, reflecting the pattern of the Silesian children's revival. The revival at Herrnhut transformed the life of the moribund community, and ignited its mission to the larger world, which Zinzendorf would seek to monitor and direct. However, it was Christian David who would be the spot person, under Zinzendorf's leadership, to itinerate internationally as an ambassador of that revival. David remained in contact with Steinmetz, as indicated in his journal, which reflected Zinzendorf's request David to seek the counsel of Steinmetz at Teschen in his own faith formation.

The persons selected for inclusion in the *Gathering* narrative numbered those who were influenced by Steinmetz in his approach to revival, and who conveyed that impulse into new fields of mission. A chief example of that influence is Samuel Lutz (1674–1750), the key revival leader in eighteenth century Switzerland, whose ministry Ward reports "as a hero with Steinmetz's circle in Germany."[74] Lutz moved Pietism in Switzerland into the direction of revivalism, based on his spirit of always being in the hand of the Savior.[75] He reflects Steinmetz's twofold soteriology (1) placing pri-

---

73. Ward, *Protestant Evangelical Awakening*, 77.

74. That oppression had reached a peak there a century after the Protestants' defeat by the Hapsburgs at the Battle of White Mountain in 1620.

75. Ward (in PEA, 178) notes that Steinmetz's reports of Lutz's work and writing are almost innumerable in the *Gathering*, 4–6 (1735–37).

mary focus on Luther's theology of the cross, with his republication of Luther's Commentary on Galatians in Swiss Reformed context, and (2) he hosted J. F. Rock (1678–1749), leader of the separatistic Society of the Inspired in Germany, whose group took possession of the Moravian community of Marienborn after its demise.[76] Lutz was attracted by Rock's prophetic ministry in the Holy Spirit, but, given Lutz's strong Christological basis, he "tempted" Lutz's followers back into the church as the true home for revival.[77] Lutz reflected a twofold theme of salvation in this entry, which Steinmetz includes in his *Gathering*:

> After the people were seated we began with a resonding hymn of praises and vied in song with the forest birds. When this was over and the devotion seemed to awaken prayer, then I offered up myself and the whole company to the to the heavenly Father through our Lord Jesus Christ, imploring His sweet presence, gracious assistance, and heavenly unction, that he would open my mouth and the hearts of all . . . and the Lord answered with fire, kindled the heart with joyful flames of love, and I sat down again and spoke on a text of Scripture.[78]

Lutz was sustained in his conflict with Swiss church authorities with a sense that his work was related to the "worldwide movement of grace" which was envisaged in Halle and also by their appointed pastor at Teschen, Steinmetz.[79]

Given the tensions between Halle and Herrnhut that Steinmetz sought to mediate, he did not include the aspects of Christian David's mission as part of that narrative, even though David appealed to his loyalty to Steinmetz as his mentor throughout his ministry. Nevertheless, our examination of entries in David's journal of travels to the Baltics, Scandinavia, and Greenland report the acts of his evangelistic ministry in lands beyond Silesia, effecting the spread of that revival beyond its origin in Teschen.[80]

His extension of that twofold soteriology as the norm for a globalizing of "real" Christianity in regenerated lives developed within and also beyond the existing institutional forms in Christendom in the early eighteenth century. It developed under the complex of a Halle and Prussian initiated and financed mission in the Baltic regions of Livonia (Latvia) and Estonia

---

76. Ward, *Christianity Under the Ancient Regime*, 125.
77. Ibid.
78. Ibid.
79. Steinmetz, *Gathering*, 4 (1735) 354-404, cited in Ward, PEA, 181.
80. Ibid.
81. See this discussion Christian David's work in Part Three, 2.3.1, above.

in 1729, in which Christian David labored for a decade under Moravian auspices.

This "complex" also developed under an expanding Prussian kingdom that was working in tandem with a Protestant Christian mission based in Halle (a Prussian University), and operating independently of the Hapsburg Emperor in Vienna.[81] A university, primary schools and an Orphan House modeled after the institutions of Halle were opened in the East Prussian city of Königsberg as part of the development of Prussian influence there, and focus was given to bring the Pietist message of evangelical Christianity to a Baltic population that included considerable pre-Christian elements (devastated by plagues) within its field of mission.[82]

The Prussian government had recruited laborers from across Germany, Poland, Livonia (later Lithuania), Poland and French Switzerland to build their expanding infrastructure, and the authorities approved the work of Steinmetz in organizing missions for revival in the Baltic region, which also dovetailed with his intent of building the Kingdom of God on earth.

The outcome of this Prussian mission was a series of revivals, which "like those of English Methodism, had considerably cumulative force."[83] These missions reflected his distinctive message of salvation and style of evangelism, sanctioned by the Prussians, which had marked the original revival in Silesia.[84] The Prussians arranged there for the building of barn-like churches as "those they also built in Silesia" and resembling the "Silesian style camp-meetings put on by the children."[85] Through this line of influence, coordinated by Steinmetz, by the 1740s, when he had been transferred to the Kloster Bergen, the revival had spread into Russian lands to the east, so that "the vast majority of the clergy in the area were of the

---

82. The pattern for this mission had been developed by the Franckes at Halle and modeled in other locations, as in Teschen, Silesia, where the revival began under Steinmetz's leadership, and under his appointment to that ministry by Halle, in concert with Protestant authorities in Silesia.

83. See T. Wotschke, *Der Pietismus in Koenigsberg nach Regalls Tode in Briefen* (2 vols Konigsberg, 1929/30) 71, 81, 1112, cited in Ward, *Protestant Evangelical Awakening*, 146. Ward notes that the theological faculty at Koenigsburg included a young Halle-trained theologian, Georg Friedrich Rogall (1701-33), who, despite opposition from Eastern Orthodox authorities in the area, "trained a whole new generation of Pietist clergy, and got some 30,000 devotional tracts into circulation." Ward, *Christianity under the Ancien Regime*, 119.

84. Ibid.

85. The Prussians also facilitated transferring 14,000 Lutheran refugees, expelled from Austria by the Hapsburgs, to the Baltic region, who came with a contingent of Halle preachers/missionaries with them. Ibid.

86. "Even the Lithuanians who could not understand the [German] language came to admire the devotion and hear the songs." Ibid.

Halle stamp, and Livonia and Estonia had together become one of the great bastions of Pietism in the Russian Empire."[86]

Christian David and a Moravian colleague came to assist in the Reval area of Livonia (now Tallinn, Estonia) in 1729, working in collaboration with Zinzendorf as well as Steinmetz,[87] to organize prayer and Bible study groups. Operating from the estate of a Prussian official near Riga (present day Latvia), this initiative expanded, in cooperation with a friend of Francke who was in charge of the estate. The widow of a Prussian general, he exhibited "the Hallensian enthusiasm for dealing with serf races in a new way,"[88] meaning, one which did not diminish their humanity but approached them as full heirs of salvation in Christ. This entry led to 50 Moravian missionaries who came to Livonia and Estonia over the following decade, which was "equal to the entire clergy in the area."[89] The result was a series of revivals, with the features of children's work spreading to adults which had been the pattern of the first revival under Steinmetz in Silesia.[90] Ward observed that this revival had the novel feature, unlike the earlier ones in Silesia and beyond, that "it was in the front line of the struggle against paganism."[91]

In 1739 the year of the revival among the Letts (Latvians) began when Christian David, who continued in correspondence with Steinmetz, opened his first meeting in the Latvian language. This revival soon spread over all of northern Livonia resulting in 14,000 converted and enrolled as members of Moravian bands in that region, consisting of Letts and Estonians, which had recently overthrown the abuses of "Swedish absolutism."[92] The revival spread in 1740 from offshore islands to the mainland of the Estonians, who now reported the demise of drunkenness and crime, and the cultural repudiation of "worldly delights" (all themes Steinmetz emphasized in his Pentecost addresses). In its second generation, David's mission developed into an indigenous revival among ethnic Estonians who were then under Russian domination. It then had a life of its own by means of the clergy who had invited them, as well as the Russian

---

87. Ibid.

88. See his correspondence with Steinmetz from this period, reflecting his intent to follow his lead in mission, as discussed in Part 3, chapter 2. Section 1.

89. Ibid, 120.

90. Ibid.

91. Ibid, 120.

92. Ibid.

93. The results of this revival led to the first schools for peasants and the translation of the Bible and Lutheran hymnal into the native Estonian and Latvian languages. This was done by a Pietist pastor in Reval, associated with Zinzendorf. Ibid,

Tsaress Elisabeth, who rejected them. The result was the Russian imprisonment of its leaders, including the Pietist pastor Gutsleff who had invited David to come to Estonia.[93] As our study has shown, David's itineraries extended as far as Greenland.[94]

4.7 Concluding Reflections

In this chapter the context and the content of Steinmetz's composition of his *Gathering* periodical have been observed, with an eye to the influence of his influential Pentecost Addresses, which stem from the historic revival under his tenure as pastor of the Grace Church in Teschen, Silesia. While under duress as the engaged pastor, caught up in an unprecedented awakening in his Silesian parish, he was constrained by circumstances from publishing his homilies on Pentecost which provided the theological motif for the first awakening movement in Protestant Christianity. It was only after his removal from that scene turbulent and transformative that he was permitted a season of reflection, when such academic work might be completed. He was then at work in his appointment by the Prussian King Frederick I as Abbot of Kloster Bergen (1732–1761), as the final chapter of his ministry, that this occurred.

Ever poised for ministry with the laity, Steinmetz built a comprehensive educational and resource center at the Abbey for personal and parish renewal in mid eighteenth century German Lutheranism. In this setting, he published several educational series, and the published *Pentecost Addresses* was the most influential among them.[95] That title first appears in English translation, with annotated text, in this volume.

Renner reports incidents in his life mid nineteenth century era of persons who presented testimonies, a century removed from the events, which remembered the transformative impact of his addresses upon their families and communities of faith. In reading his text as presented in this volume, with the interpretive chapters which follow, it is important to read it as a product of the historic children's revival from a dark era of early modern history, which became the living message of the decade long event which represents the largest and most pervasive awakening in pre-nineteenth century Europe. It gave rise to subsequent revivals in several localities throughout Europe, India, and North America where its impact was felt. The

---

94. Ibid, 121.
95. See 3.2.2 above.
96. Renner (pp. 101–129) notes that these addresses were the most popular and often reprinted title in the series.

Gathering is the narrative which establishes reciprocity between these points of light, in a world then in the throes of transition from a traditional Christendom contained in Europe to an ever actualizing global movement of redeemed persons and communities of faith through the ministry of the Holy Spirit. There is a connection between Steinmetz 's heralding the gift of the final and unrepeatable work of Calvary now sealed through the Holy Spirit's sanctifying empowerment upon human hearts, and the moving of that same Holy Spirit of the Triune God in the harvests of lives which followed that event in its global outreach.

Finally, this study has introduced the volume which Steinmetz produced in the aftermath of the revival, as the message is heard anew of the preacher who promised to "gather" the fruit of that awakening for the building of God's kingdom unto the ends of the earth, from the era of his lifetime (to 1762). It is an unfinished narrative, to which the Wesleyan message of a twofold soteriology encompassing Calvary and Pentecost bore witness in its world ministry a century later. This study is presented as an exploration of the origin of that important theme in the development of Christian thought, and of the theme of a globalized Christianity which was built upon it. We may hear less of its import in our day, but the hour is late, and a fresh reading of Steinmetz may yet awaken an urgency for earnest seekers in this day of travail within global Christianity to reclaim anew the whole gospel bequeathed to the people of God by their Lord.

A Final Addendum

David's Foundations for a Global Ministry Based on the Twofold Soteriology that He Learned from Steinmetz and Conveyed to John Wesley

The British Wesleyan historian W. R. Ward first noted the significance of Christian's David's conversations with John Wesley at Herrnhut as conveying to him within a revival context what Wesleyans call the two staged view of salvation, encompassing justification and sanctification. This conversation was the revival based source of that central motif in the theology of John Wesley, which would provide the definitive theological grounding for the revival led by the Wesleys in Great Britain and America. What Ward missed was the Pentecost connection to Wesleyan soteriology inherent in David's exposition to Wesley, because he did not have access to the Pentecost addresses of Steinmetz, which was the source of the two staged soteriology then conveyed by David to John Wesley, as recorded in Wesley's Journal.

The present study is indebted to Ward for his distinction between renewal and revival, being a key component in our exposition of the significance of Steinmetz's contribution to the Wesleys. Ward's great contribution was to demonstrate in several volumes (especially in *The Protestant Evangelical Awakening*, 1992) that revival in early modern Christianity had its origin in central Europe, in the context of the demise of the

Christendom model of Christianity occurring in the wake of travail from the Counter Reformation. He also showed that it was distinct from earlier efforts of parish renewal which were the hallmark of German Pietism.

However, Ward was not able to show the Wesleyan theological character for that revival because he did not have access to the Steinmetz sermons on Pentecost which defined the theological character of that revival. The seventeenth century Pietist leaders had worked for renewal of the parishes of the corpus Christianum through the means of the proclamation of the new birth in Christ and the introduction of conventicles for laity within parish structures. Francke, the leader of the great Halle mission enterprise, was Steinmetz's mentor and provided him with the resources for advancing Steinmetz's ministry in Silesia which resulted in bringing to fruition the first revival in Protestant history, based in the awakening among the Silesian children. Unlike efforts for renewal of extant structures of Christendom, revival first appeared not with Francke but in the awakening preaching of Steinmetz, coming as the theocentric incursion of the Holy Spirit in the midst of hopeless human conditions.

Our study of Steinmetz's Pentecost addresses is foundational for understanding the outcome of that awakening, which was to bring together the redemptive events of Calvary and Pentecost embodied in a message of a two-staged soteriology. This extraordinary event would for the first time in Protestant history ignite new communities of faith across the borders of nations and cultures. The Methodist movement was a significant outcome of that multicultural and sovereign divine human movement. The burden of this study is to recover the rightful place of the legacy of John Wesley within this trajectory.

Here we offer a closing summary of the steps of David's discovery. He began to build a global ministry based on his spiritual roots in the Silesian revival under Steinmetz's leadership in the wake of the children's revival there. When that revival spilled into Bohemia and Moravia in 1722, he addressed its leaders there concerning the "marks of God's children"—"The children of God in Silesia are very much awakened on account of our institutions, particularly on account of our order of prayer. I beg for you all very urgently not to omit it: there is a great blessing for it in Silesia, and it causes great rejoicing." He continues, "We can become a true light in the whole world, if our conduct be worthy of the gospel. God has made a good beginning with us and paved a way for us. God grant us to see clearly how we should walk."¹

He writes to the "awakened" at Augsburg (Germany) in 1733, God is trustworthy, and brings his help at his own time, just as now—For he knows the right time, when he can give his little children a real joy and put to shame the unbelievers...Now we proceed to the upper part of the structure, to purification and sanctification both of the body and the spirit, to the fruits of faith, love and hope. And there one must search and learn to know souls, whether they bring forth fruits out of faith or love or hope.² From Livonia he wrote in 1740: "The Savior's cause is doing well and is spreading constantly . . . . Many thousands have come to the faith,...but there are some of them who have obtained grace to enter the holy of holies by the blood of Jesus . . . . I long to have the simplicity of Christ, to pull the yoke equally with my brethren in my activities, as to my age to be a child . . . .to point souls to the serpent that was lifted up. Thus the heart of poor sinners will be cleansed by faith, the warrior's hearts however in the faith. The former by way of imputation, the latter in his experience as a regenerate man."³

He follows this trip with a letter to his mentor, Abbot Steinmetz, in July 1741: "Now, my dear old father and brother, this is what I can report to the Brethren. But what should I, according to your wish, say about myself, how I stand with the Lamb? I am a poor sinner, the Savior knows that well, but one who has found grace . . . in One who is my mediator and surety [the sign of Pentecost sealing], and yesterday and today and in all eternity will be and remain my all."⁴

Here is the legacy of the twofold soteriology announced by Steinmetz, which bore fruit in David and in his spiritual heir, John Wesley.

---

1. *Memoirs of Christian David,* (November 1727), 35.
2. To the awakened at Augsburg, January 18, 1735, 45.
3. *Europaeische...Gemein-Nachrichten.* Bettag in Herrnhut, 30 April Anno 1740, der dritte Theil, XV, f, in *Christian David, Servant of the Lord,* n64, 52.
4. To Abbot Steinmetz [place?], July 1741, in *Christian David, Servant of the Lord* (memoir), 56. [The question of place was supplied by the editor of David's memoir, Vernon H. Nelson. It can be reasonably added that the place where Steinmetz was then serving when he received this letter from David was the Kloster Bergen, Magdeburg, Germany, where he was appointed to serve as Abbot following his expulsion from Silesia in 1740].

BIBLIOGRAPHY

Primary Sources

Arndt, Johann, *True Christianity* (1605), in Peter Erb, editor, The Library of Christian Classics (Paulist, 1978).
Arnold, Gottfried. *Unparteiische Kirche und Ketzer Historie*. Zwei Bände. Franckfurt: Thomas Fritsch, 1699–1700.
Böhme, Jacob. *The Way to Christ*. Peter Erb, editor. Paulist: Library of Western Spirituality, 1977.
David, Christian. *Christian David: Servant of the Lord* (Memoir compiled by Count Nicholas von Zinzendorf). Vernon H. Nelson, editor. The Archives of the Moravian Church, Publication 11. Bethlehem, PA: 1962.
Edwards, Jonathan. *The Surprising Work of God in the Conversion of Many Hundred Souls in Northampton*. Dunning and Spaulding, 1735.
⎯⎯⎯. *Treatise Concerning Religious Affections*, Ed. John E. Smith. New Haven: Yale, 1959.
Lampe, Friedrich Adolph. *Geheimnis des Gnadenbundes*. six volumes. Bremen: Sauermans, 1712–19.
Luther, Martin, "Freedom of a Christian" in John Dillenberger, editor, *Martin Luther: Selections from His Writings*. New York: Anchor Double Day, 1961.
⎯⎯⎯. "Pagan Servitude of the Church" in John Dillenberger, editor, *Martin Luther: Selections from His Writings*. New York: Anchor Double Day, 1961.
⎯⎯⎯. *Small Catechism*, Philip Schaff, editor. "The Creeds of Christendom Volume III." Grand Rapids: Baker, 1996 Reprint.
Otterbein, Philip William, et al, in J. Steven O'Malley, editor, *Early German American Evangelicalism: Pietist Sources in Discipleship and Sanctification*. Metuchen, NJ: Scarecrow, 1973.
Petersen, Johann Wilhelm. *Die Macht der Kinder in der Letzten Zeit, auf Veranlassung der Kleinen Prediger/oder der Betenden Kinder in Schlesien/aus der Heiligen Schrifft Vorgestellt von Johann Wilhelm Petersen*. Frankfurt und Leipzig. In Verlegung Samuel Heil und Johann Gottfried Liebezeits, 1709.
⎯⎯⎯. *Mysterium Apokatastaseos, oder das Geheimnis der Wiederbringung Aller Dinge*. Band 1, Berlin, 1700.
⎯⎯⎯. *Das Geheimnis des Erstgebohrenen aller Creatur von Christo Jesu dem Gott-Menschen*. Frankfurt/Main, 1711.

Pierre Poiret, *L'oeconomie divine ou Systeme universel et demontre des ourvres et des desseins de Dieu en verles hommes.* Amsterdam, 1687.

Spener, Philip Jakob. *Pia Desideria.* John Tappert, editor. Philadelphia: Fortress Press, 1964.

Steinmetz, Johann Adam. *Von der Versiegelung der Glaubigen mit dem heiligen Geist. In einigen Pfingst-Erbauungsstunden aus Epheser 4,30.* Frankfurt/Main: Brönner, 1857, third edition.

――――. *Die Sammlung auserlesener Materien zum Bau des Reich Gottes: zwischen 1730 und 1760.* Selectively edited and interpreted by Rainer Lächele. Halle: Verlag der Franckeschen Stiftungen, im Max Niemeyer Verlag, Tübingen, 2006 . [A selected and interpretive study of the content of the original text in its historical context.]

Tersteegen, Gerhard. "True Godliness," in Samuel Jackson (translator), *Spiritual Crumbs from the Master's Table* (1837). Reprinted Whitefish, MT: Kessinger Publishing, 2009.

Wesley, Charles. *Manuscript Journal of the Reverend Charles Wesley M.A*, edited S.T. Kimbrough, Jr. and Kenneth G. C. Newport, 2 volumes. Nashville: Kingswood Books, 2008.

――――. Unpublished Letters transcribed by Gareth Lloyd, The Methodist Archives and Research Center (MARC), John Rylands University Library of Manchester, England.

――――. *The Letters of Charles Wesley. A Critical Edition with Introduction and Notes.* Volume I, 1728–1736, edited by Kenneth G.C. Newport and Gareth Lloyd, Oxford University Press, 2013.

Wesley, John, *John Wesley: A Library of Protestant Thought*. Edited by Albert Outler. Oxord University Press, 1964.

――――. *The Works of John Wesley.* Edited by Thomas Jackson. Fourteen Volumes. London, Wesleyan Conference Office, 1872. Reprinted Grand Rapids: Baker Publishing House, 1978.

――――. *The Works of John Wesley, begun as the Oxford Edition of the Works of John Wesley. Oxford. Clarendon Press, 1973–1983*; continued as "The Bicentennial Edition of the Works of John Wesley" 35 volumes. Nashville: Abingdon Press, 1984, with focus upon W Reginald Ward and Richard P. Heitzenrater, editors. Vol I, *Journal and Diaries*, (1735–1738).

Zinzendorf, Count Nicholas von. "Nine Public Lectures (1746)" in Peter Erb, editor. *Pietists: Selected Writings.* New York: Paulist Press, 1983.

――――. *The Herrnhut Diary.* May–August 1727. Printed in Zinzendorf und die Herrnhuter Brüder, edited by H C Hahn and H. Reichel: Hamburg, 1977.

Secondary Sources

Abraham, William. "A Barrier to Revitalization: Ecclesial Alienation," in J. S. O'Malley, *Interpretive Trends: Christian Revitalization for the Early 21st Century.* Lexington: Emeth Press, 2006.

Albright, Raymond, *History of the Evangelical Church* (Harrisburg: Evangelical Press, 1956)

Althaus, Paul. *The Theology of Martin Luther* (Philadelphia: Fortress, 1966).

Bayer, Oswald. *Martin Luther's Theology; A Contemporary Interpretation* (Grand Rapides, Eerdmanns, 2008).

Behney, Bruce, and Eller, Paul, *History of the Evangelical United Brethren Church.* Nashville: Abingdon, 1979.
Benz, Ernst. *Die Protestantische Thebais. Zur Nachwirkung Makarius des Egypters im Protestantismus 17. Jhdt 18 in Europa und Amerika.* Wiesbaden: Franz Steiner Verlag, 1963.
Beyreuther, Eric. *Zinzendorf, in Selbszeugnissen und Bilddokumenten.* Hamburg: Reinbek, 1965.
Bloom, Robert L. "The Two Swords in Theory and Practice. Pt. III: The Medieval Church" in *Ideas and Institutions of Western Man.* Gettysburg College, 1958.
Bornkamm, Heinrich. *Luther und Böhme.* Bonn: DeGruyter, 1925.
Calvin, John. *Institutes of the Christian Religion,* Edited by John T. McNeill. The Library of Christian Classics Volume XX. Philadelphia: Westminster Press, 1960.
Collins, Kenneth J. *The Scripture Way of Salvation: The Heart of John Wesley's Theology.* Nashville: Abingdon, 1997.
Conrads, Norbert. *Die Durchführung der Altranstädter Konvention in Schlesien.* Wien: Bohlau Verlag, 1971.
Drury, A.W. *History of the Church of the United Brethren in Christ.* Dayton: UB Publishing House, 1924.
_____. *Life of the Reverend Phillip William Otterbein.* Dayton: UB Publishing House, 1884.
Eberlein, Gerhard. "Die schlesischen Betekinder vom Jahre 1707/8" in *Evangelisches Kirchenblatt für Schlesien.* Zweite Jahrgang. Liegnitz; Druck von Oscar Heimze, 1899.
Eller, Paul, *These Evangelical United Brethren.* Dayton: Otterbein Press, 1957.
Erb, Peter, editor. "Nine Public Lectures (1746)" in *Pietists: Selected Writings.* New York: Paulist Press, 1983.
Finney, Charles Grandison. *Lectures on Revivals of Religion,* edited by W. G. McLaughlin, Boston: Harvard University Press, 1961.
Heidelberg Catechism with Commentary. Philadelphia: The United Church Press, 1963.
Hempton, David. *Methodism: Empire of the Spirit.* New Haven: Yale, 2008.
Jenkins, Philip. *The New Face of Christianity: Believing the Bible in the Global South.* New York: Oxford University Press, 2006.
Johnson, Todd, and Kenneth Ross, editors. *Atlas of Global Christianity.* New York: Oxford, 2009.
Kammel, Richard. "August Hermann Francke's Auslandsarbeit in Südosteuropa" in Ernst Schubert, editor. *Auslanddeutschtum und evangelische Kirche, Jahrbuch 1939.* München: Kaiser Verlag, 1939.
Kerr, Hugh. *Readings in Christian Thought.* Nashville, TN: Abingdon, 1990.
Löwith, Karl. *Meaning in History.* University of Chicago Press, 1964
Marshall Jr, Peter, David Manuel, *The Light and the Glory of God.* Old Tappan, NJ: Fleming Revel, 1977.
Matthias, Markus, Johann Wilhelm, and Johanna Eleonora Petersen. *Eine Biographie bis zur Amtsenthebung.* Vandenhoeck und Ruprecht, 1992.
Meyer, Dietrich. "Cognitio Dei Experimentalis oder 'Erfahrungstheologie' bei Gottfried Arnold, Gerhard Tersteegen, und Nikolaus Ludwig von Zinzendorf," in Dietrich Meyer und Udo Sträter, *Zur Rezeption mysterischer Traditionen im Protestantismus des 16. Bis 19. Jahrhunderts.* Köln: Rheinland-Verlag GmbH, 2002.
_____. with Christian-Erdmann Schott and Karl Schwarz. *Über Schlesien Hinaus: Zur Kirchengeschichte in Mitteleuropa, Festgabe für Herbert Patzelt zum 80. Geburtstag.*

Nordmann, Walter. "Im Widerstreit von Mystik und Föderalismus: Geschichtliche-Grundlagen der Eschatologie bei dem pietistischen Ehepaar Petersen," in *Zeitschfift für Kirchengeschichte (1930)*.
Nuelson, John L., *John Wesley and the German Hymn*. Calverley, 1972.
Neumann, Caspar. *Unvorgreifliches Gutachten*. Breslau, 1708.
Otterbein, Philip Wilhelm. *Die heilbringende Menschwerdung und herrliche Sieg Jesu Christi über den Teufel und Tod*. Lancaster, Pa, 1763.
O'Malley, J. Steven "The Distinctive Witness of the Evangelical United Brethren Confession of Faith in Comparison with the Methodist Articles of Religion," in Dennis M. Campbell, William B. Lawrence and Russell E. Richey, editors. *Doctrines and Discipline: United Methodism and American Culture*. Vol. 3. Nashville: Abingdon Press, 1999, 55-78.
_____. Translator, "William Otterbein Stresses Repentance in a Sermon at Conference of German Reformed Preachers in Philadelphia (1763), in *The Methodist Experience in America: A Sourcebook*, Russell E. Richey, Kenneth E Rowe, Jean Miller Schmidt, editors. Vol II. Nashville: Abingdon, 2000, 45-47.
_____ "The Influence of Pietism upon the Christliche Botschafter, the American German-Language Periodical of the Evangelical Association, in *Theologie für die Praxis*, 28, 2002, 35-45.
_____. "Merging the Streams: Pietism and Transatlantic Revival in the Colonial Era and the Birth of the Angelical Association and the United Brethren in Christ," in *Methodist History*, 57 (October 2018 and January 2019), 8-25.
_____. "Pietistic Influence on John Wesley: Wesley and Gerhard Tersteegen," in *Wesleyan Theological Journal*, Volume 31 n 2 (1996), 48-70.
_____. "The Otterbeins: Men of Two Worlds," in *Methodist History*, 15 (October 1976), 3-21.
_____. "Pietism and Wesleyanism: Setting the Stage for a Theological Discussion," *Wesleyan Theological Journal*. 53:1 (Spring 2018), 56-78.
_____. with Jason E Vickers, editors. *Methodist and Pietist: Retrieving the Evangelical United Brethren Tradition*. Nashville: Kingswood, 2011.
_____. "The Evangelical United Brethren Church: A History," in William J. Abraham, James E Kirby, editors. *The Oxford Handbook of Methodist Studies* (Oxford, 2009), 104-121.
_____. *On the Journey Home: Mission History of the Evangelical United Brethren Church*, in The History of United Methodist Missions Series, The Board of Global Ministries. New York: Sunshine Press, 2003.
_____. "Pietism and the Transatlantic Revival," in Douglas H Shantz, editor. *A Companion to German Pietism, 1660–1800* (Leiden: Brill, 2015, 256-292.
_____ with Thomas Lessmann, *Gesungenes Heil: Untersuchung zum Einfluß der Heiligungsbewegung auf das methodistische Liedgut des 19. Jahrhunderts am Beispiel von Gottlieb Füßle und Ernst Gebhardt* (Stuttgart: Christliches Verlagshaus, 1994).
_____. *Pilgrimage of Faith: The Legacy of the Otterbeins*. Metuchen, NJ: Scarecrow, 1973.
_____. *Early German American Evangelicalism; Pietist Sources for Discipleship and Sanctification* (Lanham, MD: Scarecrow, 1995).
Pachuau, Lalsangkima. *World Christianity: A Historical and Theological Introduction*. Nashville: Abingdon, 2018.

Pelikan, Jaroslav. *From Luther to Kierkegaard: A Study in the History of Theology*. St Louis: Concordia, 1950.
Plass, Ewald M. Ed. *What Luther Says: An Anthology.* St. Louis Concordia, 1959.
Renner, L. *Lebensbilder aus der Pietistenzeit: ein Beitrag zur Geschichte und Würdigung des späteren Pietismus.* Bremen: C. Ed. Müller, 1886
Scharlemann, Robert. *Thomas Aquinas and John Gerhard.* New Haven: Yale, 1964.
Schneider, Hans. *German Radical Pietism.* Tr. Gerald McDonald. Metuchen, New Jersey: Scarecrow, 2007.
Schrenk, Gottlob. *Gottesreitch und Bund im Älteren Protestantismus vornehmlich bei Johannes Cocceius.* Giessen: Brunnen Verlag, 1985. Reprint.
Schubert, Ernst. *Auslanddeuchtum und evangelische Kirche Jahrbuch 1939.* München: Christian Kaiser Verlag, 1939.
Shantz, Douglas H. *An Introduction to German Pietism*. Baltimore: John Hopkins Press, 2013.
Stoeffler, Ernest. *The Origins of German Pietism*. Leiden: Brill, 1966.
_____. *German Pietism in the Eighteenth Century.* Leiden: Brill, 1973.
Stoudt, J.J. *Sunrise to Eternity. A Study in J. Boehme's Life and Thought.* Philadelphia, 1957.
Svensson, Eric Jonas, *Kinderbeten: The Origin, Unfolding and interpretation of the Silesian Children's Prayer Revival.* Eugene, OR: Wipf and Stock, 2010.
Tuttle, Robert. *Mysticism in the Wesleyan tradition.* Grand Rapids, 1989.
Van Dusen, Henry P. *World Christianity: Yesterday, Today, Tomorrow.* New York: Abingdon-Cokesbury, 1947.
Wallmann, Johannes. *Pietismus.* Vandenhoeck und Ruprecht, 2005).
Ward, W. Reginald, *The Protestant Evangelical Awakening.* Oxford, 1992.
_____. *Early Evangelicalism: A Global Intellectual History*, 1679–1789. Cambridge, 2006.
_____. "Mysticism and Revival: The Case of Gerhard Tersteegen," in Jane Garnett and Colin Matthew, editor. *Revival and Religion since 1700; Essays for John Walsh.* London: The Hambledon Press, 1993.
_____. *Christianity Under the Ancien' Regime, 1648–1789.* Cambridge, 1999.
_____ with Heitzenrater, Richard P. "The Bicentennial Edition of the Works of John Wesley". Volume I, *Journal and Diaries*, (1735–1738). Nashville, TN: Abingdon, 1984 to Current Date.
_____. "The Making of the Evangelical Mind", in Geoffrey R. Reloar and Robert O. Lindor (editor.), *Making History for God.* Sydney, N.S.W., 2004.
Wood, Laurence W, *Pentecost and Sanctification in the Writings of John and Charles Wesley, With a Proposal for Today.* Lexington: Emeth Press, 2018.
_____. *The Meaning of Pentecost in Early Methodism: Rediscovering John Fletcher as John Wesley's Vindicator and Designated Successor* (Metuchen, NJ: Scarecrow, 2003).
Weigelt, Horst. *The Schwenkfelders in Silesia.* Translated by Peter Erb. Pennsburg, Pa: The Schwenkfelder Library.
Wright, N.T. *Paul: A Biography.* New York: Harper One, 2018.

Index

Adoption 29, 34, 54, 65, 211
Aldersgate 8, 29, 132, 220, 239
Altranstädt 10, 32, 184–85, 189, 191
Anfechtung 31, 62, 72, 80–81, 88, 165, 241
Arndt, Johann 22, 80, 147, 151, 159, 183, 255
Arnold, Gottfried 4, 5–6, 8, 47, 65, 79, 131, 174, 180, 211
Assurance 29–31, 34, 36, 38–39, 52, 56, 58, 60, 63–64, 70–72, 77–79, 81, 82, 84, 86–87, 88–89, 93, 95, 97, 105–106, 108, 121, 138, 153, 186, 202, 207–208, 211, 220–23, 225, 233–34, 235, 239, 241–42, 245–46, 249
Austria 125, 130, 137–138, 211

Bohemia 10, 137, 146, 148, 200–201, 208, 227, 249
Böhme, Jacob (Jakob) 99, 162-7, 174-176, 203, 231, 261, 279, 285
Breslau 146, 148, 150, 183, 193–95

Calvary 8, 9, 16, 123, 132, 135, 168–69, 207, 223–25, 235, 238, 240, 241, 243–44, 245, 247–49
Calvin 41
Calvinism 124, 206, 249
Children (in relation to the Kinderbeten) 3–6, 8–9, 11, 27–29, 53, 55, 57–58, 61–63, 65–66, 72–73, 77, 79, 81, 83, 86, 88, 93, 97, 103, 112, 114, 115, 117, 119, 125, 127–28, 130–32, 134–35, 137–41, 146, 148–62, 165–67, 170, 173–74, 176–177, 180–84, 186, 201, 206, 209–10, 212, 217–18, 222, 224, 226–28, 230–31, 234, 236, 240, 244, 248–49, 251, 253, 256
Conventicles 9, 136, 152–53, 185, 186, 191, 203–204
Conversion 8, 23, 29, 48, 55, 59, 60–61, 78–79, 96, 122–25, 132, 159, 169, 184, 202, 210, 212–13, 217, 220, 222, 229, 239, 242, 244, 255
Counter-Reformation 125, 149, 152, 191, 224
Covenant/covenant theology 79, 97, 115, 121, 145, 167–73, 177–78, 233–34, 248
Creation 72, 106, 162, 173, 178, 207, 250
Creator 167
Creeds 6, 142
Cross 6, 32–34, 37–40, 43, 45–46, 49, 62, 65, 70, 74, 75, 85, 89, 91, 97, 122, 125, 130, 132, 135, 140–44, 159, 163, 169, 175,–79, 181, 190, 215–16, 218–19, 223–26, 229, 232, 235, 237–41, 243–44, 246, 248–52, 254
Crucified 9, 23, 34, 45–46, 48, 72, 81, 89, 97, 125, 162–63, 202, 238, 240, 243
Crucifixion 221
Cultures 15–17, 149
Czech/Czech Republic 4, 130, 188, 191–192, 200–01, 254,

David, Christian 8, 10, 14, 29–31, 64, 69, 77, 84–87, 95, 99, 125, 132, 193, 199–281
Depth 6–8, 11, 37, 70, 97, 113, 119,

129–30, 132, 134, 148, 155–56, 175, 231–2
Devil 26–27, 30–32, 36, 40, 47–49, 61–62, 65–66, 71, 75, 80, 85, 88, 100, 102, 106, 113–14, 116–18, 122–24, 141, 163, 238
Devotion 80, 131, 216, 229, 256,
Dillenberger, John 7, 30, 47, 56, 116, 142–43, 163, 176, 223
Disciples 8, 52, 57, 118, 132, 134–35, 155, 157, 165, 233, 243, 244–45
Disobedience 97, 113–14
Divine 6, 17, 23, 25, 30, 32, 37, 140–41, 153, 166–68, 171–73, 177–79, 184, 217, 230, 239, 247, 249
Doddridge, Phillip 71
Doubt 32, 34, 36, 49, 51, 56, 62, 71, 74, 80, 82, 89, 91, 113, 220
Dualism 29, 99, 162–66, 174
Durchbruch 132, 229, 244

Ecclesial 3, 16–18, 56, 139–40, 147–48, 160, 187, 228, 231
Ecclesiology 175, 217
Economy 168–73, 175–78, 207, 208, 216, 250
Elect 207, 212
England 8, 10, 58, 132, 137, 140, 149, 163, 175, 196, 215–16, 220, 222, 228, 245, 250, 255
English 11, 21, 65, 81, 99, 130–31, 140, 171, 174, 182, 196, 210, 219, 222, 239
Education 5, 22, 182, 196, 200, 254
Edwards, Jonathan 57, 71, 132, 187, 271, 285
Erweckung 137, 225–26, 228, 247–48
eschatology 161,166–167,172–175,161,166–67,172–73,175, 178, 234, 270
Estonia 215, 220, 277–279
Eucharist 40, 41, 57–59, 73, 160, 242

Federal 7, 97, 153, 161, 167, 169, 172, 234, 251
federal theology 97, 153, 160–61, 165, 167, 172, 234
Fletcher, John 199, 222–32, 235–36, 245

Forgiveness 29, 34–38, 43–45, 47, 51–52, 55–57, 63–64, 69–71, 78, 80, 83–86, 89, 90, 95, 100–101, 105–106, 118, 120, 125, 127, 153, 186–87, 208, 220, 229, 241, 249
Francke, August Hermann 5, 23, 32, 55, 57, 61, 121, 137, 143, 147, 149–50, 152, 181, 188, 190–91, 193, 195, 200, 211, 213, 220–21, 228–29, 244, 248, 255
Frankfurt 10, 19, 21, 131, 147, 152, 160, 178, 214, 221

Gathering, The.. 11, 87, 125, 196, 233, 263–64, 268–75, 276, 279–80
Germany 65, 130, 132, 136, 139, 145, 174–75, 183, 186, 193, 201, 211–12, 218, 227, 229–30, 248, 254
German 4, 8–10, 21, 25, 44, 47, 53, 58, 65, 71, 81, 121, 125, 130–32, 137, 141–42, 147–49, 152, 158–62, 167, 175, 177, 179, 181, 184, 188, 192–93, 196, 200,–203, 205, 208, 211, 215, 220, 227, 231, 234–35, 249–51, 254, 281
Global 4, 6, 7–9, 11, 13–18, 49, 64, 81, 91, 97, 101, 129, 131–32, 134, 136, 147–48, 150, 155–58, 162–65, 169, 170, 173–74, 176, 178, 180–81, 188, 213–14, 220, 224, 227–28, 250, 252, 281
Globalization 3, 8–9, 11, 13, 15–17, 39, 45, 81, 91, 111, 129–30, 136–47, 149, 152, 154, 156, 199, 224, 253–54
Gospel 3, 7, 13, 16, 27, 30, 41, 42, 45–46, 56–57, 65, 66, 91, 97, 106, 119, 132, 134, 149, 153, 157, 163–65, 169, 174, 184–85, 190, 194, 202, 206, 214, 219, 224, 229, 232–33, 237, 240, 245, 250, 251–52, 254, 256

Görlitz (Germany) 29, 202,-203, 205, 211, 249
Greenland xiv, 10, 215, 219-20, 235

Halle 5, 10, 28, 32, 55, 57, 61, 71, 121, 132, 137, 139, 143, 147, 149, 150, 152, 188, 190-91, 195, 200, 211-14, 217, 220-21, 228-30, 244
Hapsburg 4, 32, 125, 128, 135, 138, 140-41, 146, 148-59, 167, 183-84, 188-90, 191, 193, 195, 200-202, 205, 208, 211-13, 221, 227-28, 255-56
Heaven 30-31, 33, 36-37, 45, 76, 84, 86, 91, 101, 105-106, 115, 118-19, 124, 132, 161, 169-70, 174, 230, 233, 235, 241, 246, 249
Heidelberg 9, 121, 286
Heitz, Johann Georg 205-206
Herborn (Germany) 174, 200
Herrnhut 8, 29, 64, 82, 99, 125, 132, 139, 201, 205-16, 219-21, 226-27, 229, 232, 235, 239, 243, 245, 248-50, 254, 281
Herrnhuter 206
Holy Spirit 7-25
  Spirit-Anointed 202
  Spirit-Convicted 106
  Spirit-Endued 5
  Spirit-Guided 165
  Spirit-Sealed 69
Holiness 5, 9, 31, 33, 49, 59, 97, 116, 125, 179, 208, 221, 224, 234-42, 245, 254
Hope 26, 30, 32-34, 36, 71, 76, 78-80, 87, 95-96, 100, 108, 111, 119-20, 123, 145, 147, 149, 164, 174, 178, 189, 195, 200, 218, 228, 239, 248, 250
Huguenots 28, 137, 139
Humanity 10, 16, 31-32, 38, 43, 45, 47, 72, 86, 91, 97, 115-17, 125, 129, 132, 135, 142, 144, 148-49, 156, 161-67, 170-71, 173-74, 176-79, 182, 196, 212, 225, 230-31, 235, 247, 254
Hungary 130, 137, 150, 191

Hussite 137, 192, 200, 205, 209, 226-27
Hymn 41, 99, 108, 149, 151, 202, 233-34, 246, 252

Inspirationist 132, 226, 228
Intercession 135, 143, 190, 230, 256
Irenaeus 97, 167-73, 234

Jerichovius 10, 191, 263, 265-274
Jesuit 4, 125, 130, 167, 195, 201, 203, 205, 208, 203
Joachim of Fiore 7, 170, 223m 234
Joseph I (Emperor of Holy Roman Empire, Vienna) 32, 138, 257
Judgment 26-27, 29-40, 46, 76, 88, 95, 101, 111, 113, 118-19, 121, 131, 142, 148, 157, 161-62, 164, 166, 168, 173, 176, 194-95, 246-50
Justification 5, 31, 37, 47, 64-65, 149, 171, 208, 219-21, 229, 232, 236, 239, 249, 254, 281

Karl XII (King of Sweden; also Charles) 138, 182, 257
Koenigsberg 204
Kinderbeten 53, 130-31, 137, 140, 152, 181, 185, 286
Kingdom 7-8, 11, 13, 18, 38, 64, 66, 70, 76, 86, 112, 115, 118, 124-25, 132, 141, 148, 157, 160, 162, 167-69, 171, 176, 180, 183, 196, 212, 217, 230-31, 237, 246, 247,-51, 254, 256
Kloster Bergen 10, 20, 196, 214, 263, 267, 270-1, 274, 278, 280

Lächele, Rainer 10, 87, 263-269
Lampe, Friedrich Adolph 79, 132, 147, 177, 251, 253, 285
Latvia 215, 218, 244, 276-7
Law 6, 30, 32, 45-46, 56, 65, 84-85, 121, 125, 142, 163, 175, 180, 185,

191, 223, 224, 229, 232, 237, 241, 243, 255–56
Leade, Jane 148, 174–5, 211
Leipzig 10, 18, 22, 57, 61, 132, 152, 183, 194, 188, 228, 253, 255, 258, 264
Liberda, Johann 189, 209, 276
Litany 8, 129, 151, 229, 232–233, 240
Lithuania 20, 204
Livonia 215, 218–19, 244
Luther 6–7, 14, 30, 32–33, 37–38, 43, 45–47, 56, 58–60, 62, 65–66, 75, 80, 83, 87, 97, 99, 116, 128, 130, 136, 141–151, 153, 160, 162–65, 174–78, 185, 217, 223, 224, 228–29, 231, 237–43, 247–48, 252, 256
Lutheran 3–5, 10, 21, 31, 45–49, 53, 60, 65, 74, 79, 97, 103, 123, 125, 130–31, 141, 146–256
Lutz, Samuel 215, 232

Marburg 131, 174, 177, 209, 210
Marienborn 227, 267, 276
Mediator 216, 219, 226
Medieval 5, 13, 70, 124–25, 131, 137, 145, 158–59, 168, 170–71, 200, 231
Melanchthonian 146, 149
Memoirs 203, 205, 215, 249–50
Methodism 8, 11, 18, 65, 77, 106, 114, 125, 132, 149, 199, 200, 254, 255
Merit 32–34, 39, 44, 47, 53, 99, 102, 111, 141–42, 239, 241
Migrate 193, 165, 205, 215
Millennialism 148, 166, 168, 171, 175
Ministry 8, 41, 47–48, 61, 64, 66, 87, 106, 114, 117, 125, 130, 132, 134, 135, 147, 149, 152, 159, 173, 183, 185, 187–89, 191–96, 203, 208–209, 211–12, 214–15, 217, 219–20, 222–23, 227, 229–30, 235, 240–41, 243, 245, 248, 255–56, 281
Missio 9, 11, 17, 39, 91, 129, 136, 148, 156, 178, 195–96, 208, 210, 212, 214–29, 240, 244
Monism 99, 164–65, 174
Moser, Johann Jacob 284
Moravia 10, 132, 137, 146, 148, 192, 200–208, 218,–19 221, 227, 249
Mystical 7, 37, 70, 119, 131, 144–47, 149, 158–76, 179, 224, 231, 238
Mystical-Spiritualist 5, 9, 70, 99 158, 161–180

Nordmann, Walter 99, 161–62, 164–80, 230–31

Oikonomia 171, 172, 178
Origen 169–70
Orphans 130, 135, 141, 143
Otterbein, Philip William 9, 65, 132, 200, 234, 251
Orthodox (Lutheran) 3–8, 28, 31, 53, 60, 103, 146, 152, 158–59, 161, 165, 184, 185, 189, 191, 193, 195, 203, 206, 214, 217, 235, 240, 254

Papacy 158
Pennsylvania 149, 174, 220, 235, 242
Perfection (Christian) 5, 46, 64, 97, 99, 180, 222, 234, 236, 239, 245
Philadelphia 73, 121, 148, 165, 174, 212
Philadelphian 148, 174, 175, 211, 212, 213, 216, 226, 256
Pietism 13, 37, 47, 55, 79, 128, 131–32, 135–36, 146–47, 149, 152, 158–59, 161, 181, 184–85, 189, 192–93, 195, 228, 230, 234, 251, 254, 281
Pentecost 6– 9, 11, 16–19, 21, 25, 28–29, 35, 37, 46–48, 51, 57–58, 61–64, 66, 69, 72, 74, 83, 91, 111, 113, 115, 127, 129–36, 148, 152–53, 155–59, 162, 166, 169,
Petersen, Johann Wilhelm 5–6, 8, 131, 139–40, 153, 156–57, 160–80, 209, 218, 230–31

Philosophy 152, 168, 171–72 /
Poiret, Pierre 171–75, 177
Poland 130, 132, 137–38, 254
Polish 4, 188–90, 192, 203
Post-Christendom 14, 156, 162, 204
Promise 27, 30–32, 37, 43, 52, 56, 58, 62–63, 65, 91, 97, 115, 142, 145, 157, 163, 169, 174, 179, 202, 206, 218, 222–24, 230, 238, 240, 243–44, 246–47, 249 Prophecies 9, 182, 221, 242
Prophecy 3, 4, 9, 28, 79, 130, 141, 143, 182, 242
Prussian 5, 137, 220
Puritan 28, 58, 251

Quietistic 160

Radical (Pietism) 4, 5, 47, 65–66, 131–32, 147–49, 152–53, 155–60, 171, 174, 212, 226, 254
Reborn 5, 23, 106, 115, 137, 167, 213, 217
Recapitulation 97, 169
Recatholicization 141, 189, 193, 201
Redemption 8, 21, 25–27, 33, 35, 39, 78, 91, 97, 113, 134, 143, 162, 168, 171–73, 177–78, 225, 238
Reformation 4–5, 9, 14, 17, 28, 32, 128–29, 131, 135–36, 140–41, 144–48, 158, 159–60, 164, 168, 177–78, 182, 193, 214, 228, 235, 252–54, 256, 281
Reformed 8–9, 49, 65, 79, 97, 114, 121, 147, 152, 167, 172, 177, 179, 200, 206, 213, 220, 226, 228, 232, 251
Restorationism 161, 174–175
Rosamunde 160
Rothe, Richard 202, 204–206

Savior 25, 26–30, 32–33, 37, 39, 41–43, 45–47, 49–50, 52, 54, 60, 63–64, 71–73, 76, 79–80, 83–84, 86–91, 96, 102, 104–105, 118, 121, 216–218, 226, 238, 242, 244
Saxony 10, 132, 137, 139, 183, 193, 195, 202, 208, 227
Scandinavia 204
Scheffer 29, 203
Schleiermacher, Friedrich 57
Schlesien 131, 138, 146, 149–150, 183
Scholasticism (Protestant) 158, 165–67
Schwenkfelder, Caspar 58, 149
Scotland 10, 196
Scripture 10, 27–29, 51, 53, 58, 86, 112, 139, 151, 163, 167–68, 171, 173, 225, 229, 239–40, 242, 254
Seal (of the Holy Spirit) 27, 30–32, 35–36, 39, 46, 50, 52–115, 186, 223–51
Seligkeit (blessedness, the holy and sanctified life) 31, 242, 54, 59, 78, 208, 229, 236, 241
Silesia 4, 5, 8, 10, 32, 57, 79, 81, 104, 106, 119, 125, 127, 130, 136–159, 170, 181–256
Silesian 8, 21, 28, 53, 58, 86, 125, 128, 130, 135, 138, 140, 143, 146, 148, 150, 152, 156, 162, 170, 182, 183, 187–89, 195–96, 201–18, 221–22, 229, 242–43, 249, 251–52, 254–55
Soteriology 8–9, 11, 15, 127, 135, 157, 169, 178, 199, 203, 208, 217–18, 253–56, 281
Soul 61–64, 70–71, 74–75, 77, 79, 81, 84, 86–87, 89–91, 95–96, 100–101, 104, 106, 113, 115–16, 118, 123–, 125, 141–42, 159, 180, 183–84, 186, 202, 216–17, 219, 223, 225, 229–30, 242
Spener, Philipp Jacob 21, 22, 73, 136, 147, 149, 152–53, 159–60, 181–82, 193, 211, 214, 228, 248, 255
Steinmetz, Johann Adam 6, 8–11, 19, 21, 22–23, 29–34, 37, 39, 46–47, 49, 53, 55, 57–66, 70–71, 74–75, 79–87,

298 Index

91, 96, 97, 99, 104, 106, 114, 115, 116, 119, 124–125, 127, 129–32, 134–35, 143, 152, 157–59, 180– 281
Stoeffler, F. Ernest 147
Swensson, Eric 53, 130–31, 138–141, 146, 149–54, 183, 185
Sweden 10, 130, 137, 138, 140, 143, 146, 151, 182–83, 200
Switzerland 145, 215 222, 232

Taborites, 200
Tallinn (Estonia) 215
Tauler 145, 159
Temptations 31, 48, 62, 80, 85, 88
Tersteegen, Gerhard 9, 75, 79–80, 96, 99, 131–32
Teschen (Silesia) 5, 8, 10, 19, 22, 28–29, 32, 48, 57–58, 61, 74, 103–104, 106, 114, 125, 127, 130–32, 135, 143, 150, 152, 157, 159, 182, 187–89, 191–92, 194, 195–96, 200–201, 203, 205–209, 212, 214, 216–18, 221–22, 225, 227, 229, 235, 249, 253
Testament 26, 30–32, 132, 168, 184, 221, 234
Theology 6–7, 9, 11, 15, 22, 29, 34, 37–38, 45–46, 70, 75, 93, 97, 125, 130–31, 141–42, 144–45, 158–59, 161–63, 165, 167, 169–70, 172–73, 175–76, 179, 180–81, 189, 195, 200, 222, 224, 229, 231–32, 234–35, 237, 239–40, 242–43, 244, 247–50, 252, 254, 256, 281
Theodicy 6, 158, 162, 164, 171
Thirty Years War (1618-48) 10, 14, 32, 118, 131, 136–38, 144, 156, 162, 168, 182, 192–93, 196, 200, 205, 248 118, 131, 136–38, 144, 156, 162, 168, 182, 192–93, 196, 200, 205, 248
Töppliwoda 22, 152, 184, 186, 188–89, 194

Underworld 159
Unfaithfulness 6, 101, 238, 241

Ungodliness 216, 241, 243
Unitas Fratrem (Unity of the Brethren) 200, 212, 227
United Brethren in Christ 250, 254
Untereyck, Theodor, 147
Utopian 204

Versiegelung (sealing)19, 21, 86, 130, 208, 221, 238–40, 247

Wallmann 150
Walther 10
Ward, W. Reginald 9, 29, 37, 41, 58–59, 80, 82, 99, 104, 106, 136, 139, 143, 144, 146, 152, 158–59, 163, 167, 180–81, 188, 190–91, 200–228, 245, 256, 281
Wernigerode 21
Wesley, Charles, 222, 232–235, 236, 246–47, 251-2
Wesley, John 8, 29, 31, 37, 46, 49, 64, 97, 99, 114, 132, 199–200, 203, 205, 206–208, 212, 214–16, 219, 220–22, 226, 232–36, 239, 243–48, 250, 251-52, 254–55, 281
Wesleyan 11, 15, 18, 29, 38, 49, 131, 180–82, 196, 199, 254, 281, 199, 233, 234, 235, 236, 237, 239, 252, 254, 256, 281
Westphalia, Treaty of (1648) 32, 138, 144, 153, 205, 214, 220
Wetterau (Rhineland region)132, 152, 226–27
Wiederbringung (aller Dinge) (restoration of all things)131, 157, 161, 166, 171, 173–74, 176–79, 230
Will 3, 5, 6, 8, 14, 17, 22, 25–27, 31, 33, 35–84, 87–91, 94, 97, 99,–101, 104, 105–106, 108–109, 111, 114, 116, 118–25, 132, 134, 142, 145, 152–53, 165–166, 169–70, 172–80, 185, 189, 194, 196, 205, 210, 215–16, 218,

220, 226, 230-31, 233-34, 238, 241-42, 244, 249-50, 254
Witness (to God's work in the Spirit) 9, 18, 22, 26, 28, 44, 52, 54-55, 62, 64, 69, 74, 84-87, 112-13, 115, 117, 119, 125, 145, 167, 216, 220, 223-24, 231, 233-36, 238, 244, 246, 250, 256
Wittenberg 7, 145, 195, 217
Wittgenstein-Berleberg 204
Wood, Laurence 37, 46, 64, 196, 199, 222-239, 245, 247, 254.
World 3, 7, 10, 13-15, 18, 26, 28, 31-32, 35, 37, 40, 45-46, 49-51, 53, 57, 60, 62, 65, 71-72, 74, 76-77, 81, 84-6, 88-89, 91, 94, 97, 101-103, 106, 114, 117, 121, 123-24, 129, 132, 134, 138, 149-150, 155-58, 161, 163, 165, 167-68, 170-71, 174, 178-80, 187, 195-96, 199, 210, 212, 214, 216, 223, 226, 228, 230, 235, 238-39, 252-53, 254,-55
Worship 3, 32-34, 60, 63, 74, 104, 106, 127, 132, 135, 137-39, 141, 143, 147, 149, 150-51, 160, 183, 185-86, 188, 190, 191, 194, 200, 227, 256
Wrath 28, 112, 119, 163, 250
Württemberg 204

Zinzendorf 29-30, 34, 58-59, 80, 82, 195, 201, 205-217, 219, 226-229, 232, 235, 248-250, 256

www.ingramcontent.com/pod-product-compliance
Lightning Source LLC
Chambersburg PA
CBHW051629230426
43669CB00013B/2238